WHITE TIE AND DECORATIONS
SIR JOHN AND LADY HOPE SIMPSON IN NEWFOUNDLAND, 1934–1936

In February 1934, a financial emergency created by the Great Depression forced the suspension of self-government in Newfoundland. Britain guaranteed Newfoundland's debt and appointed a Commission of Government. Among the first members named to the new government was Sir John Hope Simpson, whose portfolio included responsibility for fishing, forestry, mining, and agriculture. This book is a selection from the many letters written from Newfoundland to family members in England by Sir John and Lady Hope Simpson (familiarly known as Quita). It recalls in vivid detail the terrible decade of the 1930s. The reader relives the era through the eyes of a couple who had a unique and informed perspective on events in Newfoundland and Labrador.

Sir John Hope Simpson was a man of wide international experience and exceptional administrative ability. His correspondence is candid and direct – that of an insider. Quita's letters reveal a perceptive and inquisitive nature and a pervading social concern. Both write about their progressive, even utopian, ideas. They travelled extensively in the country, met a wide range of people, and recorded their experiences in letters that capture the essence of the time.

Peter Neary's edition is based on the collection of Hope Simpson papers at Balliol College, Oxford. His selection from the Newfoundland correspondence is complemented in the book by maps and photographs. Neary's introduction lays the groundwork for an understanding of the letters and the milieu of the Hope Simpsons.

PETER NEARY is a professor of history and dean of the Faculty of Social Science at the University of Western Ontario. He is the author of *Newfoundland in the North Atlantic World, 1929–1949*, and has published a number of other works on Newfoundland. His most recent book, co-edited with J.L. Granatstein, is *The Good Fight: Canadians and World War II*.

Edited by PETER NEARY

White Tie and Decorations
Sir John and Lady Hope Simpson
in Newfoundland,
1934–1936

UNIVERSITY OF TORONTO PRESS
Toronto Buffalo London

© University of Toronto Press Incorporated 1996
Toronto Buffalo London

Printed in Canada

Reprinted in paperback 1997

ISBN 0-8020-0719-8 (cloth)
ISBN 0-8020-8085-5 (paper)

Printed on acid-free paper

Canadian Cataloguing in Publication Data

Hope Simpson, John, Sir, 1868–1961
    White tie and decorations : Sir John and Lady Hope Simpson
in Newfoundland, 1934–1936

Includes bibliographical references and index.
ISBN 0-8020-0719-8 (bound)   ISBN 0-8020-8085-5 (pbk.)

1. Newfoundland – History – 1934–1949.*
2. Newfoundland – Description and travel.
3. Newfoundland – Social conditions – 1900–1949.*
4. Hope Simpson, John, Sir, 1868–1961 –
Correspondence.   5. Hope Simpson, Quita, Lady,
1870–1939 – Correspondence.   6. Newfoundland –
Commission of Government – Biography.   I. Hope
Simpson, Quita, Lady, 1870–1939.   II. Neary, Peter,
1938– .   III. Title.

FC2174.3.H66 1996   971.8'03   C95-932307-4
F1123.H66 1996

University of Toronto Press acknowledges the financial
assistance to its publishing program of the Canada Council
and the Ontario Arts Council.

FOR MARY ELIZABETH NEARY
1930–1995

Contents

All the hills round St. John's used to be thickly afforested; now there are only patches & fringes of old forest here & there in the gullies & dotted about the more distant hills. Signal Hill & South Side Hills are quite bare. But – how beautiful it is! There is a quarry up on the side of Signal Hill, but the road has been so roughly hewn that it is no disfigurement; the sun is on it now, and it is golden & purple & silver. Above it are higher slopes, with Cabot Tower & the Marconi aerial and the guns & the old arsenal; below are cultivated fields sloping steeply to quaint wooden houses climbing winding roads. I find these wooden houses most picturesque; the colours are delicately lovely – faded reds & blues & greens & greys – & the roofs all up & down, & no two houses ever alike or quite in line. And all along the shore of the hill are the fishermen's flakes, and on the rocks at the entrance to the harbour the waves dash up & fall back in white foam that spreads far out over the blue. There is a lovely red-sailed schooner tacking through the Narrows now.

Lady Hope Simpson, 26 October 1935

We have not had much this week in the way of social engagements and have little in prospect. There is a big dinner at Government House the 21st – *white tie and decorations* – and that is all.

Sir John Hope Simpson, 17 November 1935 (emphasis added)

Quita is very well and very happy. She loves this island and, above all, the view from our bedroom window over the harbour, with the myriad schooners coming and going through the Narrows.

Sir John Hope Simpson, 1 June 1936

Preface

My interest in the family letters from Newfoundland of Sir John and Lady Hope Simpson goes back to 1983, when I visited the late J.B. (Ian) and Daphne Hope Simpson at 'Craig-y-Dorth House,' Mitchell Troy Common, Monmouth, Wales. Thereafter, until his death in 1989, Ian generously answered many questions for me, and Daphne has done the same ever since. I am most grateful to them both, and I remember Ian fondly. I am likewise thankful to Jacynth Hope-Simpson, Ian's literary executor, for permission to publish the selection from the Hope Simpson Newfoundland correspondence included in this book. I also acknowledge with sincerest thanks the research assistance I received from Mary (Hope Simpson) Macaulay, with whom I spent a memorable afternoon in Cornwall, Ontario; her son and daughter-in-law, John and Margaret Macaulay, also of Cornwall; Edgar and Eleanor Hope-Simpson of Cirencester, Gloucestershire, England; and David Hope Simpson of Wolfville, Nova Scotia. I thank the Master and Fellows of Balliol College, Oxford, for permission to consult the Hope Simpson papers, and Dr Penelope Bulloch, the college librarian, for making the papers available to me and for helping me over many words and phrases that eluded me. T.J. Procter of Balliol College kindly answered my questions about Sir John Hope Simpson's university career.

In St John's, I was helped in my research first and foremost by Melvin Baker, Gertrude Crosbie, Carla and Richard Furlong, and Patrick O'Flaherty, each of whom has extraordinary knowledge of the rich and diverse past of Newfoundland and Labrador. The list of my other individual informants is long, and I trust that all those who so willingly and ably assisted me will accept this general word of thanks as a token of my appreciation. I was also well served in preparing this work by the staffs of the Centre for Newfoundland Studies, Queen Elizabeth II Library, Memorial University; the Provincial Archives of Newfoundland and Labrador; the Provincial Reference Library, St John's; the Law Library, Department of Justice, St John's; the Serge A. Sauer Map Library, Faculty of Social Science, University of Western Ontario; and the Reference Desk of the D.B. Weldon Library, University of Western Ontario. Anne Hart, Director of the Centre for Newfoundland Studies, had personal knowledge relevant to my subject, which she generously shared with me. I acknowledge special help and encouragement from Sandra Gwyn, Cyril Fox, David Twiston Davies, Richard and Susan Wallington, and the late George Story. I have also benefited greatly from the lively interest in my work shown by colleagues at Western and elsewhere, especially Sam Clark, J.L. Granatstein, Erich Hahn, Roger Hall, W.B. Hamilton, A.M.J. Hyatt, W.J. Kirwin, Doug Link, Rod Millard, S.J.R. Noel, Craig Simpson, James Struthers, Emöke Szathmary, and R.A. Young. Busy scholars and administrators themselves, they nevertheless always made time to hear me out and urge me on. Michael Bassett of Auckland, New Zealand, who was J.B. Smallman Visiting Professor of History at Western in 1992–3, kindly undertook research for me in Washington. I salute him for this and for our continuing dialogue about matters imperial and political. For assistance with translation, I am grateful to Beate Gundert, David Higgs, David Keypour, Paul Potter, and Marjorie Ratcliffe. I thank Glenda Hunt for exceptional word-processing advice and help. My research for this edition was made possible by grants from the Social Sciences and Humanities Research Council of Canada and the British Council, and I thank both organizations for their support. This book has been published with the help of a grant from the J.B. Smallman Publication Fund, Faculty of Social Science, University of Western Ontario.

Most of all, I thank my own immediate and extended families. Mary, now sadly gone, and John, Steve, and Gerald made my way easy in St John's, where Steve now also writes Newfoundland history. Margaret will know me better when she receives this book. On a clear August day in 1993, Anne and Dave and I picked our way along the shore of Gander Lake to the site of 'Gleneagles' to see the view that had so captivated the Hope Simpsons in the 1930s. To our delight, we found it as pristine in the 1990s as it was sixty years ago. Jock Bates and the late A.P. Bates once more gave me the benefit of their sharp editorial eyes, and Margaret Bates solved several puzzles for me. I thank them all most sincerely and trust that the finished product will repay their many efforts on my behalf. As always, Hilary, Nicholas, and John have been with me in every word.

In the preface to his celebrated *The Children of Pride: A True Story of*

Georgia and the Civil War (New Haven and London 1972), a selection from the family papers of the Reverend Dr Charles Colcock Jones (1804–1863), the American scholar Robert Manson Myers wrote that 'nothing so graphically conveys the essence of an age as its letters.' In letters, history 'is miraculously brought to life by a rehearsal of the particulars of every day.' That is what I experienced when I first read the Hope Simpson Newfoundland letters and it was to share my excitement in discovery that I set out to prepare this edition. Robert Manson Myers's purpose was to select letters 'which, when brought together in chronological order without editorial links, would form a coherent, independent narrative related entirely in the words of the characters themselves.' My intent was the same and, as Myers did in his work, I see in mine 'a true story told in letters – something akin to an epistolary novel.' It is, then, to history relived that I invite my readers.

Personae

THE HOPE SIMPSON FAMILY

J.H.S. Sir John Hope Simpson (1868–1961). Commissioner for Natural Resources, 1934–6.

Q.H.S. Lady Hope Simpson (1870–1939). Born Mary Jane Barclay. Known in family as Quita.

Daughters and Sons of J.H.S. and Q.H.S., and Their Spouses

Maisie and **Blair** Mary (Maisie) Hope Simpson (1902–) married Blair Macaulay (1903–1985) in 1928. They were both graduates of the medical school of the University of Liverpool, where they had been classmates. They were in practice together at Great Crosby and resided at 'Shubra.'

Greta Margaret Barclay (Greta) Hope Simpson (1903–1993). A graduate of Newnham College, Cambridge, she was secretary to Captain Cecil Graves, first director of the Empire Service of the British Broadcasting Corporation, London. She was later program director for the British Broadcasting Corporation's World Service.

Ian and **Sheila** John Barclay (Ian) Hope Simpson (1905–1989) married Sheila Gonner (1907–1948) in 1928. A graduate of Worcester College, Oxford, he was teaching at Clifton College Junior School, where he became head of Hartnells House in 1934. Sheila Gonner was the daughter of Sir Edward Gonner (1862–1922), professor of Economic Science in the University of Liverpool.

Edgar and **Eleanor** Robert Edgar Hope-Simpson (1908–) married Eleanor Dale (1906–) in 1932. He had studied medicine at St Thomas's Hospital, London; was in practice in Beaminster, Dorset; and resided at 'Gable End.' Eleanor Dale was the daughter of Sir Henry Dale (1875–1968), who in 1936 was awarded (with Otto Loewi) the Nobel prize for physiology and medicine.

Betty Elizabeth Noton (Betty) Hope Simpson (1910–1986). While her parents were in Newfoundland, she matriculated and began studies as a home student at St Anne's College, Oxford. She was later a schoolteacher.

OTHERS

Frederick C. Alderdice (1872–1936), Prime Minister of Newfoundland 1928, 1932–4, Commissioner for Home Affairs and Education, 1934–6.

Admiral Sir (David) Murray Anderson (1874–1936), Governor of Newfoundland, 1933–6.

William R. Howley (1875–1941), Commissioner for Justice, 1934–8.

Thomas Lodge (1882–1958), Commissioner for Public Utilities, 1934–7.

John C. Puddester (1881–1947), Commissioner for Public Health and Welfare, 1934–47.

(Everard) Noel (Rye) Trentham (1888–1963), Commissioner for Finance, 1934–7.

Vice-Admiral Sir Humphrey T. Walwyn (1879–1957), Governor of Newfoundland, 1936–46.

Abbreviations

a/c(s)	account(s)
A.D.C.(s)	aide(s)-de-camp
B.B.C.	British Broadcasting Corporation
C. of E.	Church of England
C.P.R.	Canadian Pacific Railway
cwt.	hundredweight
d.	pence
D.V.	*Deo volente* (God being willing)
H.E.	His Excellency
H.M.	His Majesty's
H.M.G.	His Majesty's Government
H.M.S.	His Majesty's Ship
H.Q.	headquarters
I.C.S.	Indian Civil Service
inst.	instant
I.P.P.	International Power and Paper Company of Newfoundland Limited
J.H.S.	Sir John Hope Simpson
J.P.	Justice of the Peace
M.V.	motor vessel
N.F.L.	Newfoundland
N.F.L.er(s)	Newfoundlander(s)
Nonia	Newfoundland Outport Nursing and Industrial Association
N.S.	Nova Scotia
o'c.	o'clock
P.A.	personal assistant
P.G.s	paying guests

Q.H.S.	Lady (Quita) Hope Simpson
R.A.F.	Royal Air Force
R.C.	Roman Catholic
R.C.M.P.	Royal Canadian Mounted Police
R.M.S.	Royal Mail Steamer
R.N.	Royal Navy
S.O.S.	international distress signal
S.S.	steamship
T.B.	tuberculosis
v.	*vide* (see)
V.A.D.	Voluntary Aid Detachment
w.c.	water-closet
Y.M.C.A./Y.M.	Young Men's Christian Association
Y.W.C.A./Y.W.	Young Women's Christian Association

Mary Jane Barclay and John Hope Simpson on their wedding day, 29 September 1900. 'She is a delightful person with whom to live ... ' (J.H.S., 29 September 1935).

Quita with her daughters, Mary (Maisie) (left) and Margaret Barclay (Greta) (right), June 1904. 'Domestically, our one drawback is absence from home and all of you' (J.H.S., 26 September 1935).

John Hope Simpson outside Buckingham Palace on the day King George V conferred his knighthood. The knighthood was announced in the King's birthday honours list of 3 June 1925. 'By the way, while I am Commissioner, I am "the Hon'ble Sir J.H.S."' (J.H.S., 8 February 1934).

ABOVE: St John's in 1936 (watercolour) by the English artist Rhoda Dawson. Saltfish is being dried in the foreground. Longshoremen can be seen at work on Harvey's wharf, where the ships employed in Furness Withy's transatlantic service docked. Prominent in the skyline are the twin towers of the Roman Catholic Cathedral (now Basilica) of St John the Baptist. 'I do love living above a harbour' (Q.H.S., 26 October 1935).

OPPOSITE: Rhoda Dawson's cartoon of Newfoundland society, 1936. From top to bottom, the serried ranks feature: the governor and his lady; representatives of the business and professional élite of the country; clergy and academics; working people; relief recipients; and (wearing balls and chains) members of the Commission of Government. The harpist is Fred Emerson. ' ... St. John's is a microcosm of a unique type – 40,000 people divided into watertight compartments' (J.H.S., 21 March 1934).

The Newfoundland Hotel, Cavendish Square, St John's, c. 1926. 'These rooms are the greatest comfort – the coolest suite in the hotel, on the N.E./S.W. corner & 5 stories up on a hill high over the town & harbour, so that we get every breeze that blows … ' (Q.H.S., [June 1936]).

Beside the Salmonier River, 1934. Left to right: Charles Pascoe Ayre, Lady Hope Simpson, Janet Murray, Charlotta P. Ayre, and Andrew Murray. 'We stopped for tea at Salmonier with friends who have a weekend summer bungalow on the river there' (Q.H.S., 29 May 1934).

Claude and Ruth (Taylor) Fraser and their daughter Sandra Fraser (now Gwyn) at 11 Winter Avenue, St John's, Coronation Day, 12 May 1937. 'I have just got a very capable personal assistant. His name is Claude Fraser. ... A man of ... great ability' (J.H.S., 19 April 1934).

In the grounds of Government House, St John's, August 1934. Front row, left to right: Lady Anderson, Prime Minister Ramsay MacDonald, Governor Sir David Murray Anderson, Ishbel MacDonald (daughter of the prime minister), and Lady Hastings Anderson. Back row, left to right: Captain H.D. Robinson, R.N. (private secretary to Governor Anderson), and Lieutenant-Commander J.A. Dicken, R.N. 'Ramsay MacDonald ... is here, at the moment, and I fear for another five weeks, with Ishbel' (J.H.S., 14 August 1934).

The first Markland schoolhouse. 'The first schoolhouse is up on a knoll, with terraced steps leading up to it at an angle from the road, & it looks down the road and over a valley through which the Rocky River runs' (Q.H.S., 27 June 1935).

Children at the Markland school took turns planning, preparing, and serving the daily meal. 'The school is to be educational in the sense of preparing them for being useful members of this colony' (Q.H.S., 11 September 1934).

Clare Cochius and her Markland pupils on a nature outing. 'The school is modelled on the Danish folk schools' (J.H.S., 31 October 1934).

Group of Markland enthusiasts at the settlement. Left to right: Harry Renouf, Harold Buxton, Clare Cochius, Helene Cochius, Monnie Mansfield, Marie Cochius (wife of R.H.K. and mother of Clare, Helene, and Daisy), and Daisy Cochius. Monnie Mansfield was later registrar of Memorial University College and (from 1949) Memorial University. She was succeeded in this position by Harry Renouf, who was a student at the college when this picture was taken. Harold Buxton was an English volunteer worker at Markland. 'It is a great experiment' (J.H.S., 31 October 1934).

The Grange, the Bond residence at Whitbourne. 'We walked over the fields ...
& loved the wide views over fields & lakes & forests to the distant hills – such a
glorious Sunday we had' (Q.H.S., 10 October 1935).

The first contingent of the Newfoundland Rangers, Whitbourne, July 1935. 'The
disciplinary standard demanded from the Rangers is infinitely more severe than
anything that the police have so far contemplated' (J.H.S., 29 September 1935).

Robin and Jean Reid at 'Gleneagles,' 1936. ' ... Mrs. Reid is equal to everything, and the food is quite a feature of the place' (Q.H.S., 4 August 1934).

Cecil Pelley, a Newfoundlander's Newfoundlander, c. 1940. 'My man is Cecil Pelley, a one-armed man. It is a marvellous triumph of intellect over disability' (J.H.S., 23 August 1935).

Emily and James Sparkes, who ran the Commission of Government's demonstration farm at Mount Pearl, near St John's. 'We take all our friends out to see the farm, and it is becoming so popular that I think we shall have to start a café there!' (J.H.S., 31 July 1936).

J.B. (Ian) Hope Simpson (left), in mining gear, at Buchans, August 1936. ' ... I do want Ian to see the country as near its best as can be after the first exquisite spring & summer flush of leaf and flower is over' (Q.H.S., 4 August 1936).

Vice-Admiral Sir Humphrey Walwyn and Lady Walwyn. 'He is an admiral with a fine quarterdeck manner, and an astonishingly free use of the broadside' (J.H.S., 16 February 1936).

WHITE TIE AND DECORATIONS

Introduction

The decade of the 1930s was a hard, unforgiving time in the history of Newfoundland and Labrador, and is remembered there as such. Small in population but large in area, the Dominion of Newfoundland was quickly overwhelmed by the events of the Great Depression. Individually, many Newfoundlanders were skilled and seasoned survivors, but as a people they depended on a precarious export trade, with a narrow range of goods produced in the country's basic and interconnected industries of fishing, forestry, and mining. The fishing industry was the largest user of labour. It was seasonal in nature, organized on a family basis, and devoted mainly to the production of salt cod. This was sold in distant markets – southern Europe, the Caribbean, and South America – and the trade was built on lines of credit that linked the merchant houses of St John's with regional firms and the fishing population. Local merchants supplied fishermen and took their production in payment. This was a truck or barter system. Very little cash changed hands, and many fishing families were constantly in debt. The revenue of the Newfoundland government came mainly from customs duties, and so was highly sensitive to shifts in price and demand in international markets.

When the Great Depression struck, the premier of Newfoundland was Sir Richard Squires, a Liberal. He was a promoter of industrial development and a man who had known many personal and political ups and downs. He had first become premier in 1919 but had been forced from office in 1923 by a major financial scandal. Returned to power in 1928, he initially benefited from the big North American investment boom of the second half of the 1920s, but, after the Wall Street crash of 29 October 1929, he soon found himself in a tight financial corner. In short order, the business of government in Newfoundland came to be dominated by one overriding issue: how to keep up interest payments on the country's debt while feeding the poor, whose ranks quickly multiplied as the economic downturn caught hold. Relief in Newfoundland was given in kind, and the diet of relief recipients scarcely allowed them to keep body and soul together. Nevertheless, by the winter of 1932–3 one-quarter of a population estimated at 282,000 were living on the meagre public hand-out.[1]

As financial and social conditions deteriorated, Squires attempted a series of increasingly desperate measures. His first plan was to borrow more money to keep the country going until market conditions improved. Although Newfoundland had not joined the Canadian confederation, Canadian banks in the 1890s had taken over most of the country's banking business, and the Bank of Montreal had become banker to the government of Newfoundland. In 1930, a syndicate of Canadian banks led by the Bank of Montreal gave Newfoundland a substantial loan, but the country's credit with private lenders was soon exhausted. Negotiations aimed at selling Labrador to Canada for an amount that would redeem Newfoundland's entire debt, which in 1931–2 reached $97,638,772 Canadian, also failed. The boundary between Newfoundland and Canada in Labrador had been fixed in 1927 by the Judicial Committee of the Privy Council in London after the question had been referred to it jointly by Ottawa and St John's. The decision of the Judicial Committee, which awarded Newfoundland a territory of some 112,826 square miles, rankled in Canada, especially in Quebec, but in desperate times there was no will in Ottawa to make a cash deal. All these events in Newfoundland raised the spectre of default, and this in turn led to British intervention. In Whitehall, the precedent of a financial failure by a dominion was viewed with alarm, even though the sum of money involved in this case was relatively small. This thinking led the British to become directly involved in Newfoundland's financial affairs. The British approach was to help Newfoundland in cooperation with Canada, in order to spread the burden and keep alive the idea of Newfoundland one day becoming part of Canada. The price Newfoundland paid for the Anglo-Canadian help thus received was to pass into a form of receivership. A Treasury official was sent from London to St John's to superintend the country's finances. Retrenchment became the order of the day, so as to balance the budget and keep up the contractual semi-annual payments to bondholders.

In return for the financial assistance offered to St John's at the end of 1932 to meet the next round of interest payments, the U.K. government put forward a new condition – that Newfoundland agree to the appointment by London of a royal commission to work out a long-term solution to the country's continuing financial problems. In June 1932, the government of Newfoundland had changed, and the premier now was Frederick C. Alderdice, a physically disabled St John's businessman who had been born in Northern Ireland. Alderdice, who led the United Newfoundland Party, was a Tory's Tory. He believed in small government, balanced budgets, a free hand for business, and, above all, the British Empire. Yet, on assuming office, even he had contemplated a radical act: to reschedule Newfoundland's debt. Obligations would not be repudiated, but bondholders would be told that the schedule of payments would be adjusted to take account of changed economic circumstances.

The British came down hard on this idea: a British dominion, Alderdice was told in no uncertain terms, had no choice but to honour its contractual obligations to bondholders. Every effort must be made to make payments in the amount promised, and on time. The dutiful Alderdice quickly desisted and, with no alternative policy, grasped enthusiastically the lifeline of the royal commission proposal. Its acceptance was made easier, moreover, by the fact that Newfoundland and Canada would each name a member to the three-member commission which London would appoint. The British choice to chair the Newfoundland royal commission was William Warrender Mackenzie, first Baron Amulree, a Scottish Labour peer. The Canadian nominee was C.A. Magrath, the chairman of the Canadian section of the International Joint Commission. Amazingly, Alderdice put forward the name, not of a prominent local figure, but of a financial adviser to his government, Sir William Stavert, a Canadian banker with close ties to the Bank of Montreal. The commissioners, all of whom were in their seventies, began hearings in St John's in March 1933 and eventually went to Ottawa to make soundings there. The royal commission was coolly received by the Canadian authorities, and, to the dismay of the British, Ottawa cut off all financial assistance to Newfoundland during the summer of 1933. This was done on the grounds that Newfoundland was a British problem and that Canada had too many financial problems of its own to take responsibility any longer for Newfoundland's troubles.

The Canadian pull-out put the British on the spot: should they support Newfoundland alone and, if so, at what price? Whitehall's answer was given in the report of the Newfoundland royal commission. The United Kingdom, the commission recommended, should assume 'general respon- sibility' for Newfoundland's finances.[2] In return, Newfoundland should agree to the suspension of parliamentary self-government in favour of administration by a commission of government, to consist of the governor and six commissioners, all appointed by London. Three of the commissioners would be drawn from the United Kingdom, three from New-foundland. The commission would have both executive and legislative power, and would be answerable to the Parliament of the United Kingdom through the Secretary of State for Dominion Affairs. The governor would chair the commission of government, and decisions would be taken unanimously or, if this was not possible, by majority vote. The justification advanced in the report of the royal commission for this drastic change was that Newfoundland's troubles were at root not caused by the Great Depression. No doubt the economic downturn had hit the country very hard, but Newfoundland's inability to stand up to the fierce gale that had started blowing through the markets of the world in 1929 was the result of foolish and profligate public spending in the past and the consequent accumulation of public debt. In order to win elections, party politicians had bribed Newfoundlanders with borrowed money and had embarked on get-rich schemes that made no economic sense. Sir Richard Squires was not singled out in the report, but an informed reader could decipher the message that he personified all that had gone wrong. What the country needed now was 'a rest from politics'[3] and administration that acted according to principle rather than partisanship. This is what a commission of government would provide. Once restored to economic health and reformed in outlook, Newfoundland would get self-government back.

Alderdice welcomed this proposal as one of deliverance and hope. He quickly got legislative approval for the scheme proposed by the royal commission, whereupon the U.K. Parliament passed the Newfoundland Act, 1933.[4] This received royal assent on 21 December 1933 and specified the terms on which the commission of government would operate. It promised the restoration of self-government when Newfoundland was self-supporting again and on a request from its people. The latter was a vague formulation that gave the British great freedom of manoeuvre for the future.

Recently, much has rightly been made in Canada of the concept of aboriginal self-government (declared an inalienable right by the First Nations themselves). Self-government, it is believed by supporters of this concept, would enhance the self-esteem of those affected, allow them to realize their full human potential, and usher in a reign of justice and peace. People grow, so the argument goes, by taking charge of their own affairs and escaping colonial dependency. In the calamitous events of the Great Depression, Newfoundlanders experienced the opposite of all this. True, the Commission of Government came in the clothes of imperial solidarity and Tory idealism; the dream of government above politics and with only the public good in mind had (and indeed still has) its allure. But, at another level, Newfoundlanders were in effect told that they had been betrayed by their own leaders, had made a flop of governing themselves, and needed a period of wardship before they could ever attempt to do so again. Here were the seeds of self-doubt, self-hate, and low self-esteem. It is not possible to be specific about the traumatic effect of the loss of self-government on the outlook of the Newfoundland people, but it can scarcely be doubted that such events left psychological wounds. Perhaps the Newfoundland writer Margaret Duley went to the heart of the matter when she dedicated her 1941 novel *Highway to Valour* to 'Newfoundland, a country which the author loves and hates.' In any event, Newfoundland suffered a loss in the 1930s that cannot be found in the history of any other present-day province of Canada.

The Commission of Government, which administered Newfoundland until it became a province of Canada on 31 March 1949, actually took office on 16 February 1934. The first governor under the new order was Admiral Sir David Murray Anderson, who had been in Newfoundland since January 1933. The first three Newfoundland members of the Commission of Government were former premier Frederick C. Alderdice, John C. Puddester, and William R. Howley. For all the high-minded rhetoric of the time, they were clearly chosen with an eye to denominational balance and political realities as well as administrative ability. Thus, Howley was a Roman Catholic, Alderdice a member of the Church of England, and Puddester a member of the United Church of Canada. Since Roman Catholics, Anglicans, and Nonconformists (United Church of Canada, Salvation Army, etc.) each formed a large group in the population, the reasoning behind the denominational selection was clear enough. The first members named to the commission from the United Kingdom were Everard Noel Rye Trentham, Thomas Lodge, and Sir John Hope Simpson. At the time of his appointment, Trentham was already in St John's, where he was busy representing the interests of the Treasury in relation to Newfoundland's accounts. At the first meeting of the Commission of Government, held 17 February 1934, portfolios were distributed. The British commissioners were given the financial and economic jobs, and the Newfoundlanders the rest. Alderdice became Commissioner for Home Affairs and Education, Howley Commissioner for Justice, and Puddester Commissioner for Public Health and Welfare. In continuation of his earlier duties, Trentham became Commissioner for Finance. Thomas Lodge became Commissioner for Public Utilities. His background was in government and business; he had recently lost a lot of money and needed a job. For his part, Sir John Hope Simpson became Commissioner for Natural Resources.

This portfolio comprised 'Marine and Fisheries, Forests, and Agriculture and Mines' and in essence involved the administration of the basic industries of the country.[5] In May 1934, the Commissioner for Natural Resources (Powers) Act, 1934, became law, and in November 1934, the Department of Natural Resources Act, 1934, was passed.[6]

It was over this department of government that Hope Simpson presided. And it is out of a collection of the family letters that he and Lady Hope Simpson wrote between February 1934 and September 1936, when they left Newfoundland for good, that this book has been made. The letters are mainly to their adult sons and daughters and their spouses, but nine of the letters excerpted here were written by Lady Hope Simpson to her spinster sister, Isabel Barclay (known as Bel), and one was addressed by her to her businessman brother, (Robert) Noton Barclay, Lord Mayor of Manchester, 1929–30.

When Hope Simpson sought the Newfoundland post, he was sixty-five years old and had behind him a remarkably diverse career. Born at Newby Terrace, Everton, Liverpool, on 23 July 1868, he was the fourth of eleven children, seven boys and four girls. His father was a well-to-do banker. Hope Simpson attended Liverpool College to age sixteen and then studied in Germany. In 1887, he entered Balliol College, Oxford, but after two years there went to India in the Indian Civil Service. Accordingly, he did not complete his Oxford degree until 1908. In September 1900, while on 'extraordinary leave without allowances'[7] from his multifarious and geographically scattered Indian duties, he married Mary Jane Barclay. They had met at a house party and he had proposed after knowing her only three weeks. They were then engaged for eighteen months while he was back in India. Mary Jane Barclay belonged to a large and prosperous mercantile family. Her father was the head of the firm of Noton Barclay at Oldham near Manchester. This firm had an office in Buenos Aires, and it was in that South American city that Mary Jane was born on 3 December 1870. As a result, she was known in the family as 'Quita,' a short form of the Spanish 'Mariequita' or 'dear little Mary.' She grew up in 'Sedgley New Hall,' Prestwich, Manchester, a large and well-appointed residence. She was educated at Laleham School, and then at Girton College, Cambridge. She did not get a degree from Cambridge, however, because this honour was still denied women. After their marriage, the Hope Simpsons lived, first, in India, where Quita fitted easily into the life of the colonial administrative élite. John Hope Simpson had been raised as a Congregationalist, but, while he and Quita were living for a time at Pyrford, Surrey, they joined the Church of England because there was no Congregational church nearby. Within the Church of England, they were decidedly low church and evangelical.

When the Great War began, Hope Simpson was acting as chief commissioner of the Nicobar and Andaman Islands, which were used for penal settlement. In October 1914, he was moved back to a previous posting at Gorakhpur, United Provinces (now Uttar Pradesh), but in May 1916 returned to the Andamans for a second term. He left India in December 1916 at age forty-eight, hoping that, because the age-of-enlistment rule had been relaxed, he would be able to join the armed forces. He did not succeed in this ambition and went instead to the Intelligence Department of the newly created Ministry of Labour. After the war, he and Quita sailed to New York and then undertook a most extensive Canadian tour. This whole trip is described in a lengthy diary Quita kept, which gives a foretaste of the style to be found in her Newfoundland letters. John Hope Simpson went to Canada because he was considering taking up farming there, but he eventually opted for Somerset instead. There the Hope Simpsons lived at 'Blagroves,' near the village of Oake. In the general election of 1922, Hope Simpson was returned to the House of Commons for Taunton as a Liberal. As a member of Parliament, he was notable for his contributions on agricultural and imperial, especially Indian, topics. He took a special interest in the affairs of Indians transplanted to East Africa and chaired a committee on overseas Indian communities (the India Colonies Committee).

Hope Simpson was defeated in the general election of 1924 and returned to private life. He was knighted the following year. After living for a time at Grenoble, France, he and Quita returned to the United Kingdom in 1926 and established themselves at 'Dolguog,' a spacious house which they rented near Machynlleth (Montgomeryshire) in Wales. Sir John's next appointment was in Athens as vice-president of the Refugee Settlement Commission, which the League of Nations had established in the aftermath of the 1920–3 war between Greece and Turkey. In 1930, he undertook a special mission to Palestine for the U.K. government. The ensuing report on immigration, land settlement, and development was completed in April 1930 and was published as a parliamentary paper. The next year, he became director general of the National Flood Relief Commission, established to deal with the destruction caused by an immense flood on the Yangtze River in China. At the end of this work, which involved the construction of a system of dykes, he hoped to become high commissioner of the Free City of Danzig, another League of Nations post, but this position did not materialize. In this period, he seems also to have had a job prospect of some kind in Romania, but since this also came to nothing, he turned to the Dominions Office and volunteered for service with the Commission of Government.

John and Quita Hope Simpson had five children, born as follows: Mary (Maisie) in 1902, Margaret Barclay (Greta) in 1903, John Barclay (Ian) in 1905, (Robert) Edgar in 1908, and Elizabeth Noton (Betty) in 1910. All but Edgar were born in India, where, shortly before Betty arrived, the other children contracted but survived bubonic plague. As a young adult, Betty Hope Simpson, who had been disabled by an attack of polioencephalitis in babyhood, found inspiration in the work of the Oxford Group (later Moral Re-Armament), as apparently did her parents (especially her father). Sir John began each day with a 'quiet time,' in which he sought God's guidance and the spiritual resources to carry out the tasks of the day. In the Newfoundland of the mid-1930s, at the trough of the Great Depression, the strength he found in such reflection would be severely tested.

After a busy round of preparatory engagements, the Hope Simpsons left Liverpool for Newfoundland on 2 February 1934, on board the R.M.S. *Montclare*. Alderdice and Thomas Lodge and his wife, Isobel, were also among the passengers, and the voyage gave them a chance to take the measure of one another. The Hope Simpsons and the Lodges got on well together from the beginning, and Sir John and Thomas Lodge became close allies in all the affairs of the Commission of Government – and the leaders of the new administration in its first phase. Sir John's initial impression of Alderdice was of a man of limited outlook and ability, weighed down by sickness, and nothing that happened subsequently changed his mind about him. The *Montclare* was supposed to go direct to St John's, but because of ice conditions the captain went to Halifax instead. From there, the Hope Simpsons travelled on to St John's aboard the *Silvia* and arrived in the Newfoundland capital on 15 February. From the *Silvia* they went to the Newfoundland Hotel, which was their home base for the whole of their stay in Newfoundland.

Located in Cavendish Square in the east end of the city, the Newfoundland Hotel had been opened on 30 June 1926, and in 1934 was being run at a loss by the Newfoundland government. Beginning in mid-March 1934, the Hope Simpsons occupied rooms 501, 502, and 503 on the northeast/southwest corner of the building and had 'a lovely view of the Narrows & Signal Hill.'[8] E.N.R. Trentham was already living in the hotel, and the Lodges moved in as well. Other long-term residents of this way station of empire included Andrew and Barbara (Rapsey) Grieve, the latter a relative of Sir John.[9] Life in the Newfoundland Hotel, with its potted plants, chintz coverings, and lace curtains, was easy and comfortable, and fitted into a pattern that would have been familiar to officialdom throughout the British Empire. Government House and the Colonial Building, the seat of the now-defunct Newfoundland legislature, were just along Military Road from the hotel, and much of the day-to-day life of the Hope Simpsons in St John's revolved around these three buildings. Here was the locus of power in Newfoundland, a colonial enclave where afternoon tea was served, bridge played, laws made, orders issued, and, as occasion required, white tie and decorations worn. The Commission of Government was inaugurated in the ballroom of the Newfoundland Hotel and held its first meeting at Government House. As Commissioner for Natural Resources, Hope Simpson established his office in the Colonial Building.

In March 1934, the Hope Simpsons went across Newfoundland with the Lodges and the Puddesters and a party of officials, on a familiarization tour. They travelled in style and comfort on a special train of the Newfoundland railway that was rather like the Newfoundland Hotel on wheels. The railway itself, which was of narrow gauge and had several branch lines as well as the main line from St John's to Port aux Basques, was one of the big sources of the debt that had brought Newfoundland to the edge of bankruptcy. The trans-island line had been pushed to completion in 1897 by Sir Robert Gillespie Reid, a Scottish-born engineer who had done well in the railway business in Canada. For many years, the railway and related ferry and coastal boat services had been run by the Reid Newfoundland Company, but in 1934 this whole transportation system was being operated by the government, again at a loss.

When spring, almost invariably late in Newfoundland, finally came in 1934, the Hope Simpsons got out a dark powder-blue leather-lined Austin 16.6 automobile they had brought with them from England and began exploring the Avalon Peninsula beyond the confines of the self-absorbed and gossipy capital of about 40,000 souls. The Avalon was the oldest settled part of Newfoundland and had the most extensive road network on the island. But even here there were isolated outports, as the coastal communities of Newfoundland were called, and many roads were scarcely worthy of the name. Elsewhere in the island, roads were few and far between, and highly localized. Not until the 1960s was it possible to drive on pavement across Newfoundland from St John's to Port aux Basques through the same territory traversed by the railway. None the less, the Hope Simpsons got a great deal of seasonal use and enjoyment out of their car, and, just as they hoped and intended, their knowledge of the country and its people grew apace as they went about. Their travels by car also gave them rich subject-matter for their letters to England, a steady stream of which began while they were still on their way to Newfoundland.

In July 1934, the Hope Simpsons again went across country by train, this time to visit George Simpson and family at Lomond, Bonne Bay, and to give Sir John an opportunity to inspect the settlements in that region. George Simpson, a Scot, was manager of the St Lawrence Timber, Pulp and Steamship Company, Limited, which exported pit-props to the United Kingdom. The next month, Sir John and Quita had their first full-scale Newfoundland holiday, which they took at 'Gleneagles,' an inn with a celebrated Scottish name, on Gander Lake, near the entrance to the Gander River. This inn had been opened the previous year by Robin and Jean (Knowling) Reid. Robin Reid was a grandson of Sir Robert Gillespie Reid. 'Gleneagles' was approached along a path through the woods from a halt on the Newfoundland railway. Quita mainly enjoyed the rustic charm of the inn itself, but for part of the time, Sir John, who was an avid fisherman, went down the Gander River with a guide.

Also in August 1934, Betty Hope Simpson came out to St John's to visit her parents. Her touring was confined to the Avalon, but during her stay Sir John went off on the *Daisy*, a government-owned forty-ton former minesweeper, to visit the northeast coast of Newfoundland and the coast of Labrador. At St Anthony, the headquarters of the famous medical mission Sir Wilfred Grenfell had established, he encountered not only Grenfell but Ramsay MacDonald, the prime minister of the United Kingdom, who was on holiday in Newfoundland aboard H.M.S. *Scarborough*.

On the Labrador coast, Hope Simpson went as far north as North West River, where he stayed with Dr Harry L. Paddon, whose enterprise and achievements he greatly admired. Another of his Labrador ports of call was at the mouth of the Alexis River, where the Labrador Development Company had started a logging operation. At the request of the company, he named the site of its headquarters 'Hope Simpson' (Port Hope Simpson). In September 1934, Sir John saw Quita and Betty off to England from Botwood aboard the *Geraldine Mary*, a paper carrier. He then continued on to Ottawa, where he met with various Canadian officials. In November 1934, he went over to London for a round of meetings at the Dominions Office, and he and Quita, who had gone home to close up 'Dolguog,' were able to enjoy Christmas *en famille* in England. Sir John returned to Newfoundland in February 1935, and Quita in April. In May, they resumed their Newfoundland travels, this time on the South Coast, a part of the country that could be visited only by ship. From Placentia, which could be reached by road, they travelled aboard the *Malakoff*, the government bait ship, which had been cleaned up for the occasion. They arrived in Port aux Basques after many ports of call; boarded the *Terra Nova*, the private car of the Newfoundland railway (it is now in the National Museum of Science and Technology, Ottawa); and went by the main line to Stephenville Crossing. After visiting a number of nearby places, they reboarded the *Terra Nova*, which was then connected to an eastbound express. Among its passengers were Captain Cecil Graves and his wife, Irene. They were in Newfoundland so that Captain Graves, the first director of the Empire Service of the British Broadcasting Corporation, could advise the government on the future of radio broadcasting in the country. Graves's secretary in England at this time was Margaret Barclay (Greta) Hope Simpson.

In July, after a busy social round with their English visitors, the Hope Simpsons made a second South Coast tour. As before, on the *Malakoff*, they left from Placentia and ended up at Port aux Basques. On the return journey this time, however, Sir John left the train at Deer Lake in order to explore up the Humber River with Ken Goodyear, a local businessman, and party, while Quita retreated to the domesticity of the Newfoundland Hotel. Reunited in August at 'Gleneagles,' the Hope Simpsons completed their summer 1935 rambles with an extended canoe and fishing trip on the Gander River. They were poled along and generally looked after by two remarkable river men: Cecil Pelley, who as a lad had suffered the loss of an arm from a shooting accident; and his half-brother, Sandy Parsons. This particular trip was a high point of the Hope Simpsons' Newfoundland touring, and is described in minute detail in their letters. Quita even wrote from her canoe as they were being poled along. Yet all was not idyllic. While they were on the Gander, a big forest fire was burning nearby. In the summer of 1935, moreover, life at 'Gleneagles' was disturbed somewhat by the antics of one of the parties of the Public Schools Exploring Society, a British body founded and led by Surgeon-Commander G. Murray Levick. The Hope Simpsons were not amused, and wrote scathingly of the advantage the English visitors took of the hard-working Reids.

In October 1935, Sir John gave notice to the Dominions Office that he wished to resign on 16 February 1936, the second anniversary of his swearing-in. His resignation was eventually accepted, but for September 1936 rather than February. In July 1936, Robert Benson Ewbank, who had been secretary of the India Colonies Committee chaired by Hope Simpson, was named as his replacement.

The Hope Simpsons' last months in Newfoundland were as busy and as eventful as those that had gone before. In November 1935, they went back to England, where Sir John, Thomas Lodge, and William R. Howley were involved in discussions at the Dominions Office over a sticky constitutional issue that had arisen between London and St John's. This started with the dismissal of Westbury Kean, the son of Newfoundland's most famous sealing captain, Abram Kean, from his job as master of the *Portia*, a government vessel which plied between St John's and Halifax. Wes Kean had been charged with smuggling and, even though acquitted in court, was fired by Thomas Lodge, the commissioner responsible for transportation. The commission as a whole backed Lodge's decision, but public opinion in moneyed St John's and in the Kean family's fiefdom of Bonavista Bay swelled in favour of the aggrieved captain. When the Dominions Office, feeling the heat, asked for information on the matter, it was refused by the commission on the grounds that it alone was responsible for what had been done and, by constitutional right, did not have to answer to London in detail for its actions. At root, the Kean affair posed the question of who was ultimately in charge in Newfoundland: the Commission of Government or the Dominions Office. Not surprisingly, given the financial relationship of the two parties, this question was settled at the London talks in favour of Whitehall.

The Hope Simpsons returned to St John's in January 1936. Their fellow passengers on this trip included a new governor of Newfoundland, Vice-Admiral Sir Humphrey T. Walwyn, his wife, Eileen Mary, and his son, James, who had followed his father into the Royal Navy. Hope Simpson's initial impression of Sir Humphrey was very favourable, but over time, as Walwyn tried to assert authority over the commission, Sir John came to have a very different view of him. In March 1936, Quita went back to England on short notice to visit her ailing sister Isabel. She returned to Newfoundland in May and on the way over enjoyed the company of Victor Campbell and his Norwegian wife, Marit. Campbell had been a mate on the *Terra Nova* when that vessel, now in use at the seal fishery, was a supply ship with the ill-fated 1910–12 Antarctic expedition of the English explorer Robert Falcon Scott. Campbell had also come close to losing his life in the Antarctic and was a legendary figure in his own right. The Campbells owned a big house at Black Duck on the west coast of Newfoundland and went to stay there every summer. In June, the Hope Simpsons went by train to visit them at a retreat that was manifestly more sylvan than rural. In July, the Hope Simpsons made another satisfying visit to 'Gleneagles.' The next month, their son Ian visited from England, and on 3 September Sir John gave over his office and he and Quita left by train for Deer Lake. From there, they set off on their last big Newfoundland adventure, an extended trip up the Humber River. This expedition was organized for them by Josiah Goodyear, a brother of Ken Goodyear and another compleat Newfoundlander. On 14 September 1936, the Hope Simpsons boarded the *Caribou* at Port aux Basques and left Newfoundland for a round of American and Canadian visits before returning to England and semi-retirement.

In July 1935, before he and Quita set off on their first South Coast tour, Sir John wrote that once this particular trip was completed they would 'have been round the whole of the island' and would 'know more about the coast of N.F.L. than 99% of the population.'[10] This was probably no exaggeration. In general, Newfoundlanders were rooted in locality, and while itinerancy was a feature of their world of work, their movements tended to be within well-established bounds. Travel for leisure and holiday-making were rarities in a country where subsistence and survival were for many the foremost considerations. By contrast, the Hope Simpsons could command the best means of transport Newfoundland had to offer, and, given Sir John's responsibilities, they had good reason to tour extensively. They were also seasoned travellers and lovers of the landscape, which, in the case of Newfoundland and Labrador, they found visually stunning. They often favourably compared the physical features and natural attractions of Newfoundland to those of Greece and Scotland, and description of the land itself and discussion of environmental matters are important themes in their letters. If anything, their appetite for Newfoundland as a place grew the longer they were there and the more they were able to explore. Quita in particular rhapsodized about the sights of Newfoundland and never tired of the view from the Newfoundland Hotel onto St John's harbour. There the age of sail lingered on, and schooners and sealing vessels mixed with paper carriers and the passenger and freight ships of the Furness Withy Line: the *Incemore, Newfoundland, Nova Scotia*, and, beginning in February 1936, *Fort Amherst*. The Furness Withy ships, which docked at Harvey's wharf, provided service between Liverpool, St John's, Halifax, Boston, and New York, and their movements absorbed the Hope Simpsons, for whom letter writing was second nature and the arrival of mail from England an eagerly awaited and very special event.

If the Hope Simpsons found much to admire scenically in Newfoundland, they also found much to criticize in almost every other respect. Indeed, their letters continue the harsh critique of Newfoundland society found in the report of the 1933 Newfoundland royal commission. They were shocked by the dilapidated appearance of much of the island, by the numbers and condition of the poor, and by what they regarded as a general lack of energy and enterprise in the population. And in line with the thinking of the royal commission, they concluded that the root problem of the country was moral. Patronage, denominationalism, and undue reliance on government were the symptoms of this malaise, the vices the Commission of Government must stamp out if Newfoundlanders were to become fit to govern themselves again. Inevitably, this would be a slow process, and success would hinge on a reformed and improved education system in which the existing state-supported denominational schools would have to give way to public schools. In practice, the Commission of Government was divided on this issue, and the critics of denominational education were able to make only limited headway.

One of the big surprises at the outset of commission rule was the attitude of Hope Simpson and his fellow British commissioners towards St John's businessmen. The latter had been all for the Commission of Government and fully expected that an administration above politics would naturally listen to them, since, by definition, they had the same perspective on the world. In this, they were badly mistaken. Thus, although the Hope Simpsons mixed a great deal socially with the St John's upper crust, they were severe critics of the role this small élite played in the life of the country, and regarded this group, along with its spokesmen, the Newfoundland commissioners, as obstacles to progress. In the case of the fishing industry, the cutthroat individualism of the Newfoundland exporters undermined prices in overseas markets, with the consequent loss being passed on to fishing families. A similar situation existed in forestry, where the two foreign pulp and paper companies operating in the country, the British-owned Anglo-Newfoundland Development Company (Grand Falls) and the American-owned International Power and Paper Company of Newfoundland Limited (Corner Brook), enjoyed enormous advantages while loggers toiled for near-starvation wages.

The way forward for Newfoundland, Sir John believed, was to provide opportunities for the people to help themselves. 'It is a case,' he wrote in May 1935, 'of building up from the bottom.'[11] Hence the emphasis of the commission from its inception was on leadership, cooperation, and education. Hope Simpson's analysis of the fishing industry was that too many people were trying to make a living from it, with the result that it produced a miserable return for almost all. His prescription was to reduce the labour force in the industry, raise the productivity of those who remained in the business, and compel the merchants into orderly marketing arrangements (i.e., supply management) that would lead to better prices and higher returns to individual fishermen. The high point of his administration of the fishing industry was the creation in 1936 of the Newfoundland Fisheries Board. This entrenched the regulatory approach he favoured and was one of the most far-reaching changes ever made by the Commission of Government. As a first step towards doing something about conditions among loggers, Hope Simpson launched an enquiry, which was carried out by Gordon Bradley, who had been leader of the opposition in the Newfoundland legislature after the election of 1932. Bradley produced a scorching indictment of the practices of the foreign-owned pulp and paper companies, but his report was buried by the commission. The government was, however, able to extract some ameliorative concessions from the companies for the loggers. But this whole episode highlighted the practical limits of the commission's authority when it came up against an interest group with the means and will to defend itself.

For the many Newfoundlanders who would be displaced from the fishing industry as it was rationalized and modernized, Hope Simpson looked to land settlement as the panacea. On this issue, he and Lodge were of one mind and strong backers of a land-settlement experiment that was started with government assistance in 1934 at Markland on the Avalon Peninsula. The Hope Simpsons visited this developing community again and again and saw in it a new beginning for Newfoundland and a model that could be emulated throughout the country. Their observations in 1935 at Lourdes, a resettlement community on the west coast of the island, reinforced their faith in the direct link between assisting people to move and the opening up of new economic opportunities and the broadening of social horizons.

Another of Hope Simpson's pet projects was the creation of the Newfoundland Ranger Police Force. Known as the Newfoundland Rangers, this unit was formed under the authority of legislation that took effect on 21 September 1935, and its members were intended to be general agents of the government and social animators in rural Newfoundland. Hope Simpson had high expectations for the Rangers and gave top priority to their training, which was conducted at Whitbourne, and to their posting. In the same spirit, he was at the fore in pressing for the reform of the magistracy and the civil service. If Newfoundland was to progress, he believed, its administrative machine would first have to be made equal to the task at hand. At the Department of Natural Resources, Hope Simpson's own secretary (the equivalent of deputy minister in the Commission of Government) was Claude Fraser. He exemplified all the qualities of efficient administration –

reliability, creative policy making, hard work, and dedication – that Sir John hoped would eventually come to characterize the whole of a revitalized Newfoundland public service.

The Hope Simpsons were convinced that Newfoundland had a rich tourist potential, so another of Sir John's purposes was to develop facilities that would allow this potential to be realized and thereby create a new source of employment in the country. He was full of praise for the efforts of the Reids at 'Gleneagles' and promoted a make-work scheme that was designed to open up the Salmonier Line area of the Avalon Peninsula for holiday-makers. He also planned a national park and had trails cut along the Humber to facilitate the more adventuresome form of tourism that could be developed there. Again, he sought to enforce tougher regulations than had ever been known before for hunting and inland fishing. In this latter regard, the Hope Simpson letters are a reminder of just how pristine the natural world of Newfoundland still was in the 1930s and just how much it has been disrupted and, in some measure, despoiled since that time.

When Sir John left Newfoundland, he was convinced that an economic corner had been turned there and that the country was at last on the road to modest but solid well-being. In truth, he somewhat misjudged the situation. Newfoundland was hit hard again by the big recession that struck the North American economy in the late 1930s, and, as the terrible decade drew to a close, the proportion of the country's population on relief remained shockingly high. But all this changed suddenly for the better with the coming of Second World War, which ushered in the greatest prosperity that Newfoundland had ever known. This prosperity, based on military spending, moved Newfoundlanders away from the Nordic and folk type of future that the plans of the Commission of Government in the 1930s had envisaged for them and towards a more characteristically North American mode of living. The glad bright day that Sir John had hoped for and forecast truly came, but it was quite unlike the one that he and his associates had had in mind. Yet portents of that very different future appear in the letters that he and Quita wrote: for example, in their many references to the growing influence of radio and in their account of the breaking of ground in the summer of 1936 for the Newfoundland Airport at what is now Gander. This area, so empty in the 1930s, became a focal point of wartime military activity. But perhaps the shape of the future as seen in the letters is found best of all in Quita's account of driving down to Beachy Cove on a fine summer day in 1936 to attend a picnic with some ladies from St John's. En route, from what was in many respects still a nineteenth-century world, they stopped and looked up at that striking symbol of twentieth-century progress, the German zeppelin *Hindenburg*, as it cruised down Conception Bay on one of its transatlantic flights. Here was a quite new connection for Newfoundland with the larger world, and implicit in it was the promise of a better, if as yet scarcely imaginable, tomorrow.

On their return to England, the Hope Simpsons settled in Oxford, and Sir John was active in the affairs of the Royal Institute of International Affairs, a branch of which he had helped launch in St John's. In the 1930s, the main focus of his work for the institute was on refugee questions. After the war started, he became director of the research program of the institute when much of its work was transferred from Chatham House in London to Balliol College. In April 1940, Sir John resigned his research position, though he continued with other work for the institute and remained on a committee dealing with Newfoundland affairs. One of his colleagues on this commit-tee was Thomas Lodge, who had been replaced on the Commission of Government early in 1937, and in 1939 had disgraced himself with the Do-minions Office through the publication of his *Dictatorship in Newfound-land*. The continuing interest in Newfoundland of the Royal Institute of International Affairs would bear fruit in 1946 in the publication of R.A. MacKay, ed., *Newfoundland: Economic, Diplomatic, and Strategic Studies*. By this time, Sir John was living in Worthing, Sussex. Quita had died in 1939, and in 1941 he had married Evelyn Brookes, the widow of one of his colleagues in the Indian Civil Service. They had known each other since his days in the Andaman Islands in 1914. Sir John died on 10 April 1961 at age ninety-two after a fine evening of bridge in which he had made a grand slam.

After his father's death, Ian Hope Simpson, who finished his own career as a history master at Rugby School, undertook to write an account of Sir John's life after his return from India. Ian completed this work, which he entitled '"Jack of All Trades": An Indian Civil Servant in Retirement. Sir John Hope Simpson,' but it was never published. Shortly before his own death in 1989, he deposited the typescript of his study, together with a collection of his parents' papers, in the library of Balliol College, Oxford. In 1990, I published an annotated edition of Ian's chapter on his father's Newfoundland days. My edition is entitled 'J.B. Hope Simpson's account of Sir John Hope Simpson's Newfoundland career, 1934–6,' and it appeared in *Newfoundland Studies* 6/1 (Spring 1990), 74–110. With the permission of Ian's literary executor, his daughter-in-law Jacynth Hope-Simpson, I then undertook to prepare a select edition of the family letters in the Balliol

College collection which Ian had used in writing his Newfoundland chapter. The result is the present work.

In making my selection from the correspondence, I have concentrated on the information that I believe will be of most interest to students of Newfoundland and imperial history. I have in general omitted family information unless it bears directly on the public lives of the Hope Simpsons and is therefore of larger historical interest. Ellipses indicate text I have omitted. I have tried to avoid repetition of material, but I have occasionally included his and her accounts of the same episode in order to present a full picture. I read 317 letters at Balliol, 161 by Sir John and 156 by Lady Hope Simpson.[12] The passages I have chosen are taken from 244 of these, 132 by Sir John and 112 by Lady Hope Simpson.[13] They are arranged in chronological order, and here and there I have silently added or changed punctuation, adjusted capitalization, corrected obvious spelling errors, and so forth, in the interest of readability. For the same reason, I have also expanded many abbreviations and removed some underlining. Words underlined in the original letters which I have chosen to highlight here appear in italics. I have likewise put all ships' names in italics. Generally speaking, however, the letters are as they were written, with my added words in square brackets. In my explanatory notes, I have given birth and death dates, where they are useful, whenever possible. For the benefit of readers who may wish to consult the original correspondence in its entirety, I have deposited a rough typescript of this, on disk, at Balliol College library. Readers who want a narrative account of the history of Newfoundland in the 1930s may wish to consult my 1988 book *Newfoundland in the North Atlantic World, 1929–1949.* My bibliography summarizes the state of knowledge about Newfoundland and Labrador in the 1930s.

The Hope Simpson letters excerpted in this book were clearly written from a special perspective, but they are just as clearly an important source for understanding the history of Newfoundland during the Great Depression. The view of a hard-pressed little country to be found here is from a window on the fifth floor of the Newfoundland Hotel and is, by extension, that of the governing class. But the window sash is of generous proportion and the window-pane is clean and clear. For the student of the Newfoundland past, these are no small advantages.

NOTES

1 Newfoundland Royal Commission 1933, *Report* (London 1933), 4, 50.
2 Ibid., 224.

3 Ibid., 195.

4 United Kingdom, *The Public General Acts*, 1933–4, 5–14.

5 See my *Newfoundland in the North Atlantic World, 1929–1949* (Kingston and Montreal 1988), 47.

6 *Acts of the Honourable Commission of Government of Newfoundland 1934* (St John's 1935), 46–7, 181–8.

7 Balliol College Library, Oxford University, Hope Simpson Papers, J.B. Hope Simpson, '"Jack of All Trades": An Indian Servant in Retirement. Sir John Hope Simpson,' vi.

8 See below, 52.

9 Barbara Grieve's mother and Sir John were first cousins.

10 See below, 184.

11 See below, 156.

12 The totals by year are as follows: 1934 – J.H.S., 54, Q.H.S., 55; 1935 – J.H.S. 58, Q.H.S., 56; 1936 – J.H.S., 49, Q.H.S., 45. The 317 letters I used at Balliol include 13 letters from Q.H.S. to her sister Isabel; 1 letter from Q.H.S. to her brother Noton; and 1 letter from J.H.S. to Q.H.S.

13 The totals by year are as follows: 1934 – J.H.S. 44, Q.H.S. 41; 1935 – J.H.S. 44, Q.H.S. 39; 1936 – J.H.S. 44, Q.H.S. 32.

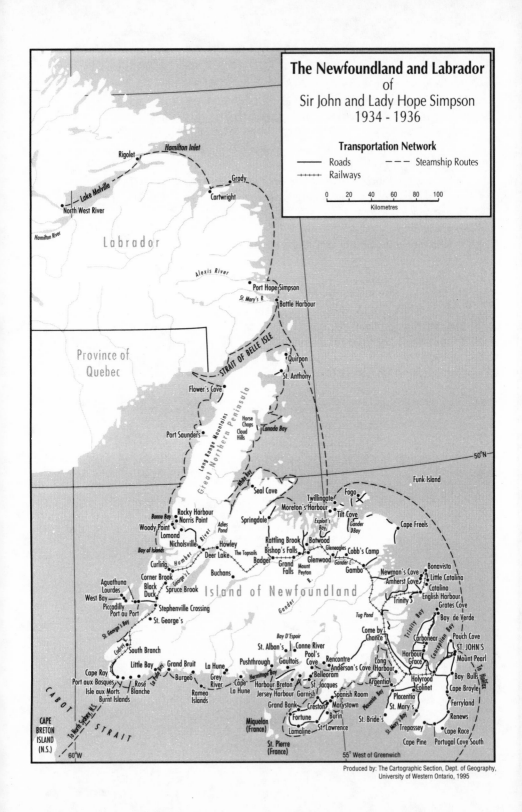

The Newfoundland and Labrador
of
Sir John and Lady Hope Simpson
1934 - 1936

Transportation Network

— Roads   - - - Steamship Routes
+++++ Railways

0   20   40   60   80   100
Kilometres

Produced by: The Cartographic Section, Dept. of Geography,
University of Western Ontario, 1995

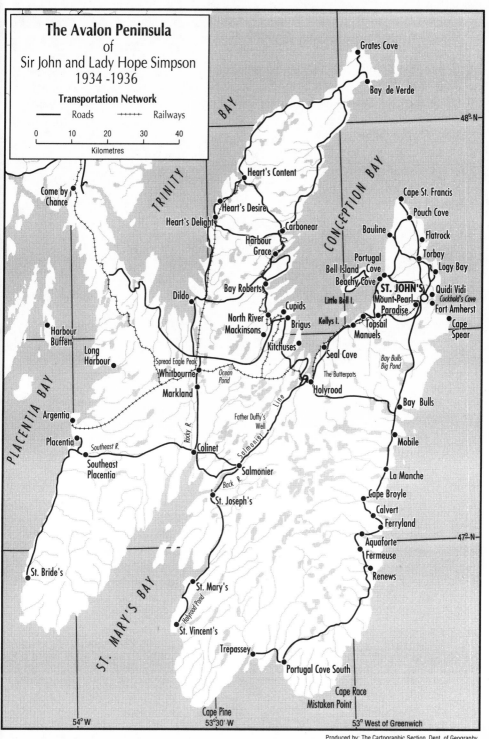

The Avalon Peninsula
of
Sir John and Lady Hope Simpson
1934 -1936

Transportation Network

——— Roads   +++++ Railways

0   10   20   30   40
Kilometres

Grates Cove

Bay de Verde

48° N

Come by Chance

TRINITY

Cape St. Francis

Pouch Cove

Heart's Content

Bauline

Flatrock

Heart's Desire

Torbay

Carbonear

Portugal Cove

Logy Bay

Heart's Delight

Harbour Grace

Bell Island

Beachy Cove

Dildo

Bay Roberts

Little Bell I.

ST. JOHN'S

Quidi Vidi

Cuckhold's Cove

Mount-Pearl

Fort Amherst

Cupids

Paradise

North River

Brigus

Kellys I.

Topsail

Cape Spear

Mackinsons

Manuels

CONCEPTION BAY

Kitchuses

Seal Cove

Harbour Buffett

Long Harbour

Spread Eagle Peak

Whitbourne

Ocean Pond

Bay Bulls Big Pond

The Butterpots

Holyrood

PLACENTIA BAY

Markland

Father Duffy's Well

Salmonier Line

Bay Bulls

Argentia

Rocky R.

Mobile

Placentia

Southeast R.

Colinet

Salmonier

La Manche

Southeast Placentia

Back R.

St. Joseph's

Cape Broyle

Calvert

Ferryland

Aquaforte

47° N

Fermeuse

St. Bride's

ST. MARY'S BAY

Renews

St. Mary's

Holyrood Pond

St. Vincent's

Trepassey

Portugal Cove South

Cape Race

Mistaken Point

Cape Pine

54° W

53° 30' W

53° West of Greenwich

Produced by: The Cartographic Section, Dept. of Geography,
University of Western Ontario, 1995

1934

J.H.S. to Betty, 1 February 1934, Royal Hotel, Waterloo, Near Liverpool

You have sent me exactly what I need. I shall have unlimited engagements when I get to St. John's, and when I come back, I shall show you them in my book. Very many thanks.

We have had a hectic week. On Monday morning, I had engagements and had lunch with Sir Wilfred Grenfell.[1] You know about him and Labrador, where he runs a mission. He has done magnificent work. Both he & Lady Grenfell[2] are very much excited about this new government, and hope for great things. ... There are two good items of news. Our ship is to call at St. John's, so we shall not have to go to Halifax and then come back by ferry boat. The other is that the government may want me home in October to consult.

There is one bad item. The temperature at St. John's is 10 degrees below zero. ...

[1] 1865–1940. Founder of medical mission in northern Newfoundland and Labrador, with headquarters at St Anthony, Newfoundland.

[2] Anna (MacClanahan) Grenfell (1885–1938), an American, known as Anne.

Q.H.S. to Betty, 2 February 1934, R.M.S. *Montclare*

Here we are, started but held up in the river. ... We hear now that we go direct to Halifax & on by train. It is a great disappointment, as yesterday the ship had orders to go direct with us to St. John's. By the bye, don't forget to address us Newfoundland Hotel, St. John's, Newfoundland. There is a St. John in Nova Scotia or New Brunswick,[1] so don't leave out the Newfoundland. There is so much ice in St. John's harbour that they dare not venture this big ship into it. ...

1 Saint John, New Brunswick.

J.H.S. to Ian and Sheila, 3 February 1934, off Greenock, R.M.S. *Montclare*

We are just, 10.30 a.m., about to anchor off Greenock, after a perfectly lovely sail up the Clyde[1] estuary. The sea is brilliant, and there is a cool south-west breeze, though the sun, and the ship, are both hot. There are only 21 passengers in the saloon. They have given us a cabin with a bath-room, another cabin for my dressing room, and a third for our baggage. So we are in clover. The other members of the Commission, Mr. (and Mrs.) Alderdice,[2] and Mr. (& Mrs.) Lodge,[3] and we compose the captain's table. Given decent weather, we shall be most comfortable. ...

Yesterday, we went into Liverpool, where I paid for the new car.[4] ... I did not have much time with the family as there were reporters and interviewers and the Lord Mayor[5] in top hat and gold chain to see us off. We left at 4.30 on the tick & anchored off New Brighton till 9 o'clock. We had a sea like a mill-pond all night.

Your letter, Ian, was on board. Many thanks for it. I hope that the Christ's Hospital[6] appointment may materialize. It is just possible that the publicity I have had in the press may have some slight influence, though that is questionable. ...

1 River Clyde, Scotland.
2 Frederick C. and Harriet (Carter) Alderdice.
3 Thomas and Isobel (Scott) Lodge.
4 The Austin 16.6 they brought to Newfoundland.
5 George A. Strong.
6 English public school, known as the 'Blue Coat School.'

J.H.S. to Ian and Sheila, 8 February 1934, south of Cape Race, en route to St John's via Halifax, N.S.

... We are hoping very presently, though not by any means expecting, favourable news about Christ's Hospital. Even though you may not get it, you will at least be known in a new quarter as looking for a post of the kind. That is to the good. It was very wise to apply. There is a motto ...

'Don't wait for your ship to come in. Take a boat and go out to meet it.' I did that in the case of my present appointment. I wrote to J.H. Thomas,[1] telling him that, as Romania had fallen through, I was free, in case my services might be useful to the government in connection with this Commission, and was sent for by return of post. There can be no possible harm in informing people, who cannot otherwise know, that you are willing to accept a vacant post. ...

The Atlantic has certainly been kind to us. We have had quite a lot of sun and, till Tuesday,[2] mild southerly wind. It was rough on Monday night, and again very rough last night. Today is perfect. ...

Yesterday morning, the captain took me up to the chart room and, swearing me to secrecy (which I have observed, not even repeating it to Mum), showed me on the chart the icefields and icebergs in our path which have been reported from Cape Race[3] by wireless. He changed course at 8 o'clock & came south. A Newfoundland skipper, Capt. Whiteley,[4] who is on board, told me yesterday morning that he 'smelt'[5] ice. The captain had not told him anything, so I suppose there must be something in it. We are past the ice now. It does not travel west past Cape Race.

I have now done a lot of work on board, writing up and finally dictating notes on the various interviews and conferences in London, and consulting Mr. Alderdice, the N.F.L. prime minister. ... He is a *very* sick man. ... He has no feet and only one leg. The other was amputated high up as the result of septicaemia owing to a kick at rugger. He was a great player. The septicaemia affected the other foot also & that was amputated. Altogether, he had 18 operations in an attempt to save the leg and foot. He is a very courageous man, and has a fine memory and a highly developed sense of humour. Altogether an attractive person, but with an outlook restricted to the coasts of N.F.L. For instance, he has no use for their marine biological station,[6] which is the best on the Atlantic coast. He says, 'What can the scientists teach us? We have been curing fish for the last 300 years & know everything there is to be known about it.' Yet the Labrador fish is badly cured and suffers from 'pinkeye' – red lines each side of the backbone. The despised scientist has discovered the microbe that causes pinkeye and that the reason for it is dirt!

Mr. & Mrs. Lodge are also on board. He is one of the British members of the Commission. A pretty good man he must be, as he was secretary of the shipping control in the war. He is very lethargic. We play bridge with them each night after dinner, and Mum is playing *very* well. Also, she is beating me repeatedly at piquet.[7]

We should be in Halifax tomorrow evening, D.V. Thence we travel by a local steamer – the *Silvia* – 2,000 tons, – to St. John's. We hear that she is a professional roller, so we are praying that the weather may be very kind. ...

By the way, while I am Commissioner, I am 'the Hon'ble[8] Sir J.H.S.' That is satisfactory, for now I know that I am honourable.

1 Secretary of State for Dominion Affairs.
2 6 February 1934.
3 Southeast Avalon Peninsula, Newfoundland.
4 George C. Whiteley (1874–1961),

member for St Barbe, Newfoundland House of Assembly, 1932–4.
5 Smelled.
6 At Bay Bulls, near St John's.
7 Another card-game.
8 Honourable.

Q.H.S. to Betty, 12 February 1934, The Nova Scotian, Halifax

Here we are just finishing our 2nd stage. Tonight we sail ... for Newfoundland. We saw such a magnificent N.F.L. dog today – a perfect darling. You would love them. They are trying to breed them all black now, but this fellow has two white forepaws, as his master wanted to ensure that he would not easily be stolen.

We have had such a lovely time here. ... The people ... have been so hospitable & kind. ... On Saturday[1] Daddy was taken round the fisheries & lunched with some of the leading men & the ladies, & I went to a tea-party of Halifax ladies arranged to meet us. It is rather like Athens.[2] People seem to go from one tea-party to another. ...

Yesterday ... we had about 36 people to lunch – we being the Commission – all the Newfoundland students we could get hold of who are working at the Dalhousie University here – boys & girls. It was a delightful lunch. We had a private room & a horseshoe table. Daddy presided, & the rest of us scattered among the students. They were such nice young folk – a very fine example of what N.F.L. can produce – all children of Dr. Paton's[3] teaching there. They say that each boy who goes out from his school bears his stamp. Such an insignificant-looking little man, but a great schoolmaster. After the lunch, John spoke to the students, telling them that the future of the country lay in their hands. At present, all the best men go to Canada & America to make a living – there is nothing for them in N.F.L. But if this Commission can do its job, & if the young men will do their part, there must be a future for N.F.L., possibly a great future. We are greatly impressed with the character of their lads & of the men we are meeting. ... This afternoon, I have to get our boxes off to the *Silvia*, while

Daddy is up at the school for the blind,[4] where there are some N.F.L. people. Then we all go to tea at Government House, & from there to a cocktail party, & after dinner to our ship. ...

1   10 February 1934.
2   The Hope Simpsons had lived in Athens, Greece, in the late 1920s.
3   John Lewis Paton (1863–1946), High

Master of Manchester Grammar School, 1903–24, President of Memorial University College, 1925–33.
4   The Halifax School for the Blind.

Q.H.S. to Edgar and Eleanor, Newfoundland Hotel, 17 February 1934
We really are having a marvellous time and just wish we could share it with our children. ... I fancy there is plenty of hard work ahead and many disagreeables & troubles to be faced. But – just now – the clear, crisp cold makes one feel so happy and so full of energy, and so ready to enjoy everything. ...

Our voyage from Halifax was not exactly pleasant – the ship rolled horribly & we were in the wake of a big storm. But we enjoyed it – we had a luxurious cabin with bedroom, tho' the hot water did not work at all & the cold not always.

We had a crowd to meet us when we arrived – mayor & corporation & ministers & A.D.C.s & police. Then on the jetty was a crowd of poor folk – pitifully poor & half-starved they looked. But they say that it is these poor people who are feeling stirrings of hope.

I have just had the Y.W.C.A. secretary[1] in for about 2 hours. She has been telling me that her greatest anxiety is for the girls who are so poor they can't live without going on the streets, and it is to keep them in the Y.W. hostel that she is straining every nerve – and cash is so short that it seems as tho' the Y.W. and the Y.M. would have to go. ...

Well, I must tell you about Friday.[2] It was a historic day here. The ceremony was held in the ballroom of the hotel, as it is the largest room in the town. It was most impressive, not to say funereal – until Daddy did his part. The procession of Commissioners came very slowly up the aisle to the platform, as Mr. Alderdice is so crippled he has to walk with 2 sticks. Then a pause, and then the Chief Justice,[3] followed by the Governor[4] & his A.D.C. in full blaze of naval uniform & medals. All this in dead silence. First, the Letters Patent were read – that took almost half an hour. Then, the King's Proclamation. Then, the Governor read his speech, & then the Prime Minister, Mr. Alderdice, read his. Then Daddy spoke direct to the people, and it seemed really as tho' a breath of reality & humanity blew through the hall & all the people stirred & breathed again. He spoke simply & naturally, tho' he had prepared very carefully. And he took the hearts of the people at the last by a very apt story illustrating the spirit in which the British Commissioners would do their work. Do you remember the story of the local circumstances? Two men walking in a field met an angry bull & one shinnied up a tree; the other bolted into a cave. The man bolted out again & tried to reach the tree, but the bull chased him back to his cave. The tree-man watched the cave-man make [a] second sally only to be chased back. 'Why don't you stop in your cave, Mike – the bull will get tired of waiting & go away.' 'You don't know the local circumstances – there's a bear in this cave.' The audience shouted with laughter, but saw the point & realized that the Commission are not out to dictate but to understand and sympathize & be guided by local circumstances. I have no doubt that that story is now circulating with huge enjoyment in the outports & these far-off lonely people feel themselves brought into touch with the new government.

Afterwards, they all had to go to Government House to take the oath, & ladies followed to tea. ...

The hotel is right out on the edge of the country – a snow-covered land at present. In front is the open space, where there is a monument & a circle where the trams[5] turn in their tour of the town. Below is the harbour & inlet, & the town lies on the hill along this inlet. It is a dreary-looking town because the snow makes the wooden houses look so dirty & dilapidated. Bright paints would make all the difference. Can you hear the sledge bells? I am sitting with the windows wide open, as it is very mild today & the hot pipes give a very oppressive heat. It was raining all night, and the streets are so slippery that it is amusing to watch the schoolchildren sliding round corners & anxious work for elderly people & cars even with chains. The steep streets make glorious toboggan runs, & there seems to be no check on the joyous activities of the youngsters. It is dreadfully dangerous really – but very gay. The country to [the] north & east of us looks most attractive. ... And we have a lovely view of the harbour and of the hills beyond the town too, so we don't feel a bit shut in.

The first thing we had to do was to get 'creepies'[6] put on our galoshes & snow boots; 'creepies' are rather like the suspender fasteners you clip onto your belt. You open them when you [go] out, so that you grip the slippery surface, & you close them when you come in, so that you do not spoil your floors. But on a day like this even 'creepies' do not seem to be sufficient. But the air is delicious; it makes you feel so fresh, & when the sun shines, it is a heavenly world. ...

But the accounts of the condition of the people are simply appalling. They are so apathetic – they have suffered so long that there seems to be no energy in them. They stand by with their hands in their pockets & watch men trying to fight a forest fire when their help would control it. In many of the outports, in the winter, the women don't get up till about 1 o'c. because they have nothing to do. Work amongst these people is most disheartening. They have been practically serfs & have no traditions – no moral impetus. They are apparently charming to meet – very friendly, but there it ends. Even Dr. Paton was discouraged. Most people seem to be in despair.

Well well! They say no one can stand more than two years of this. Is it just a question of sticking to it and leadership? ...

Here comes the sun. I don't think we have had more than one day without sun since we left England.

1 R. Cheswright was General Secretary of the Y.W.C.A. in St John's.
2 16 February 1934.
3 Sir William Horwood (1862–1945), Chief Justice of the Supreme Court, 1902–44.
4 Admiral Sir (David) Murray Anderson (1874–1936), Governor of Newfoundland, 1933–6.
5 Of the street railway.
6 Creepers (see G.M. Story, W.J. Kirwin, and J.D.A. Widdowson, *Dictionary of Newfoundland English*, 2d ed. [Toronto 1990], 120–1).

Q.H.S. to Greta, Newfoundland Hotel, 17 February 1934

I can hardly believe that it is only a fortnight ... since we left England. ... It seems such a long time. ...

Dear, this is such fun! We have a very comfortable little suite on the 5th storey. A long sitting-room ... with 2 windows looking out on the harbour & the rather dingy, dreary town to the hills. The bedroom is a long room too, with a hanging-cupboard room off it. The sitting-room has a large hanging-cupboard too. And the bathroom communicates with both rooms, so it is compact & complete. When John moves his books & papers into his office, we shall get rid of the last of our trunks. The walls are plain light buff, & the furniture is covered with plain dull green nap & is comfortable. So all we have to do is to add a few plants & flowers & touches of colour. We are really very comfortable. We each have our own dressing-table, chest of drawers and writing table, & hanging-cupboard, so we don't get our things mixed up & John's watch-chain entangled in my hair net. The beds are heavenly & the linen good, & we have rose du Barry silk eider-downs. So we are much more luxurious than at home. We feed in the big dining-room, & the food is excellent & served by the prettiest doll-like waitresses, who wear light blue linen with pretty white aprons [and] caps & cuffs in the morning & black frocks for dinner. They all talk prettily too, as everyone here does, with a strong Irish accent. One table maid is Flora, the kindest loveliest little thing – far too pretty – who looks as tho' there must be delicacy behind those great eyes & long dark lashes. She is like a little friendly timid bird flitting round, but she is a very well-trained waitress. ...

Everyone is most friendly – the maids, the lift[1] boys – the shop people. This hotel is very well run. When we go down to breakfast at 8, the maid comes along at once, & by the time we come up, the three rooms are all swept & dusted. I think they give us clean pillowslips every day; I know the table napkins are clean for every meal. And the terms are 12/.[2] a day each, inclusive of everything – board, rooms, & service, and the manager[3] told John that if we give our chambermaid 1 dollar a month (4/.) tip, she will be delighted. So it is not going to be anything like so expected for our up-put. ...

Yesterday, we went to tea with Mr. & Mrs. George Whiteley.[4] ...

Tomorrow, I suppose we must expect all the world & his to call.

I have enjoyed these quiet days, getting settled & finding out a bit about things.

Barbara Grieve & her husband[5] & boy are living in the hotel [and] so are the Lodges & the other British Commissioner, Mr. Trentham. Mr. T. has been here 1½ years, trying to get some order into the finances. ...

I like the Lodges. She is such a keen little woman; he is very shy and silent, but John likes him more & more. I think they are very much in sympathy in their aims & ideals.

We went to the cathedral[6] this morning. It is a fine building – most surprisingly large for this little island community. Various well-known faces look down from the opening of the arches. Queen Victoria, I think, is the first. The place was full, & the majority of the congregation were men & boys and young people.

Can you hear the sledge bell? There are cars, but they have to have chains. All the business is done on sledges. There are lots of dogs scampering about – Newfoundland, Alsatian, Collies. The children use dogs to draw their toboggans, I notice. ...

Here is someone's harking. I am longing to have the wireless[7] & to hear Big Ben[8] again & feel near you. But we must collect some cash first. ...

1 Elevator.
2 Twelve shillings.
3 Bennett B. Stafford.
4 George C. and Mary (Canning) Whiteley. The same George Whiteley who had 'smelt' ice from the *Montclare* (see J.H.S. to Ian and Sheila, 8 February 1934).
5 Barbara and Andrew Grieve. The Grieves had three sons: John, Henry, and Walter. Andrew Grieve was connected with the firm of Baine Johnson in St John's and had business interests in Labrador.
6 Anglican Cathedral of St John the Baptist, Gower St and Church Hill.
7 Radio.
8 The great bell in the Houses of Parliament, London.

J.H.S. to Ian and Sheila, Newfoundland Hotel, 18 February 1934

Here we are, very comfortably installed in a small suite ... looking out on a landscape covered with snow. It is a bad day – trying to rain and with thick mist. ... This is a squalid town, very poor, built almost entirely of wood. Yet there are all the amenities – electric trams, taxis, telephones of course (mine rings 50 times a day), central heating very pronounced every-where, even a picture house and, I believe, an opera house which is never used. ... At Halifax ... I had lunch with ... the Provincial Superintendent of Education.[1] I had three hours with him after lunch – most interesting. Here all education is in the hands of the churches and is sectarian. There they have state schools. We hope to succeed in undenominationalizing education here, but it will be peculiarly difficult, as the R.C. community is very strong and very bigoted. ...

Yesterday was the first meeting of the Commission, and we steered dextrously round two very rocky headlands, though it is obvious that we are going to have great difficulty with some of our N.F.L. confrères. ... I got my private secretary[2] after lunch and commenced work. ...

I had a very bad night last night, lying awake, thinking, – a very bad habit – for four hours. So now I am going to have a snooze. ...

1 Henry Fraser Munro (b. 1878).   2 Alice Butt.

J.H.S. to Edgar and Eleanor, Newfoundland Hotel, 19 February 1934

It is 8.20 a.m. I have had my quiet time and am waiting for Mum's arrival for breakfast. It is a misty, rainy morning. The streets are, quite literally, a sheet of ice. People can only get along by walking on the tram-lines, and I have just seen a car, with chains on both back wheels, figure skating. It did a beautiful S. The night before last, it was zero. Today, I should think it is not less than 40° F. The changes of temperature are very rapid and large. ... It may be that these changes are the reason for the undoubted exhilaration of the atmosphere here. We both feel extraordinarily well and very vigorous. ...

Q.H.S. to Ian and Sheila, Newfoundland Hotel, 20 February 1934

We are wondering whether you have any news yet. No letters from home have reached us yet. It does seem such a long time. I am just going to post as I finish a letter, so that our letters will come at uncertain intervals but will catch the next mail, whenever & wherever that may be. One mail left by train yesterday. You might note how long this letter takes. There is a mail direct from here to Liverpool on the 23rd, so maybe it will not go till then. We shall have to find out the quickest route. ...

We have had all sorts of weather. ... Yesterday, there was thaw & rain, & ... today, it has thawed still more & is raining hard at present. ... I can see Daddy ploughing along through the slush to the old parliament building¹ which is to be his office – a magnificent building with Grecian portico. Now he & his secretary have got into the tram-line. ... John has another room at the hotel at present for his office, but hopes to get into the Colonial Building tomorrow. There is no building available to house all the offices of the government & they are scattered all over the town, but at least John will have all his staff under one roof, I trust. Perhaps some day the country will be in a position to build proper government offices grouped together. ...

1   The Colonial Building, Military Rd.

J.H.S. to Greta, Newfoundland Hotel, 21 February 1934

... Tomorrow, it will be a week since we arrived. ... We are very well in health. Mum is extraordinarily well. She seems to enjoy life in this one-horse place, though the weather has been disgusting since we arrived. Alderdice said he had never seen a fog on land before he saw it in London. There is not fog here, but a great deal of white mist, which is almost as bad. ...

We had our first meeting at Government House ... and since then we have been very busy getting into the saddle. The great difficulty is offices. These are scattered all over the town. Each minister has had a separate staff, which he put in himself and which went out of office with him. There is no registry and no record room and no list of files or of papers. Absolute confusion. No one knows anything about indexing. It is a case of starting from the bottom and creating offices. I have already amalgamated all four of mine, and have appointed a record keeper, but whether this will work or not, heaven knows. ... One of our jobs will be to keep in touch with the people. I expect a large part of our leisure will be spent in visits to various organizations to speak & let them know the kind of people we are and the kind of work we are doing.

Now it is tomorrow morning at 8.15. The days are very full. Yesterday evening, after dinner, we went to another hotel[1] to see a film shown to us by a Catholic priest, Father O'Brien,[2] who works in the summer among the Indians in Labrador. It was a wonderful film for an amateur. ...

I am thankful to say that I have a very good secretary. She is a young girl named Butt – quick, quiet and methodical. And I think she is able to keep her mouth shut. There is a great deal of preliminary work to do, and she has been dealing with a mass of work. But it is being done. I wish you could see my engagement book. Lots of people want to see me, and I want to see lots of them. I also want to keep the people informed of what we are doing, for we have to replace the politician in this respect. The people must be told not only what we are doing but why we are doing it. That means public meetings and speaking.

Today, there is a gale of wind and brilliant sunshine.

I have to go to my new office – the Colonial Building ... by 9.30 – then at 10.30 to another office, and at 12 to call on the R.C. Archbishop.[3] In the afternoon, I have a meeting at 2.30, and men to call at 4.30 & 5.30.

We have had two meetings of the Commission, and tomorrow have another. Gradually we are getting through the strangeness of the situation and used to one another. It was quite difficult at the start. Naturally, the N.F.L. members were suspicious and on their dignity. ...

1 The Crosbie Hotel,
   260 Duckworth St.
2 Edward Joseph O'Brien (1884–1986).

3 Edward Patrick Roche (1874–1950),
   Archbishop of St John's, 1915–50.

J.H.S. to Ian and Sheila, Newfoundland Hotel, 25 February 1934

We have so far had no letters from the family, except from Betty. I expect that we shall get some this week, when the direct steamer from Liverpool arrives. She will have a job to get in, as there is a N.E. wind which has driven the ice up against the coast. ... I walked to the cathedral for early service, and it was so cold that I thought very seriously of a frost-bitten face. There are three methods of transport in addition to foot-slogging. We have a tram. There are motors[1] – and there are sleighs. One of the reasons against sweeping the snow is the necessity for leaving sufficient for the sleighs. The tram-line is kept clear & used very much as a footpath. The sides are not cleared & are used by the sleighs. ...

On Thursday,[2] there was an official dinner at Government House – all the Commissioners & their wives, the Chief Justice & his wife,[3] the Mayor[4] & his. Decorations. Lodge, one of the British Commissioners and a C.B.,[5] had his decorations put on astonishingly. The C.B., which should have been hanging just under his collar-stud and with the ribbon under the white tie, was swinging low down on his tummy with the ribbon outside his tie! His foreign decorations were sewn onto his coat – one on the lapel, one between lapel and coat and the third on his left breast. He has a large head & was wearing an opera-hat at least two sizes too small. ... He looked like a music hall turn. And he appeared not to know it at all. The Governor is Sir D. Murray Anderson. They are first-class people. She[6] is a terror to work & has organized the Service League[7] marvellously well. Though there is intense religious bigotry & jealousy between R.C., Anglican & Nonconformist in this island, she has 238 undenominational committees at work. That is a triumph. The poverty of the island is appalling. 25% of the population are on the dole. And the dole is a real dole – so much bread, meat, tea, molasses every month, and they eat it up quickly & then have nothing till the next month comes around. I am very much afraid that there is widespread physical deterioration going on. Beriberi[8] is exceedingly common.

On Friday night, I went to the ice hockey match between St. John's & a Canadian team.[9] What a magnificent game that is – very fast & very skilled and the skating is beautiful. ... I was with the Governor's party in the royal box. There was of course no heat, and you can imagine how cold one got in an hour and a half of watching. ...

Next ... Sunday[10] evening, we start across the island by train. We get back the following Saturday.[11] ...

---

1 Automobiles.
2 22 February 1934.
3 Julia (Hutchinson) Horwood.
4 Andrew Greene Carnell (1877–1951), Acting Mayor of St John's, 1932–3, Mayor of St John's, 1933–49. His

wife was Mabel (Payne) Carnell.
5 Companion of the Order of the Bath.
6 Edith Muriel (Teschemaker) Anderson.
7 The Service League of Newfound-

land distributed clothing, etc., to the needy.

8 A polyneuritic disease caused by a deficiency of Vitamin B.

9 At the Prince's Rink, Factory Lane. The game featured the City All-Stars and a team from the Nova Scotia Technical College, Halifax. The City All-Stars won 4–2.

10 4 March 1934.

11 10 March 1934.

Q.H.S. to Greta, Newfoundland Hotel, 25 February 1934

The weeks are beginning to skim along again. You know how the first day or two in a journey or in a new place, time seems almost to stand still before it rushes on again. ... I am staying in bed today, as I have got a touch of laryngitis. ...

Mrs. Lodge, the other British Commissioner wife, is a very friendly nice woman. Her daughter Ruth, aged 19, is on the stage. ... Mrs. Lodge sprained her ankle two days after we arrived. We were walking to the shops together, & she trod on a piece of false ice & nearly broke her ankle in a rut, so she has been laid up all the week, & I looked after her & now she looks after us. ... She has a sense of humour and a good capacity for enjoyment, and we really do enjoy ourselves going about together. We shall not be able to be friendly with anyone else, so it is lucky we like each other. 'Tommy' is a beggar for thinking. He sits & glowers & then suddenly a smile flashes out. He is ... untidy ... but he is a good fellow & very able & upright – & downright. They have two other daughters, both Girtonians[1] & both married. ... Mrs. Lodge told me that 'Tommy' put £40,000 into a Romanian mine (the big man in it was dying & 'Tommy,' to prevent the man knowing things were difficult, put more & more of his money into it), & they have never had a penny out. And at the same time, all their other investments went wrong, & from being very wealthy they were so reduced that she put her money into a small tomato farm, & 'Tommy' ran it & she did all the housework – laundry & all, with her married daughter as cook & occasional help. ... They had been living in Paris for 10 years, & she had her own maid & the girls had their own maid, so it was a change! But she is a plucky little woman. ... He was one of Nansen's[2] right-hand men. ...

We like the Andersons very much. Lady A. is, I think, an Australian – rather beautiful – very fair & tall & slight, with a beautiful head & great clear brown eyes & lovely hair & brow & nose – rather big & delicately well shaped. I admire her very much. He is good-looking too, & they make a fine couple. Their sister-in-law, Lady Hastings Anderson, is the most shadowy person I have ever seen – but at night, with a touch of rouge, she looks quite lovely. Both these women are working themselves to death on behalf of the poor outport people. They have committees & individuals organized all over the island & central offices here – the whole of the top floor of this big hotel – & a big packing & storage room in the basement. Lady Hastings Anderson is here every day & all day, at the head of the work here, & Lady Anderson comes a lot & supervises the whole work. They send clothes & blankets to the outports. It is difficult to get to many of them in the winter. But the need is terrible. In some places, the people never go to bed because they have no blankets; they huddle together round any fire they may have. In others, the women don't get up because they have nothing to do all winter. The dole, & 25% of the population are on the dole, is so little that it is starvation – I think it is 2d.[3] a day.

And the politicians have so demoralized the people that it has not been worth their while to make efforts to help themselves. There is an island where there is lots of peat just for the digging. But coal is sent to these people, & the 2 decent families who *have* worked & dug peat for the winter get no coal. 'Why are you such fools as to dig the peat?' say the others. 'You're worse off than us.'

Many of the fishermen are so reduced by years of a diet of molasses & tea that a man who knows tells us that it will be 2 years before they will be fit for the work again. Many fishermen when things were so bad went off to work in mines in Nova Scotia;[4] these have closed down & the men have come back to nothing – the boats are sold – their tackle is rotted & destroyed, & they have no means to start again.

And there has been such waste. On one bank, when the fishery used to be good, the fishermen threw away their stale bait onto the bank, and the fish were driven away from the bank.

There has been incredible immorality in the public business. And the treasury of the country has been squandered – its resources left underdeveloped – its land gambled or given away – its people exploited beyond belief. ...

We had a very jolly, tho' official, dinner at Government House on Thursday.[5] We all – most of the ladies – wore black on account of the death of the King of the Belgians.[6] The guests all gathered in the drawing-room; the A.D.C.s lined us up in order, & then the doors were thrown open & the A.D.C. announced H.E. & Lady Anderson, and they passed along the line shaking hands with us all. Then the big doors to the dining-room were flung open. It is a jolly old home – like an English country home in dark red brick. I can see it from my bed – standing in the snow about ¼ mile away – with a group of trees about it. I think these must be the only decent-sized trees in St. John's. But to return to the interior and our dinner. I sat on the left of H.E., opposite Lady Anderson, with John on her right. I had Mr. Alderdice on my left. H.E. is a good host, so kindly & interested & interesting. We had such a dainty dinner, so simple: soup, a wonderful fish jelly (green), a dish of tongues[7] done in white sauce, & vegetables & fresh green peas sent with it, & a trifle. The peas were delicious – their own growing last summer; they pack them in cartons & they are pressed & kept in one of the big ice stores. Such a dainty short dinner. There must have been about 24 of us.

After dinner, Lady Anderson did a sort of general post with the ladies, giving all the ladies a few minutes with me. When the men came in, the A.D.C.s took on the job, and all the men moved around in the same way every 7 minutes. It gave us the chance to get to know every one of them – all the old ministers & the officials. I think there are some nice people here.

The 3rd British Commissioner, Mr. Trentham, ... is a great help to us. He is a nice fellow I think – a very typical civil servant: [a] well-bred, well-mannered man with musical taste & interested in literature – a friendly, modest sort of man. I think he has had a bad time here & welcomes us all. He is about 40 – has either divorced or been divorced – the sort of man I think to bear the brunt whoever was in fault. He has a grand piano in the bedroom, & we had a jolly party in his rooms – H.E. & Lady Anderson & Lady Hastings Anderson & the Lodges & ourselves & Mr. & Mrs. Emerson.[8] Mr. Emerson is a most interesting & gifted person who sings & plays beautifully. ...

Next Sunday,[9] we are planning to go out into the country. We are to have a special train & stay where we want to stop. I hope we shall not get snowed up, but it will be very interesting. We are to be away about a week.

It is all so interesting. One night we went to the Y.W.C.A. & Y.M. They are both in the Seamen's Institute,[10] the foundation stone of which was laid by the King;[11] the first thing he did after his coronation[12] was to go back to Buckingham Palace (I believe it was there) & touch a button which lowered the first stone into place. The fishing has left St. John's now – driven away by the rapacity of the longshoremen. So the Institute was handed over by the Grenfell Association[13] to the Y.M. & they rented part of it to the Y.W. Like all other institutions here, they are in difficulties, but such devoted women are running the Y.W. – a Miss Cheswright & Miss Sharpe[14] with the help of one cook & a few most devoted maids. About 650 girls use the place & they could take many more if they had room. But the girls are so poor now that the Y.W. is carrying many of them as a form of

preventive work. There would be nothing for them but the street otherwise. And the men have no secretary or leader, & their affairs are in a
muddle. The women were paying their way & had no debt, but they took
on the men's debt as a condition of keeping on their premises but the
whole situation is at the last financial gasp. I do hope we can save it. It was
really wonderful to see the work that was going on there. And nothing is
being done for the lowest class of lads & girls.

1 Former students of Girton College, Cambridge.

2 Fridtjof Nansen (1861–1930), Norwegian explorer, scientist, diplomat, and humanitarian. Directed famine relief program for Russia, 1921–3.

3 Two pence.

4 Sydney, Nova Scotia, was a magnet for Newfoundland itinerant workers.

5 22 February 1934.

6 King Albert I of Belgium was killed in a rock-climbing accident on the evening of 17 February 1934.

7 Probably cod tongues.

8 Frederick Rennie Emerson (1895–1972) and Isabel (Jameson) Emerson (1892–1981).

9 5 March 1934.

10 Located in the King George V Seamen's Institute, Water St.

11 George V (1865–1936).

12 22 June 1911.

13 The International Grenfell Association.

14 R. Cheswright and Elsie Sharpe.

J.H.S. to Edgar and Eleanor, Newfoundland Hotel, 26 February 1934

... I have had my breakfast, but it is now only 8.40 and too early for office.
Incidentally, that office has caused consternation. Last Monday,[1] I decided
to amalgamate at the parliament house (which is of course not now needed)
three offices of my various departments, which were scattered in separate
buildings about the town, and so were incapable of effective supervision.
There has been feverish activity. The parliament buildings had not been
cleared within memory of man – nor cleaned. They have now been washed
from roof to basement. ... St. John's has never seen such activity! However, it is done, and I go in today. I am going to be there every day at 9.25, &
at 9.30 I shall go round the rooms and see that everyone is there. I am
going to start an attendance book at the door and make all the clerks sign
as they arrive, with the time of arrival. This morning, I am going to meet
all the staff at 12 o'clock and talk to them about the organization and try to
stimulate them to regularity and industry.

Tuesday 27/2. And almost dinner time. I am dressed. Mum is dressing,
and in half an hour we are due at the Alderdices'. The climate here is very

extraordinary. Yesterday morning, it was about zero & clear cold weather. In the evening, it commenced to snow hard, and I came out from an inter-outport ice hockey tournament (which we were attending officially) to find about six inches on the ground. An hour later, the temperature rose and snow changed to rain. This morning, it was very mild and all the snow melted. Then the wind went round to N.W. and rose, and now there is a gale and I suppose 10 degrees of frost and all the water frozen in the streets. Changes like this occur almost every day. The harbour yesterday was full of ice. This morning, there was just a fringe. Now, doubtless, it has all blown out to sea. ...

On Thursday, we had a dinner at Government House – ... white ties and decorations.

The days are very full. I have to see a large number of people – usually three interviews in the morning and three in the afternoon. It sounds a waste of time, and I sometimes grudge it, but as there is no parliament, we must keep in touch with the people the best way we can. ...

1 19 February 1934

Q.H.S. to Betty, Newfoundland Hotel, 26 February 1934

... Darling! It is so lovely today. The children are sliding & tobogganing about & shouting & skating along the streets & the sledge bells ring so merrily, and there is fresh-fallen snow over everything & the sun shining on all.

But it is terrible to know of the awful poverty behind this joyous scene. It is unbelievable. The dole is so small that it is only just sufficient to keep life; it is given in kind (food) once a month, & of course a hungry family finishes its ration long before the end of the month. And it does not allow for clothes or rent or anything else. There are poor creatures living in the town in shacks without doors & without any heating in this bitter cold. That is why Lady Anderson & other people are at work & working their fingers to the bone. And it is not just here. All over the island, the poor people are in desperate case. Women stay in bed till 1 o'c. because there is nothing to get up for. In other places, the people never go to bed because they have no blankets, so stay huddled together round whatever fire they have. One trouble here is that there are so many tiny communities scattered along the coast – fisher folk whose ancestors settled just here or there because there was enough fishing for perhaps one or two families. And many of the villages, & towns even, are so inaccessible in the winter – they can only be reached by sea & in the winter it is almost impossible to get to them. There has been terrible misgovernment – worse, terrible immorality in the government. The people have been exploited – the natural resources have been wasted & gambled away. Wealthy men hold huge tracts of land – hundreds of thousands of square miles & pay 2/. an acre & do nothing to develop it – just hold it in the hope that sometime it will be wanted & they can demand huge prices for it.

The politicians have demoralized the people – they say, 'Appoint me & I'll give you this & that.' So that the people have grown accustomed to having everything done for them. ...

The stories we hear!

And yet – they are a fine people really, & if they get a decent government and a chance to recover, they will do well.

Lunch-time, & Daddy will be in directly.

He is in his own offices today – in the Colonial Building. H.E. told him, 'It is nothing to build 7,000 miles of dyke[1] compared with getting the Colonial Building ready for use in 4 days.' Lady Anderson says she & H.E. have been down several times & have been tremendously interested in seeing what was going on – the cleaning up of rooms that have not been touched for years. ...

1 A reference to Hope Simpson's work in China.

Q.H.S. to Betty, on the train en route for Port aux Basques, 6 March 1934

I don't think I shall be able to write while we are travelling, but we have stopped for a moment & so I will get on as well as I can. ...

We started yesterday morning at 10 o'c. in snow after three days of glorious mild sunny weather. We have a special train and are most comfortable; Daddy & I have cabins with beds next door to each other & a washstand – just like a tiny ship's cabin. We are sitting in an observation car and we have a dining saloon and our own kitchen. There are 6 of us – three Commissioners & three wives – John & I, Mr. & Mrs. Lodge & Mr. & Mrs. Puddester.[1] There are also the General Manager & the Chief Engineer,[2] but they have their own special quarters & kitchen. We are just having this trip to see something of the country outside St. John's & to meet some of the outport people. It must be a very beautiful country in the summer – the coast is wild & rocky with delightful beaches and it is so 'accidentée'[3] ... and so varied. Our train has run up & down inlets of the sea, & along lakes & in & out of coves. ... The land itself is ¼ water. I must send you a map that will show you how wild it is. Of course just now it is all covered with snow, & the lakes are frozen. A fortnight ago, the temperature up here was 54° below zero! It was terribly cold. ... Just now the land is covered with snow out of which young pine trees[4] spring, & here & there woods of pine and birch – and everywhere, lakes & inlets & what must in summer be jolly little streams – here & there, you could see them beside the line by deep holes in the snow with the stream rushing black below. ...

1 Mary E. (Moores) Puddester.
2 Of the Newfoundland railway.
    They were, respectively, H.J. Russell
    and W.F. Joyce.

3 Uneven, bumpy.
4 Evergreens.

Q.H.S. to Greta, on the *Terra Nova* carriage on the special train, Port aux Basques, 6 March 1934

... This letter will go by the *Caribou*, which leaves here tonight. She was stuck in the ice half-way between here & Sydney (90 miles) on her last trip & could not move for 3 days; I hope she will not have the same trouble going back. We are lying beside her now, & the men are busy hammering plates & making all ready for a hard passage. ...

The great excitement in St. John's just now is the departure of the seal fishers tomorrow. The men came in to St. John's last week to get outfitted. They lie between decks 18 inches to a man – packed like sardines, I believe. But they get good food – fish & seal flesh – & they improve in health. They aim to get to the sealing grounds a fortnight after the birth of the babies. Poor lovely babies. They are born white and are just balls of fat – very pure fat. And of course their pelts are valuable for drying. They say it is a dreadful scene. The seals cry pitifully just like babies, & tears come from their eyes. The big seals are shot; the babies are killed with one blow of a club. It must be ghastly.

On Saturday night,[1] at 5 o'c., someone suggested John should have a meeting for the sealers, and, at 8 o'c., the theatre[2] was packed. Such grey, hungry-looking fellows. But they seemed so pleased to have the meeting. John & Mr. Lodge told them about the work of the Commission & appealed to them for the help every N.F.L. man can give the work. An old sealing captain[3] of 78 spoke so well, & the men evidently love him. We had about 6 of the captains on the platform. They told us the men will talk of this meeting all the voyage.

I have just written to the Canada Women's Institute headquarters for advice about starting them here. They must have just the same conditions in the outports of eastern Canada. It will be extraordinarily difficult here, for the women are so ignorant & so lethargic from years of low feeding & spoon-feeding by the government. ...

1   3 March 1934.   3   Abram Kean (1855–1945).
2   The Casino Theatre, Henry St.

Q.H.S. to Edgar and Eleanor, on the train at Grand Falls, 7 March 1934
No letter from you yet, but we hope for news of you when we get back to St. John's. There is only one direct ship from Liverpool to N.F.L., the Furness Withy line, and at present they run only one ship, the *Nova Scotia*.[1] ... So that really we sometimes got our letters in China by the Trans-Siberian mail as quickly as we get them here now! It will be better in the summer, when there are more frequent direct ships. ...

Such an empty land: we never see a living wild thing – not even a crow or a seagull. There are a few moose & caribou & partridge & lots of white hares, but we have seen nothing. The N.F.L.er kills everything. Nearly everyone here talks Irish!

1   The *Nova Scotia* was built in 1926 by   same company in 1925. The ships
    Vickers-Armstrong. Her sister ship,   were designed to accommodate 183
    the *Newfoundland*, was built by the   passengers plus crew.

J.H.S. to Betty, Newfoundland Hotel, 11 March 1934
Mum and I were at early service this morning in the Old Garrison Church,[1] a wooden church, built, I suppose, nearly a hundred years ago. ...

It is snowing hard, and the snow is drifting – it blows along like steam. It is quite dry, and the flakes are very small. By tomorrow morning, if it goes on like this, there will be feet of snow in the street. The church is quite close to us, but we are going to lunch and we shall have quite a walk to get there. Yesterday morning, we were at a place called Argentia[2] and walked from the station to the priest's house to call. It was only a mile, but the snow was deep & we had had quite enough exercise by the time we got back. I slipped & fell, and Mr. Puddester, who was with us, went up to his waist in a drift.

I have not written to you since 20th February,[3] I am afraid. I am very sorry, but the train was much too shaky for writing, and when it stopped, I had always work to do seeing people. I expect that Mum will have told you all about it so you must forgive repetition. ...

We are sending you a map showing the railway, so that you can follow the journey if you like. We ran straight through to Bishop's Falls the first day, arriving there about midnight and leaving first thing in the morning.

That was Monday.[4] We travelled all day through snow, an undulating country with low rocky ridges and a lot of spruce and fir. At the highest point, there is a place called [the] Topsails, where trains are often snowed up, and there we passed through a drift where the snow was level with the top of the carriages. We took photos of that. I only hope they will come out. We got to Port aux Basques, the terminus on Cabot Strait opposite Nova Scotia, about 2 o'clock Tuesday morning. ...

That morning we spent in inspection and having a meeting with the merchants. As everywhere else, they want the government to do everything for them. We left at midday and came back along the same line to St. George's. There we got out and had a public meeting and called on the R.C. Bishop. His name is 'Simpson Renouf.'[5] He was called Simpson after the Dr.[6] who discovered the use of chloroform, who was a friend of his father.

While we called on the Bishop, Mum had a good time with the girls, and there was quite an open-air meeting going on when we came out. Our meeting was good fun too, and was very useful. Then we got on the train again and arrived at Corner Brook early on Wednesday morning.

At Corner Brook, there is an enormous paper mill that turns out between 500 and 600 tons of paper every day and provides the paper for the *Evening Standard* and the *Daily Express*.[7] We inspected the mill. It was very interesting. The wood goes in in the form of 4 foot logs at one end & comes out in rolls of paper at the other end. We lunched with the manager and then had a meeting at the court-house, at which we heard complaints and suggestions. Then we got back to our train and left at 6 o'clock.

Next morning, Thursday, we were at Buchans – a lead & zinc mine. There we walked round the town and called on the clergyman & the Methodist[8] parson. It was a very cold day, freezing hard and the snow was in deep drifts on the road in places, but was frozen hard so that you could walk on top. All the houses & churches & schools were of wood, & there are only 100 houses of five or four rooms each for 1,000 people. Quite a housing problem.

That night we got to Grand Falls, the headquarters of the paper mill owned by the *Daily Mail*.[9] We left the train and stopped in very luxurious quarters in the staff house. After dinner, we played bridge. Next morning, Friday, I inspected the schools, interviewed the heads of all departments of the mill & inspected the mill. Then, after lunch, we inspected the model farm, and then had a meeting in the court-house. We met all the people who wanted to meet us to make any suggestion or complaints. ... After the meeting, we rushed back for a cup of tea and then on to the train.

We arrived at Argentia on the morning of Saturday, did an inspection, called on Father Dee,[10] and then came on, getting home at 5 yesterday afternoon. ...

1 St Thomas's Anglican Church, Military Rd. Opened in 1836.
2 Placentia Bay.
3 Letter not included in Balliol College collection.
4 5 March 1934.
5 Henry Thomas Renouf (1872–1941), Bishop of St George's, 1920–41.
6 Sir James Simpson (1811–1870).
   Discoverer, in 1847, of the use of chloroform as an anaesthetic.
7 Of London, England.
8 United Church of Canada.
9 Also of London. Founded in 1896.
10 Adrian Joyce Dee (1895–1951), parish priest at Oderin, 1919–22, at Argentia, 1922–41, and at Argentia–Freshwater, 1941–51.

J.H.S. to Greta, Newfoundland Hotel, 11 March 1934

This afternoon I went into another man's room to hear the weekly news bulletin broadcasted by your department.[1] Reception was *excellent*, though a snowstorm with a gale of wind was in progress at the time. When we get a little money together, we must buy a radio set. Here everything is very dear, owing to the tariff. You know that Mum had a dress and hat sent after her, as they were not ready when she left. They cost £7-11 – in England. We had to pay $18.75 = £3-15 in import duty before we could get them out of the post office. The all-round tariff is 50%; then they have added a general surtax of 5%, and on certain articles a further 12½%. Can you wonder that the poor are suffering? There are about a quarter of the population on relief, and the relief is by no means sufficient to support life. We are increasing the relief by a very little, but even so the physique and the morale of the people are steadily deteriorating. And it is a dreadful problem. If you reduce the import duties, the deficit will increase. And the British Government is responsible for the deficit, and the British Treasury naturally watches every additional penny spent with a most jaundiced eye.

Mum must have told you about the trip across country to Port aux Basques on the Cabot Strait. I have sent a map to Betty which you may see if she is anywhere near you in the Easter holidays. The centre of the island is most sparsely populated. You go for miles without seeing a house. It is a country of low rocky hills – ridges rather – with a great deal of rather monotonous pine forest between them. When you touch the coastline, it is most lovely. There are deep narrow bays with steep rocky hills right to the water's edge, and these hills covered with pines. With blue-white ice floating in the bay and the trees sprinkled with snow and the ground white, you can imagine what it looks like in the sunlight. Quite lovely.

Everywhere we stopped, we had meetings with the people and we had a great welcome. Of course, they all hope that we are going to do something for them. There was a firm conviction, for instance, that the dole allowance was to be doubled. They think that the whole of the money of the British Treasury is at our disposal. Naturally, they are disappointed, but even so they trust us. One thing they are now getting is a perfectly honest government. Graft and favouritism are of the past, as much as we British Commissioners can ensure it.

Some of our meetings had amusing incidents. We invited the people to come, not to hear us talk, but to put their case and to ask questions. At Grand Falls, one man said that he seized the opportunity to say what many people thought but what no one had had the pluck to put into words. He objected entirely to the constitution of the Commission. He thought that better U.K. Commissioners could not have been chosen (!!!), but it was a scandal that the Newfoundland Commissioners were nothing but politicians tainted with all political vices. One of the N.F.L. Commissioners was sitting listening to that tirade. Then another man got up. He said he was an officer in H.M.'s Army. He had fought in Flanders and in Gallipoli and in Mesopotamia. His pals were all lying dead there. He welcomed the Commission and hoped, for the sake of the memory of his pals, that the Commission government would continue in N.F.L. until every existing voter is dead. Then he said goodbye and walked out of the court-house.

I expect that Mum told you all about the enormous paper mills at Corner Brook and at Grand Falls. ... Between them, they turn out over 1,000 tons of paper every day. The trouble is that they pay no taxes & pay very low wages. The men in the woods cannot keep themselves and also their wives & children. While the men are working, the families are on the dole. When the men cease to work, they also come on to the dole. It is a scandal. I am tackling that question at once. We shall commence with the outside contractors, & stop them cutting altogether unless they pay adequate wages. At the same time, we shall compel the American company[2] to raise their wages to the same level as the British company[3] (*Daily Mail*). Then, next year, we shall start from that level and try to push the whole lot higher.

There is *crowds* of work. ...

1 The Empire Service of the B.B.C.
2 International Power and Paper
  Company of Newfoundland Ltd, a
  subsidiary of the International Paper
  Company of New York.

3 Anglo-Newfoundland Development Company. Owned by the
  Harmsworths.

J.H.S. to Edgar and Eleanor, Newfoundland Hotel, 13 March 1934

It is nearly a month – indeed, it will be a month on the day after tomorrow – since we arrived here, and we have yet no letters from you. I expect that you are both very busy, but we also are busy people. And we are very thirsty for news of all our loved ones. A letter is like a spring in a thirsty land.

I am not innocent either – for it must be a fortnight since I last wrote. But my time is very much occupied. Not only is the work very heavy, but my particular department touches the interests of practically the whole population, and a very large number of people want to interview me. I have perhaps been rather too liberal in granting interviews. This was deliberate. I want to get to know the people, and their problems, at first hand. Now I shall have to be less accessible or I shall never get any farther with the office work of the files. Incidentally, I have been teaching a very dull lady the art of record keeping. It is a merciful Providence that has granted me the gift of patience. Otherwise, we should have come to grief in the record room. Hitherto, there has been no system of records at all, and papers are untraceable.

14/3 – and twenty to eleven. Mother has gone to bed and I should also – but I want to get this off by Friday's mail.

I have a very great deal to do, and that is not confined to daytime. I begin before breakfast, as a rule, then get to office before half past nine. ... I work till one & get back as soon as possible after two and work till six or half past. Then, most evenings, after dinner there is some engagement. Yesterday, we had a meeting of the young people between 17 & 30, and had over 1,200 in the Casino Theatre. All the three U.K. Commissioners spoke. It was a great meeting and was broadcasted all over the island. Today, I have had telegrams of thanks from many places. Tonight, I had a meeting of the Game and Inland Fisheries Board. Tomorrow & Friday, I have after-dinner engagements. On Sunday, I speak at a Catholic meeting in the morning and in the evening for the British & Foreign Bible Society, and have speaking engagements next Tuesday & Wednesday. A dog's life.

I expect you have heard all about our cross-country trip from Mother. It was a very useful tour, as we met all sorts and conditions of people and heard all their suggestions & complaints. The people generally are dreadfully depressed. 25% of the population is on quite inadequate relief. This must have an effect on the future of the children and has already had upon the physique and the morale of the adult population. In certain parts, they have lost all energy and all initiative, and throughout the island there is far too much reliance upon the government and far too little local effort. Restoration of morale will be the most difficult problem. ...

Q.H.S. to Greta, Newfoundland Hotel, 15 March 1934

... I wrote to you last from Port aux Basques. I am enclosing for you a rather dramatic map that will give you a better idea of the kind of island this is – the land mostly water. ... When we left Port aux Basques, we came first along the coast and saw the arctic ice – so lovely – pale green. It comes down through the Cabot Strait at this time of the year and makes that western coast cold. But the villages on that side look much more comfortable. The houses are clean-looking, & some are painted & there are small farms attached to many. We saw hens & then half a dozen sheep & sometimes a few cows huddling in the shelter of a building. But, of course, in the winter weather you can get no idea of what animals there are.

Until the beginning of this century, the interior of the island was uninhabited – the only village off the coast was a little place called Whitbourne. Now, there are 3 little model towns dumped down in the country – at least I should except Corner Brook, which is in a very long inlet. ... All three are made towns – dumped down in the wild. Tied towns – financed by outside capital. Corner Brook & Grand Falls are both paper towns. ... Buchans is a mining town, & the mine (zinc & lead) was never expected to last more than 25 years, of which about 12 are gone. There are about 6,000 people at Corner Brook & 5,000 at Grand Falls, and 364 babies were born at Grand Falls last year – the same at Corner Brook, I expect. There are 1,500 people at Buchans, and 54 babies were born last year. So you can imagine that the question of population & employment & housing becomes more acute every year. These towns cannot absorb their increasing population into employment – in fact the island itself seems to offer no prospect of employment at present; all the best-educated young people have to go to Canada or the States.

We had a delightful visit to Corner Brook in spite of the weather being bad – snow falling all the time. But the manager's wife[1] came at breakfast time & invited us all to lunch & tea. Daddy & the other men had to inspect everything, but I had a heavy cold & stayed in the carriage till lunch-time. Even through the falling snow, we could see what a lovely setting Corner Brook has. The Elderkins' house stands on a hill above a lake, & the forests around have not been cut. The wood is brought from farther away. It has such pleasant houses too – here, all the houses have rooms with wide doorways opening one into another & are so well heated that there is cosiness combined with space & air, even in small houses. Dining-room, drawing-room & sun parlour round half a corner led into a conservatory that was gay with flowers – the house was full of daffodils & geraniums and nasturtiums! I have never seen nasturtiums grown in a conservatory before to come out, in the middle of winter too! It was a gay homey house with its flowers & its two children & the adoring maids and happy parents. Mrs. Elderkin is a Canadian, & most of the ladies she asked to meet us for tea were Canadian or English. All these 3 model towns strike me as foreign towns stuck down in N.F.L. – so different to shabby, dilapidated St. John's & the outport villages we have seen. It is, of course, partly the difference between an artificial town & one that has grown. But no doubt the old town & the outports represent, too, something of the demoralization of the people of this island.

We got over the Topsails with difficulty during the night; with the rotary plough on our engine, we grunted & groaned & stopped & started, but we got to Buchans on time and wakened to a glorious day. That is not such a happy community. The manager is a squinting, meagre, bitter American 'Swede'[2] – most unattractive. We were not invited to his house. We saw something of the mine & mill – most interesting. The zinc & lead are extracted from a glory-hole – a deep punch-bowl – and the stuff is immediately dropped through the holes in the floor of it to trucks waiting 500 feet below, & then it is hauled to the surface. I suppose it must be found in the mine too. We saw the stuff being loaded into great crushers & from one machine to another – till it was liquid. Then some precious chemical is added drop by drop to the mixture, & this separates the zinc from the lead – the zinc falling, the lead rising in great silver bubbles.

We ladies & Mr. Puddester (originally Poindexter, if you please!) then went to see the Service League committee. We were all seated round a room, & the C. of E. padre sat in 'the chair' &, for a minute, we waited in silence, wondering what to expect. Then he explained that he had expected all the Commissioners to come, so that they could lay their case before them. They had not received any publicity at Buchans, but he thought they had done their part – yes, they had looked after their own poor and had sent help to outlying places. We hastened to assure him that their work had not gone unnoticed by Lady Anderson – that she had spoken of it to me, etc. However, I noted down all the details & passed them on here and found that the committee³ ... here had no idea what they were doing! (I had mixed up Buchans & Grand Falls in my memories of Lady Anderson's appreciation, luckily!)

Then we tramped through the snow to call on all the other padres – United Church⁴ & R.C. We had heard of them having difficulties – 100 houses for 1,500 people – and the exorbitant prices charged by the only stores allowed in the place. Life certainly is hard for the people there; & it is not just the fault of the mean-looking, bitter manager.

That evening, we got to Grand Falls; that is the nicest town of the lot – a very jolly place – a very English community – rather like an Indian station with its club & all its life complete in itself. We spent the night ashore⁵ here & had a most delightful & interesting time. ... Mr. Jones⁶ ... is of Quaker stock & comes from Kendal.⁷ He is a wonderful host. His wife & daughter are in Sussex just now – the daughter having a season. We were entertained at the staff house, & the Lodges & we had delightful little suites – bedroom, bathroom & sitting-room. We sat down about 40 to dinner & played games after. Next day, we were shown the mill & saw the huge new engines turning out paper about 30 ft. wide by the mile. One of the ladies had a tea-party for us, & we liked the people we met – all so friendly & happy. They must often feel very cut off, but I should think that it is as happy a society there as here. We were told that, when we come in the summer, we are to stay at Lord Rothermere's⁸ own house, but in the winter it is closed now. ... Snowing all the time still. All that night, we travelled & woke to an exquisite morning as we ran along the south coast – the sun shining on dazzling, snow-covered cliffs, and a dancing, tumbling, dark sapphire-blue sea breaking below the line. You never see anything very long because the coast is so indented. ... We stopped at Argentia & then at Placentia. It is glorious country. I long to see it in summer. Placentia was the ancient French capital, & a great many of the names round there are French. There is still one little island – not far from Placentia which is French – St. Pierre⁹ & [it] is a centre for smuggling. ...

1 The manager at this time was Karl O. Elderkin (1895–1966). His wife was Elizabeth Eleanor (Lea) Elderkin.

2 Percy William George, an American national born in Sweden. Arrived in Newfoundland in 1930.

3 Of the Service League of Newfoundland.

4 United Church of Canada.

5 Off the train.

6 Vincent Strickland Jones (1874–1967). Arrived in Newfoundland in 1910 to be mill manager at Grand Falls for the Anglo-Newfoundland Development Company.

7 In Cumbria, England.

8 Harold Sidney Harmsworth, first
   Viscount Rothermere (1868–1940).
   Brother of Alfred Charles William

Harmsworth, Viscount Northcliffe
(1865–1922).
9 French-owned island off the south
   coast of Newfoundland.

Q.H.S. to Edgar and Eleanor, Newfoundland Hotel, 19 March 1934
... I have just finished a removal from one suite to another on account of
getting a better sitting-room & better water. In our old suite, the water
was so full of rust that I hesitated to wash in it. We are better off here, but
the walls are a horrible yellow. I tried yellow curtains, but they were not a
success – now I am having very pale rose that throw an apricot tinge onto
the walls. But there is nothing for it but to change the walls, so we shall
have them colour-washed next time we go off for a few days. Anyway, I
don't feel so jaundiced with the rose light. *And* I have such a lovely view
of the Narrows & Signal Hill & can watch for the mail coming in, & shall
see the sealers returning from their seal harvest. We have lovely wide
windows here, looking over the hills – all covered with snow now. I can lie in
bed in my bedroom & watch the beacon light coming & going on the water.

I expect you are enjoying your second spring in Dorset. I wish we
could go primrosing with you. We shall have to wait till June for our
spring, and it is apt to be a treacherous, dangerous month, with icebergs
bringing down the arctic cold to our very gates when the sun is getting
really hot. ...

The doctor[1] at the General Hospital has come to see me this week. He
wanted to enlist my support for introducing some sort of nursing service
for St. John's. Do you know that they have no nursing service, except in
the hospitals. (For the outports – on that 6,000-mile coastline – there are
now only 9 Nonia[2] nurses.) Dr. Keegan did his training in Dublin. He is a
Catholic – he is about 70 (his wife[3] is 71) & he has a wooden leg. Mrs. Lodge
& I went to see the hospital next day. It is a dreadful old building, but
Dr. Keegan has done his best to equip it well. I don't understand the
machines, but they strike me as very up to date. But – but – the nurses for
the most part don't look old enough, and many of them look over-worked
& ill, except when they are rouged. Dr. Keegan is dreadfully troubled
about the increase of cancer among young people; there were 4 men in when
we went round – inoperable cases, tho' he had operated on one just to
prolong his life a little (a man of 29 with 3 little children). But the hospital
was dreadfully overcrowded, & there were beds down the middle of the
ward & children among grown-ups. The operating theatre had doors from

which the paint was peeling off, & cracked floors. 'No money to do any-thing! It is heartbreaking. I have to keep the people in because I know they'll die for want of nursing if they go out, & I often have to send them out in any case to make room for others.'

Conditions in this country are beyond belief out of date – almost savage in many cases. Do you know, in the outports it is the usual thing to keep a bucket in the middle of the floor for sanitary arrangements & not to empty it for weeks – & when they do empty it, they just tip it out beside the door! And the flies are awful. Savages have better arrangements. And savages manage their social morality better. The moral conditions are ap-palling. No wonder their is so much idiocy. O dear! O dear! What is to be done! Reformation of everything – sweeping away of religious divisions that make a squabbling ground of every public service – good interde-nominational schools & decently paid teachers – decent housing (this little town has appalling slums) – nursing services. I hope great things from the reform of the customs – that is what keeps prices up. I had to pay 75% on a frock & hat that followed me out; everything is taxed & highly taxed – just killing trade. ...

1 Lawrence Edward Keegan (1859–1940), Chief Surgeon and Superin-tendent, General Hospital, St John's, 1909–35.

2 Nonia was founded in 1924.

3 Mary (Walsh) Keegan.

J.H.S. to Ian and Sheila, Newfoundland Hotel, 21 March 1934

... St. John's is a microcosm of a unique type – 40,000 people divided into watertight compartments. The wealthy and ex-wealthy business class – the religious circle – the poor. ...

The work is very heavy. You cannot imagine the conditions here. Thousands are working in the woods. They cannot earn more than enough to keep themselves during the time they are actually working. During that time, their families are on the dole, and when they come out of the woods, they also come straight on to the dole. A quarter of the population is on the dole. I am in charge of natural resources – including forests – and we U.K. Commissioners are agreed that no industry should be allowed to exploit the need of the community by sweating labour. It is the Congo[1] over again. So we are putting on a commission of enquiry into the labour situation in the forests.[2] Lord Rothermere and the *Daily Mail* are likely to have something to howl about, and we are going to be most unpopular in high quarters. But this cannot be helped. You know that the Anglo-New-foundland Development Company is the *Daily Mail* and they have a large pulp & paper mill at Grand Falls. They are not so bad as the International Power & Paper Company at Corner Brook – an American concern. These two companies have hitherto been all-powerful. And they have lived on sweated labour the last two years.

I have just proposed the fisheries development programme. It will cost the Colonial Development Fund[3] about £135,000 if it is accepted. But it will put 10,000 people off the dole and into work again. Incidentally, it will mean work for boat builders and cordage and sail manufacturers and food suppliers. I am busy with my agricultural development programme, and we have secured a man to take charge of the forests. I am in communication with a man for the geological section.

And I have no doubt that with all this activity I am no busier than you two. Probably you use your time more methodically than I do. A great deal of mine is spent – I was going to say 'wasted' – in interviews. It is sometimes difficult to be patient. ...

1 Refers to the notorious Belgian exploitation of the Congo (now Zaire). Leopold II of Belgium, independently of his own govern-ment, ran the Congo as a personal empire, and allowed the most brutal conditions of exploitation of the population there. Finally, he was brought to heel, in part by interna-tional indignation, in part by the Belgian government taking over the territory.

2 Conducted by F. Gordon Bradley (1888–1966), the former leader of the opposition in the Newfoundland House of Assembly.

3 Provided for in the U.K. Colonial Development Act of 1929.

Q.H.S. to Greta, Newfoundland Hotel, 25 March 1934

... We are plunged back into midwinter again here – storm raging and snow piled high & whirling around the town. Yesterday, we had an inter-val – a glorious day of sunshine – keenly cold but hardly any wind. It was simply glorious. I went for a walk round the streets that the snowplough had cleared, & it was a real joy to be out again. This has been the worst storm of the winter. I have kept indoors most of the week, as it really was too much of a battle to venture out. I have been trying to get rid of a cough that followed on a cold I had about 3 weeks ago. ... I had one of those dizzy attacks[1] again this week too – not a bad one but disappointing to have one at all after so long. ... Mrs. Lodge was so kind; she came & stayed with me – sitting in the next room all the time & rushing to put a mat under my feet when I got up. I did not really take to her much at first, but we have come to be very fond of them both. She & I have great fun calling together & exchanging our experiences at parties, etc. I think her accent put me off, and he is so untidy & loutish in appearance. But both are sterling people – really kind & good, & both are clever. It is great luck to have as our closest companions a couple we both really like & who like us. Mr. Trentham ... I don't know yet whether I like. ... He seems to me to be far too much impressed by the local gossip. 'They say! – What do they say? – Let them say!' But he seems a bit merry about it all the time. ...

Midday gun! Now, Mrs. Lodge has just been in to tell us the latest news: the Squireses[2] – the villain & villainess-in-chief of this place are coming back from Jamaica, where they have been hatching plots, & will be coming to call on us. Mr. Lodge says he will not receive them. John says we shall have to, as he, Sir Richard Squires, is a Privy Councillor, & we are official. So here's a pretty kettle of fish. We had this same sort of position once before in India.

As a matter of fact, we are in the room the Squireses occupied before. Lady S. used to have the curtains arranged to cover the whole window, & they were never drawn. I believe they are a very clever couple but horribly unscrupulous and have piled up enormous fortunes for themselves at the expense of their country. They attracted followers by paying them liberally out of public resources. He was nearly as possible pitched into the harbour during the riots.[3]

Everyone is very friendly and most people are related, so that you have to be on your guard not to let your friendly response draw you into gossip or you are certain to put a foot into the dangerous territory. I am trying to be very careful. I don't gossip with anyone except the Lodges & the Government House people. The other day, I went to a tea-party and almost the first serious remark was 'We're none of us Newfoundlanders so we can say what we like' – and there was a pause. I gather I was expected to welcome an opportunity to unburden myself. I did not.

The Commissioners are bound to make themselves unpopular. Mr. Lodge is in charge of communications etc., and this hotel. He found all sorts of scandalous arrangements made by Squires. The manager, a very decent fellow, I should think, is really a chemist, & he was put in by Squires. All Squires' friends had to have special terms. One couple paid 1/. a day for their *two* rooms while they were away all summer, & they used to come in from their shack in the country several times a week for baths & they would sometimes stay a night or two. Lots of people paid only 1 dollar a day (4/.), all included. Mr. Lodge has put up the prices & instituted all sorts of changes & he is looked at with a sour eye. ... It *is* a queer country. But I wonder, were we any better 100 years ago? I believe our Victorian fore-fathers were the men who worked a revolution in public morality in one lifetime. We are so accustomed to the standards they set up that it is a shock to us when public men fall short of them. What was done for us by them can be done somehow for this island. ... The Lodges have bought a wireless set, & I listened to Vernon Bartlett[4] this week. I also listened to the Boat Race.[5] It made me feel in touch with you. ...

We have central heating in this hotel, but most houses have fires as well. Dressing for the house is continental style more than English. ... The houses are so well heated you need nothing extra warm for indoors, & the ladies wear semi-evening dress a lot in the afternoon. But, for going out, you must have a fur coat and 'gaiters' (snow boots) or galoshes. Everyone wears galoshes here & in America. I notice too that, when we go out to tea, we are shown to a bedroom, & the girls take off their coats & snow boots & then fling up their skirts & take off their thick woollen knickers they put on for out of doors. I have not felt the need for them, but they say we shall feel the cold more next year. ...

1 She had a history of these.

2 Former prime minister Sir Richard Anderson Squires (1880–1940) and his wife, Helena (Strong) Squires (1879–1959).

3 Of 5 April 1932.

4 James Vernon Bartlett (1863–1940), ecclesiastical historian and promi-nent Congregationalist.

5 The annual race between Oxford and Cambridge universities.

Q.H.S. to Edgar and Eleanor, Newfoundland Hotel, 26 March 1934

I picture you two rejoicing in the wildflowers again this spring. Will you go down that lovely little wild primrose lane we found – all grass grown with great bunches of kingcups growing in forgotten ruts, & the black-thorn making a veil of white lace to hide its beauty from preying eyes? And have you found lots of white violets this year? I do love them. Won't it be interesting to see what wildflowers are hidden under the snow here. We shall not know that till well on in June, or possibly July. Then the spring is so short – the heat of summer follows too close on its steps.

We are back to winter again here. We had a blizzard last week and the streets are not clear yet, tho' the snowplough is at work every day. There was quite a heavy fall again last night. But we very seldom, if

ever, have a day with no sunshine. Even last week, we had exquisite days –
lulls in the storm – & often a few hours of sunshine – exquisite hours. The
sun is so warm that it is really hot unless there is a wind; the wind is very
keen. ...

Daddy is having a busy time, but he is very well. He is up nearly every
morning about 6 and gets through a lot of work before breakfast. He is
doing a lot of talking & he is very fully reported & usually he is broadcast.
It lets the people know what the government is doing. In the old days,
they had their M.P.s & candidates – lots of people to listen to politically,
& I suppose it was the one or one of the chief interests of their lives. They
will miss that. So it is up to the present governors to do what they can to
make up for that by talking a lot. The people are certainly very apprecia-
tive of this. But it adds tremendously to the work. Then he is seeing
everyone he can, and these personal interviews take a lot of time. Holy
Week is kept very strictly here – I did not realize this, & as we have some
men from Grand Falls and Corner Brook up for conference, I arranged a
dinner party last night. I wanted two extra ladies. The first ones I asked
were tremendously keen to come – but drew back when they remembered
it was Holy Week – tho' they are Protestants. We can't even go calling this
week.

Mrs. Lodge & I went to the Colonial Building one day ... & I remembered Daddy had told me I should have a look at the library. There are three
rooms full of all sorts of books, some most interesting. But in the midst of
them sits an old grey lady[1] in possession. Nothing will move her – this
found, little, dusty antiquity. There she sits amongst the big books; she is
far too frail to move – just looking at them – & remembering old times.
She is supposed to be the librarian, but she has never even catalogued the
books. But she will talk by the hour about the history of the island.

I have just discovered that the mailbag is closing, so I must send this as
it is. Daddy has just gone off to office after [a] ten-minute snooze in his
chair – not uninterrupted. Mr. Lodge came in with suggestions for a few
minutes. But now he is off battling up the road to his office in the teeth
of the wind & snow. I hope he will get a little rest tomorrow, Good
Friday. ...

1 Lizzie Morris.

Q.H.S. to Ian and Sheila, Newfoundland Hotel, 26 March 1934
... We had one of the nurses down from St. Anthony.[1] ... She came by the

mail route by dog team all the way to the railway. It took her 6 days, & she met a blizzard & her driver injured himself & she had to doctor him before he could go on. But she knows her way around – a fragile-looking, dainty little lady & devoted to her work. She lunched with us, & another woman who was with us was inveighing against the thanklessness of the natives & their dislike of any outsiders. She said: 'Well, that is not my experience. Last time I went back from my holiday, the people said, "Welcome home, Mrs. Hutton" & that went right to my heart.'

We had a Nonia nurse in from one of the southern outports too and she told me something of her experiences. She is a New Zealander – Miss McKeague,[2] a stout, hefty woman of about 50 – very weatherbeaten but healthy & strong. She is a power in the land. She has no companionship at all, as she cannot make any intimacies with the outport people or she would lose her power for influencing them for their good. She is making the people round her fence & dig the ground about their houses & is getting seed for them to plant so that they will grow vegetables, as beriberi is very bad in the island. She makes jobs for the people on the dole; government is helping you, you must do something to help other people. If a man has a cow, she tells him to send 1 pint or 1½ pints of milk to one of her sick patients or a child, & if they don't do it, she sends warning that she will come, & she never had to warn them twice. She goes tremendous distances on a 'slide' – the kind of sledge that men use for hauling wood. It has upright poles, & to them she lashes boards on their sides – fills the bottom with hay with two hot rock-salt stones (just seaside stone) at the foot, & she sits with her feet straight out against the stone & another rail over her, & off she goes drawn by a horse with a driver. I don't know how they even get women to take on these jobs – the life is so lonely and so terribly hard. There is no doctor anywhere near – she has to be the doctor herself – & if the case is beyond her, she brings it to St. John's, a two-day voyage across a bay in a little coasting boat & on in a guard's van with beds rigged up and a fire & cooking stove. She had just brought in two terrible cases that had nearly died on the way. These Nonia nurses go to cases in weather the doctors & priests won't face, we are told – 40 miles on lakes in the teeth of a blizzard all alone. The pay is small, but the spirit is great. There are real heroes and heroines in this land. So far, the Nonia nurses have been all from the old country – the Newfoundland girls don't carry the weight of influence necessary. But funds are so low that instead of 30 there are only 2 Nonia nurses in the whole island now. The Grenfell nurses only work in the hospital at St. Anthony & in a small district round about there. ...

I have my sitting-room full of flowers today. We had a big dinner party last night & I had to get flowers for the table – daffodils. And then I had a presentation bouquet of scarlet carnations a few days ago. I have passed some on to Mrs. Lodge but have a gay show myself – such a joy. Even the common marigold is $2 a dozen – 8/. No flowers are less; they all seem the same price, so I don't buy them except for special parties. ...

The 12 o'c. gun!

Mrs. Lodge & I went to see some wine vaults yesterday. Andrew Grieve ... wanted John to go but he could not, so [we] went instead. Have you heard of Newman's Port? In the old days the merchants of Oporto[3] used to trade port for fish, & our navy found that the port they brought here was marvellously matured – the further rolling of the voyage over here & the effect of the climate seemed to have a wonderful effect on the wine. Newmans were merchant venturers of Dartmouth[4] & they buccaneered out to Newfoundland & began taking codfish to Portugal in the 1500s. In Portugal, they bartered fish & oil for salt & wine ... ; the salt & wine were taken to Newfoundland & the wine was stored there until a ship was going to England, and much of it was then re-exported to Devonshire. But I think the navy very soon discovered that the wine matured in N.F.L. was the best in the world, & so it became customary for Newmans to send all their port to mature here. One of these Newmans built Mamhead Park, near Exeter.[5] The original firm was Hunt, Roope & Teage.[6]

They often had to fight for their freight, specially with the French. The vaults where the wine is matured are very old – the outside is like a prison. The windows are high up & open-grilled, so that it is bitterly cold & the snow comes drifting in to the great barrels. Those huge barrels are called pipes. Some of the wine was being drawn off the lees from one barrel to another & we were allowed to taste it. I think I must try to get hold of one of Newman's advertisement booklets for you. The illustration is beautiful. ...

1 Headquarters of the Grenfell Mission.
2 (Clara) Beatrice McKeague (b. 25 June 1889). Arrived in Newfoundland in 1929. Stationed at Lamaline.
3 Portugal.
4 In Devon, England.
5 Also in Devon.
6 Through history several firms incorporated the names Hunt, Roope, Teage, and Newman. Newman, Teage & Co. of Dartmouth, for example, traded at Bay Bulls, c. 1776–97.

J.H.S. to Edgar and Eleanor, Newfoundland Hotel, Maundy Thursday, 29 March 1934

I brought home the wrong file cover from the office last night and I have no work with me. Is that not luck? But if I had only known it, I should not have been up at 6.30 this morning. ...

We are having the usual N.F.L. spring weather. About a week ago, we had very heavy snow. The last two days, it has been thawing fast, but last night it snowed again, & this morning is sharp frost. However, we get a great deal of sun, which makes up for much. ...

You can have no conception of the poverty of this island. It is not only that 25% of the population is on the dole. The dole is a curse. The people have become so demoralized by the politicians that anyone will get the dole, if he thinks he can get away with it, even though he may be well able to look after himself. And very many are making no attempt whatever to support themselves. The classic case is one where the relieving officer put himself and his own family on the dole. Apart from the dole, there is an extraordinary cleavage between the haves and the have-nots. There is a crust of wealthy merchants. There is a class of small merchant, battening on the people in the outports, which is rapidly becoming more wealthy. Then there are the self-supporting fishing class & small agriculturalist, who have a very low standard of comfort. And, finally, there are the real poor, who have nothing and are practically 25% of the whole population.

I am having exceedingly heavy work. I get up each morning about 6, have my quiet time, & then put in a couple of hours before breakfast & get home about 6.30. Then, most evenings, I have engagements at which I speak. As a rule, they broadcast my speeches. I think that my colleagues – especially my N.F.L. colleagues – think that I have two faults – indeed, three – in speaking. First, that I do it too often. Second, that I tell the people too much of what we are doing, and third, that I give them too much hope. I do not agree except in the first. I have been speaking too much.

Last night, we had a dinner. I had called the managers & woods managers of the two big paper mills to discuss lumbermen's wages (which are far too low), & we gave them a dinner last night. There were 12 & we played bridge after dinner. ...

J.H.S. to Betty, Newfoundland Hotel, Easterday, 1 April 1934

... This is the evening of a very lovely day. Mum and I were at church this morning at St. Thomas's. ... There must have been over 200 taking communion ... and we were not back till after one. This afternoon, we should have been at tea at the Emersons,[1] but Mum has had one of her turns and is now in bed trying to sleep it off. ... Yesterday afternoon, a man named Harold Macpherson[2] took us to see his farm.[3] He has a herd of Ayrshire cows. He drove us out nearly to the farm in a motor, and then we got into a sleigh and drove up to the barn, where we were joined by the dogs – four great bouncing black Newfoundlands. They ran with us as we drove over the fields in the snow. One of them took great mouthfuls of snow as he ran. And they all jumped up and tried to get into the sleigh with us. They were such affectionate beauties. Mr. Macpherson also has two goats – one black, one chocolate – and each of them has had twins. The kids are charming. We drove back to his brother's[4] house (I think he lives there also) for tea and had a great blowout. ...

1 Either Fred and Isabel Emerson or L.E. and Ruby Emerson.

2 1884–1963. President of the Royal Stores, St John's, 1921–63.

3 Westerland, just west of the present-day site of Memorial University of Newfoundland.

4 Cluny Macpherson (1879–1966), a medical doctor.

J.H.S. to Greta, Newfoundland Hotel, 1 April 1934

... I think that we are really making some progress, though the place is an appalling mess. All the assets of the country, the forests and the water-powers and the mineral areas, have been given away with both hands, and are now largely held by speculators waiting to sell them to financiers. ... We are planning to put heavy taxation on all undeveloped concessions. That will compel people to do one of three things: develop or pay or return to the state. Most of them will return them to the state.

I have engaged a forest officer,[1] the first Newfoundland has ever had, though the whole country is, more or less, forest. I have also engaged a first-class geologist.[2] Then we are now putting in district fishery officers and are preparing the plan for an agricultural service. They have no agricultural service of any kind. ...

I went to a stag bridge party after dinner the other night. Never again. There were eight. I wanted to get home to bed by eleven. But supper was at eleven – coffee and Welsh rarebit and celery and sardines and sandwiches. And whiskey soda, if you wanted it. And then they went on with the bridge. And I could not well break up the rubber. So that is the last time I go to after-dinner bridge. ...

1 Jack Turner (1889–1948), Chief Forestry Officer, Department of Natural Resources. Went overseas with the first Canadian contingent in 1914. Winner of the Military Cross.

2 Claude K. House (1907–). Became assistant government geologist in 1934.

Q.H.S. to Greta, Newfoundland Hotel, 5 April 1934

A horrid day – grey & raining. It was quite nice this morning tho', & I enjoyed a run down the town to see the office of the Nonia. ... Then we had Mr. MacDermott,[1] a Congregational padre, to lunch, & he sat on with Mrs. Lodge & me till 4 o'c. while we pumped him. It was hard work; the pump is not much used & is terribly rusty & stiffly set in its determination not to be pumped. And yet that was what he came for! He sat there glowering at us with blue eyes under red eyebrows. I sat & laughed in my intervals at Mrs. Lodge doing the pumping. She is not easily beaten, but she was today. I was warned that you had got to get him started, so I rang up Mrs. Lodge as soon as Daddy had left & tempted her with 'I think you would like to come to meet Mr. MacDermott from Fortune Bay.' She rose to the bait. ... He is bitter about the St. John's people, who sit in comfort and know nothing of the hardship of the island dwellers. It is truly terrible; mismanagement – selfishness – greed have ground the faces of the poor in the ice of the island. A little instance: the outport people will not use brown flour – they must have white. And beriberi is rife here. It sounds like folly and stubbornness. The real reason is that brown flour has more life in it, & therefore it gets weevily & sour easily. The shopkeeper of an outport keeps his flour anywhere, mixed up with fish & stale fish, so he keeps the flour that will taint less easily & the people demand the flour that is less easily soured. They have no choice of shops either; they must buy from *the* shop & they are in the hands of the shop – the shop is owned by the merchant who hires them to fish for him & he pays them in orders on the shop.

Friday. 6. ...

I have seen the first snowdrops here! – just a few tiny ones coming up in a bit of lawn from which the snow had drained away. The rain is washing the snow away fast now, but I expect we shall have snowstorms till June; it is not likely to lie now tho'. I went to see our car last week. It is a real beauty – a dark powdery blue, almost a navy, but brighter & lighter & softer. I am longing to go out in it, but the roads will not be fit for some time yet. You know there are practically no roads except in this peninsula. Isn't it extraordinary? At Corner Brook, up at the mouth of the Humber, they have about 10 miles of roads altogether – they can go about a mile out in several directions – the furthest, to the golf course, is a dreadful road along the side of a precipice, I gather. And they can't go for walks because it is thick scrub jungle with bogs. If the people can afford a motorboat, that takes them to lovely spots along the Humber estuary, but the current is too swift for a rowboat, and the charge for having a motorboat is £2 a day. So life is not easily varied in the places outside the Avalon Peninsula. It takes the Corner Brook people 22 hours to get to St. John's too – & costs about £4 return, I believe. I think it must be simply deadly to be shut off in an outport or in one of these paper towns, in spite of the beauty of the country. The interior of the island south of the railway is about as unexplored as Central Africa used to be in Livingstone's[2] youth.

I think the Commission is really getting on wonderfully with this job, and the people realize it here at any rate, and in many of the more accessible outports where they can hear the wireless talks & have people educated enough to read the papers when they can get them. I think it is astonishing what they have done already. I expect Daddy will tell you about the work. We hear on all sides expressions of confidence in the Commission, and occasionally the more enlightened express their acknowledgement of the wonderful generosity of England. But I think the mass of people are so accustomed to having everything done for them by the government that they rather take for granted that the mother country should shoulder the difficulties the Newfoundlanders have created for themselves. If England had refused to help, I can't imagine what the conditions would have been now. Bad as they are (I don't believe the St. John's people know how bad they are in the outports) ... there would have been no money for further doles; it would have meant sheer starvation and a population mad & out to massacre the politicians & merchants who had landed them in such a position. I have never been in a position before to see what selfishness & greed in commerce mean to the people. Here the merchants have exploited the fishermen, as you know – grown richer & richer while skinning the people who work for them, and then going away to spend & enjoy their wealth in England or America. The money made here is not, as a rule, spent here. The country is lacking in the simplest amenities that that wealth should have provided – roads, for instance, decent education – libraries. The poor people have nothing but their sects & the gambling game of the fishing – killing something & the rivalry of the sects. One thing I got out of our rusty pump: he started weaving in many villages besides the one in which he actually lives.³ But only there has it gone on; everywhere else, the people lost interest & dropped it. They have not the particular kind of grit for going on with a task when it ceases to be interesting & becomes monotonous & has no gambling element to give spice to it. The morale of the people has been undermined by all the conditions of their lives – the low standard of living – the starvation food, really – the isolation of the little outports, with lack of interests & incentives. I think the character of the people is going to be the greatest problem here. What is the good of putting things right if, as soon as the Commission's work is done, the people slip back into their old ways? It is a reformation that is needed – a moving of the spirit – the in-pouring of new waters of life. It is a miracle that happens in the case of peoples far further removed from any such attitude to life as is required here – as, for instance, the changes in the Chinese who become trained. So it is not impossible.

I have just been watching a banker going out (that is, a schooner that goes to the banks for the codfishery); she must be the first to start, I think. It was so pretty to watch her tacking through the Narrows. Now she has passed the point where the Atlantic waves break below the lighthouse. Now she is out to sea.

There was great excitement here the other day when the wireless told that old Captain Kean (the 80-year-old⁴ man with a golden wig who spoke so well at Daddy's meeting for the sealers before they sailed) has got his millionth seal (during his life, of course). He is a public character & everyone likes him, & the sealers evidently like him enormously so the papers had big headlines. John sent him a telegram. The sealing this year has been a success. The first ship is in: the *Eagle*, with a full load and the others will not be long after. The ice is breaking up now, so the seals go off some-where else. On Monday, there is to be a flipper⁵ supper, & all the Commission have to go to it. The flippers are considered a great delicacy. ... We have been having some dinner parties – important people first, with a few unimportants to lighten the weight. People here are very friendly and easy to entertain.

It is such a lovely afternoon after a morning of rain, but there is a fog out at sea & the foghorn is going all the time – a most doleful sound. But the sky is blue with fleecy clouds, & I am sitting at the open window with the heat turned off. It is jolly to see the harbour free of ice, the blue sky and the snow-patched hills. Had my hair washed this morning in the hotel. All the shopkeepers – indeed, everyone in the place – seems to know us, & all have a friendly welcoming word & the burden of their song is 'Things will be all right now that the Commission is here – our hard times are done.' ...

Saturday. 7. I fear you will have had a long wait for letters. The *Incemore* broke down and has been delayed and so will not take on letters today. Such a hooting & booming: one of the sealers has just come in. I have been watching her – just a little steamer – her decks piled with dories packed one inside another & heaped with seals & the men all crowding on top.

1 Hugh J.A. MacDermott (c. 1880–1949), author of *MacDermott of Fortune Bay* (London 1938). Arrived in Newfoundland in 1904.
2 The British missionary and explorer David Livingstone (1813–1873).

3 Pool's Cove, Fortune Bay.
4 He was in fact seventy-eight at the time.
5 The webbed foot of the seal.

Q.H.S. to Edgar and Eleanor, Newfoundland Hotel, 8 April 1934

Sunday again – the first after Easter, and we are having a quiet day. Daddy went out to early service, but, ... the morning was wet, so I stayed in. Now he is having a quiet but busy morning at home, writing to the home government. ... I can hardly imagine how far on the spring is with you now. Here, we have had a week of much milder weather and quite a lot of rain, and the snow has melted a lot. The country is motley now instead of a mantle of white. The snowplough has cleared the main streets, but five minutes out the snow is four feet deep on either side of the track cut by the plough. We called on a lady who lives 'out in the country' yesterday & settled ourselves for half an hour's drive, as we were told the road was open now. We were there driving between 4-foot snowbanks or cuttings in under five minutes. They call it 'living in the country' when they are just outside the main roads. And this is true in the case of this lady. She has a sweet old farmhouse – about 150 years old & fields all round. When the snow was lying, her garden was level with the tops of the fences, & she simply walked down to the town over the fences of garden & field – I mean that all boundaries were below the snow. ...

The great excitement here just now is the return of the sealing fleet. One ship, the *Neptune*, came in on Saturday with sirens blowing & flags flying & all the sealers gathered on the poop on top of the piles of pelts. At 2.30 the sirens were blowing hard again & the flags strung up on the signal tower[1] & we saw the smoke of a ship blowing round cross the Narrows from the north. But a banker, a fishing schooner, was starting out on her voyage & she had to get through the Narrows before the sealer could come in. Then she came – ship dressed with flags and siren blowing – the *Imogene* with 50,000 pelts & the poor little *Thetis* in tow. The *Thetis* broke her propeller in the ice almost before she had got 1,000 seals – such a disappointment to the sealers, who are paid by results and not much at that. But it is a sport to them; they love the excitement of hunting for the seals & then the spice – no, real danger – of the scramble over the ice & of the chance of fog & blizzard coming down & cutting them off from their ships (there was a terrible disaster with that, one year).[2] And they enjoy the full meals of seal meat after their long winter of starvation rations.

Daddy is working very hard, but he is happy to have a job that is so much worthwhile. Things are in a horrible mess. But the mass of the people are behind the Commission – at least at present. It must be an immense relief to see that even already the Commission is getting a move on – has embarked on schemes for helping to put the fisheries on a more modern & scientific basis, to ensure good standards and receptive markets, and readjust the labour conditions so that the fisherman gets his fair share of the profits. Many fishermen who have lost their boats & their gear are to be restarted, & their boats will be built & give labour to carpenters & cordage labourers & the men who make the fisherman's outfit. The dreadful conditions in the woods, where lumbermen work hard all winter while their families live on the dole & come back with nothing – these conditions are being changed. The companies are being forced to pay a decent wage – a living wage. Lands & forests & rights in water-power that have been given away are being reclaimed when possible or taxed to get something back for the country. Schemes of land development & agriculture are being developed for the employment of the unemployed, & families are going to be settled in communities. The country has depended far too much on the fisheries, & the land has been neglected. This has affected the morale of the people, as it is such an uncertain trade that the gambling instinct [has] encouraged. And the fishermen have been entirely in the hands of the merchants. Do you know that in most of the outports money is unknown? The merchant pays in notes for goods on the shop that he himself owns! It is the old truck system. The merchants are not altogether to blame – the custom arose out of necessity. But the fact remains that he has grown wealthy, and the fisher folk have grown poorer & poorer. The merchants go away & live in big houses in England & come back occasionally or send their agents just to see to their interests here. They do little for the country from which they draw their wealth. It is unbelievable how backward this country is. There are no roads worth mentioning outside this Avalon Peninsula. I believe they have about *10* miles of roads in & about Corner Brook & Grand Falls. Other where, there is no means of communication except by boat. Imagine having to go about in an open motor or rowing boat in winter & being likely to be frozen. North of the south coast right up to the railway is unexplored practically.

We have had a Congregational minister in from Fortune Bay this week, a Mr. MacDermott. He has been 30 years here. When he found he had to come to N.F.L. & learnt about the conditions, he went & 'did' medicine and he married a trained nurse. He & his wife[3] are the only doctor or nurse within about [a] 100-mile area &, as he says, the people get their doctoring for nothing. I said to him, 'It seems to me that the life of a Nonia nurse is too hard for any woman – absolutely alone because she cannot make friends with the people if she would, and forced to undertake terrible journeys in terrible weather, etc.' 'It *is* too hard. And the worst is they don't know what they are coming to.' Newfoundland girls won't do – they have no authority with the people, & the Nonia nurse, an Englishwoman, must be an authority among the people. Women are of no account here, & a Newfoundland girl is just a woman. A Nonia nurse is something different if she comes from England. Besides, Newfoundland girls get married. There is a shortage of women here. Mr. MacDermott has two children, 21–23, but he sent them back to England at 7. 'Wouldn't [it] be a comfort to you & your wife to have your daughter to help you?' He glowered. 'We chose the life for ourselves; there's no reason why we should condemn our children to it.' I stupidly said: 'It seems to me that yours is the ideal arrangement – you & your wife have each other.' 'Not much! She is mostly alone or she is delivering a child in one direction & I in another.' 'I don't know how she stands the loneliness,' I said. 'Not another woman I've known could have stood it all these years.' He is a funny, rusty old pump. Mrs. Lodge & I pumped & pumped, & he sat & glowered at us. But he did talk to John. He told him that things in the outports are dreadful. ... There is no leadership and no cooperation among the people. If 2 men are fishing together in a boat & one gets into trouble, the other will not help him.

But then! There *are* fine men and the people are so friendly & kindly in spite of all. A third of the people are on the dole, but John had fishermen in yesterday & they told him that they would rather see their sons drown than on the dole & the sons would rather drown. ... P.S. or N.B. Don't repeat what I tell you in case you have people connected with N.F.L. So many come from Dorset & Bristol.

1 Cabot Tower, Signal Hill.

2 Probably a reference to the *New-foundland* disaster of 1914, in which seventy-eight men died.

3 Gertrude (Hall) MacDermott.

J.H.S. to Ian and Sheila, Newfoundland Hotel, 12 April 1934

It is 8.15 a.m. and I have had an extra hour in bed and did not get up till 7. I had a long day yesterday – up at 6, work till breakfast at 8.30 & then in office till after 5 – then a meeting of the Game & Inland Fisheries Board from 8 to 10 & back home about 10.20. Every day means hard work. ...

I have hired a room next to our bedroom for an office room. The window faces the harbour and the Narrows at its entrance – S.E. – and at the moment there is a schooner beating out against the east wind, tacking and tacking in a very constricted space, and away out beyond her the Furness [Withy] boat, the *Incemore*, just coming in from Halifax. She will take this letter tomorrow.

There is little news. My work is absorbing, immense in magnitude and enormous in range. Last Monday,[1] I had a conference on cod-liver oil – the method to meet Norwegian competition. On Tuesday, there was a meeting of the Commission of Government in the morning, and I had conferences in the afternoon with fishermen as to measures to be taken to help men who have lost everything to restart fishing, followed by one with representatives of the unemployed of St. John's – mainly longshoremen. On Wednesday, I had up the investigator[2] whom we have commissioned to enquire into conditions of men employed in the woods, and in the afternoon I went around the outskirts of the town to devise relief works. On Thursday, I had a partner in Job Brothers[3] to discuss the supply of frozen bait, followed by a representative banking captain, who represented the need of the banking schooners – then a man who wants permission to export timber from the Labrador, followed by the representative of an American company desirous of a concession for the erection of a fishmeal factory. The whole afternoon was taken by a conference on the unemployed question. And so on. Last night, I summoned the Game & Inland Fisheries Board – a statutory body – to tell them that we are going to legislate their abolition and that I am going to take over their duties. A delicate meeting. They have been functioning very inefficiently for the last 25 years.

It is now 5.55 a.m. on Friday 13th ... and I have masses of work to do – which explains why I am up so early. We had a meeting of the Commission yesterday to consider my fishery development scheme, which leaves by today's mail and calls for immediate allocation of about £100,000 from the Colonial Development Fund. My colleagues doubt its acceptance. I have no alternative to resignation if it is turned down. *Of course this for yourselves alone*. I cannot see the British Government facing the storm if I resigned. And Lodge would resign also. ...

1 9 April 1934.   3 Prominent St John's firm.
2 F. Gordon Bradley.

J.H.S. to Edgar and Eleanor, Newfoundland Hotel, 15 April 1934
... It is ten a.m. I had a morning in bed – did not get up till 8.30 and then breakfasted in dressing gown. I am sitting in my office room at the hotel. ... It is no. 503. 502 is our bedroom & 501 our sitting-room. I face the harbour and the Narrows. The other (south) side of the harbour is a rocky hill, patched with snow. Half a gale of wind is blowing in from the east, and brings with it a mixture of hail, sleet & rain. A dirty day for boats at sea. There are masses of gulls on the water. They are devouring the refuse from the sealers, of which three have returned. The numbers of baby seals destroyed are enormous. This year the fleet has taken 190,000 – and 20,000 large seals. One ship came in with over 50,000 white-coats, i.e., baby seals, on board. They only bring the skin for the fur. The carcase is left on the ice. And this though we have got 95,000 people on the dole. The skin with the fat weighs about 50 lbs. The flaying is very roughly done, and bits of meat stick to the fat. It is when these bits are cut off and thrown into the sea in the harbour that the gulls have their feasts.

With each skin, the ship brings in a 'flipper' – the webbed foot of the seal. It is not a foot, nor is it a fin, but it is between the two. It is a culinary delicacy, exceedingly popular, and flipper suppers are now the order of the day. I had flipper at lunch one day. It is quite good, a little resembling jugged hare, and you eat it with jelly. But it is not an edible about which to rave.

We are very lucky to start our time with a first-class seal fishery. Not only does it mean that a large number of men can then fit themselves out for the codfishery. It also means that we, the new government, are looked upon as lucky. We are also lucky in the happenings of the codfishery. Our trawler[1] made £1,200 on its first voyage of three weeks. And the schooners from the banks are in from their first voyage, with catches of 25 to 35 tons apiece.

But the problem is really a terrible one. For 15 or 20 years, the government has been borrowing and pauperizing the people. Every member of parliament has been making money himself and using public money to buy votes! And the shamelessness of it is incredible. Here is an instance. A man named Dunn wrote to me offering to take the post of lighthouse keeper at £10 per annum less than is being paid to the incumbent, a man named Brown. In the course of the letter, he said that last year Brown had

left the lighthouse for five months to go fishing, that he had done it without leave and had put in one Dyke, the previous keeper, to do the work
while he was away. I started to enquire and found that Dyke had been
dismissed for no reason except that Brown was a political supporter of the
late member! A letter was written to the deputy minister in charge of
Lighthouses: 'By the desire of Mr. Quinton,[2] Member of the House, you
are requested to dismiss Alfred Dyke and to appoint David Brown as
keeper of North Island lighthouse.' 'In answer to your letter of – I beg to
inform you that Alfred Dyke has been dismissed and David Brown appointed keeper of the North Island lighthouse.' Can you imagine anything
more barefaced? I have dismissed David Brown for absence without leave
and have reappointed Alfred Dyke! But I fear that I have opened the door
to a mass of complaints and that I shall be asked to do ditto in an unlimited
number of cases, as that was the usual practice in 'political' days.

You can have no idea of the desperate poverty and of the low standard
of life in this island. In the outports, the mass of the people is living on the
dole, and the dole is quite inadequate to maintain life. And one of the
troubles is that the people have been educated into the belief that the dole
is everybody's right. A man comes home from sealing with £20 in his
pocket and goes straight onto the dole. Justices of the Peace are on the
dole. One of the relieving officers was himself found to be on relief. There
is general demoralization among a people who, a generation ago, were a
self-respecting, self-helpful people like the Scotch. The mothers of the last
generation spun and wove the cloth & made clothes for their families and
ran the gardens and cured the fish. The modern girl just lies in bed till
eleven 'because there is nothing to do,' lives on the dole – and wears
artificial silk stockings. Our chief problem is the re-establishment of
morale. ... I am very thankful for health, for strength, and for a great
capacity for work. But the work is proving more than I can manage, and I
am getting a personal assistant who will also be head of the office. ... We
have the problem of Christian living in a *very* pronounced way here. Such
wasted lives. Such failure to realize responsibility. St John's society people
live – a lot of them – to themselves alone. Bridge. Dine. Wine. And there is
such need for moral stimulation everywhere. ...

1 The *Cape Agulhas*.
2 Herman W. Quinton (1896–1952) was
   the member of the House of

Assembly for Bonavista South,
1928–34.

Q.H.S. to Greta, Newfoundland Hotel, 15 April 1934

Mid-April already. I expect you are beginning to rid yourself of heavy clothing & are tempted to run risks of chills by going out without a coat. Even here, spring seems to be a long step nearer, tho' we have snow showers every day. But it does not lie, and there is not much snow left on the southern face of the hills, and we are planning to get the new car out today. I am longing to explore, but the roads are dreadful. And there is only 800 miles of road on the island! All the roads are in this little peninsula of Avalon. There are about 10 miles in Corner Brook & Grand Falls.

Everywhere else, the people have to get about by sea or in winter by sledge over the snow. Daddy is planning for 2 aeroplanes. They will be a help for getting to inaccessible outports & for patrolling against smugglers, watching for forest fires, etc.

Another plan is to send some of the local police to England for training. They are pretty useless as they are, in spite of the fact that the N.F.L. men are absolutely fearless. With training, $1/3$ of the men now employed could do the work. ... Such a lot of schemes Daddy has on foot. The papers are full of praise for the work that the Commission is doing; they voice the rising spirit of optimism. The enthusiasm of the papers makes me rather afraid. In spite of the warnings they give that everything cannot be accomplished at once and that the people themselves will have to help themselves too, there is almost bound to be a reaction when checks to development come or something goes wrong with the fishing or the crops fail. Still, there is no question that the Commission has got to work extraordinarily quickly, & that there is a move on, and a rising spirit of hope and thankfulness & faith in the future of the land that really seemed doomed to extinction a few months ago.

It is such a lovely morning again. We have had two or three quite dull days. Last night, I was wakened by the call of a vessel and jumped up to see the lights of a big ship coming through the Narrows. It was a lovely clear night without a moon, and all the lights of the harbour & the hillsides were great jewels in the dark & such streams of light along the water. She was the *Ungava*, a sealer with 40,000 pelts.

We were dining at Government House last night – just ourselves & Mr. Trentham & the Andersons & Lady Hastings Anderson. ... She is going home for 3 months, but I think she will come back, as she is a great help to Lady A. and enjoys the work of helping with the Service League. She has it all in her hands – the organization. When we of the Commission & Government House get together, we have rather fun comparing notes. They can't talk to anyone else; neither can we – not really *talk* – you know

– say what we think. With everyone else, you have to be so careful in case of hurting their feelings or saying something that might be repeated with the wrong emphasis.

I am feeling ever so well. I should love to climb Signal Hill this morning – it is such a tempting-looking hill – about as high as the Bastille at Grenoble.[1] ...

1 The Hope Simpsons had lived at
   Grenoble for a time in the mid-1920s.

Q.H.S. to Ian and Sheila, Newfoundland Hotel, 19 April 1934

The *Nova Scotia* came in this morning direct from Liverpool. She was due last night, but a sea mist wrapped us round & I suppose she did not venture through the Narrows. I was dressing when Daddy called, 'Here she comes!' & there was her smoke blowing ahead round the Gibraltar that is our Signal Hill that guards the Narrows. Then she came, looming so large through the mist, and we watched her together wondering & hoping, 'What does she hold for us!' O dear! it is so lovely getting letters. In the Andamans,[1] we used to watch for the ship that brought our mail & could see her far away. And here again, after nearly 20 years, we watch again for a mail that comes by ship, through dangers from icebergs here instead of the cyclones & hurricanes in those tropical seas. And instead of letters from our little children & growing boys & girls, we get lovely letters still from the children – men and women now, out in the world themselves, with wives & husbands & families of their own. And the delight of those home letters is as intense as ever. They are not in yet. But they may be here any moment now. And Daddy has just rung me up to tell me that the mail bag closes at 1 o'c. I do wish they would come. ...

Conditions here are terribly difficult. *Private*. There is a place called Carbonear[2] that is full of unemployed miners. They used to go away to Sydney in Nova Scotia to work in the mines there, but N.S. can't employ them now, and there are the mines at Bell Island just opposite Carbonear & they are working with much-reduced staff. These men are regular agitators – they get on the telephone & their spokesman shouts at Daddy from about 30 miles away. We know he is shouting so that the crowds about him can hear him. Daddy is not the Commissioner in charge of unemployment – one of the Newfoundlanders, Mr. Puddester ('Pudd'), has that job. But they hate him. Everyone comes to Daddy about every single thing. The trouble is too that the dole is utterly insufficient – $1.50 a month for a man, 60 cents for a child! – that is 6/. a month for an adult, 2d. a day for a child. It is terrible. Daddy has to decide whether to tell the British Government that we must have additional money for a dole that will support life until the country can get onto its legs again. It has to be a case of this must be done or I go. The dole is bad, we know – it is abused, we know. But how can you supervise the administration of the dole on an island like this, with ⅓ of the population on the dole & that population – a population equal to about the population of Leicester – scattered round 6,000 miles of coast – settlements that are inaccessible except in calm weather & seldom accessible at all as there are so few boats. It is a fearful problem. There is a clergyman here now from Carbonear, & he tells us that these Carbonear men tried to make him and the United Church parson sign a paper to say the men on dole ought to have $12 a month. They could not do it – not because $12 is too much but because force is not the way to do it. So these rioters decided to kill them. All the merchants & the parsons were to be summoned to a meeting in the hall, and then it was to be set on fire.

Everyone says that the dole is the ruin of men. But what can you do? You can't let them starve when there is no work to give them. For work you could not pay them less than $20 a month, & the British Government would never stand for the amount needed for that. Living is so much dearer here than in England. The problems here are terrible.

The population problem is another. The Roman Catholics teach, I am told, that an R.C. who produces 7 little R.C.s is certain of his ticket to heaven. Children swarm, quite irrespective of whether there are the means of subsistence.

The island seems to be like a farm that has been thinned & left. I often remember Daddy telling us that the farmer must be the farmer's bank. The bad farmer impoverishes his land; the good farmer enriches it. The merchants here have put nothing they could help back into the land; they have taken their fortunes abroad – spent their money in England. Can you blame them? Who would choose to educate their children in an island where there is no education to be compared with what they can get in Canada or England? Who would invest money in an island when government was so corrupt!

So the island is reaping the harvest that the merchants have sown.

The faith of the people in the English Commissioners is pathetic.

It has been very thrilling seeing the sealers come in. You hear the siren blowing and you look out & there are the flags strung up by the tower³ on Signal Hill – and in comes a boat – the sealers crowded on her poop – the dories piled high on the decks & the pelts – about 40,000 in most of the boats. The men as they come off the ships are black with seal oil and coal dust. All along the road, you meet people hurrying along, with flippers for their supper. It is considered a great dainty here. But only one flipper is brought with each pelt – I suppose because there is no room for more. Last night, there was a flipper supper here. I was afraid to touch flippers; they look & taste rather like ham.

And do you know – all the good seal meat is left on the ice! The ships bring only the pelts with the fat & one flipper. Next year, Daddy plans to send a ship for the seal meat. Mr. Lodge says, 'No good' – the men would go after the seals. They are tremendous hunters. The seal meat is excellent eating.

I must stop. Daddy & I are very well. I keep having dizzy attacks, but I don't mind them so much now and I think they are getting slighter. ... Gradually, he is getting his office organized. But everyone says you can't rush anyone here. So he may be in for trouble. That can't be helped. He has to work with the best material he can find here. It is no good importing crowds of people from England even if you could afford it. ...

1 Islands in the east Bay of Bengal,   2 Conception Bay.
   Indian Ocean, where Sir John had   3 Cabot Tower.
   once been posted.

Q.H.S. to Edgar and Eleanor, Newfoundland Hotel, 19 April 1934

... Daddy is having a terribly worrying time. The difficulties of this job are extraordinary. Think of trying to control dole for a population of tiny settlements round 6,000 miles of coast with *no* roads, & the settlements accessible only by sea & only in decent weather in a climate & on an ocean like this. ... The Carbonear people are threatening to burn their town, and the parsons, & the magistrates – they mean it too. ... What is to be done for all the unemployed? Daddy is wondering – shall we ask the British Government to put down some huge sum to raise the dole to a decent living sum & stand to go if the request is not granted; or what shall he do? It is not his job, but you can't stand by and see men starve if you can do anything to help. It will be long before this country can stand on her own feet; meanwhile, you must feed the people if they are ever to be fit for work again. ...

J.H.S. to Ian and Sheila, Newfoundland Hotel, 19 April 1934

Just a line this morning. I am sitting facing the Narrows, in my study at the hotel. The gulls are in myriads, screaming over the refuse from the seals. There is a cloud of mist hanging about 100 feet above the water, and the *Nova Scotia* is just entering the Narrows with mails from England. And it is time for breakfast. ...

Here we are getting along – very seriously hampered by want of money. Conditions are in fact appalling, with over 100,000 now on the dole out of a population of 280,000. And the dole is miserably inadequate. It works out to about $1.55 per adult in a family of 5 – that is 6 shillings *a month*. For children of 5 and below, it is half that amount. Can you wonder that physical & moral deterioration has set in? The morale of the whole people is dreadful. The habit of leaning on the government has set in – indeed, it has become normal. As has the habit of failure to repay advances. Indeed, our most urgent as our most difficult problem is to stimulate a sense of honesty in the people in their relations with the government.

My own work remains intense but has been much lightened in the course of the last week. I have just got a very capable personal assistant. His name is Claude Fraser.[1] He is a lawyer and a Catholic, and a tremendous worker. A man of ... great ability. The effect has been enormous and immediate. I have been able to shed on to him a mass of detail with which I was clogged. I have also put him in charge of the office. ...

I have been speaking again. The Sergeants' Mess[2] is a great institution. I spoke there on Tuesday night, and on Thursday was guest of the chief Masonic lodge. That was an occasion. There were 190 Masons present, & I spoke on civic duty – quite straight – to a valuable representative audience. Last night, we took a party to 'The Middle Watch,'[3] excellently produced in aid of widows and orphans of ex-servicemen. ...

1 1905–1944. Nephew of Sir Patrick T. McGrath (1868–1929).
2 An organization of non-commissioned officers of the Royal Newfoundland Regiment.
3 By Ian Hay, pen-name of Major-General John Hay Beith (1876–1952).

The Middle Watch was put on at the Casino Theatre by the War Vets' Players and was sponsored by the Great War Veterans' Association. Sets were by Dan Carroll (1865–1941), Newfoundland artist and poet.

Q.H.S. to Betty, Newfoundland Hotel, 23 April 1934

... We are looking forward to having you out here. You will love the country in summer. It is so beautiful. We have had the Austin out twice this week. She had run only 4 miles when we started, and of course we have to go carefully for the first 500 miles. But she travels so sweetly already. These roads would try any car, but she takes the bumps like a bird skimming on the waves. She is an Austin 16.6., dark powder-blue inside & out – leather lined. Daddy loves driving her. I fear he exceeded the 30-mile pace set for her first 500 miles; it is difficult not to when you hardly notice the pace.

Daddy took his first day off since we arrived, and we drove to Holyrood – about 30 miles. The road is only just open, and the frost is not out of the ground yet. But it was such a joy to get out of St. John's and to see the country. ... Topsail ... is about 12 miles out on the road to Holyrood, & you climb up on a pass ... & you come down between stony mountains covered with scrub pine & a shrub they call 'Indian tea'[1] (which has very red dead leaves just now) & below you is spread the great bay[2] with Bell Island & a distant coast. It just wanted the sea to be blue and we should have been coming down to Salamis & Eleusis.[3] As a matter of fact, the road was much more beautiful. There are the most beautiful streams & waterfalls; Topsail itself is just a long scattered village along the shore, but there are a lot of pleasant little houses where people come for the summer – rather like at Sunium,[4] but the houses are smaller & of wood.

Further along the road to Holyrood, there are fine mountains – 'Butterpots' they call the peaks that are knobby like the Butterpots in Ireland. These mountains have sheer, solid rock faces – precipices with no hold even for little plants. ... Holyrood is another long village along another bay – very like a Greek village. We saw a few cows out – so thin, poor creatures, after the long winter on low rations in stalls. And we saw some miserable sheep too & some darling lambs skipping about like lambs all the world over – such a joyous sight.

We took Mr. Trentham & a Mrs. Emerson[5] with us, & he did host for lunch at a jolly little place, where they gave us excellent food. Mr. & Mrs. Godson[6] are English; they came out to farm but could make nothing out of that under the old regime, so they started this wayside café. She is quite a girl still, I think, but she is an excellent cook, and they are such nice people. They have a good little N.F.L. maid too – & lots of dogs & puppies; they heed. After lunch, we sat out on the verandah (having had a walk before lunch) & I tried to sketch without any success. Then I penetrated to the kitchen, and the maid taught me how to do a hooked mat. All N.F.L.ers are very clever with their fingers. They can do almost anything. Their mats are wonderful – so fine that the Americans will not believe they can be hand-done. And they are all, rich & poor, wonderful cooks. The cakes at tea parties are a dream – also all the sandwiches & hors-d'oeuvres. And the men can build their own houses & ships.

Yesterday afternoon, Sunday, we went again to Holyrood for tea &

took two men, the Woodses,[7] who are here reorganizing the customs. ...
They did so enjoy the trip. We did not dare venture on any other road yet,
as they are still pretty bad with snow & mud. But really it does look as
tho' spring were coming – the grass that was so dead brown when the
snow melted is coming to life, & there is a green sheen on the hillsides &
flashes of green here & there where grass is growing at last. There are
crocuses in flower in gardens too. But everyone warns us not to be misled
– there is lots of cold & snow to come yet, & we must beware of icy blasts
again after this spell of warm weather.

Do you know that there are only 800 miles of roads in this island and
those 800 are mostly in the Avalon Peninsula where we are – you know
that lump on the end of the island. There are no roads along the coasts,
tho' all the settlements are along the 6,000 miles of coast. And the interior
of the island is practically unexplored. So we shall not be able to get far in
our car. Still, it will be a real joy to get about here. An open car would be
hopeless – the roads are so dusty. ...

1 A low-growing evergreen. Also
   know as Labrador tea (*Ledum
   groenlandicum*; or *Rhododendron
   canadense*.)
2 Conception Bay.
3 In Greece.
4 A cliff in Greece, near Athens. Also
   spelled Sounion.
5 Either Isabel Emerson, wife of Fred
   Emerson, or Ruby Emerson, wife of
   L.E. Emerson.
6 Frank and Evelyn Godson ran the
   Beach Cottage Tea Rooms at
   Holyrood.
7 B.M. Wood and A.C. Wood, known
   as 'Gin and Bitters' and 'Sunny Jim.'

Q.H.S. to Ian and Sheila, Newfoundland Hotel, 26 April 1934

... Here all goes as well as could be expected. Every day seems to unfold
new revelations of wickedness in the past, & misery & maladministration
in the present as a result. It is all very startling to us. I don't think any of
the Commissioners would have taken on the job if they had known what
the conditions really are.

For instance. Yesterday, I was at the Y.W.C.A., which is doing splendid
work under dreadful difficulties. Their finances are at the lowest ebb; it is a
question, from day to day, whether they can carry on. And yet they are
carrying girls who are employed by the best shops in the town and are not
being paid enough to support life. The Y.W. is in fact helping the merchant to get his labour for almost nothing. But how can they turn these
girls out? There would be nothing for them but the streets. There are 640

girls in the streets in this little town – a town of about the population of Oxford.

It is a horrid little town really. The surroundings & the position are beautiful. It might be a beautiful little capital of this beautiful island. But it is just a dirty, foul-smelling slum. Water St., the main shopping street, is about the level of the streets behind Euston Station[1] (the fried fish shop level but less lively); the shops often have nothing in the window, or are boarded up, or a few tinned goods & a few vegetables – or half a dozen mangy hats. Even the best stores, very 4th rate, look very shabby & unpainted and are mixed up with the meaner shops, and with very slummy little dwelling houses. Duckworth St. is wide & better laid, but is less alive. Gower St., the best residential street, [is] drab & slummy. I came along there this morning and the street was unswept, & every gust blew filthy dust & bits of straw in my face – old buckets & tins full of garbage stood outside every house at 10.30 o'c. in the morning! These Gower St. houses are inhabited by wealthy merchants, & inside they are surprisingly comfortable and well furnished. And the back streets & the side streets are worse still – dreadful. The harbour always fascinates me – I love watching the ships coming & going, but I have never been nearer than Water St. except to get onto a ship, and the smells that are wafted up are sickening – cod-liver oil & seal fat! That is inevitable – it is the living of the people and one does not resent that. But the dirt & carelessness are preventable. We begin to see what conditions will be when the hot days come and the winds blow all this dirt & dust about the town. It is a town without self-respect. No one seems to have cared enough for it to think & plan & spend for it. I think that ten years of government of the island by the Commission may transform this town into a place of order & beauty. But so many things must be done first. $\frac{1}{3}$ of the population of N.F.L. on the dole!

Things are moving pretty quickly. The seal fishery has been good, and the codfishery has started well, so money is coming into the town. Buchans, the mines in the north, has paid a good sum to the government for the first time for years (somebody probably pocketed the money or was paid not to demand it before). New industries are springing up, old industries are waking up. There is a spirit of hope abroad. Under the old regime, it was useless to try to do anything. Now the people feel there are honest men at the helm, & it is worthwhile not only to back them up but to try to help themselves.

And yet – and yet – the people are so well worth helping – the trouble has been that the population was too small and too uneducated to have self-government. A population altogether about the size of Leicester scattered round 6,000 miles of coast, no aristocracy or cultured or leisured class with traditions of service and public responsibility – just a population of hard-working fishermen some of whom amassed wealth and took command. They have succumbed to the temptation of power or have kept out of politics because they were so dirty. I have never before realized how great is the duty of every man to play his part as a good citizen. The good men here have got what they asked for by shirking their duty. If they had played, it is possible that the island might have won through to some form of decently ordered community life. As it is, the mess is appalling. ...

Here is a sea mist sweeping over the town. But the sun is shining through it still, so I expect it will soon pass. We have been having lovely weather – so mild and so sunny. But, [as] there are icebergs within 6 miles of us, we have to be careful of sudden chills. We see mists driving past the entrance to the harbour & sometimes lying on the hill, but they don't often envelop us. ...

1 London, England.

J.H.S. to Edgar and Eleanor, Newfoundland Hotel, 28 April 1934

... Our Commission has commenced operations with a good deal of what people call 'luck' but what we may perhaps call 'blessing.' There has been an excellent sealery.[1] The spring fishing is very good. Our government trawler has come in twice, and we made $7,000 from the first catch and $9,000 from the second. The total outfitting charge so far has been $12,000 ... so we have a profit already of $4,000, & there is one more voyage before she goes on biological work. Then a mine[2] which has only paid once before in its history has paid us over $1,400 in royalties, and the price of wood has gone up, so that we shall get royalties of perhaps $50,000 this year from that source. But, best of all, the people generally are gaining in confidence. They are working after years of slackness and dependence on dole. If we can but stimulate that feeling and induce people to exert their own effort in place of depending on the government, the chief problem will have been solved. To give you an instance of the kind of thing that happened. Men of the sealing fleet always got free passes from the government for the railway journey to and from St. John's. This year, one of the ships paid each man $110-odd as his share after a month's work. Directly they were discharged, five of the men came to my office for free passes and were much surprised when they did not get them. Meanwhile, the railway has natu-

rally been showing a heavy deficit every year. ... We are having a deal of
wind, but also a deal of sunshine. The climate is not to be despised. ...

1 Seal fishery.   American Smelting and Refining Co.,
2 At Buchans. Operated by the   Ltd.

Q.H.S. to Betty, Newfoundland Hotel, 2 May 1934

... I often long for you to be here when we do something specially nice.
The weather is so lovely – day after day we wake to glorious weather. We
wake regularly at 5.30 now and see the world at its freshest & loveliest. The
dawns are beautiful. Our bedroom window faces the east, & we sleep with
the blind up – sometimes with the window wide too, but it is usually too
windy & too cold to have the wind blowing across our beds, so we have
the bathroom & sitting-room windows open & the two doors open & are
very fresh & comfortable. There is no heat on at night. But it is lovely to
wake to see the sunrise over Signal Hill, our Gibraltar, and the beacon
light still winking on the Narrows & perhaps a banker (a schooner) slip-
ping out to the Atlantic to the codfishery. I never weary of watching the
ships coming & going. These sailing ships are such lovely things and so
live. A few days ago there was such a gale blowing, & I watched ship after
ship try to make the Narrows. They were like horses jibbing at a fence.
They came sweeping in so swift & brave; then, suddenly, the sails flagged
& ragged, & you saw the men straining at the tiller as she swept round &
out again, just shaving the rocks below Gibraltar. I watched schooner after
schooner try again & again, but only one out of 6 got through, & she tacked
& tacked and, every tack, I thought she was going to be swept onto the
rocks or out to sea again. The sails of these bankers are cinnamon brown
usually. ...

Daddy wants me to tell you all that he is having such a busy time he is
leaving me to do the letter writing for the moment. He is looking very
tired. These first three months have been very strenuous. I shall be glad
when he can get away from St. John's to the outports; it will not be a
holiday, but it will be a change and a relief to get away from the office.
The Lodges sail tomorrow by the boat that takes this letter. We shall miss
them very much, and Daddy will have to take on some of the work, so he
will be busier than ever till they return. But I have suggested that he visit
some of the outports in the Avalon Peninsula when there are roads and we
can get out by car whenever he gets a chance. The roads are open pretty
well now – the snow is melting fast everywhere. I can't *see* any now, but
when roads have been kept dug out with snow piled at the sides, that is

not clear yet, &, as it melts, it makes the road very soft & almost impass-
able. But it is a very early spring for this country. Did I tell you that we
have seen two icebergs passing the mouth of the Narrows – on such lovely
sunny days? ...

Q.H.S. to Edgar and Eleanor, Newfoundland Hotel, 4 May 1934

The *Nova Scotia* is lying beneath our windows ... and this letter will go by
Mrs. Lodge & she will post it in England. How we wish we could go with
it to see you all. Only 6 days! But the fare is a big mouthful. It costs close
to £60 to go & come again – quite that with tips, etc., as much as going to
Greece. But! how nice it would be! We seem to be almost as far away from
you here as we were in China, the mails are so infrequent. There is so little
traffic between here & England that it does not pay to run the boats.

The harbour is quite lively now – there are two large steamers going out
now – the *Silvia* & the *Glencoe* – one to Halifax, the other round the south
coast of the island – good ships both of them. Then there are the sealers.
They are all safely back in harbour now. The *Beothic* had a great reception.
She arrived in the middle of the night, & all the sirens hooted a welcome to
old Captain Kean bringing home his 1,000,000th seal. He is 78 and a hero
to the sealers. A dear old man too & so amusing, with his golden wig and
his marvellous memory for poetry. The sealers all follow him, as he seems
to have a special seal sense and finds the best sealing grounds. ...

Daddy is having a busy time & is getting very tired. But there is a new
spirit of hope & enterprise in the island. This week we saw 9 men off early
in the morning to start an agricultural settlement¹ at Whitbourne. They were
such a decent lot of men – half-starved they looked, but they were full of
hope & enthusiasm & thankfulness. 'We've got our chance! They've been
good to us (the Commission). We'll have our ups & downs, but we're
bound to make good – we can't let them down anyway.' They are picked
men, men who are fit in every way & who have proved themselves eager
to help themselves & had been working for this even before the Commission came. We saw the spades & picks & food & axes & saws & tents &
mattresses piled on the lorries, & then the men shook hands heartily all
round, & climbed on top, & off they went on their 100-mile drive, waving
cheerily. They expect to have three houses ready for their wives & families
in 5 weeks. We had such a nice letter from them, thanking Mrs. Lodge &
me for going to cheer them off.

John has been prospecting for another settlement of about 50 men. The
idea is, in the first place, that these men should be able to grow enough to
feed their families. They can't even do that now. And the fishing is such a

gamble, and there are far too many men in it. This is a great wild berry country & there should be a market for their canned fruits. The strawberries are marvellous, I am told – also the blueberries & raspberries.

I want to change for dinner tonight. We are going to dine on the *Nova Scotia* with the Lodges. ...

1 Markland.

J.H.S. to Ian and Sheila, Newfoundland Hotel, 4 May 1934

... We are having beautiful weather – lots of sunshine, frequently with high wind. Last Tuesday,[1] I took the afternoon off and went trout fishing on Big Pond,[2] about three miles south of St. John's. ...

We have laid in a stock of a million pounds of frozen herring for bait, in case the bait supply fails again, as it did last year. The bait was caught in the southern bays and frozen as it was caught, on the *Blue Peter*, a refrigerating ship belonging to the Hudson's Bay Company. Yesterday, I went down to their premises to see the bait unloaded and stored in the cold storage. The fish were as hard as a board, and the cold storage has 25° of frost. So they should keep well. The job will be the distribution. We are building four subsidiary freezing depots at various points on the coast, but the fish will not keep frozen for the 24 hours necessary to transport them. We shall have to get a modern cold storage boat of a small type for the distribution.

There is lots of interesting work to do. And a great deal of it is most difficult. My department is the largest, and it is the department on which the material prosperity of the country depends. I am engaged in getting back what is possible of the various concessions granted by the government of graft which brought N.F.L. to its present pass. Yesterday, I cancelled 23 concessions of 100 square miles each in the gold-bearing areas of the Labrador. The concessions demanded a report on operations, to be submitted each year before 31st December. Fortunately, the concessionaires failed to carry out this term of the agreement, so I cancelled them *en bloc*. I have also got back sundry other mineral & forest areas and a lot of water-powers. And I have put a royalty on export of cut timber. Altogether, things are looking more rosy. But the fishing population is in desperate poverty and appallingly indebted. That is the next great problem. Rafta, rafta, as the Persian says. 'Coming, coming.'

1 1 May 1934.   2 Bay Bulls Big Pond.

Q.H.S. to Greta, Newfoundland Hotel, 10 May 1934

... It is just a week tomorrow since I wrote last to you, and today Mr. & Mrs. Lodge should be landing. I do hope you will see them. ...

They have lent us their wireless while they are away, and I am trying to get the good of it. It is rather complicated & difficult to understand how to get the stations at different hours of the day, but I am gradually finding out how to do it, and 'London speaking' thrills me. ...

We have just come in from a tour of inspection of roads under repair in the country. 100 men, who had been on the dole for months, & some of them for years, have just started this week. It was lovely to see how happy they looked to have a chance to get down to a job of work and a chance of earning something to buy food & clothes for their family. In one place, a bucket of soup was being ladled round into their cups. They are so starved, poor things; I don't know how they can do a day's work, especially in this terribly stony ground. It is like our soil but worse – more slaty & harder stuff than slate & huge stones & boulders & stones big & little. The ground grows stones. ...

We had the weekend combining business & pleasure – not any relaxation for John, however. One of the Water Street merchants, Chesley Crosbie,[1] took us with his wife in the car to see what is going on along part of the coast. 'Ches' is only 29 but he is more like 40 in maturity. His wife[2] is rather like Sheila.[3] ... He talks all the time; she is quiet, a nice girl. They have 3 children, a girl of 6 & 2 small boys.[4] 'Ches' is not beloved of the rest of 'Water St.' He is a keen, good businessman, but he is not greedy or selfish. He sees the men's side & is sympathetic & generous in his treatment of them. He is a fish merchant. His brother[5] has a very up-to-date butterine factory & supplies milk & butter to the hotel – excellent, all standard & so good. Mrs. Ches, this dainty little lady, is the unbelievable daughter of the undertaker, who is also the Mayor[6] – a dreadful person who accentuates his broad Irish & is a public buffoon. Mrs. Ches was wearing the most beautiful coat I have ever seen – a leopard baby fur, I should think, with some light fur for collar & cuffs. 'Ches had to be away in Canada when baby was born & he just heaped gifts on me when he came home; he was so sorry.' They were such kind hosts. We started on Saturday at 3 and went by Holyrood & Salmonier away down to St. Joseph's to see the lobster catchers at work. It was a dull afternoon & turned to heavy rain, so Mrs. C. & I stayed in the car mostly. But the lobster men brought us gifts of tinned lobster hot from the pot and we warmed our hands on them. From there, we turned back up to Salmonier, & from there across another arm of the peninsula to the Placentia coast. We stopped short of the coast at

Southeast Placentia on the eastern arm of the inlet at a place called
'Phippards.' Mr. & Mrs. Phippard[7] were waiting for us under the light of
the porch as we drove up to the funny old wooden house – such kindly
welcome & entertainment – all very simple – bare oilcloth floor & no
furniture in the bedrooms except beds & a dressing-table - but all spotlessly clean & warm, with big fires and good food and comfortable arm-
chairs. It smelt of sweet spruce wood. We were not the only guests; there
were 14 others, but some sat with their hosts in the kitchen. There was
actually indoor sanitation (which is most unusual even in private homes in
the outports).

Next morning, we were up at 6, but it was misty & dull, so I decided
not to go with them further down the coast. ... John & Mr. Crosbie went
away down the coast visiting every settlement down to St. Bride's. Soon
after they left, the sun came through & the mists swept out to the 3-mile
limit, where it usually stays, and we had a marvellous long day.

I went for a walk along the road – pine-wooded hill on one side, sloping lawn-like little holdings with neat wooden houses and the blue, blue
inlet with wooded hills beyond, and away in the distance, 7 miles down, a
line of shingle with houses along it, and beyond that the sea. The sea is just
the colour of clear sun-shot sapphire – all the lakes & ponds are a wonderful colour – almost a royal blue – & the air is so clear that everything is
sharp-edged & vivid. In the afternoon, a Mrs. Emerson[8] (wife of a lawyer
who was member for Placentia)[9] took me to Placentia itself, which lies on
& across that line of shingle. It is the old French capital – a most beautiful
spot – the two arms of the inlet meet & rush through the narrows there –
one inlet runs about 28 miles inland – the other 7 miles – they are so like
Scotch lochs. Placentia is only a scattered village of wooden houses, but it
is rather quaint. The English church is closed now because the last Protestant has died, but we went in & looked at the little graveyard – a cheery
little spot with little white headstones & the sea breezes blowing on it. ...

1 Chesley Arthur Crosbie (1905–1962).
2 Jessie Elizabeth (Carnell) Crosbie
   (d. 1982).
3 Sheila (Gonner), wife of John
   Barclay (Ian) Hope Simpson.
4 Joan (1927–1981), John Carnell
   (1931–), and Andrew (1933–1991).
5 George Graham Crosbie (1907–1984).
6 Andrew G. Carnell.
7 John and Rose Phippard.
8 Ruby (Ayre) Emerson.
9 Lewis Edward Emerson (1890–1949),
   member of the House of Assembly
   for Placentia East, 1928–32.

J.H.S. to Betty, Newfoundland Hotel, 10 May 1934

... This is a perfectly lovely morning. The gulls are screaming in the harbour. I suppose that they have discovered a shoal of small fish. Schooners are coming and going and are so beautiful with their white or brown sails. There is one just passing up now, opposite my window, with furled sails and under auxiliary motor. There is a great deal of local traffic by schooner, as the coastal boats sail at fortnightly intervals and are expensive. Schooner traffic is very cheap.

Last night, Mum and I went to the annual meeting of the church – St. Thomas's – where we worship. ... The Mayor was there. He is a professional funny-man – rather a horror – and is the local undertaker. I have heard him speak in public and in private and say the most outrageous things. He spoke two or three times while we were there, and each time there was general laughter, in part I think because of his reputation as a funny-man.

Mum and I had a very interesting weekend. We went out on Saturday afternoon with Mr. & Mrs. Ches Crosbie in their car. ... He is a fish exporter and rather a rough diamond, but very straight and strong. And he knows the country thoroughly. Sunday was misty when Crosbie and I started at 7.30 for St. Bride's at the south end of Placentia Bay, but by 10.30 the sun had come out and we had a glorious day. We stopped at every settlement and I saw the people. As a rule, they are miserably poor and they had learned to depend entirely on the government for everything. We are giving them advances for the fishery, as far as we can, and the lists are coming in. Some of them are astonishing. One man asked for four pairs of ladies' boots, size 8 laced, & four pairs [of] rubber-soled shoes ... ! And they ask for enormous amounts of tea and flour and sugar and butter and tobacco. Tobacco is really an essential for the fisherman. Our chief difficulty is going to be to make them independent once more.

We started relief works for the unemployed last Monday,[1] and have had a good deal of difficulty with a labour union, which wanted us to pay union rates of labour and objected very much to one arrangement we have made. We pay 2 dollars a day and for the first month cut 50 cents a day, which is saved up for the man, and the second month one dollar a day. At the end of 8 weeks, he will have $36 saved up. That we are going to pay, after the work is over, at $6 a week to the man that earned it, so that for a further six weeks he will need no help. We hope thus to break them of the dole habit. They objected very strongly, but we insisted. I think the work is going smoothly now, but the union is an unreasonable factor.

Dr. & Mrs. Olds[2] of Twillingate are here. Twillingate is ... on the N.E. coast, and we are having considerable difficulty there. Local politics are very strong and there are two factions, one working against the other. And everyone is on the dole, though probably not a quarter of the people really need it. The whole population has come to look upon the dole as something to which they have a right, whether they would otherwise starve or not. That is a terrible habit, and a most expensive habit for the government. It will take a great effort on the part both of the government and of people to break them of it. And you can imagine how popular our government is going to be when the breaking-off process commences in earnest. People are always suspicious of us – especially, I think, the old-fashioned merchants who think us socialistically inclined. They suspected us from the start. And the people who used to get anything they wanted done for them at government expense by asking their local member are beginning to wonder whether the change is advantageous to them when they are asked to do things for themselves. ...

1 7 May 1934.
2 John and Elizabeth (Arms) Olds. An American, John Olds (1906–1985) was a graduate of Johns Hopkins University. First worked in Twillingate, as a medical student, in the summer of 1930.

J.H.S. to Greta, Newfoundland Hotel, 13 May 1934

... It was good news to hear of your promotion,¹ though your salary sounds small enough – about £250 a year. My private secretary here, who has not any of your educational qualifications (though she is very accurate, quick and good, and, above all, keeps her mouth shut), gets £216. Here the lowest-grade salaries are quite good, but the top men are very inadequately paid. The head men in my department get £540 and £360, respectively. The former is a man well over 70. We have just introduced the 65-year rule for retirements and find that, out of about 230 civil servants, 68 are over 65. And, of these, one man of 68 was put in seven months ago – probably the last political job before the Commission arrived. ... You cannot imagine the wholesale bribery that went on. At one election, the outgoing party spent $500,000 on public works, quite futile, to bribe the electorate – bits of road that connected nowhere with nowhere but paid the voters good wages for little work – hundreds of jetties which were a convenience to local fishermen & which they should have built themselves. And the people have got into a dreadful habit of leaning on the government for everything. The most serious problem facing us is the re-establishment of public morality and private morale. They are a very attractive people, and I have no doubt that things will improve in time. They need leadership very badly.

The work is very varied, very interesting and far too heavy, though it is gradually lessening now that I have a good P.A. in Claude Fraser. He is overworking too, but that is the common complaint. Yesterday, I wrote a long memorandum on the habits of the lobster! I am trying to get reliable information on that interesting crustacean, to decide on what months of the year should be the open season for the lobster fishery. I also wrote a long letter to the local Board of Trade[2] on the method of fishery supply. We hope to get about 2,000 fishermen to work. A great many of them can get no supplies from the merchant. They have no credit. So the government will have to do the supplying, and the merchants are kicking at my proposal that they should allow the government half the profit on all supplies bought from them. In fact, they do not want us to supply at all, as they fear that will mean more fish, lower prices and less profit to the merchant. I fear that I shall have to tone down my letter. It makes me angry when they offer that criticism and no alternative suggestion for getting these fishermen off the dole. The St. John's merchants are a reactionary crowd. They see no further than the ends of their noses, and have no interest outside their own profits. They dislike me & they dislike the Commission of Government, because our main interest is prosperity among the common folk.

Another subject in which I am deeply immersed at the moment is game preservation. The murder of the wild beast has been appalling. This island used to swarm with caribou. They were killed by the thousand and the carcasses left to rot, and there are now only a few hundred where they used to be by the thousands. Even now there is constant poaching and no sense of law breaking. The government took little interest & left preservation to a 'Game and Inland Fisheries Board' whose only connection with the government was a small annual grant. Things are looking up already, and I expect that within five years there will be a different tale to tell. But I have myself to draft the regulations, as no one else seems capable of it, and that is a big job. I got the Department of Justice to prepare a draft and it came in a document of somewhere about 60 pages of type! So far I have drafted four sections of the regulations. They contain all that would be found in 25 of those drafted by the legal people.

One of our troubles is the distrust of the N.F.L. Commissioners. As a result, everyone with a grievance comes to us and tries to induce us to influence our colleagues. That may be complimentary, but it is a great nuisance. I have refused to allow any of my colleagues to interfere in my department's affairs. So I have a certain delicacy in interfering in theirs, even when I know that things are wrong. Yet it is inevitable. Labour, for instance, always comes to Lodge or to me because organized labour is regarded as anathema maranatha[3] by Puddester and Alderdice. They stand just about where employers stood in England in 1832. ...

This afternoon we drive with the Puddesters. A penance, but inevitable. It is a sea-misty day, & we shall not even have the pleasure of the view. ...

1 At the B.B.C., London.
2 Newfoundland Board of Trade, founded in 1909.

3 A portentously intensified form of anathema.

J.H.S. to Edgar and Eleanor, Newfoundland Hotel, 14 May 1934

... We have to thank you, Eleanor, for a jolly long letter, which arrived yesterday and brought us a vivid whiff of an English spring. ... You may imagine how it made us long for home, though we also have the spring. The fields are green and there are lambs everywhere and the fishermen are busy caulking and painting their boats and repairing their schooners, and the little leaves are coming out with the lilacs and the wych-elms and presently it is going to be unpleasantly hot. ...

Here all goes well. The work is still exceedingly heavy, but I am having more efficient assistance, and shall have still more efficiency in the office when we bring in the 65-year rule and get rid of the fossil crust which is ubiquitous. That happens on 30th June. And in June, we are to hold the first public competition examination for the civil service in the history of N.F.L. Incidentally, that is a much more important reform than appears on the surface. Hitherto, one of the criteria of appointment has been religion. If you appoint a Catholic, a similar appointment must be earmarked for a member of the Church of England and another for one of the United Church of Canada. Now we are asking for education rather than for religion in our candidates. This religious question has been one of the banes of the island. A contract given to a Methodist implied one to a Catholic and another to a C. of E., and because two Catholics running have been in charge of the General Hospital that position is now regarded as a Catholic preserve. ...

This weekend, I am going to make a short tour down to Trepassey & then back & out to St. Mary's & back again via Whitbourne, where we are settling 10 ex-service unemployed families on the land as an experiment. They have been out there a fortnight now & have one house nearly completed and the foundations of three others laid. I trust very heartily that the experiment will succeed, as it will then be the first of 50 others of the same kind. The trouble is that once we began the experiment, there are scores of other unemployed ex-servicemen who want to do the same. ...

Q.H.S. to Betty, Newfoundland Hotel, 14 May 1934

... *May 17* ... St. John's ... is coming out much more attractive now that the snow has gone. The snow, so lovely in itself, makes everything else look so dull & dirty & hides so much. Now we see how quaint & pretty the old wooden houses are climbing up & down the hills: one roof a little higher than the next; some roofs so flat that the snow blows off as it falls; some gabled so that the snow slips off; some with curved roofs & dormer windows. All the houses are painted wood & are faded to dim reds & blues & greys & greens. And down on the harbour are the wharfs & stages where the fishing schooners bring their harvest. The lumbermen are bringing in great loads of pine branches, which are strewn on the stages where the cod are dried. The talk here is all of fish now that the sealing season is over.

This afternoon we are going to Bay Bulls to see the biological station. We took the Governor & Lady Anderson out there last week, & she & I went & saw some dreadfully poor people. I must take some sweets with me again. ...

Q.H.S. to Ian and Sheila, Newfoundland Hotel, 17 May 1934

... We are getting about a lot now that the snow has gone. We can't get far away from headquarters until Mr. Lodge gets back, but we can do a lot in the Avalon Peninsula with the car as there are nearly 800 miles of roads here. ... Last weekend, the Puddesters took us in their car round Conception Bay to Bay Roberts – such lovely places all along that coast. Great inlets open off Conception Bay – beautiful harbours many miles deep into the land. The country is most varied. Above Bay Roberts it is so wild and bare and almost torrid-looking – just what I imagine it would be like among the mountains of Arabia – crumbling, rocky ground & crumbling cliffs & knobby hills like knuckle-bones sticking out of the crumble & splashes of rose-red in the detritus, and then round a corner you look down on a long deep sapphire sea & lakes & green fields and peaceful settlements of gay little wooden houses. Those settlements round Conception Bay – Carbonear, Brigus, Bay Roberts – must have been very prosperous; they look so comfortable even now – & they have large populations – 2,500 to 3,000 in some of them – & beautiful schooners lying in the bay ready for the fishery. But the majority of the people are on the dole. We spoke to a fine-looking man who was standing with his four big sons, leaning on his garden fence, watching our struggles with a boiling radiator. He is a carpenter & has had no work for 10 years! The sons have never had any work. His 5 daughters are all away in America; they can all get work. But these men were tidy & well clothed (it was Sunday evening). 'We've got a bit of land; we live on the vegetables.' I expect the daughters help. The women were all indoors (a mother & grannie & a young child at the window). ...

Q.H.S. to Edgar and Eleanor, Newfoundland Hotel, 29 May 1934

I am writing at the wide-open window with the sun streaming in and glittering on the harbour water. No heat on and I am hot. ... I expect you are revelling in summer weather and the spring flowers.

We are seeing quite a lot of this Avalon Peninsula now. We did a tour from Friday afternoon to Tuesday[1] afternoon, encircling almost the most easterly tongue of the Avalon. St. John's & Cape Race are the only names you will recognize, & we cut across Cape Race so did not see that this time. The first afternoon, we went as far as Ferryland, where Lord Baltimore established his settlement and built a big house at the beginning of the 17th century – about 1620. ...

We stayed that night (Friday) at Calvert with a dear little fisherman's wife – everything very simple but spotlessly clean. The coast from St. John's is most beautiful – one inlet after another – deep fissures running inland & about 1 or two miles wide & so lovely. We saw a large iceberg stranded just inside Mobile inlet. La Manche was the loveliest of all. We came on a hill into an enchanted valley – wooded hillsides & a string of blue lakes & islands threaded on a wide stream that rushed & splashed along among white & yellow boulders, and at the end of the valley huge cliffs almost enclosing the valley with just a flash when the river leapt to the blue sea far below.

At Ferryland, I saw a boy with an egg in each hand. I asked what he was going to do with them – exchange them for a cake of yeast. Barter is the medium of exchange in these outports.

Next day, Saturday, was a long day and a dull rainy day for once. We went on to Cape Broyle & Aquaforte, beautiful places both of them, & picked up the constable at Renews. The doctor at Ferryland has 60 miles of coast for his practice, & the constable at Renews has 60 miles to look after. The doctor is also the magistrate for that district, & doctor & constable are the only 2 people in the whole of these 60-mile districts to whom one can turn for assistance in government. From Renews, we travelled on the road of the old railway line that has recently been taken up because the St. John's to Trepassey branch did not pay. I don't wonder, the people are so poor. Many would starve but for the dole. After Renews, the line cuts across the country, missing Cape Race & the settlements there, so we shall have to return & go along the shore another time. And such a desolate country we drove through for about 20 miles. First through a forest of skeletons; as far as the eye could see, mile after mile, nothing but burnt forest, the trees bleached white by summer suns. Then for miles over a barren waste of boulders & peat bog. So much of Newfoundland looks as though it has lain for an epoch under the icecap or under a great glacier. We did not see a home the whole way I think (there may have been one shack), and we met only one group of road men at work & one lorry, which carries them to & fro along the road, & one car. We asked the man in the car if there was anywhere we could get a meal in Portugal Cove[2] or Trepassey. 'I could not get even an egg,' he said. Portugal Cove looked desolate indeed in the rain but our business was at Trepassey & we went on, crossing lovely coves & magnificent cascades. The coast is wild & grand. Most of these inlets & coves are almost land-locked by shingle beaches like the Chesil Beach.[3]

We called on the constable, who is also the magistrate here – a very decent fellow. The two constables & John had a long talk & I invaded the kitchen when the wife was getting some tea & biscuit for us, & I had a talk with her. The people there are in terrible case: so dreadfully poor & the land so poor in most parts of the coast. The reason the people have settled on rocky points is for the fishing; there has been no thought to anything else, & once settled in the far-back past nothing will make the present settlers move. And some of the settlements are so small; there was only fishing to support one or two or half a dozen families perhaps & in the days before motorboats you had to live on top of your fishing if you were a small man. We were thankful for a hot cup of tea and we ate our sandwiches on the way back. The railways in this country are narrow gauge & the track was narrow & muddy & we nearly slipped off into the bog more than once – in fact, we escaped with a load of mud over. It was a trying drive for John – no help within many miles if he had slipped off the road. We were glad to get onto a rough but fairly hard road at Renews & got back to St. John's that night.

Sunday, we went off again down the western side of the same tongue of land. It was a lovely day again. We stopped for tea at Salmonier with friends[4] who have a weekend summer bungalow on the river there. ... Little bedrooms with berths one above the other for children & practically no furniture. But the living room had a long hooded stone fireplace & wide windows with plate glass 'because,' Mrs. Murray told me, 'I was warned that the mosquitoes are so bad you can't sit out and enjoy the view, so I determined I should be able to sit in and enjoy it.' So we all sat around the window with a great blazing log fire on the old dogs behind us. Mrs. Murray is a great gardener, & later on delphiniums look in at all the windows, tho' it is raised on piles. We looked out over a wide quiet pool of bluest water to a mass of golden logs banded in a bay below a pine wood. Three muskrats were playing about in the reeds quite close to us and there was a beaver dam not far away. ...

Then on down the estuary of the Salmonier – very like the Clyde, but poor little wooden houses pitch along the hillsides with ribbons of cultivation running up behind. All these parts much better off on account of the land. Then, along St. Joseph's, the houses strung along about five miles of shore, & all along these shores of the Avalon the people are Irish & Catholic & have huge families, so that any idea of women's institutes seems almost impossible of achievement; the women are too far apart and much too busy to leave their houses.

Then on across barrens that are rich in berries and partridges – marsh berries, blueberries (whorts), partridge berries, bakeapple,[5] raspberries. N.F.L. is a wonderful land for berries, and that is one of the industries that has to be developed. St. Mary's is another long, stretched-out settlement. We stayed the night there with a nice young couple, Dr. & Mrs. McGrath.[6] He too is a magistrate as well as doctor for 60 miles of coast. The people are so poor that often, when he is called to a maternity case at night, there is no lamp in the house & not even a basin for him to wash his hands in. He is seldom paid, but when he was building his house, his patients flocked to help him. He had over 70 at work on it. Mrs. McGrath told me that the people who have a cow will not sell her milk. 'We don't sell milk – we will be glad to give it you.' So she has to devise ways of repaying them by gifts. He was educated in Ireland & ... used to spend his holidays tramping in eastern France. Their new house – not nearly finished – is full of interesting books & their two babies. It was a pleasant visit.

Next morning, the doctor came on with us to St. Vincent's on Holyrood Pond. This is an inlet 25 miles long & is land-locked by 2 miles of another of these Chesil beaches. The other side of the 'pond' is uninhabited & looks almost inaccessible, the cliffs are so steep. But I don't suppose it is, for there are forests. St. Vincent's is only about 12 miles from Trepassey, but there is no road – only a track. Otherwise, we might have come round from Trepassey. A road would be very expensive as in storms the sea pours over these Chesil beaches. I think St. Vincent's was the poorest place we have been to. And yet, even here the priest has built himself a good presbytery and there is a big church. Father Battcock[7] is a nice fellow – quite young and very keen. He has been there 10 years. We walked &

talked together on the Chesil beach while John talked with the fishermen. I saw dreadfully white-faced women & children at the windows. I tried to buy some candies at the one little store, but there was not such a thing to be had. Everywhere along these coasts, the magistrate & constables said the same thing: 'But for the dole the people would starve.' The dole is 2d. a day, & food is dearer than in England. When I come home, I am going to collect all the toys I can beg, borrow or steal for these outport children. They have nothing. And when they are sick there is often no help for them – some of the doctors charge prohibitive prices to come 60 miles – the cost of the petrol alone is prohibitive to most of these poor people & the doctors are not wealthy – we should think them very poor. And there are very few nurses – only about half a dozen, even in the peninsula. And there are no toys. I shall begin making scrapbooks as soon as I can, so please save Christmas cards for me. For such children, they would be an unspeakable boon. Keep coloured magazine pictures too – anything for a bit of colour in their drab lives. We sat a long time with Father Battcock in his house & talked & talked. Then back to St. Mary's, where the fishermen of that shore had gathered to see & talk to John. Then a late lunch, & we said goodbye to the McGrath family & retraced our wheel marks as far as Salmonier & saw the fishermen drawing their nets on the Salmonier estuary, their dories gleaming gold in the sunshine on the blue water. Then across country to Colinet, a pretty place on another estuary, where we stayed the night with an ancient dame called Diddums[8] and a great-grand-child who was not apparently called 'Do it.' The sanitary arrangement was about [a] mile up the road – most sanitary but somewhat inconvenient. We were just thinking of going to bed when it seemed that we were plunged into the thick of a revolution. Guns went off under our windows: 'It's the boys giving you a welcome.' John went out to talk to them; I stayed in safety, but the revellers thought I should be entertained, so they kept it up under my window, so that I had to hang on to my common sense and try not to leap at every explosion.

Next day, we went north up the Rocky River to Whitbourne – or rather to 'Markland,' the new settlement where 9 of the unemployed are making homes for themselves & their families. The Commission is helping them, but they are doing everything themselves. We heard the tractor at work miles away singing at the top of its voice as it hauled the trees out of the ground. The men have been out only 3 weeks, but they have cleared quite a lot of land already – enough for the first planting of the potatoes that are to keep them next winter. It is lovely land but thickly afforested. They have also cleared land for their houses, & one is practically finished &

another is just getting the roof on & a third has its platform & sides up. The homes are quite far apart – one is nearly two miles away. I can't understand that – you would think the women would want to get together to help each other, especially in the long winter days. Someone lent them the tractor; before that their poor hands were in ribbons.

From there, we came back across another barren waste – with lovely ponds & islands with here & there a fishing shack or huntsman's little home – to Conception Bay at Brigus, and so round those beautiful inlets & across to St. John's again by lunch-time on Tuesday.

I forgot to tell you about a queer thing that happened near St. Vincent's. A family lived in a very isolated spot & the parents had to go away; they left the children, ages up to 10, in charge of the grandfather. While they were away, he died. The children had never seen death in a human before but had had experience of animal deaths & were expert in dealing with the bodies. So they skinned the grandfather. The people in these parts are still called 'Skin Daddies,' but you don't mention it to them. ...

1 25–9 May 1934.
2 Portugal Cove South.
3 On the coast of Dorset, England.
4 Andrew Hamilton Murray (1876–1965) and Janet Morrison (Miller) Murray (1891–1946). Andrew Murray was a St John's businessman. The property described here is now owned by the artists Christopher Pratt (1935–) and Mary Pratt (1935–).
5 Cloudberry (*Rubus chamaemorus*).
6 James Michael McGrath and Anita (Kearney) McGrath. James McGrath (1902–1975) practised at St Mary's, 1928–38. He was Minister of Health in the government of Newfoundland, 1956–67, and Minister of Finance, 1967–8.
7 George William Battcock (1892–1984). Ordained 31 December 1919.
8 Anne Didham, wife of John Didham and sister of John Phippard.

J.H.S. to Greta, Newfoundland Hotel, 31 May 1934

... It is a heavenly morning. The sun got up about 5 this morning, and the sky was emerald shading into opal – and the fleecy pink clouds floating in it – so lovely. My window looks out over the harbour to the Narrows, and there are schooners coming and going and the motorboats coming home from the night's fishing. When you look out on to this, you are apt to forget all the desperate poverty and misery both of St. John's and of the outports. There is one dreadful skeleton in our cupboard here that occasionally protrudes a bony indicative finger. We have a Longshoremen's Protective Union, which has become immensely powerful because the employers never hang together. Occasionally, they decide to fight. Then some individual firm sees an advantage in blacklegging,[1] and the whole resistance collapses. The employers are now making valiant efforts to induce the Commission to pull its chestnuts out of the fire. This matter should be dealt with by one of our N.F.L. colleagues, but this morning I have spent nearly two hours concocting a diplomatic letter to the Employers Association, which will go before the Commission for approval & then be signed by J.C. Puddester as his contribution! Any minute we may have a strike, and in N.F.L. strike has always meant riots. That is because the head of the police[2] is a lawyer and a coward. The police are not disciplined in any way. When we asked him whether he had any plans cut-&-dried in case of a strike, he said it would take a fortnight to drill them to be ready! Is that not a confession of incompetence? He was a political appointment, and there are lots of people who will think that we shall do him injustice when we retire him compulsorily next October, as we shall do because he then reaches 65. This government would be infinitely more efficient were there no N.F.L. members of the Commission, and I think we three U.K. Commissioners could quite well run the whole show. Our N.F.L. colleagues have the habit of trimming. ...

All kinds of things have happened since last I wrote. On Wednesday last week, I addressed the senior children of the United Church College[3] about Empire Day.[4] Thursday was Empire Day, & we spent it out at the Big Pond near Bay Bulls – 12 miles south of this – in pouring rain – I fishing, Mum sitting in the car. I caught four trout. ...

Friday, we dined with the Alderdices, and Saturday, with O'Halloran[5] & the two Woodses. O'Halloran is a British Post Office official, & the Woodses British custom house officials. They are all here to put things right. They found them in an awful mess. For example, the money order accounts have not been audited since 1875! On Monday, we gave a farewell 'stag' dinner for Davies,[6] who has gone home to be Trade Commissioner. He left on the *Newfoundland* next day. On Tuesday, we gave a dinner to six friends out at Holyrood – 30 miles away – and on the way back had a puncture! At midnight. Fortunately, a car behind us came up & contained two engineers of one of the garages. So that was all right & we were put right in ten minutes. Was that not luck?

Yesterday, I spoke to the combined Orange lodges – and now I must rush to breakfast. – Breakfast is over, and I am off to the office. Such a jolly little schooner is sailing into the harbour – just under my window. This is a dreadful town of squalor, but nothing can spoil the beauty of the harbour on a fine day. ...

1 Breaking ranks.
2 Charles H. Hutchings (1869–1946).
3 Prince of Wales College.
4 24 May.
5 H. O'Halloran arrived in St John's on 19 April 1934. Appointed Secretary for Posts and Telegraphs as from the same date.
6 Daniel James Davies (1880–1946), civil servant and scientist. Born in Wales.

Q.H.S. to Ian and Sheila, St John's, 3 June 1934

Look at the date – and it has just been snowing! What an extraordinary climate! I hear that there has never been a month of the year when snow has not been recorded. And yet we have such lovely weather – far more sunshine and clearer weather than we ever have in England over a period of four months. Of course, we are south of the latitude of Paris, I believe, and the sun is very warm. Things are growing so fast. The daffodils which were a show in the gardens are over now and the hyacinths are marvellous. We were one month behind England a week ago – in another month we shall have caught you up. Imagine us in iris time – a month from now (I think) – blue irises growing like buttercups here, I am told. The green of the grass is the thing that startles us. I suppose it is like Ireland. The land holds the moisture of the melted snow that has sunk deep down, & then the hot sun draws on all vegetation most astonishingly fast. ...

This is June 6. Wednesday. I must tell you something that will be of interest to you as a teacher, Ian. How do you think French is taught in nearly all schools here? – Every word is spelt. The teacher asks: 'What is "I am" in French? – "J.e.s.u.i.s."' There is no attempt at pronunciation. It is a new language! They spell so fast that a teacher unaccustomed to this method imagines a new language is being spoken. And any attempt to alter this meets with stubborn opposition. Dr. & Mrs. Hunter[1] told us about this. Pupils coming from schools to the Memorial College have to start over again, and the attitude is often 'that's just silly.' It is a sad fact but true that 17% of the population are illiterate, & the standard of education even among those who have had a chance is very low. The system of having 3 schools where one would be sufficient is wasteful of the money available, but the different denominations will have their own schools – R.C., Anglican, United.

Adult schools have been started on a small scale during the last two years and they are a great success. But they work under tremendous difficulties. At present, the teachers are all women, but the men crowd to the schools & the teachers also go into the houses. Women are so busy in their houses with their large families & often so poor they can't go out in the winter, [so] that the teachers spend much of their time in the homes. The women welcome them eagerly. But it is hard work for the teachers. Getting about is so difficult in the snow & the intense cold & with prehistoric means of locomotion. Even the trains on the branch lines take 20 hours to do a short journey, & there is no heating & no food to be had on them. We had the luxury of the special train & restaurant car when we went across country in the winter. And the accommodation the teachers have to put up with is dreadful in these outports as a rule – no sanitation & the coarsest food. One of the finest of the staff of six was burnt to death when the house she was staying in caught fire last winter.[2] Life is not easy for those who try to carry help to these isolated, neglected outports.

Do you know why the interior of this island has not been developed? Why the settlements are so backward? Why the fishermen are so much in the hands of the merchants? Because for hundreds of years the settlers were not allowed to develop the interior – were not allowed to do any agriculture to improve their conditions; at one time there was an attempt to prevent women from landing & a law was passed to deport any women there were here. It is really one of the worst examples of the abuse of wealth & power. The merchant princes wanted to keep the island simply as a base for their own trade. Settlers improving their conditions might develop into rivals. No wonder there is bitterness between the outport people & the merchants of St. John's; these latter are the descendants of the people who used the settlers so wickedly and they have inherited systems of trading which still depress & harass these fisher folk. The story of Newfoundland is not one of which we as English people can be proud. We owe her a debt long overdue. The Newfoundlanders made a great name for themselves for their courage & hardihood – but their courage was born of despair I reckon and their hardihood of conditions that made life a case of the survival of only the physically fittest.

We are seeing a lot of the Avalon Peninsula now. I told you of our expedition on this tongue of the land. On Friday, we went up to Trinity Bay to Dildo to see the salmon freezing on the *Sunset Glow*, the government's railway ship that is equipped for this purpose. Lord Sempill[3] is here and he came with us. He is a nice fellow – very modest & very able. He made all the arrangements for the Everest flight[4] & he is going into the question of aviation for this island. He came with us last night to Government House too & he looked so jolly in his 100-year-old kilt. ...

The salmon freezing was interesting – fish about 30–35 lbs. – heads cut off – a hole slit for cleaning – cleaned – then 5 in a line pushed into a wa-

terproof bag – the necks inserted onto a cylinder filled with freezing mixture & the whole plunged into the freezer. After 1½ hours the bags are
taken out & the salmon thawed off the cylinders, and then they are solid as
rocks ready for transport. ...

1 Alfred and Harriet Hunter. An
   Englishman, Alfred Hunter (1892–
   1971) was vice-president of Memorial
   University College, 1933–49. When
   Memorial was made a degree-
   granting institution in 1949, he
   became Dean of Arts and Science.

2 The teacher was Ida Parsons. She
   died at Harbour Grace.

3 William Francis Forbes-Sempill,
   nineteenth Baron Sempill (1893–1965).

4 The first flight over Mount Everest
   took place in 1933.

Q.H.S. to Betty, on Butlers Pond, near Portugal Cove, 5 June 1934

Here we are out for a holiday. We started after breakfast. We are only
about 7 miles from St. John's but we might be 100 miles away. This is a
lovely spot – just a big pond, as blue as the sky & the sky blue above it and
balsam firs all round it. Daddy is out in a boat fishing. I sat in the boat all
morning – on a little narrow seat on the bow. Daddy caught two trout.
This afternoon, I thought I should enjoy a seat in the shade, so I have
spread [a] rug on the floor of my green pasture and shall write some
letters. ... Tonight there is an official reception at Government House – 500
people asked – so I don't want to be too burnt. Today is a holiday for the
King's birthday – that is why we are here. ...

  My dear! Can you smell the pines? ... And the atmosphere is so clear –
every detail is so clearly defined – sharpened as tho' through a magnifying
glass that magnifies colour as well as detail. I think you will enjoy painting
here. ...

J.H.S. to Edgar and Eleanor, Department of Natural Resources, 5 June 1934

... The Austin is an outstanding success – very sweet to drive and very
comfortable. Everyone admires her. In this island it is commonly said that
English cars cannot climb a hill! That fiction is maintained by the garages,
which have close connections with the American manufacturers & do not
wish to change. ...

Q.H.S. to Greta, Newfoundland Hotel, 6 June 1934
I have just had a lovely gift – a large bunch of lily of the valley, fresh from the garden, barely in flower. They are like the wild lilies that grew in our woods at Sedgley[1] when I was a girl. They came to me from Mrs. Andrew Murray, the lovely blue-eyed, white-haired woman who loves her garden down on the river at Salmonier. ...

I listened in to Australia on Empire Day. It was excellent – came through so loud & clear. I listened at 11.15 here to the news, & the Australia programme followed. ... I keep your little silver clock at English time beside the wireless! ...

1 'Sedgley New Hall,' the Barclay
   family home in Manchester.

**Q.H.S. to Greta, Murrays Pond, about 8 miles from St John's,
13 June 1934**
... We have just had one sitting-room redecorated. ... We seem to be settled in the hotel, so we may as well make our rooms as attractive as we can. It suits us to stay on here; we are not tied – if we want to come home we just lock up everything & pay 4/. a day for any room we keep on & we know just what our expenses are all the time. ... We have been having interesting &, for Daddy, very busy days. Last night,[1] we had a dinner of 18, a farewell to Lord Sempill. He is a nice fellow. ... I expect you know he is a great airman. I think he is visualizing this as the Clapham Junction[2] of the American continent air service of the future. ... Last night, we all went on to hear a lecture he was giving at the Memorial[3] school hall. It was packed to hear him. He gave us a wonderful account of the history of air development & the present condition, showing pictures & statistics by lantern slides. It was thrillingly interesting. I had no idea how far it has got and what tremendous services are being rendered. ...

1 14 June 1934. This letter was written   2 A major railway junction in
   13–15 June 1934.   London, England.
                                              3 Memorial University College.

J.H.S. to Greta, Newfoundland Hotel, 14 June 1934
... Lord Sempill ... leaves tomorrow. ... He is to be our Honorary Aeronautical Adviser. You know that we are starting an air service, and I guess

that it will rapidly prove quite indispensable to the administration. I expect that once it is started we shall have every department calling on it for inspection purposes. I sincerely hope so.

Puddester, Lord Sempill and I made a rapid tour of the Bonavista Peninsula last weekend. On Thursday night, we travelled to Bonavista and spent Saturday there and in the neighbourhood. They are a Bolshie crowd down there with an *âme damnée*[1] in the person of the self-appointed president[2] of a fishermen's union. He has developed a sincere dislike to myself. He gave out that he was my *fidus Achates*[3] at least. Indeed, I believe he thought that I was his personal assistant. It was also given out that the government had provided him with a schooner. Of course, that was quite untrue. He tried to create trouble for me without success. In the afternoon, we drove out to Amherst Cove and saw some very fine fishermen go out in small boats in a heavy sea to get the salmon out of their nets. One boat got 400 lbs., one 300. We bought a 10 lb. fish for 50 cents = 2/. It is very remarkable that in one village you find active, hard-working, self-reliant fishermen, and in the next a degenerate, lazy crowd. That was the case there. At Newmans Cove, a couple of miles away, they were doing nothing. Not a man had gone out salmon fishing. It is true that it was rough, but no rougher than at Amherst Cove. During the night, we went on to Catalina, where we found the same phenomenon. People there are hard-working and content, though of course poor. Everyone is that. At Little Catalina, three miles away, they are feckless, lazy and all on the dole. Until we get them off the dole & can put a stop to it, things are not going to be right. But that is dependent on an extension of other work besides fishing.

Sunday we spent at and around Trinity. The bay is most beautiful, and the villages neat & self-respecting with the exception of a deteriorated population at Dunfield. Puddester and I went to service at the C. of E. It was an appointed day of prayer for the fishery which has just commenced. Sempill is a Catholic & went there, so we were appropriately represented in each place. The C. of E. church records go back to 1757, and I signed my name in a book in which the first signature was in 1825. They look upon themselves as quite an aristocratic community. ...

It is a misty, dull morning and the fog alarm is going all the time at the point. How the ships find St. John's in this kind of weather, I cannot imagine. Last Friday morning, the whole country was white with snow. That is unusual in mid-June, even for N.F.L. ...

1 A zealot.

2 Joseph Roberts Smallwood (1900–1991), Premier of the Province of Newfoundland, 1949–72.

3 Devoted follower.

Q.H.S. to Ian and Sheila, Colonial Building, 15 June 1934
I am writing here for a few minutes. We are having a rather hectic time
with many visitors and parties. There are three specialists here just now
advising the government – Lord Sempill, on air – Mr. Baird,[1] agricultural
aspects – & Dr. MacDonald,[2] adult education (& cooperation). [And] ...
we have Miss Digby,[3] a cooperative expert from England – sent by
Dr. Grenfell. Lord Sempill is a great scoop for N.F.L. He is going to be
president of the London Chamber of Commerce next year & he will bring
N.F.L. onto the map then. It is up to N.F.L.ers to bring their products up
to the best standards. They have been losing markets because their goods
were badly prepared for the markets & so badly marketed. The fishermen
do their own canning in the simplest, most unhygienic ways & there has
been no attempt to cooperate. 'There or thereabouts' is good enough they
think. An excellent tin of salmon – finer than anything produced elsewhere – will be followed by a tin labelled salmon & found to contain cods'
heads! So now the Commission, or Daddy in this case, are making great
efforts to standardize goods & find markets for all. Lord Sempill is going
to be a great help, both in the marketing & in advising & helping about the
air service. He is tremendously keen & has been coming everywhere with
us and with anyone who can show him conditions. Last weekend, he went
with Daddy ... round a lot of settlements. ... He told me he was enormously impressed with Daddy's patience with & understanding of the
people, & with his wide outlook & scientific attitude to the development
problems. He was horrified at the conditions; could not have believed if he
had not actually seen for himself. The thing that impressed him most was
the high percentage of 'poor fools.'[4] There is so much inbreeding & such
terribly large families that mothers have no chance to produce healthy
children. Lord Sempill is a Catholic himself, so I dared not enlarge on this
subject. ...

I took the Nonia industrial superintendent[5] & one of the nurses for the
afternoon last Sunday, & Nurse Phillips[6] told me something of her work.
She has been out only 8 months & she came from a slum district in London. She loves her work, tho' it is terribly hard. She is such a fragile-
looking little creature. She says the people are wonderful – so poor & so
clean & brave in one of her centres – so nice & so good & so dirty &
shiftless in another. They have no toys & never see a doctor. She gave all
the children (56) between 6 and 12 a tiny present for Xmas, & the excitement of the village was tremendous & most touching. She hopes to give
them an Xmas tree this year.

Her story of going to sea 5 hours 'vomiting all the way' to a poor soul
who had been in labour for 5 days: a man came to fetch her – not her

district – but there was neither nurse nor doctor anywhere nearer. She tried to get a doctor, but the weather prevented anyone attempting it. Wired to St. John's to send a cutter with doctor 400 miles – but no cutter could venture. She had to operate herself after 2 more days. ... The mother was dying, & she could not let her die 'like that.' It was a terrible case, & how she had strength to take her dead child away with her hands I do not know. The mother lived. The child had been dead 4 days. ...

1 Whylie Wellington Baird (1886–1960).

2 Professor Angus Bernard MacDonald (1893–1952), educator and cooperative leader. Joined the extension department of St Francis Xavier University, Antigonish, Nova Scotia, in 1930 and became a key figure in the Antigonish Movement, which promoted cooperative activity.

3 Margaret Digby (b. 1902). Her visit led to the publication by the Horace Plunkett Foundation, London, England, of her *Report on the Opportunities for Co-operative Organisation in Newfoundland and Labrador* (London 1934).

4 Simpletons.

5 Margaret Beckett, an Englishwoman.

6 Mary Phillips (b. 31 August 1906) was the nurse at Burgeo.

J.H.S. to Edgar and Eleanor, Newfoundland Hotel, 17 June 1934

... An ecclesiastical orgy is in progress here at the moment. The Anglican synod and the conference of the United Church of Canada are both in session. In addition, we have the advantage of Dr. MacDonald of the St Francis Xavier College (R.C.) of Antigonish. He has come down to talk cooperation, and addressed an audience of Anglican clergy, United Church ministers and R.C. priests on Thursday. A unique audience. I was there to propose the vote of thanks. ... On Friday, there was a large reception on the Canadian S.S. *New Northland*. It was a horrible night. We drove down to the wharf in our car and, as I was walking up the gangway, I discovered I had on my ordinary leather slippers, so had to return to change. Pelting rain – puddles underfoot everywhere. They had a radio concert, having brought artistes from Canada, with whom they brigaded certain local talent. It was all poor-quality stuff, and the speeches were poor quality also. Mother & I escaped home at 10 o'clock. ...

I am having rather an anxious time. We have fitted out a large number of men for the fisheries and are getting about 170 of them off to the Labrador. There has been a tremendous rush, & the steamers have been overcrowded. We chartered a special steamer for our men, & it was rushed by the crowd & filled up by others who wanted to go, with the result that our men were left behind! We got almost all of them off by another boat. There is not much difficulty about the men, though they will take their families & hens & goats with them. The real problem is their motorboats. Hundreds of them had to be transported. The great rush is over, but we shall have to have a relief steamer to send down the disgruntled balance. ...

The last week has been horrible weather – cold, rain, sleet, fog. It is not fog like that in England, but more like Welsh fog, – a cloud settling down on the land. ...

Q.H.S. to Greta, Newfoundland Hotel, 21 June 1934

We have got the Lodges safe back again, & Mrs. Lodge tells me of her lunch with you. ... Mr. Ashley Cooper,[1] the governor of the Hudson's Bay Co., has been here, & there was a lot of entertaining in connection with his visit. ... Mrs. Lodge tells me it was absurd the way the man was treated on board ship – just as the captain's right hand; there were other ladies (including herself!) there at the table, & the ladies ignored at table. She says A.C. was always half an hour late for meals, & they all had to sit & watch him eat, the captain never daring to leave till he finished & terrified of being later than he coming to dinner meals. A regular little Lord God Almighty. ... Mrs. Lodge *is* inquisitive. I am often confused by her questions to people. But she says, 'I'm so interested in people I want to know all about them & I forget that they may not want to tell; I expect them to be as eager to tell as I to hear.' She is a dear. She makes her husband say, 'Isobel! You really are the limit.' But he enjoys her enormously. I am afraid Mr. A.C. was not treated quite with such royal honours as he expected here. ... I heard another rather nice story also peculiar to this peculiar island. Bowring Brothers & Job Brothers are the two chief fish merchants here. A Christian brother (a sort of Plymouth Brother) was going round one of the outports and a fisherman asked him, 'What are you?' – 'A Christian brother' – 'A Christian brother! I've heard tell of Bowring Brothers & I've heard tell of Job Brothers but I never heard tell of Christian Brothers. What price is fish in St. John's?' (the fishermen have to keep a sharp watch on the outport merchants & they compare the price they give for fish with the price given in St. John's, which also is kept dark & not published except as it suits the St. John's merchants).

I wish you had been with us last night – all the girls were having a gay time. We went to dinner on the *Dragon*, which was here for a few days. It was a jolly show. The captain is a nice fellow. He is a good artist too and a great fisherman.

We are just off to Placentia on the west coast of the peninsula for the weekend, as Monday[2] is a holiday ...

1 Sir Patrick Ashley Cooper (1887–   2 25 June 1934.
   1961), Governor, Hudson's Bay Co.,
   1931–52.

Q.H.S. to Ian and Sheila, Newfoundland Hotel, 29 June 1934

... Last weekend we were down at Placentia and John tried the river at the head of the loch but it was no good. The salmon were leaping at the sea end of the loch – just fresh in from the sea, but nobody was catching anything.

We had a lovely time however. We stayed at Fulfords,[1] about 5 miles up the loch – the Southeast Arm: a lovely spot, rather like Loch Katrine,[2] but I think more beautiful. This country is more colourful than Scotland; the atmosphere is so intensely clear that all the outlines & colours spring sharp cut & intensely vivid to the eye, so that the beauty catches you by the throat. And it is so intensely green & the sea & sky so deeply blue. And in addition there is here that quality of light you find in Greece – an indescribable radiance of dawn & sunset. You will think I exaggerate; I only tell you my experience. Every day I am here I seem to feel the beauty of this country more intensely. There is an old story that the only people who have to be chained to heaven are the Newfoundlanders; they always want to get back to their island.

Placentia itself is the old French capital. It is built on the barachois, a kind of Chesil Beach that almost land-locks the two arms of the loch. Standing on this beach looking inland, you feel as tho' you were in Scotland looking up the Gare Loch[3] & Holy Loch,[4] with a great wooded rock dividing the two & lovely islands dotting the lochs. Seaward, you look across the blue to a rocky, jagged coast, all opalescent between the blue of sea & sky; that way you are in Greece.

The inhabitants of Placentia are not French, but they are all Roman Catholics. William IV[5] was stationed there for 6 months when he was Prince of Wales, and he built the little Anglican church on the site of an old Catholic church. There was a court-house beside it, & he acted as magistrate. We got the key of the enclosure & church & found much of interest – old tombstones, some inscribed in Basque. But the altar was covered with dead flies, and the surplice was green with mould. An old tombstone served as a table in the vestry.

One of the women who showed us round very volubly was a Bradshaw, one of the old Protestant family who married the Catholic magistrate & is a Catholic herself now. The story of the Bradshaws is interesting. William IV was stationed at Placentia for 7 months when he was Prince of Wales and only 17 years old. The doctor of the ship was a Bradshaw who also was new to N.F.L. They had a quarrel[6] one night, and ... Prince William had him put off the ship – marooned at, Placentia; & there he married & lived & died and his descendants after him. But they are all gone from there now except a few women who have married Catholics. Another Bradshaw, wife of Dr. Mitchell[7] of St. John's, was staying at Fulfords too & she told me some queer stories. The Placentia people are very proud of their royal blood! She says there used to be a tombstone in this little old churchyard inscribed 'Sarah – illegitimate daughter of William IV.' Someone has caused it to disappear now. King William sent a silver communion service to the little Protestant church which he built while he was there. That is now preserved in the Protestant cathedral[8] at St. John's. The Bradshaws claim they ought to have it, but it is inscribed to the church. The Prince also acted as magistrate in the little old court-house that used to stand beside the church.

It is a queer thing having the village built on the barachois. There is some surface soil now about the houses, & the people make little gardens but it is all imported soil. Mrs. Mitchell told me that an old uncle of hers, who was evidently a pretty heavy toper, left instructions in his will that he should be buried with his ancestors in this churchyard & that his coffin should be waterproof lined. And so it was. You get to water when you dig the graves, and I suppose he did not want raw water mixed with his elements.

When we got back to Fulfords, ... I said to Mrs. Mitchell, 'We have been visiting the tombs of your ancestors.' Dr. Mitchell said: 'We're not going near there! We don't want to visit the tombs of her illegitimate ancestors!'

July 2. At Salmonier, staying with the Andrew Murrays for the holiday weekend. Yesterday, July l, is the anniversary of Beaumont Hamel, when the N.F.L. regiment was almost wiped out.[9] ... Mrs. Murray's 1st husband, one of the Ayres,[10] was killed there, and 3 other of the Ayres[11] were killed the same day. So it is a day of remembrance in St. John's, the great day of the year & always a holiday. So the holiday is today instead. We go back to St. John's tonight.

This is a lovely spot & a lovely house. ... It has ... a long room with wide plate glass windows on 2 sides; in fact, 2 sides are all window and it is like being on the river outside without the bother of the flies. The bungalow is facing a wide pool in the river, & the river flows below on the south side – so close that we can actually see the salmon moving up – make out their forms even when they do not break water. And I can hardly do anything at times for watching them leaping in the pool. But will they bite! I watched Daddy fishing early this morning, & the fish were leaping beside his boat, but he did not have even a nibble. He & Mr. Murray are out now casting from the bank – no, from an island in mid-stream. There are islands of yellow water lilies too. And there are muskrats playing in the reeds just below the window. We saw a beaver dam yesterday. At Placentia, on the famous salmon river,[12] there are 57 beaver dams this year! It is so lovely here! There's a scarlet & green Canadian Indian canoe swinging on its rope beside the reeds – a cape of reeds runs out into the pool beyond; across the blue water, dotted with islands of yellow lilies, there are green meadows and [a] mass of golden timber shining in the sunshine in one bay, and the hillside beyond reminds me of that picture my father was so fond of – of a hillside in Wales – all the trees so massed – young birch & larch & the deeper greens of spruce & fir tree.

I thought Daddy had got a big fish there! Such a commotion in the water, but I got the field glasses on to it & he is still casting & the fish sitting up and wagging their tails at him.

This room is charming with its great open fireplace (grey) & a stone chimneyhood. A long ship's table at one end and eight easy chairs and two sofas, all placed for watching the river. ... We have a tiny room with just room to pass between the beds close up to the window looking down into the river. The Murrays' room is almost as small & looks onto the pool, where the sound of the salmon leaping at night keeps Mrs. Murray awake! ... Yesterday, we went away up the coast seeing the Markland settlement of the unemployed (who were) and we did not get back till 9 o'c. ... 'Markland' is getting on wonderfully. The 10 men have built 5 of the 10 houses & got the families in, and they have cleared about 6 acres as well and have planted potatoes and cabbages & turnips for their next winter's food and they are so happy & improving in every way physically & morally. They were not picked men – some of them were not good characters. But they have risen to their chance.

The success of the venture has encouraged the trustees[13] to go on. 50 more of the unemployed of St. John's are to be settled at Markland. Mr. Cochius,[14] a Dutchman who has been out here for many years & has taken a tremendous interest in the scheme & has helped in laying out, etc., is to be manager for the trustees. His wife[15] is a splendid little woman, I believe; she will be an inspiration & a help to the women, & Miss Cochius,[16] who has just done splendidly at college[17] & wanted to be a missionary, is going to take charge of the school and adult education. Everyone is so eager & so happy about it.

We went away round the coast about 50 miles & saw a beach white with whalebones & a whale rolling up a bay. We saw magnificent great cliffs – rose-red & green & grey (some of the oldest rock in the world we were told) and marvellous jagged cliffs across the seas.

I must get out & join Mrs. Murray in the garden. She has just finished preparing our dinner. The day gets lovelier & lovelier. The flies are the only drawback to sitting out of doors. There is a beastly little beach fly that gives me stings that last for weeks & form wounds if I do not guard my hands from scratching.

I must tell you one more little detail. We were talking about the fines for breaking the law. Before the Commission came, a man who was fined for fast driving (for instance) just said: 'Put it to my account' – just like any other bill. ...

1 Edward J. and Mary (Kelly) Fulford.
2 Perthshire and Stirlingshire, Scotland.
3 Right arm of the Firth of Clyde, Dumbartonshire, Scotland.
4 West arm of Firth of Clyde, Argyllshire, Scotland.
5 1765–1837.
6 Legend has it that Bradshaw accused the prince of cheating at cards.
7 Timothy Mitchell and Jen (Bradshaw) Mitchell.
8 Anglican Cathedral of St John the Baptist.
9 On 1 July 1916, the first day of the Battle of the Somme. 1 July 1934 fell on a Sunday; hence the holiday on 2 July.
10 Eric Stanley Ayre (20 October 1888–1 July 1916). The Ayres were a prominent St John's business family.
11 Eric's brother, Bernard Pitts Ayre (28 November 1892–1 July 1916), and their cousins, Gerald (29 October 1891–1 July 1916) and Wilfred (15 July 1895–1 July 1916).
12 Southeast River.
13 The Markland settlement was run by trustees under the chairmanship of Fred Emerson.
15 Rudolf Hugo Karel Cochius (1880–1944), landscape architect and designer of Bowring Park, St John's.
15 Marie (Aarsen) Cochius (1888–1960).
16 Clare Cochius (b. 1915). Later married Allan Gillingham.
17 Memorial University College.

Q.H.S. to Edgar and Eleanor, Newfoundland Hotel, 3 July 1934
... We have had an interesting time since I wrote last. The most important event here is the arrival of the caplin – a fish like a smelt but sweeter – excellent eating. It comes in millions to the beaches for spawning. The people ladle them out in buckets & shovel them onto carts. We saw them at work yesterday at Topsail. It is such a sight. The fish are carted straight away to the fields and spread just as they are. Such a waste. They would be infinitely more valuable made into fishmeal. We stayed for two days at Fulfords, an inn about 5 miles up the Southeast Arm of the Placentia inlet, & we had tough beef and chicken rag[1] but never a fish, with fresh smelt & cod & salmon & lobster all around. We actually brought in some smelt to be cooked but found them flung out to the children for bait. These people won't eat smelt & think lobster too common for the guests. Fish is cod here – nothing else is considered worth eating except salmon & that comes after cod. 'Fish and salmon' is the way it is mentioned. ...

1 Possibly ragout.

J.H.S. to Ian and Sheila, Department of Natural Resources, 3 July 1934
... We have arranged for Betty to come out by the *Nova Scotia* on 3rd August, and Mum will go back with her in September to close up Dolguog.[1] That is an economy measure. At present, we are paying income tax on our income in England and on that here and, I presume, super-tax! The income tax on the income here is a matter of contract and cannot be escaped. That makes it quite reasonable to escape it in England if we can. After all, we pay £450 on the income here, while we are receiving nothing at home. ...

   Yesterday was a holiday, so on Saturday evening we drove out 50 miles to Salmonier, to stay with the Murrays. ... I saw literally thousands of salmon coming up the river on the tide and disporting themselves in the enormous pool opposite the house. I spent most of the two days fishing and enjoyed it very much, though without success. On Sunday afternoon, the Murrays drove us along the coast of Trinity Bay – such a drive – most lovely coast scenery. The rocks in some places are blood-red precipices into the sea below. And the sea was as blue as the Greek Mediterranean.

1 Their house near Machynlleth,
   Montgomeryshire, Wales.

Q.H.S. to Greta, Newfoundland Hotel, 3 July 1934
... We are off ... to Bonne Bay & further. ...

We are going to have quite an interesting trip, I think, but I hope we shall have good weather for the part of our journey that we have to do in a motorboat on the west coast.

J.H.S. to Ian and Sheila, Newfoundland Hotel, 13 July 1934
... We have had a very wonderful week. ... It began on Thursday the 5th, when we left by the evening train for the west coast. We had our own saloon – the 'office car' – with two sleeping cabins, a dining-room and an observation compartment at the back. We were tacked on to the end of the express. It was a perfectly heavenly evening, but the first part of the journey was spoiled for us by Professor Fraser Bond,[1] who travelled in our car to pour into my unwilling ear his grievances about Markland, our new agricultural settlement adjoining his property. He has a constant fire nightmare – day & night. He wants us to close it up – which is impossible. It is in fact a great success. He left us in an hour, & then I got a telegram saying that a detachment of police were following us in cars & that we would wait for them at Holyrood. A gang of discontented lumbermen, 40 strong, were threatening to rush the train to get unpaid passages home. Meanwhile, we meandered along the shore of Conception Bay in the lovely evening sunlight – the sea blue as blue and the mountains in the west purple in their shadows. Mum thinks this is the most beautiful country she has ever seen, and I agree. It is most lovely. The police caught up in 25 minutes, & we got going again. We got to Badger, where the men were, at 7.30 in the morning, and I held a little enquiry. They were quite decent fellows, but should never have been sent to the woods. Lumber work is really skilled labour, and these men could not earn anything at it. I gave them passes home, but wired the magistrate that they were not to get the dole. The delay at Badger threw us an hour and a half late.

We got to Humbermouth at 2, instead of 12.30. There we were met by Mr. George Simpson[2] of Lomond, to whom Uncle Frank's David[3] is going. He had brought in a motor launch for us, and we started down the Bay of Islands – 25 miles to the open sea – in a fresh westerly wind. It was very beautiful – wooded hills each side and islands dotted about – some big, some small, and all except one uninhabited. When we got outside, it was dead calm & we ran north for 25 miles along a bleak & precipitous but very beautiful coast ... to Bonne Bay. That is a beautiful spot – a narrow entrance to a very great big bay with arms running inland in three directions, like Scotch lochs, with thickly wooded hills running up to 2,000 feet. We called at Norris Point at the mouth of one of these arms (if an arm can be said to have a mouth) to see a new motor launch just built for Mr. Simpson – a beauty – and then 12 or 15 miles up the Lomond Arm to Lomond, where the Simpsons live. They are a nice family – Mr. & Mrs., Mrs. Fleming (elder daughter) & Miss Simpson.[4] A man named Boyd[5] – his right-hand man – lives with them. On Saturday, in the morning, it rained, so I did my visits to Woody Point (the H.Q. of the bay) and Norris Point in the afternoon – of course by water, as there are no land communications. One of the troubles of that remote part is that life is monotonous, and drink easily smuggled from St. Pierre and so cheap – and both magistrate and doctor are addicted.

On Sunday, there was no service as the padre was away, so we spent the day on the river. I caught three grilse and a sea trout and lost a salmon, which I had brought as far as the net. It is a lovely river, but the salmon are not yet in, though the officers of the *Dragon*[6] caught 14 of them the previous week. That was evidently an advance guard. The water is very low this year.

Monday morning, I inspected logging camps and operations, and in the evening tried the river again and got three more grilse. At one time, I had a grilse & a trout on at the same time, but the grilse threw the trout off the hook when it leapt into the air.

The next day, we left & drove an appalling road to Deer Lake, about 30 miles. They provided a motorboat for the worst part – at the Big Pond[7] – and we did 8 miles by water and met the car again at the other end. Then they had arranged for a horse & wagon to follow us, lest we should get bogged. We did. The car went through the road up to the axles & was towed out. At one place, we passed a logging camp with several very dirty children and one quite well-turned-out girl. She turned out to be 20 and already the mother of three children. Then her mother came out. She has 14 children, all alive! The women were very well turned out, but the children were dreadful. I do not believe their hair had been brushed for months.

At Deer Lake, we were tacked onto a goods train, which left at 8 and came along almost as fast as the express, so that we were in St. John's by 5 on Wednesday evening. ...

1 (Frank) Fraser Bond (1891–1965). Taught at the School of Journalism, Columbia University, New York. Nephew of Sir Robert Bond (1857– 1927), whose estate, 'The Grange,' at Whitbourne, he had inherited.

2 Born 1875 in Scotland. Arrived in Newfoundland in 1916. Manager of

the St Lawrence Timber, Pulp and Steamship Company, Ltd.

3 Frank Hope Simpson was Sir John's youngest brother. Frank's son, David, came out to Newfoundland to work with George Simpson at Lomond.

4 The Simpson daughters were Margaret H. (b. 1901) and Ella Cooper (b. 1903). Their mother was Jean Aitken Simpson (b. 1876). All three were born in Scotland and arrived in Newfoundland in 1918.

5 Duncan K. Boyd. Born in Scotland in 1888. Arrived in Newfoundland in 1916. Married Ella Simpson.

6 Cruiser of the Royal Navy.

7 Bonne Bay Big Pond.

J.H.S. to Greta, Newfoundland Hotel, 15 July 1934

... Since we got back last Wednesday, I have been working off arrears. Two evenings I did a little fishing. ... Thursday, ... when I got to Butlers Pond, I found a crowd there and a doctor the other side of the lake working away with a little girl who had just been drowned. That put a stop to the fishing. She was one of 11 children & there was nothing in the house – not even a shift in which to clothe the poor little body for the coffin. The poverty of the people and the size of their families are both appalling problems. ... Murrays Pond is the fishing club. There are two lakes, Murrays Pond and Butlers Pond, and the clubhouse – quite a jolly little place – is on the bank of the former. You can get simple meals: ham & eggs, fruit salad and Devonshire cream. It is 8 miles from here, and we go out pretty often for our evening meal. Last night, I ran out after dinner and fished about an hour & caught a large trout, 1 lb. 2 oz. ... I think we are really making progress here, though there are very great difficulties. The revenue has increased materially and the railway receipts are up 20% on last year. These are good signs. And now we are having a good codfishery. So tails are up. We advanced about £50,000 to help the fishermen in their outfit, and I do not think that we are going to lose it. In one district, we have got back the whole of it already, and there are still over two months' fishing for the men to earn enough to keep them through the winter. Last year, they were on the dole, and would have been all this summer, & then indefinitely, had we not helped them to go fishing. So it looks as if our advances would take about a thousand families off the dole permanently.

Then we have started ... Markland, which already has a population of about 358. They are doing excellently, though of course we are only at the beginning of things. But the change in morale is the encouraging feature. The people were on the dole – had been for years – and the change is incredible from hopelessness to courage & anticipation. They are working so keenly now.

Yet we have a long row to hoe before we can begin to think that things are going right. Never mind. A good beginning is a great thing. ...

Q.H.S. to Greta, [Newfoundland Hotel], [20 July 1934]

... The weather is delicious; I wish you had it like this – glorious days ... but always a cool breeze so that you don't swelter, and the evenings most refreshing and such marvellous sunsets.

We have an arrangement for flies here that would be fine for moths: a wooden frame in two pieces that pull out to fit the width on any window & fitted with wire gauze. It is just what you want. It would lie in the bottom of your bag, and you could use it anywhere. I think I must send you one by the next ship. ... We are both keeping very well. Forest fires have been awful – a great anxiety. And the men on the dole who accepted jobs in the logging camps are jumping trains & steamers and returning to their houses in hundreds – the work too skilled for them to be able to earn enough and the flies unbearable in the woods. But Markland men are doing magnificently, and they and their families stick the flies. There is a men's side as well as a master's and that will have to be examined. But it is discouraging to hear of a man taking advantage of the trip to Labrador and not even bothering to land & look at the work! ...

J.H.S. to Greta, Department of Natural Resources, 26 July 1934

... We are going off on Sunday for a week's leave!!! The only leave I shall get this year. We go to Gleneagles – a small inn not far from Glenwood on the Gander River. I am looking forward to it intensely. ...

I told the post office people that Graves[1] was willing to advise on the broadcasting question. Trentham, Commissioner for Finance, who is also in charge of the post office, is going home next month & will look up Captain Graves and discuss the matter with him direct. We are convinced that we shall have to take over broadcasting ultimately – I think myself, the sooner the better. ...

1 Captain Cecil Graves (1892–1957) of the B.B.C. First director of the Empire Service, 1932–5. Margaret Barclay (Greta) Hope Simpson was his secretary at this time.

J.H.S. to Ian and Sheila, Glenwood, 3 August 1934
Here we are at a log cabin inn, Gleneagles, about half-way across N.F.L. by rail from St. John's. We are having a week of holiday and are doing a real loaf – breakfast in bed every day! I go out fishing every afternoon. So far, I have caught one grilse and lost one salmon. That was yesterday afternoon. I got him on & he jumped out of the water and then ran out 30 or forty yards of line – then there was a jerk & the salmon was in the air and my line slack. I reeled in & found that the fly had broken off the cast just above the shank. So much for the tackle you buy in St. John's. It was probably old stock.

We are on the Gander River, just near the bottom of the Gander Lake. We look up it – south – seven or eight miles. The lake is about a mile wide, with low wooded hills on either side and higher hills at the far end. But the main lake runs at right angles to this one, and from this one 26 miles east to Gambo. Today is Friday – incidentally, the day Betty sails from Liverpool. Last Wednesday, we went right up the lake by motorboat, to where the Gander River runs in. There we got into small boats which we had towed with us and went a couple of miles up the river. I tried fishing, but got nothing. We had tea on the bank at a place that was covered with moose tracks. The river was very lovely, but just like all these forest rivers, some-what monotonous. There were a lot of water-lily beds.

We came out by last Sunday's express, and they gave me a special car so that we were cut off at Glenwood at 3.49 a.m. when we arrived, and slept until 7. Glenwood is a wretched little village. A lot of the men have been living on dole, not attempting to work, and the energy and morale have been sapped out of them. There are scarcely any gardens, the reason being that should any energetic people run a garden, the loafers steal all the produce! That is pretty awful, and it shows how the people have degenerated. Truly our problem is largely a moral problem. That means a long row to hoe before things are right. The next generation is the hope, but will be no better than the present one if we cannot get to a better system of education. We have a population about 280,000, we guess (there has been no census since 1921). Last year, $500,000 was spent on education. This year, we have raised the estimate to $725,000; but we shall not be in a position to demand a reformed and higher standard till we can spend at least $1,100,000 on teachers' salaries. There are 1,600 teachers, so that sum will only mean an *average* salary of $687.50 = £137.10, and expenses of living in this country are just about double those in England. The first educational problem is a salary for the teacher which will make the profession at least as attractive as lumbering. When we have attained that object, the next problem is denominationalism. You, at home, cannot imagine the state of affairs here. Every denomination demands a school in every village. So in Moreton's Harbour, for example, with 120 families, you have a Catholic school, a United Church school, an Anglican school and a Salvation Army school. That is incredible but true. Education is not my pigeon, but the government is bound to be judged by what it does in this matter, and the Commissioner in charge[1] is doing nothing at all. He has done nothing for the past five months. His department is causing the U.K. Commissioners great anxiety. And they have sufficient of anxiety in their own departments. I have myself volunteered for more work! The police is in a dreadful mess. We are retiring the Inspector General[2] (much against his will), but the department concerned, Justice, is incapable of organizing and controlling the police, and, in any case, the executive should be separated from the judicial. So I am to take over the police, and, given three or four months before the row begins, I hope to have it an efficient force. There are too many on the strength, but it is a mob – not a trained force.

I seem to have wandered somewhat from the story of our doings. We got out of the train and Mum started in talking to the children and finally visited one of the shacks, where a mother, threatened with T.B., has five little children, and a husband who earns $50 a month in the summer and $30 a month in the winter. Mr. Reid,[3] who runs this hotel, came to meet us with a motorboat, and we arrived about ten o'clock on a lovely morning – such a contrast to Sunday, which was a wretched day of rain. I went down the river fishing after lunch and caught a grilse – that was Monday. On Tuesday, I went out in the afternoon and did not have one rise. That was another lovely day. On Wednesday, we did our trip with the Reids to the Gander, the other end of the lake. A lovely, lovely day, though it came to blow on the way home, and we had quite a dusting when crossing the mouth of the Gambo Arm. That night, at about three o'clock, Quita woke with one of her dizzy attacks, and was sick and miserable for an hour – then got to sleep and was quite herself in the morning. That was yesterday. I fished again in the afternoon and lost my salmon. I am going to try again this afternoon and have mounted some flies myself. ...

The Reids started last year and the place promises to succeed. There are five of us here at present – tonight another comes, and on Sunday two more – but we go away that day. Of course, the season is very short – only three months of effective fishing. Reid's grandfather[4] built the railway and was almost owner of N.F.L. He was a great man, but his progeny was not of the same calibre, and the whole of the property has gone, though enormous areas are still held by Alan Butler (chairman of de Havillands),[5] who married a Miss Reid[6] and bought it up. ...

1 Frederick C. Alderdice.
2 C.H. Hutchings.
3 Robin Reid (d. 1958), husband of Jean (Knowling) Reid.
4 Sir Robert Gillespie Reid (1842–1908).
5 Alan Samuel Butler (1898–1987), chairman of the de Havilland Aircraft Company, the British aircraft manufacturer, 1924–50. Invested in a seal spotting company in Newfoundland run by the Australian Sidney Cotton.
6 Lois M. (Reid) Butler (d. 1970), daughter of William D. Reid (1864–1924).

Q.H.S. to Edgar and Eleanor, 4 August 1934, 'Gleneagles,' on the Gander Lake

We wonder what you are going to do for a holiday this year? How you would like to explore this country. I should be terrified if you did! People get lost so easily in these trackless forests. Even Jack Turner,[1] the man in charge of the forest, who is a real N.F.L.er & knows the country so well, lost himself not long ago, tho' he travelled by compass. What happened was that a lake he thought he had left behind him twisted & turned across his path seven miles ahead and threw him out. But there are lots of lovely 'ponds,' as they call the lakes here. ... There is no other habitation on the [Gander] lake. The Reids ... are a plucky couple and deserve to make a success of the venture. I don't doubt they will. He has cleared two acres of forest for his crops, has made a cart road for more than half a mile to the railway & has built them a log cabin halt, 'Gleneagles,' where trains will stop on request for their P.G.s. In a little, lovely, sheltered bay, he has cleared the land for settlement. The main cabin is just above the shore, with a little garden (Mrs. Reid's) and a paved path with baby poplars planted on either side to the top of the shore – about 10 yards! – but it gives such a pretty air of precision to the place. Little paths lead to cabins dotted about – the bedrooms for the guests; a bathroom & wash-houses up on the hill; the servants' quarters; the bachelors' quarters perched on a knoll with glorious views up & down the lake; and, further in, the barn & the cow-house & pigsties.

It is all so simply done – the cabins are of peeled logs laid horizontally, caulked with sphagnum moss to keep the insects out, and all the windows and the verandah are wired against them. The main cabin has a gable at either end with a verandah between. Behind the verandah is the lounge, with a great stone fireplace & chimney built of lovely coloured foot-big stones from the shore and with a curb of stones set in the cement in the hearth.

All, or nearly all, the furniture is home-made and made from the freshly felled wood of the settlement. Red & white check curtains with little frilled valances make the cabins gay & homey. The beds are laid on peeled log-steads, & the washstand is a box lid laid on the forked branches of a pine. The dressing-table is made of packing cases covered with chintz, with curtains to cover the shelves below. Nails in the logs are for your hangers.

In the gables of the main cabin are, on one side, the dining-room, opening without partition to the lounge, &, behind it, in the wing, the kitchen premises. In the other gable & wing are the Reids' quarters. It is all so nicely planned, and the Reids are such hard-working hosts. Most of the guests are fishermen, & every day they go off with guides, taking sometimes food for the day, sometimes tents & food for a week or fortnight. Their nearest neighbours are a poor little settlement of half a dozen houses, four miles down the lake. ... All their supplies have to come from St. John's, 12 hours away, & there are only 3 trains a week, so catering needs skill & foresight. But Mrs. Reid is equal to everything, and the food is quite a feature of the place. ... People complain of the difficulty of getting their supplies at St. John's!

The train passes at awkward times too – the outward mail to Port aux Basques passes at 4.30 a.m., the inward to St. John's at 12.30. That means that supplies & guests have to be met during the night, & Mr. Reid has busy nights guiding guests over the rough road, and always there is a blazing log fire and a meal to welcome them.

John went off yesterday with his guide & tent to explore down the Gander River. It is 30 miles down to the mouth and there are rapids, but the guides are very expert river men. I did not go because they wanted to travel light & get as far as they could. There is a lot of netting on the river, & none of the big salmon are getting up. So John is going down to see to that himself. The river wardens seem to be useless here. All the salmon taken up here has borne the marks of the nets. It is no good advertising the salmon fishing and making a place like this if people can't get the salmon. And the tourist trade is one of the opportunities for revenue for this poor country that John is anxious to develop. The people are so pennywise – always sacrificing tomorrow to today. And they have no respect for law. A magistrate had to fine a man for some breach of the law & he said, 'I'd have done the same myself, & I hope you make enough to more than cover the fine.' A young clergyman boasted to John that he had been eating caribou (which is protected by law) all winter – 'every day.' John wrote to the Bishop about it. 'If the leaders of the people defy the law & encourage the people to defy it, what can the Commission do!' So the Bishop spoke strongly on the subject at the yearly convention. It is all a

matter for patience & firmness & steadiness of purpose. The people have
for so long been badly governed and have seen their politicians playing
always for their own hands, their own aggrandisement, their own enrich-
ment, helping themselves openly from the public purse – no wonder they
have no sense of public morality – public duty.

But they are a fine people. There is a strong body of public support
behind the Commission. The more intelligent people realize that if England had not come to N.F.L.'s help, there would have been an appalling
catastrophe – the island must have starved. And they see that the Commissioners have nothing to make for themselves out of their job – that they
are impartial, not to be deflected from what is just by any consideration of
friendship or convenience. And they see that the affairs of the country are
being put in order as quickly & as well as is possible & that capital is
coming back & [that] gradually work is being found & the country is
being developed. But it cannot all be done in a hurry, and another bad
winter must be faced. That awful load of debt incurred by the immoral
politicians is something that cannot be wiped off the slate; it has got to be
paid for by years of industry & thrift. But for that, the problem of recovery
would be easy. But how for the interest of that debt and for all the running expenses of the government & for the development schemes that are
necessary to recovery! These are the basic problems that have to be faced &
dealt with. ...

1 Chief Forestry Officer, Department
   of Natural Resources.

J.H.S. to Ian and Sheila, S.S. *Daisy*, 14 August 1934

If you look at the map of N.F.L., half-way between St. John's and the
northern point, and on the east coast of the island, you may see an island
marked 'Fogo Island.' At this moment, I am on board a 40-ton ex-mine-
sweeper, running west along the south coast of that island. Presently, we
shall round the western end of it and so into Fogo Harbour.

I am one of an inspection party consisting of Lodge, Jack Turner (Forest
Officer), Robinson (Chief Engineer),¹ Fudge (Chief Fishery Officer)² and
myself, which is en route down to the Labrador, calling in at various small
settlements on the way. Today, for example, we call at Fogo & Twillingate
and, at the latter place, inspect the Grenfell Hospital, which is mainly
supported by government grant. Tomorrow, it is Tilt Cove copper mine
& Seal Cove, a fishing station; next day, Canada Bay, and, on the 17th,

St. Anthony and Quirpon. St. Anthony is the Grenfell H.Q. in N.F.L. I fear that we shall find the *Scarborough* (H.M. ship – a sloop) with Ramsay MacDonald.[3] He is here, at the moment, and I fear for another five weeks, with Ishbel.[4] He arrived on the *Dragon* – a cruiser – on Friday, and is staying at Government House. On Saturday, he sent for me, and I had 1¼ hours with him – largely indiscreet confidences on his part. My impression is that R.M. is approaching the end of his public career. He is suffering from acute brain fog. FAG, but also FOG. That night, there was a dinner at Government House – just the six members of the Commission and their wives. I was on the right of Lady Anderson, the hostess, and had Ishbel on the other side. ...

18th. Saturday at 6.40 a.m. at St. Anthony, where we arrived about an hour ago on a lovely morning. ...

Yesterday, we were in Canada Bay – v. map – about 80 miles south of here. We wanted to explore possibilities and so stayed a day there. It is a quite perfect touring centre, five salmon rivers, lovely creeks and lakes and bays, mountains (Clouds,[5] Horseshoe,[6] Long Range) to climb, birds and bear and caribou to shoot. From the key spot of the bay, a 15-mile radius takes one to most places. Also, there is good agricultural land – so we are planning a second – or third – or fourth – Markland. I have had Dr. Curtis,[7] already, & now it is breakfast time & I must stop. ...

1 William J. Robinson.
2 Philip Thomas Fudge (1884–1939).
3 (James) Ramsay MacDonald (1866–1937), Prime Minister of the United Kingdom, 1924 and 1929–35.
4 His daughter.
5 Cloud Hills.
6 Horse Chops.
7 Charles S. Curtis (1887–1963) of the Grenfell Mission.

J.H.S. to Ian and Sheila, *Daisy*, in the Gulf of St Lawrence, west of Belle Isle, 23 August 1934

... We have had a most interesting and useful trip down to the Labrador. Here you never say 'up to the Labrador.' It would be as wrong as to say that you went down to London from Bristol. The attraction of the Labrador is a curious thing. The coast is rocky and barren and strewn with barren & rocky islands. These, in the summer, are the haunt of thousands of fisher folk from N.F.L., who catch millions of fish. 'Fish' is always and only codfish. The catch this year is about 20,000 tons. Of this amount, 2,500 tons has been caught by parties organized and/or financed by the government, who would not have been able to fish at all except with our assistance. The government gets the fish & sells it, paying the fisherman the balance (if any) between the price received and the advance made. So at the moment, I am a wholesale fish merchant, looking for new markets so that we shall not compete with the local merchants. I have sold over 1,000 tons in [the] U.S.A. & Canada – both new markets – and have enquiries for another 750 from Grimsby[1] and Egypt – again new markets. If we can get rid of 2,000 tons in this way, it will take the margin off the local market, and ensure the continuance of decent prices to the fishermen generally.

We have called at a large number of small places, and so have learnt local conditions in a way that would be impossible from description or correspondence. ... At ... St. Anthony ... we met Ramsay MacDonald again and had a long conference with Grenfell. Both Ramsay & Grenfell appear to be long past their best. St. Anthony is rather a showplace. They have a magnificent hospital – a farm – industrial work and education. But the economic standards of the mission are far and away above the possibilities of the island. They get very large funds from America. They also get a great deal of volunteer service from young American plutocrats. They have 35 in N.F.L. altogether this year. They work like coolies, moving coal, digging drains, selling curios, doing a thousand odd jobs. They call them 'Wops'[2] or 'Wopesses,' and the wops and wopesses not only work for nothing but pay for their board and lodging. It is a clever system for the mission.

After St. Anthony, we called at Quirpon – pronounced Carpoon – in the extreme north and then crossed the Strait,[3] a somewhat *mouvementé*[4] passage, and went to Alexis River, where the Labrador Development Company has started timber operations. There I christened their H.Q. 'Hope Simpson'[5] – at their request. It is a most attractive spot. The river at that point, over 20 miles from the mouth, is over a mile wide, and you can go back in a motorboat for 60 or 80 miles before you come to the lowest falls. Both sides are very densely wooded. They have some big stuff. I saw two trunks 70 feet long, 27 inches at the base & 7 at the tip and straight as a die.

That night, we left – Monday last – and went to Grady, a rocky island about 20 miles off the coast – the H.Q. of one of our fishery districts and the H.Q. also of a whaling company.[6] They were towing a dead whale in as we came & had two enormous animals at the top of the slip. They haul them out of the sea by a winch, along a slip up to a platform where flensing is done & the pieces taken into the boiler houses. From Grady, we sailed up to North West River, stopping for the night at Rigolet, a Hudson's Bay Company's post at the narrow entrance. A fearful place for mosquitoes.

North West River is an eye-opener. It is 100 miles from the sea at the west end of Lake Melville on the Hamilton River. You may see Hamilton Inlet marked on the map. Dr. Paddon[7] of the Grenfell Mission is at the head of affairs at North West River, and has succeeded in creating a great community spirit. The gardens are astonishing. They have a very short season; the ice clears away about the beginning of June & frost is general before the end of September, yet they grow all kinds of vegetables to maturity. The great industry is trapping.

On the way back, we called at Cartwright (Grenfell Mission), where a plane arrived from America while we were there. It had come from Deer Lake on the west coast of N.F.L. – 500 miles away – in 5 hours. We next made St. Mary's River – another Grenfell station with hospital – and then Battle Harbour. There we crossed the Strait again & had a blow on the way to Flower's Cove on Friday morning. That day, we sailed down the coast & called at Port Saunders – a haunt of degenerate & demoralized lumbermen & at the limit of poverty – on the way to Bonne Bay. We got there Saturday morning, spent a couple of hours there & went on the Lomond, George Simpson's place ... a very attractive spot. In the afternoon, I went out on the river & caught a grilse, which got off, a small salmon and 14 excellent trout.

We left that night & had quite a dressing down in a gale of wind on a brilliant moonlight night. Fortunately, the wind was dead ahead, so it was a case of steaming along slowly and pitching into it. We got to Humbermouth at 6. The International Paper people took us for a drive from the estuary to Curling – a lovely drive – and then in a fast motorboat six miles up the Humber River. That was a great trip – very lovely. Then they gave us a slap-up lunch at the Glynmill Inn,[8] & we left for St. John's by the train in the evening. We got there at midday Monday & found Betty & Quita and Mrs. Lodge waiting to meet us.

And now the mill is running again & I am up to the neck in work. ...

1 Humberside, England.
2 Workers without pay.
3 Strait of Belle Isle.
4 Lively.
5 Port Hope Simpson.

6 Newfoundland Whaling Company, a mainly Norwegian enterprise. Managed by Olaf Olsen.
7 Harry L. Paddon (1881–1939), practised medicine at North West River, 1915–39.
8 Corner Brook.

Q.H.S. to Ian and Sheila, Newfoundland Hotel, 24 August 1934
... Betty arrived by the last direct mail a fortnight ago today. It is lovely having her here, and she is enjoying herself tremendously. Everyone is entertaining her and Ruth Lodge,[1] who came by the same boat. ... The Lodges & we had a launch to go out to meet them & there were flags flying from Signal Hill to welcome them and there was to have been a gun, but that did not come off because they arrived earlier than expected. But it was all very thrilling for them. And it was such a lovely day and the entrance to the harbour is magnificent. I had not seen it before as it was dark when we arrived in the early winter morning.

Since then, the girls have had a succession of lunches, picnics, teas, dinners, [and] cocktail parties given in their honour. Even Government House was going to have had a lunch party for them, but that was cancelled for a tea-party as catastrophe descended upon the Government House domestic regime. The butler was discovered drunk (for the 3rd & last time, having disposed of £50 worth of whiskey – emptying & re-sealing the cases with great skill), and the same day the parlour maid fell down stone stairs and smashed her face, & the cook was in bed with an attack of stone – such a tale of domestic troubles Lady Anderson told me, but she would have them come to tea. ...

[Betty] ... & I had a lovely day down at Logy Bay one day. We took our lunch & sketched – I had meant to write letters, but she was very keen that I should try my hand too & it was such fun. We sat on a green sward below some rocks that gave us comfortable protection from wind and a rest for our backs. Beside us was a stream with clear peaty pools from which we got water for our bottle – just below, the stream plunged down among boulders to a rocky funnel where the sea roared in & dashed the spray almost to our ledge. There were great sandstone headlands on either side of our bay, with the sea deep emerald-green among the rocks; beyond the bay the sea was deep sapphire with white-sailed schooners passing and sometimes a little coasting steamer. We recognized the *Blue Peter* on her way to America with the first shipment of the blueberry harvest. Betty chose a headland with the rocky bay & a schooner on the blue sea; I chose fishermen's flakes (stages for drying the fish) on pink rocks with the sea beyond – both turned out to be most effective poster effects – great fun. I shall try again.

We have had a wedding this week. John's secretary, Mr. Claude Fraser, was married at 10.30 in one of the convent chapels. Betty & I were the only outside guests, so we felt highly honoured. It was such a beautiful service – mostly in English, and the young priest[2] was so humanly nervous. I was close to him & could almost see his heart beating & how his breath failed & he had to swallow hard! After the service, we went to the convent[3] parlour & the mother superior kissed me! Sweet thing she seemed. Then we went to the bride's[4] house & had all sorts of lovely things to eat – a regular dainty breakfast served as at a tea-party – all sitting round the room. And the poor young priest had to make a speech, and Claude Fraser, almost as nervous, had to reply. One of the nicest things in this country is that there is no professionalism in their entertaining. Hostesses make their own dinners, tho' the maid serves them; all cakes are made by the lady of the house – even the wedding cake & breakfast were home-made, but could not have been better or prettier.

Another day, in a pause, Betty & I climbed Signal Hill. She loved it – so did I. We went up by the motor road which goes almost to Cabot Tower, but we scrambled down another way. It is glorious up there looking across the Atlantic with this wonderful coast at our feet & stretching away to Spear Head.[5] There are lakes up on top and lots of wildflowers in the hollows. The Marconi station is in the tower,[6] & the wireless masts are close beside it.

John has had a most interesting trip. ... We were to have gone ... but the *Daisy* is too small for the party & the cabins have no portholes – the settlement wharves having posts jutting out that poke out the ship's eyes. And the stairway is like a ladder, so it would have been uncomfortable & dangerous for Betty in rough weather. But I should love to have gone. So would she. Our regret was that we could not unfurl the flag at Port Hope Simpson – a pennant. They brought it for us to see before it was rushed up to Labrador to be ready for their arrival.

One thing John has to do is to devise a government for the Labrador. It will be extraordinarily interesting to hear what he has decided. ...

1 Actress daughter of Thomas and Isobel Lodge.
2 Ronald McDermott Murphy (1900–1985).
3 Presentation Convent.
4 The bride was Ruth Taylor

(1909–), daughter of George and Mary (Carten) Taylor. George Taylor was manager of the Bank of Commerce in St John's.
5 Cape Spear.
6 Cabot Tower.

J.H.S. to Edgar and Eleanor, St John's, 8 September 1934

You may guess how much my work has eased off when you learn that I am actually beginning this letter in my office at four o'clock in the afternoon. The reduction in work is in part due to the fact that much of our preliminary work is finished, in part to the fact that my office is now well organized. ... 12/9. I did not get far in the office that afternoon and now it is Wednesday morning at 6.30 and the *Newfoundland*, which should have left at midday yesterday, is still loading cargo, so there is just a chance that this may get away on her.

I was also too optimistic. Monday & yesterday have been dreadful days – long and anxious Commission meetings each morning and difficult cases in the afternoons and finally dinner engagements each evening, yesterday with a set speech.

Life is an interesting experience, but how much one requires judgment therein. One of my most painful problems at the moment is caused by the action of Sir Wilfred Grenfell. That is a remarkable statement. The case will give you some inkling of the class of difficulty that is created by want of judgment coupled with enthusiasm.

I think I must have told you of our visit on the tour of Canada Bay. There, Sir Wilfred Grenfell holds a forest area of 116 square miles, which he got as a concession. That has never been developed at all, though he has recently erected a small sawmill, which has let him in for a considerable loss on working.

The Canada Bay people have been kept alive by the operations of Mr. John Reeves,[1] a local merchant, an R.C. who has undertaken contracts of pulpwood during the winters, and, though he has charged the people exaggerated prices for supplies, has at least arranged that they had something to eat. All the forest in the vicinity has been cut over, with the exception of Sir Wilfred Grenfell's block. Reeves was willing to take a contract, if he could get permission to cut there, and to pay Grenfell a royalty of $0.25 a cord for permission. That would have given work to the whole bay.

When at St. Anthony, I had a long talk with Grenfell and he agreed to that proposition, I thought. However, he dislikes Reeves intensely and so made a trip to Canada Bay, formed the people into a cooperative society, & told them the government would pay them cash for what they cut, if they would take the contract. Of course, that is ridiculous. The people know nothing of the business end of cutting pulpwood for export; they have no capital, which is required in large quantities – all they expect is to be hired to cut wood for cash, instead of being hired to cut wood in exchange for supplies. They have severed their connection with Mr. John Reeves – there is no one else to supply them – and there is every probability that they will starve this winter.

And Sir Wilfred Grenfell has left St. Anthony and gone to Montreal en route to the U.S.A., and there is no one competent to help untangle the mess.

He acted in excellent good faith, but with no common sense. I am now going to attempt to secure the block of timber for the government, and then shall try to patch up things between John Reeves and the inhabitants and to induce John to take, finance, and run a contract. But the time is very short, and, as I say, Grenfell has left for a Canadian lecturing tour.

Another of my difficulties is the fact that force of circumstances have made me a fishmonger! The government had to fit out about 2,000 fishermen who could not find supplies elsewhere. This cost about £30,000 and we are paid by the men in fish. On the Labrador, I have about 2,000 tons of fish, and have to sell it at the best advantage for the fishermen. The 'Trade'[2] is dead against me, for their object is to pay the fishermen as small a price as possible and to make the largest possible profit. So they would not help in the disposal of this fish at all. We succeeded in selling 1,200 tons in new markets in the U.S.A. and Canada at a better price than has been secured for years. That took the excess fish off the market and fixed a price fair for everybody. Directly the merchants found out where we had been selling, they came to the same people and offered fish at a lower price. Was that not dirty? They could have got the same price, and probably a little more, if they had stood out. But they did not care about the price to the fishermen. All they wanted was a low price for them, and to break the price which our operations had actually fixed. I think they have been too late, for we have already sold the fish of so many fishermen at the higher price that the rest of the fishermen are encouraged to refuse any lower price by the merchant.

We, the government, are going to lose money over this fishery supply business. The fishery has failed over large sections of the coast, & there we shall get little or nothing back. But where it has been successful, there are great results in re-establishment of morale and independence. And there is a spirit of confidence abroad which is most valuable. And things generally are unquestionably better. The revenue is up 20% – the railway traffics are up – the postal service is up. The government is criticized, and in many quarters disliked, but we have certainly instituted policies which are to the advantage of the people generally. The moneyed people are the men who chiefly dislike us, as they think us a socialist government. ...

1 Eugene John Reeves (1883–1950),   2 Fish exporters.
   owner of John Reeves & Sons,
   the main supplier to fishermen in
   White Bay.

J.H.S. to Ian and Sheila, Newfoundland Hotel, 8 September 1934

... Mother and Betty are leaving next week. They go by a paper boat – the *Geraldine Mary*. She sails from Botwood with paper for the *Daily Mail*, and is the property of the Anglo-Newfoundland Development Company, which again is the property of Lord Rothermere and his group. She is an 8,000-ton boat, carries 12 passengers only and is said to be most comfortable. And the passage costs £15, against £27 on the regular line. Also, there are not so many tips to pay. So we reckon that on the whole transaction we shall save about £25, less Betty's fare to Botwood. Mother and I have a pass over the railway. They sail on the 19th and should be at Purfleet[1] on the 27th. There, the company is arranging for a car to meet them, to drive them into town. ...

Last Wednesday[2] was a whole holiday, so we went out to our experimental settlement 'Markland.'... We are hoping great things from this experiment. If successful, we hope to multiply it by ten or by twenty. After all, the salvation of this country lies in the land, though I suppose that the major industry will always be the fisheries. ... This is a dreadful country economically. The woodsmen & the fishermen are unorganized and are in fact serfs. For 300 years, they have been existing, and the major part of their earnings have gone to create about 300 wealthy families. And that system of sweating still exists. It is a dreadful problem.

Another problem is found in the lawlessness of the people. This manifests itself in every direction. It is very pronounced in the case of the game laws. Still more is the custom of 'squatting' on any government land. The land on either side of the harbour of St. John's belongs to the Admiralty. There are literally hundreds of wooden houses on that land, for no one of which has any permission been given. Within the last ten days three have been put up for which permission was asked *and refused*. Yet nothing is done. We shall have ultimately to take over the municipality. And the fun will begin when we try to regulate matters. ...

1 In Essex, England.   2 5 September 1934.

Q.H.S. to Ian and Sheila, Newfoundland Hotel, 11 September 1934

... Sunday, Betty got us up early & we got breakfast quickly, & John drove us up to Cabot Tower and we found a lovely corner among the rocks where we could sit & paint the view. ... We got down just in time for church – a lunch party & Government House, & then out again to the south side of the harbour, where we had never been before. We had to leave the car & walk over & under fishermen's flakes & along wooden ways along the rocks with the sea roaring in and out of coves below – & then up a long wooden way to the lighthouse,[1] where we found several parties of friends sunning themselves on the grass among the rocks. It is a beautiful spot; you get the sweep of the bay to 'Spear Head' & Signal Hill with Cabot Tower – a great rock with magnificent old red sandstone cliffs. And the sea so blue & the harbour water at our feet such clear deep green. The south hill is almost as fine a rock as Signal Hill – they both rise sheer 500 ft. from the sea. We had tea at the lighthouse, & the lighthouse keeper[2] rose from his bed to show us his treasures. His great-grandfather & grandfather & father had all been the keepers of this lighthouse in turn. His wife,[3] such a lovely woman of about 35, is granddaughter of old Captain Kean, who brought home his 1,000,000th seal this year. Captain Sheppard sounded the foghorn 3 times for us. It must have [been] startling to hear the foghorn on that brilliantly clear day. It is such a melancholy old cow – a minor tone.

Another glorious day last week was Wednesday, when we went to Markland – a long day, about 156 miles there & back, and walking about Markland seeing the crops & the houses & the new roads. It is a wonderful achievement. We saw the first batch of 10 men (unemployed for years) start off in the early morning one March day, so thin & starved-looking but full of hope & determination to make good – not picked men – some of them men with bad records. And they have made good. It is wonderful what they have done. The Commission has backed them & is helping them till they are started. Now there are 150 men out there and they have about 12 acres of land cleared for crops, and magnificent potato & turnip crops, & roads and 45 houses built, & most of them occupied by the men who have built them, with their families. A fine Dutchman who is an enthusiast & idealist, a landscape gardener by profession, is in charge of the development and is making a beautiful estate of it. His daughter, a fine girl who has just graduated from the Memorial College, volunteered to take the school. She has just had a camp for 15 of the children to get to know them & get some elements of discipline & decent life before school begins. It has been a great success. The 15 will be the nucleus of discipline for the rest of the school. The school is to be educational in the sense of preparing them for being useful members of this colony. ... Many of the children will have some distances to come & in the winter they will have to dine at school. Meals will be prepared by the children ... under Miss Cochius' supervision, of course. ... The idea is to develop a full, interesting, happy, self-dependent life for the community. I felt like crying when I saw the happy healthy faces & the crops & the trees coming down & the good earth being shaken from the roots before they were dragged away for burning or for use in building. ...

1 At Fort Amherst.   3 Sadie Addison Sheppard.
2 Captain Robert Sheppard.

J.H.S. to Ian and Sheila, Newfoundland Hotel, 16 September 1934
... Mum & Betty start for Botwood today, and I accompany them to Grand Falls. On Wednesday, they start for England. ... The same day, I go on to Ottawa ...

I have been having a great time selling fish! We fitted out some 2,000 fishermen who were on the dole and had no credit. Some of them we fitted on the 50/50 basis, i.e., we took half the catch in return for the outfit. Others we fitted on condition they repaid from their own fish. We have sold all but about 750 tons. But we have sold it in new markets where it will not compete with the local merchant. We sold a million pounds in the U.S.A.! It has been an anxious business. The local merchants hate us because we are paying all we can to the fishermen. We have paid $1.50 per 100 lbs. of unmanufactured fish in net bulk. The merchants want to pay $1.25 or less. For manufactured fish, first quality, we have paid $2.60 a cwt. on the Labrador. They want to pay $1.70 to $2 – in St. John's, & it costs 35 cents to get it here – so that would mean $1.35 to $1.65 on the Labrador. This will explain the bitterness they feel towards our operation. Personally, I wish that we could get out of the business, but these 2,000 whom we sent out would still have been on the dole but for the government supply. As it is, three-quarters of them are most on their own feet again.

Of course, we shall lose some money. There are stretches of the coast where there has been no fishing at all – the fish have not come. And in other places, there have been such enormous shoals of dogfish that the codfish could not stay. The dogfish are a terrible curse. If we could get fishmeal plants, we might deal with them, but that is not a venture for government.

I have people coming to lunch, and must stop.

17/9/34. Monday. Grand Falls House, Grand Falls. N.F.L.
Mother, Betty & I left St. John's in our private railway car yesterday.
While here, I am making arrangements for the reservation of a national park in the southern half of the island. We are not ambitious – as we have

not much money – and shall begin with an area of 400 to 600 square miles, which we can afford to patrol. When we get more money, we shall proclaim other areas. It seems preferable to have five parks of 400 square miles each, rather than one of 2,000 square miles. The Public Schools Exploring Society[1] did a survey of a considerable area on Rattling Brook this summer, and it is in that area that we are going to operate.

This house was built for Lord Northcliffe. The Grand Falls paper mill provides paper for the *Daily Mail*. In fact, the Anglo-Newfoundland Development Company is really Lord Rothermere. They have enormous areas of forest here in N.F.L., of which a great deal is held by them but is in fact not of any use, as it is so far from the scene of operations. I wish that we could get it back again. It would be useful to the government. We are the guests of Mr. & Mrs. Vincent Jones. He is manager of the company. His brother is assistant Bishop of Liverpool.[2] ...

1 A British society founded by Surgeon-Commander G. Murray Levick, R.N. (1876–1956). Later the British Schools Exploring Society.

2 Herbert Gresford Jones (1870–1958), Bishop of Warrington, 1927–45.

J.H.S. to Ian and Sheila, Chateau Laurier, Ottawa, 23 September 1934

... I came on from Grand Falls on Wednesday[1] morning's train to Port aux Basques and crossed that night to North Sydney on Cape Breton Island. We had a lovely crossing. Cabot Strait can afford ninety miles of solid unpleasantness when the weather is bad. It is one of the roughest pieces of water. And the *Caribou* – 2,000 tons – is not a comfortable boat in a sea. If I am as fortunate next Saturday[2] night on the return voyage, I shall be glad. The reason for this visit is that we contemplate a force[3] in N.F.L. analogous to the Canadian Mounted Police,[4] and I am finding out how that latter force is organized and trained. It has a very fine and well-deserved reputation. ... Tomorrow and Tuesday, I shall go on with my enquiries. In addition, I have various matters to discuss with other ministers. They have placed an embargo on hay and we need 12,000 tons – for which I must see the Minister of Agriculture.[5] We want the Canadian geodetic survey to undertake the triangulation of N.F.L. The Canadian government is also helping out with our new meteorological service, and I have to see them about that. Then the C.P.R. boats are starting a ship-to-shore plane service & they will use two of our posts. I have to discuss that subject with the civil aviation people. Finally, the managing director of the International Paper

Company,[6] which runs the mill at Corner Brook, has come down from New York to see me about conditions in the lumberwoods. So that in all I have a very full programme. ...

The journey from North Sydney here – about 40 hours – was interesting. ...

We reached Montreal just in time to catch the express to Ottawa and got here at 10.30 p.m. I found that my secretary had engaged a bedroom, sitting-room and bathroom, & that the charge was $15 – £3 – p. day for lodging, board being extra. I got out of that into a single bedroom next day, but it was an indication of the custom of the N.F.L. ministers under a political regime. My travelling allowance in Canada is $10 – £2 – per day, all in. So I shall be out of pocket by the visit. Before the Commission, a minister on work of this kind was actually in pocket. ...

1 19 September 1934.
2 29 September 1934.
3 The Newfoundland Rangers.
4 The R.C.M.P.
5 Robert Weir (1882–1939).

6 The New York parent company of the International Power and Paper Company of Newfoundland Ltd (Corner Brook).

J.H.S. to Betty, Scotia Hotel, Truro, Nova Scotia, 29 September 1934

... I was in Montreal on Wednesday and met some old friends – the Dales.[1] Their son-in-law[2] has been making an enquiry into the conditions of shop assistants and of the people who make up clothes for the ready-made trade. Some of the things he told me are incredible. He said that they had found cases of women who got 25 cents – one shilling – for sewing twelve pairs of trousers, including the buttonholes. One penny a pair of trousers. Is that not appalling? ... It looks to me as if, in many directions, there must be radical reform, not because there will be revolution if reform does not come, but because the present conditions are definitely un-Christian. The reason for my visit to Montreal was to discuss with the lumber people the wages of loggers in the woods. They cut for the paper companies. The price of paper is fixed by competition, and the companies in their turn fix the wages so that they can compete. The price of paper is now very low – about £8 a ton – and, as a result, the wages of the loggers are very low also. In N.F.L., a good logger working steadily and long hours every day cannot earn more than $30 a month. Out of this he has to provide his clothes & boots – heavy items, for wear & tear is heavy – and to feed his family at home. And he cannot do that. He could only do it if he got $50 a month. The companies say that if they paid any higher wages, they could not produce paper at the price at which it is sold. Yet, if the companies got together, they could demand a higher price for the paper, for the newspapers & publishers could not do without it. An effort is being made in Canada to get the producers together and to force up the price to $45 – but one concern stands out and will not agree. So all the concerns go on selling at this lower rate, which prevents a fair wage being paid to the loggers. I do not know what we shall do, but we shall have to take some steps to force wages up.

Much the same question obtains in the codfish trade. The fishermen are being paid far too little for their fish. Yet the merchants still make their profits. If they sell abroad at lower prices, they deduct the difference from the price they pay the fishermen, and make the same old profit themselves. At least, that is what they try to do. Our operations this year, during which we have sold large quantities of fish caught by men fitted out by the government, have helped to raise the price of fish for the actual fisherman. ...

1 Robert J. and Marian (Barclay) Dale.
2 Francis Reginald Scott (1899–1985), husband of Marian Dale Scott (b. 1906). Frank Scott and H.M. Cassidy filed a 'Report on Labour Conditions in the Men's Clothing Industry' with the Royal Commission on Price Spreads, which reported in 1935.

J.H.S. to Ian and Sheila, St John's, 7 October 1934

... Here summer has gone & seems to have taken autumn with it. We had snow on Thursday night & sleet on Friday, with a gale of wind. Yesterday was glorious with sunshine. Today an easterly gale with rain. ...

Yesterday, I saw one of our lighthouse keepers – lighthouses are one of my duties. This old gentleman, a man of 6 feet 2, spare, and with a white beard, is at Cape Pine,[1] a lonely spot. His family has looked after the light for over 100 years. How seldom one thinks of these hundreds of lonely men, whose faithful service saves hundreds of lives each year. I must try to institute some kind of travelling library for them.

Monday morning. 8th October. A lovely morning. The sun is quite hot. There was a terrific gale all yesterday, and one pitied the men at sea. This is a bad coast. Two schooners were wrecked last week. Fortunately, there is a lot of building going on. There are 80 schooners on the stocks, & we have a programme for another 200 to 250.

I think I told you I had been selling fish. We have sold practically the whole of the government-supplied catch – some 2,500 tons – at decent prices. The merchant community was very hostile. But the effect has been not only to help the 3,000 men whom we supplied (and whom the merchants refused to supply), but also to raise the price of fish to the fisherman generally by about $10 a ton. That of course explained the hostility of the merchant. Had it not been for our operations that extra $10 would have gone to the profits of the merchant.

I have not only been selling fish – which, by the way, always means codfish – I have also been organizing the trade in Scotch-cured herring. (That is not Scotch herring, but N.F.L. herring cured in the Scotch manner.) The trade was quite chaotic, with the result that the fishermen got dreadful prices. Now we have succeeded in creating an exporters' association, so that all sales are made through one channel. There will be competition among the buyers, but not among the sellers. The association guarantees to the fishermen a price practically the double of what he received last year. So there is gain there.

Also, we are allowing export of round-wood.[2] The government always prevented that, for some obscure reason. We are encouraging it and charging 25 cents a cord royalty on export. The results are threefold. First, the export helps to pay for our external debt. Second, we get a modest but important addition to the revenues. Third, and most important, work is provided for more than 1,000 men who would otherwise be on the dole with their families.

Altogether, there are a few gleams of sunshine. Our financial year begins on 1st July. The first quarter, ending 30th September, our revenue has been $2,543,000, against $2,035,000 last year. The railway returns are 20% up. The postal revenue is 20% up. We have a long way to go before things are right, but we seem to be heading for recovery.

I must get off to office. ...

1 Trepassey Bay, Avalon Peninsula.   2 Saw-logs.

J.H.S. to Edgar and Eleanor, St John's, 12 October 1934

... Here life is never without incident, frequently difficult, sometimes unpleasant, always interesting. At the moment, we are having a mild tug of war with the municipal council of St. John's. The Mayor is the local undertaker and the members of the Council are none of them men of any standing. The quality has steadily decreased through the years. The administration is, I believe, execrable. They have $300,000 in arrears, 25% of the rates are never paid, & they allow 10% for payment within a month. The general opinion is quite distinctly in favour of their suspension. We do not want to take drastic action, but we do want improvement. We offered to recommend them for a loan from the Colonial Development Fund, on condition that we appoint a financial controller. They have turned down the offer quite flat. One councillor' resigned in protest. Now we are awaiting the reactions of the city. If the council persists and is backed up by the inhabitants, we have naturally nothing to do, though as a government we are interested in the well-being of the capital. If the council is not backed up by the inhabitants, we shall probably legislate the council out of existence, and take over the administration ourselves. That will mean a lot of additional work, and we shall not be popular, for we shall insist on payment of dues and on efficient administration, which always connotes treading on many corns.

That is happening even now. We are unpopular in many quarters. We demand that, before a man travels by train, he shall take a ticket. In the old days, about half the people travelled without tickets and got away with it. We insist that the legal minimum size of a lobster for canning shall be observed. It is the custom to catch any lobster – down to a six-inch baby or even smaller – and to can it irrespective of the law. We insist on observation of the game regulations and prosecute for trapping beavers, for which there is a close season. This has never been done before. In a thousand ways, we are *governing* where government was hitherto a farce.

Nevertheless, things are unquestionably improving. Everyone realizes that fact. Even our enemies. ... Yet there are appalling places still, where the population is absolutely destitute and the fishery has failed. In many places now, at the beginning of winter, there is no food; there are no resources, no clothes. We have a long way to go before this island can be put right. The fishery will not do it. There are far too many fishermen, and the price of fish is ridiculously low.

One promising feature is that in several village centres they have this year organized fairs, with exhibitions of vegetables, home work, livestock, fruit &c. That we are stimulating by giving prizes. If we can create village leadership & emulation, much good will result.

We get no help from the merchant class – none whatever. They are still living in the 17th century. There is no cooperation, and all they hope for is a very low price to the fisherman for his fish and a very high price to the merchant. There are one or two who realize how appalling is the standard of life of the fisherman, but they are almost negligible. It looks almost as if the government would be forced into trade. This year we fitted about 3,000 fishermen & I have sold 2,000 tons of fish. I hoped that, next year, we might reduce our operations, but it looks much as if we might have to increase them. ...

Winter is on us – at the threshold. We have had snow already – just a threatening. Tonight, there is a northeast gale – a bitter wind with sleet. ...

1 Philip E. Outerbridge (1887–1975).

J.H.S. to Ian and Sheila, St John's, 15 October 1934
... One dreadful problem here is unemployment. St. John's is the outstanding case. There are probably 1,500 men in this small town who will never be employed again under the best of conditions. Patchwork is useless. Unemployment relief, in the form of temporary work invented for the purpose, only postpones the solution. We are planning ultimately to have 10,000 families on the land – but families increase faster than we can provide funds for settlement.

I must to office. ...

J.H.S. to Ian and Sheila, St John's, 31 October 1934
... This is a difficult job and is made no easier by vicious and virulent criticism. A regular agitation is going on against the Commission. Ex-politicians, who have lost their job, and so their living, are at the bottom of it, and they are running a paper each week called the *Newfoundlander* & full of all kinds of scurrilous personal abuse. It is unpleasant, but there is nothing to be done except to live it down. Things are really improving, and will continue to improve, but we cannot make a pigsty into a model farm in a year. Our main policies are long-range policies, whose effect will come gradually, and will chiefly be felt by the rising generation. The young people are our hope. They are a splendid crowd. Meanwhile, there is an appalling amount of distress among the poor and the unemployed, and a very large section of the population has lost the desire, and indeed the knowledge, of self-help. They have to be educated out of their lethargy, and it is a long and painful process. ...

There have been several public functions recently. I have had to speak once or twice. One speech was at the closing of the fair at Heart's Content.[1] That was a remarkable show. The village has, I suppose, a couple of hundred inhabitants. They had a show of agricultural produce and home industry. 2,000 exhibits from all over the place. At the close, Mr. Lodge gave the prizes & I spoke to about 1,500 of audience. It was in the paper sheds of the Anglo-Newfoundland Development Company (*Daily Mail*). Monday of last week, I went to open the school at Markland, our agricultural settlement for the unemployed. I must have written you about this before. The school is modelled on the Danish folk schools. It is the cultural centre of the settlement. Men, women and children attend – not of course together. The children are taught everything. School begins by them washing their hands, faces, ears & necks and brushing their hair. Then they all clean their teeth. All of this is entirely new experience for them. And they are taught deportment and chorus singing and nature study and organized games and the three Rs. In the afternoon, the women have their instruction in management of children and of the house, in cooking, dressmaking and other female arts. In the evening, it is the turn of the men, who learn the three Rs (if they do not know them), history, [and] political science. Two have asked for and are receiving instruction in physics. It is a great experiment.

We have lots of experiments in progress. Our airplanes have just come, and the first was on its trial trip yesterday. There is one snag which was unexpected – the floats are much heavier than we imagined. This reduces the effective weight-carrying capacity, which was three passengers and a fourth at a pinch. Now, it is doubtful whether they can carry two – plus pilot. They think they can improve matters, but we are not going to take them on unless they are guaranteed to carry two. Next year, we shall have to get a larger plane to carry five or six. ...

1 Trinity Bay. The fair closed on
   18 October 1934.

J.H.S. to Ian and Sheila, Hotel Vanderbilt, South Kensington, London S.W. 7, 6 December 1934

... I am having constant engagements here in London and there are many who want to see me for whom I cannot even make arrangements. The Dominions Office is, I am thankful to say, entirely satisfied with our first year's results. The revenue is a million dollars up on the first five months of this financial year – since July 1st. This means that we shall be able to face considerable financial capital expenditure which would otherwise have been impossible. We have to build a new jail, a new hospital, new police barracks, and – if we can at all manage it – a new set of government offices. ...

1935

**J.H.S. to Ian and Sheila, on board *Alaunia*, Cunard White Star,
10 February 1935**
We are within eight hours of Halifax and steaming through a perfectly
calm sea. ...

From Halifax I can travel either via St. Pierre by an old tub called the
Dominica or via Sydney & Port aux Basques. It will probably be the
former, and we pray for decent weather. ...

J.H.S. to Betty, St John's, 19 February 1935
... They have flooded the tennis courts & every day crowds come to skate
to music. The hotel charges 15 cents a person and is making a good thing of
it. The music is dreadful – ancient waltzes on a gramophone with a loud-
speaker attachment. But the skating is very pretty. There are not many
high-class skaters, but a great many quite good ones. Lady Anderson skates
& had quite an adventure the other evening when a little man whom she
had never seen in her life took her by the arm and insisted on skating with
her. She left the rink.

We are having every kind of difficulties out here. The Governor is
away, & Sir William Horwood is 'Administrator' and presides at meetings
of the Commission – very badly I hear. I shall know today, as there is a
meeting this morning. ... Then there have been organized depreciation of
the Markland effort, in which I fear some of the Commissioners themselves are implicated – though that cannot be said publicly. ...

J.H.S. to Ian and Sheila, Department of Natural Resources, St John's, 26 February 1935

... I am writing in my office room at the hotel at about nine in the morning. I have been up for three hours – have had my quiet time, have polished off the papers brought home, have written Quita and had breakfast, and in a few minutes I must leave for the office, where, I hear, the unemployed are going to make a demonstration. They are choosing the wrong shop. I am not in charge of public welfare, but they dislike the N.F.L. Commissioner[1] who is, and think me weaker or more sympathetic – (the same thing).

We are having rather a difficult time at the moment in an attempt at educational reform, which is exceedingly unpopular among the R.C. & Church of England clergy. The present system is antediluvian & radically bad. The government hands over to the churches grants for education based in amount on their respective populations – in 1921, which was the year of the last census. That is the end of the matter as far as the government is concerned. There is no audit of the money, no standard of qualification for the teacher, no inspection of schools. And, with the rest, the curriculum is antediluvian also. There are three 'superintendents' – one R.C., one C. of E., one United Church, appointed & paid, but not controlled, by the government – who hold statutory appointments & are supposed to administer the educational grant. In fact, it is denominational education in its worst form. We are making a commencement by abolishing the superintendents and bringing education directly under the Department.[2] And clerical opposition has at once begun. No one objects to this particular item of reform. But both the R.C. Archbishop[3] and the C. of E. Bishop[4] are quite clearly aware that it is the thin edge of the wedge – as in fact it is – so they are commencing their attack at once. We shall get our reform through in time, but it will be a long struggle and I fear cannot possibly be free from bitterness. Some of the churches apply a good deal of the money to purposes other than that of education. They foresee that, if any reform goes through, that system ceases. It would be much easier & more comfortable to let this sleeping dog lie, but education is one of the fundamentals, and if Newfoundland is to be resuscitated, as we all hope, it will certainly entail a radical change in the control & method of education. I must away to office. It is snowing hard.

28/2. ...

The unemployed made their demonstration, but it fizzled out before it reached my office. They went first to the Commissioner for Public Health and Welfare.[5] He would not receive two members of the deputation, whose history is unsavoury, but received others – two men & one woman. It was snowing really hard and the crowd outside – about 200 or 300 – must have had a most uncomfortable time during the hour of conference. So must the police outside. They had about 20 at the gate of my office. Apparently the deputation went away satisfied that all that could be done is being done, and that legitimate grievances will be remedied.

The whole country is deep in snow and it is difficult to imagine that in three months it will be blooming. ...

1 John C. Puddester.
2 Of Education.
3 Edward Patrick Roche.

4 William Charles White (1865–1937), Bishop of Newfoundland, 1918–37.
5 John C. Puddester.

J.H.S. to Maisie, Newfoundland Hotel, 20 March 1935

To think that Mum sails next Tuesday week! That means that I cannot get any more letters to her & that she will be here within three weeks. I very sincerely trust that she may have a good voyage. The weather has been awful – northwesterly gales with a temperature round zero. Yesterday afternoon, I struggled to my office in the teeth of it. The office is less than half a mile away, but it was quite a feat to get there, and I was puffing & panting when I arrived. I cannot imagine how the sealers survive. Fancy being out on the ice under those conditions, and often miles away from their ship. They appear to be doing fairly well, but they have lost a great many 'pans' – i.e., heaps of seal skins left on the ice to pick up later. It is a cruel trade. They kill the babies, and you can imagine the slaughter when the ship takes 10,000 in two days.

This is a cruel country in many ways. Life is maintained by killing something – fish or seals or deer or beaver – or birds – and from their babyhood the children learn to kill. The result is indiscriminate killing. The caribou is supposed to be protected. The poacher goes out & kills, not one, but as many as he can, and then leaves the corpses rotting on the ground, just taking tidbits for his consumption. The same with birds. They shoot for the sake of killing. The same with salmon in the rivers. They poach the salmon – 'jigging' they call it – and often leave them lying on the bank – just kill for the sake of killing. And yet they are a highly religious people. What is needed is education, and we are arranging for that. ...

I must stop. It is 9.10 a.m. & I am due to go to inspect the police. ...

Yesterday, the thaw came & all the streets were brooks. Then at night, while I was away dining, ... the snow came down thick again & on return to the hotel, I stepped over my ankles into soft snow. This morning it is all white. The changeable weather makes flying difficult. The forest officer[1] went off in brilliant weather yesterday morning. I hope that he got back safely. Our planes are rather too small for our work & their speed is only 80 miles an hour & their effective range about 100 miles (i.e., 200 there & back). Alas, our people are not yet air-minded & there is a certain reluctance to use the air for inspection. ...

1 Jack Turner.

J.H.S. to Ian, Department of Natural Resources, St John's, 20 March 1935

... Here we have been having samples of mixed weather of which the constant constituent is wind. ... It is sad weather for [the] unemployed and for old people and for young children. A lot of small children have died. There has been a lot of flu.

The sealers are in town, and the boats sail on Thursday.[1] I inspect them on Wednesday afternoon. One cannot well hope for such a successful voyage as last year, but I pray that they may do well, for it creates confidence for the year. We are really doing extraordinarily well. You may remember that we took a big slice off our tariff as from 1st January. Even so, this year (January, February) we are 10% ahead of last year in our revenues. So we are working out another cut in the tariff as from 1st July. These are the first reductions in taxation for over 20 years. We have a surplus over 1¼ million dollars so far this financial year (from 1st July 1934) and shall use it for capital expenditure. We are buying a new mail steamer, putting up new police barracks, rebuilding the General Hospital[2] (all of which are urgent), fitting out the Ranger force, building quarters for it & for its commandant, and buying a large estate[3] which will be H.Q. for the agricultural dept., the Rangers & the forest dept. *Of course this is not yet public.* But it shows what can be done with decent administration.

I am looking forward eagerly to mother's return on the first direct boat in April. ...

1 21 March 1935.   3 Fraser Bond's property at
2 St John's.   Whitbourne.

J.H.S. to Ian and Sheila, Newfoundland Hotel, 24 March 1935

... Today is Sunday. All sorts of luxury. I had breakfast in my own room at

9 o'clock. ... And this is a lovely day of sunshine and east wind, and the snow in the town is melting fast, though the hills across the harbour do not yet show definite signs of thaw. You cannot tell from day to day, or even from hour to hour, what the weather will do, but we do rejoice in a great deal of sunshine. That I should say was the outstanding meteorological feature of this country. I wish very much that you two could pay us a visit some time. It would be interesting to you from many angles. Not least as an instance of a microcosm very little affected by the tides of European progress. In many ways, we are here in the 18th century.

I think I must have told you of the educational struggle through which we were passing three weeks ago. It was definitely a struggle of church versus state. In matters educational, if a state ever wishes to institute progressive reform, it is, I think, almost inevitable that it will experience opposition from the Catholic Church. I forget whether I sent you anything after our Waterloo – Monday the 11th inst. That was a most anxious day. It was clear that we could not continue to administer effectively if two-thirds of the population – the Catholics & the Anglicans – were definitely hostile. There were all sorts of threats. This is not for public consumption, but in fact the R.C. Archbishop had threatened that, if we passed our bill, he would order the R.C. Commissioner[1] to resign, and would not allow an R.C. to replace him; that the action of the Commission should be formally condemned from the altar of every R.C. church in the island; that no R.C. should be allowed to take part in the Jubilee[2] celebrations or to accept the King's Jubilee medal. The Anglican Bishop was equally hostile, but evidently has not got similar dictatorial and disciplinary power. In the outports, we should have had all the Anglicans against us. In St. John's, the more liberal would have been with us. All in all, however, administration would have been so difficult as to be impossible. Trentham[3] (the other U.K. Commissioner in St. John's, Lodge, being away on business in New York) and I had sober conferences as to whether we should force the bill through & accept the challenge, or withdraw the bill. We sat in Commission that day from 10 to 1.15, from 3 to 5.30 & finally from 8 till 9.30. At the first session, we amended the bill to provide: 1. for a consultative committee with no executive functions, consisting of two members of each religion, which should serve as liaison between the heads of the churches and the Department[4]; 2. for a force of inspectors, equal numbers of each religion, but under the orders of the department and for inspection of schools, *so far as conveniently possible*, by inspectors of the religion concerned. We maintained the provision that all the power hitherto in the hands of the denominational superintendents (who were in fact dictators of education for their various faiths) should be transferred to the Secretary for Education,[5]

and that the office of superintendent should be abolished. Then we sent
Howley, our R.C. Commissioner, to interview [the] R.C. Archbishop and
[the] Anglican Bishop, to see whether these new provisions would remove
their active hostility to the bill. Neither Trentham nor I believed that
Howley would succeed. But evidently the Commission is more powerful
than we know, for at 8 o'clock Howley came back with the bill accepted!
You may imagine the relief. We at once passed the bill & it is now law.[6]
But I expect that when it is known that we are replacing the R.C. Secretary
for Education (who is really useless, partly because he is under the thumb
of the Archbishop) by a Presbyterian, who is an expert of great parts,[7]
there may be a further storm. However, there we are on much firmer
ground, for it is clear that we can allow no church, or church authority, to
dictate to us as to personnel of our civil service. We have won our Waterloo, and the subsequent skirmishes will not be of great importance.

Howley left for England next morning, and I have his work in addition
to my own. He left *appalling* arrears. Never could I have conceived an
office in such a mess as that office. In his room, Howley has a very large
table, and on it I found 5 file baskets overflowing with papers and the
whole table covered with heaps of papers. When I got to work on them, I
found important papers which had been lying, sometimes for more than 12
months, unanswered and untouched. I will give you an example. I found a
letter from one of the judges, dated 12th March, suggesting the addition of
certain words in a despatch to the Secretary of State.[8] The despatch was
going from Trentham's department. I at once sent an urgent letter to
Trentham – it was the 15th – asking that the words be added and got a
reply that the despatch had been sent on 16th March 1934, without the
additional words! The judge's letter was of the 12th March 1934, and had
been lying there ever since, without action taken. There was another very
important letter, from one of the leading firms of lawyers, dated July 1934,
which had not been acknowledged. And these are just typical instances.
Since I took charge, I suppose I have written between two and three
hundred letters dealing with these arrears. Now I am up to date, & there
are no papers on the table. But it has meant intense application for the last
fortnight, and I have my own very heavy department to administer in
addition. ... One of the features of this position is the inadvisability of
intimacy with any of the people in society. I dine out and entertain, but in
the nature of things we cannot mix. I do not belong, for instance, to the
City Club.[9] It is not that one would be influenced by any friendship, but
that the public might think that one was subject to special influence. That

fact inevitably means loneliness. It is all right when Quita is here – or the Lodges – but at present these three are all away. ...

I am going to lie down for a postprandial invitation. Tomorrow is going to be a very heavy day, with a meeting of the Commission in the afternoon. The Governor is on leave and the Chief Justice – a nasty-tempered, insignificant little man – is acting as chairman. I do not think that is likely to occur again. I have made the position quite clear to the Dominions Office. It is intolerable. ...

1 William R. Howley, Commissioner for Justice.
2 Silver Jubilee (6 May 1935) of the reign of George V.
3 E.N.R. Trentham, Commissioner for Finance.
4 Of Education.
5 Commission of Government equivalent of deputy minister.
6 The new education act became law on 6 April 1935 and came into effect from midnight on 30 June 1935.
7 Lloyd Willard Shaw (b. 1893), a native of New Perth, Prince Edward Island.
8 For Dominion Affairs.
9 At 193 Water St.

J.H.S. to Ian and Sheila, St John's, 2 April 1935
... It is a lovely day of sunshine, but your description of the crocuses and the bulbs makes me realize what a backward country this is. ... I have not yet taken out the car, and do not propose to do so until the middle of May.

We are having busy, and sometimes exciting, times. Things are I think going quite well. Of course, there are all sorts of criticism. I am being trounced now for fixing a minimum limit of ten inches for lobsters. The supply has diminished rapidly, and the alternatives were a close season for several years or a drastic minimum limit of size. The former would have entailed cutting off commercial relations abroad entirely and much deterioration of lobster-catching plant. So I chose the latter, with a consequent storm. I fixed ten inches after very careful examination.

We are just about to start our beaver farms. We are having four or five to commence with and shall extend gradually from year to year. Ultimately, I hope that we shall also have many private beaver farms & go shares with the lessees in the produce. I foresee great prosperity for these farms, and that ultimately they will become an important source of revenue. ...

I am looking forward to meeting Quita next Monday or Tuesday. The weeks normally pass with great rapidity, but I fear this first week in April will be leaden-footed. ...

J.H.S. to Ian, Newfoundland Hotel, 13 April 1935

Mum arrived, very welcome, on Thursday[1] morning, today being Saturday. ... They had a pleasant and quite eventful voyage. You will have heard or seen that they got an S.O.S. from the *Towerbridge* and went to her rescue. ...

We had a great official reception for the Governor who was on board the ship – band and guard of honour & welcome arches, top hats, uniforms and decorations. ...

We are having quite an interesting time. A good deal of progress is being made in various directions. I think that there seems a good chance that, for the first time in history, the merchants of St. John's will be got together to cooperate in marketing codfish. Hitherto, they have spent much time in cutting each the throat of his neighbour. Now I have drafted an act[2] forming them all into an association with a board on which the government nominates three representatives, including the chairman, and it looks as if the merchants were going to accept it. We did a similar thing for the herring trade with great success.

We are also just starting a scheme of district magistrates, dividing the island into six districts, each under a magistrate who will be responsible for all the administration of his district. There will be assistant magistrates under each of them. The service will be modelled on the I.C.S., though of course the magistrates will not have the same powers or be, at least at first, of the same calibre.

Another matter I am agitating [for] is a juvenile offenders colony. They have always been incarcerated with the ordinary criminals in the penitentiary[3] – a regular factory for turning out juvenile criminals. I am planning an agricultural colony[4] for them, without formal restraint, but of course with strict discipline. Our Markland experience goes to show what can be done in reform. ...

1 11 April 1935.
2 The Salt Codfish Act, 1935, of 13 June 1935.
3 In St John's.
4 On the Fraser Bond estate at Whitbourne.

Q.H.S. to Bel,[1] Newfoundland Hotel, 15 April 1935

... We had a lovely voyage – the fiddles[2] on all the way, but great rolling waves that were not upsetting to my internal economy. And we had glorious sunshine & blue seas. When we got into the ice, it was still lovelier. ... There were lots of seals on the floes – they looked like big black slugs: the babies had already changed their lovely white coats for the dark ones, tho' sometimes there would be a patch of white on the breast. ...

We crept round Signal Hill into the Narrows early in the morning. John was watching from 4.30 – so was I – and he was on board by 5.30 – as soon as we dropped anchor. He climbed up a ladder on the ship's side in his top hat and frock coat – all ready for the official reception of the Governor at 9.30.

It is good to be together again & I am very glad to be back here. Everyone is so kind & welcoming. ... It is a very friendly country. We had to be at a Rotary[3] lunch the same morning, so I met everyone at once as all the world & his wife were gathered to do honour to Lady Hastings Anderson[4] who has done splendid work in the Personal Service League.[5] ... I am very fond of her & shall miss her. She ... was shaking all over when she made her reply to the half-hour-long speech which preceded the presentation of an address.

John talks of taking me in a yacht round the south coast to see some of the outports that are terribly distressed; that will be in May. Let's hope for calm seas. ...

1 Her sister Isabel.	3 Rotary Club of St John's.
2 Contrivance for stopping things from rolling or falling off a table in bad weather.	4 Sister-in-law of Sir (David) Murray Anderson.
	5 The Service League of Newfoundland.

J.H.S. to Betty, Newfoundland Hotel, 21 April 1935

... We are losing winter at last, and the snow is melting fast. There has been a lot of mist the last few days, though yesterday was a lovely day of sunshine, and mother & Mrs. Lodge walked up to Signal Hill. Today, there is thick mist and rain and half a gale of wind. ...

I have a full and interesting life, and we are really getting on, I think, though there is a long way to go before things are right. At this time of year, there is always depression. The merchants adopt a defeatist attitude. Everything looks bad. They say that prospects are unfavourable in Portugal and in Spain, in Italy and in Brazil, and in a sense they are. But people have been crying 'wolf' every spring for the last umpteen years, and did so last year also. Yet, last year, they have had the most successful year for very many years. Almost all the fish is sold. Indeed, you could not buy any material amount of fish at any price.

We have all sorts of plans in prospect. ... We are initiating a large road programme, which, if accepted, will mean that at the end of three years you will be able to bring a car over from America at Port aux Basques and drive from there, through Corner Brook & Grand Falls to Botwood – or to Springdale on White Bay. And we are trying to buy the Fraser Bond property at Whitbourne & make it H.Q. for agriculture and Rangers and reformatory[1] and game park and forest school. Altogether, we are having a busy time. ...

1 For juvenile offenders.

Q.H.S. to Betty, Newfoundland Hotel, 24 April 1935

Thursday 25th. ...

Yesterday, I went to see the Grace Hospital[1] (Salvation Army). It is beautifully run & so different from the General Hospital. There were three incubator babies! One was a boy only *1 lb. 2 oz.*! You never saw anything so tiny & so perfect. It looks quite healthy – as much as we could see of it, & we saw its head perfectly; it is only 3 days old & it is still a very healthy red & has a crop of dark hair. It is the mother's 13th child! The other incubator babies were pale but quite healthy. Matron took off the lid for a minute or two so that we could see the babies better. She was so careful & gentle lifting it & putting it back – there must be no shaking or shock.

Some of the cases I saw were terrible – especially the children. Two starved children were brought in from the south coast; one died & it is to be hoped the other will. He is a little skeleton, 4 years old, with a big head & blind eyes and sticks of arms & hands; such a pitiful, pitiless, little forlorn scrap of humanity. He was sitting up or rather crouched over a crust at which he was picking. Matron laid him quietly down. She told me the eyes were in a horrible state when he came in: right out on the cheek hollows, the eye sockets a mass of sores. It makes one's heart ache and one's conscience burn that such horrors should be endured by little children. A very different case was an old man who had been blind for 28 years and has planted & reaped & farmed his little property all through these years & is just fretting to get back to his animals. Such pluck! I have not been able to get the smell of sickness out of my lungs since I came back – not sick smell but the smell of sick sweats & diseased bodies.

I went to the General last week with Mrs. Lodge – the cases there are dreadful; people don't come until they are dreadfully ill. ...

Darling – you should see the ships coming in. I must have seen 30 bankers come through the Narrows today. They are coming in to be fitted out for the fishing season. ...

1 St John's.

Q.H.S. to Ian, Newfoundland Hotel, 26 April 1935

... This last week the snow has been clearing fast – the hills are almost clear except for drifts & pockets. Even in the town, however, some of the roads have banks of snow 6 & 8 ft. high. But the main roads have been cleared. I can hardly believe that there was ice in the harbour less than a fortnight ago. But everyone who has a garden is thrilled to find the bulbs well up. ...

John has had a heavy week with work. He is doing the judicial work for Mr. Howley[1] while he is away for 3 months. He found mountains of arrears & he cleared them off. ...

Another thing he has done in this connection is to get all the magistrates in from the outports. These men are underpaid & often inefficient, and they have nothing to encourage or stimulate their pride in the work and they are often depressed & pretty useless. But there are fine men among them who are doing good work under difficulties. Anyway, the magistrates should be the nucleus of life in these outports, & they may be developed into a great service for the island. As a start, John called them all in, and, at the government's expense, they have had 10 days' holiday here at the hotel, meeting each other & meeting other people here. And John arranged for various people to give them talks on different aspects of their work. The finish-up was that he gave them a dinner and took them all to the cinema to see 'Bengal Lancer.'[2] The whole thing has been a huge success. Those men have gone back to their jobs knowing now that they are important links in the chain of the new government, & that at headquarters their work is watched and assessed and the value of their work & personal conduct to the community in which they work is considered of the first importance. One of these magistrates was drunk & disorderly in the hotel dining-room the first day, & he was sent back & could have been dismissed but that he has done 30 years' service & is due for his pension. Also, these are early days and new ways, and two years ago no one would have thought anything of a magistrate going on the spree when he came in to town, probably for the first time in his life. But he must have got the surprise of his life, poor fellow. Anyway, it startled other people into a realization that the days are past when an official could behave like that. This place is 100 years behind the times in every way, as you must have heard us say before. But, you know, they are such nice people – so responsive to right leadership. ...

Talking of their being behind the times, the conditions of the shop assistants here is dreadful. They are so underpaid, and the hours are unlimited. I have heard of two cases where the delivery van arrived to deliver orders for Saturday at 1.30 a.m. on Sunday. They dare not complain; there are plenty of unemployed who would jump at the job. A friend told me she had withdrawn her custom from the biggest shop because of this very instance of late delivery at her own house. She chanced to have to go into the shop for something, and the head of the firm had evidently been told she was there, for he came out and said he was sorry to find that she had withdrawn her custom; might he know the reason? She told him straight. He said: 'The men will stop for their tea; they could finish by 10.30 if they went on.'! She was furious: 'You expect men & horses to go straight on from midday without rest or food!' 'They have never complained,' he said. The shopkeepers are also the merchants – they are the aristocracy of the place, if you can call them so; but you can't call it an aristocracy of birth or ability or service in any sense as a rule. Lots of them are very nice people and duty doing up to their lights, but they have very little light. It's dawning, I think, & the process is painful; enlightenment shows such terrible wrongs. I told you about pay in the shops being so low. Girls are so badly paid they can't live on their pay. They would have to go on the streets if the Y.W.C.A. did not give them a home, for which they cannot pay. And the shopkeepers contribute to the Y.W.C.A. to some extent & they subscribe to the schools & get some kudos from it, but they don't pay their employees as they ought & they don't teach them as they ought. There is no convenience for the girls in most of the big shops! It is wicked.

It is not only the shopkeepers who are cruelly selfish & thoughtless for their employees. Women go to the cinema on Saturday evening, &, when they come out, they do their shopping for the weekend & expect the goods to be delivered that night. ...

Sunday.[3] A glorious day – the harbour water shimmering like ripple silk – Quidi Vidi Lake blue as the sky above it & not a sign of the ice that covered it a week ago and was still half over a solid mass two days ago. Yesterday afternoon, it was snowing – big flakes. Now, the air is quivering with a heat mist. I will tell you one curious thing I had not seen last year – the steaming[4] of all the roads – so nasty because they smell so, & you can't quite keep your nose above the steam. ...

1 Commissioner for Justice.   3 28 April 1935.
2 *The Lives of a Bengal Lancer*,   4 Caused by drying.
   starring Gary Cooper, played at the
   Capitol Theatre on Henry St.

J.H.S. to Maisie, St John's, 5 May 1935

... I have had a lot of work and we have all had a good deal of worry since I last wrote. As I dare say you have seen, there have been two disgraceful reports in the British press about conditions in St. John's sent by a local correspondent.[1] He is a man of no good reputation here, where everyone knows him, but he has succeeded in creating a stir in England through articles in the *Daily Herald*, which were gross misrepresentations of the position. He stated that the Commissioners had to have police protection when they went to their offices! And that we had the police armed with rifles & bayonets. I expect that he referred to the guard of honour at the arrival of H.E. the Governor – but he did not say that. He suggested that it was to overawe a starving multitude. Anyone who read the articles would have concluded that St. John's was seething with starving disaffection and on the verge of revolt. The case is exactly the reverse. Of course, there are a large number of unemployed – perhaps 1,500 – but conditions are better than they have been for the past ten years, and the dole is 25 per cent better than last year, with fewer people on it. Of course, there is lots of misery, as there is in Liverpool. And that fact is being used by disgruntled ex-politicians as a weapon with which to attack the government. And we have to waste precious time in concocting explanations to be used in answer to questions in Parliament.[2] ...

Quita & I start for a fortnight or three weeks on the south coast at the end of this week. We are going in our bait ship, the *Malakoff*, some 150 or 160 tons. It will not be comfortable, but we shall wander along from bay to bay as the weather serves, and I think we shall take one of the planes to help us out. ...

1 The journalist in question, probably   'representative of the United Press
   John T. Meaney (1871?–1943), was   and British United Press' in
   identified only as a special corres-   St John's (*Daily News*, St John's,
   pondent (*Daily Herald*, London,   11 May 1935, 3).
   17 April 1935, 1, 4). Meaney was the   2 U.K. Parliament.

Q.H.S. to Bel, Newfoundland Hotel, 7 May 1935

... I have sent you a sample of Nonia hand-weaving, which I think is a pretty thing. I expect you have heard Lady Allardyce talk of 'Nonia.' ... It was started by the wife[1] of the former Governor before Sir William Allardyce,[2] and Lady Allardyce[3] was tremendously keen on it – could talk & think of nothing else apparently. The idea was that the people in the outports should be taught to knit & weave & that the produce of their labour should pay for district nurses. In fact, it did not work out like that; the outports that were better off & more intelligent did the work for which there was a sale, and the outports that were literally on the rocks were too stupefied by poverty & poor living that their work – when they were taught – was not worth buying. As nearly always happens with these matters, as long as the Governor's wife took an interest, it went with a swing. But a new Governor came, & his wife took up some other equally or more urgent need, and Nonia declined till, from about 32 nurses, there were only 4 or 5. Now the government has taken on the whole of public welfare and has organized a district nursing service for the island ... and Nonia survives only as an industrial voluntary association to help the outport women to weave & knit & sell their goods. The hooked mats are the nicest things they do, but, unfortunately, they have to use cheap materials & cannot guarantee the colours. I meant to send you one of them, but there are none I can ... just now, and it seems such a waste to buy a rug that is going to fade at once.

I have just received a medal! *'From Buckingham Palace* by command of His Majesty the King the accompanying medal is forwarded to Lady Mary Jane Hope Simpson to be worn in commemoration of their Majesties' Silver Jubilee. 6th May 1935.' All the members of the Commission and their wives have received them – we just because we are the wives. It is rather thrilling tho', isn't it? A nice thing to have, & one need have no modesty in enjoying it because there is no question of deserts involved. ... I wonder whether there is any form of acknowledgement required – a curtsey at Buckingham Palace. I have often thought lately that it was stupid for me not to have been presented. John has done so many important jobs I think I ought not to have neglected this duty. ...

May 8. We have to put off our trip to the south coast. John cannot get away at present. The *Malakoff* was to have started tomorrow for Placentia. Well anyway, there is more chance of having calmer warmer weather. I see that only a little further north on the island logs are still being hauled by horses over the ice-bound lakes, so there's a good deal of thawing to be done yet before we can believe that spring is here. ...

1 Constance Maria (Shute) Harris (d. 1941), wife of Sir (Charles) Alexander Harris (1855–1947), Governor of Newfoundland, 1917–22. Lady Harris and Evelyn Cave Hiscock (1885–1944) started an outport nursing service which was reorganized by Lady Allardyce in April 1924 as Nonia.

2 Sir William Allardyce (1861–1930), Governor of Newfoundland, 1922–8.

3 Elsie Elizabeth (Stewart) Allardyce (1878–1962).

Q.H.S. to Maisie, Newfoundland Hotel, 9 May 1935

Just look out of our bedroom window! 'Mid-winter again!' you would say. The land is covered with snow again and the wind is whistling past my windows. The waves are flinging their spray high up the rocks below the lighthouse point, but out beyond the Narrows a band of calm greeny white – must be slob ice.[1] I can see to the horizon – a leaden sea slashed with flashing white – but the mists are whirling high now, and rain blotted out the pale radiance that showed when the sun had risen. It is early yet – not yet 7 – so the day may change. I am *thankful* we are not starting on our tour tomorrow. That wicked south coast would be horrible in weather like this in a 200-ton boat. Such a change from last year at this time when we had already had a lovely summer weekend at Placentia. ...

Luckily, we had a fair day for the Jubilee celebrations on Monday.[2] But, in spite of glorious sunshine, the wind was icy. St. John's rose to the occasion well, however – flags everywhere and illuminations at night; even the slums seemed to have managed to raise a few coloured lights to put in the windows.

We started with the official thanksgiving service in the cathedral.[3] The Commissioners all sat in a row with their wives and made a joyful noise. The cathedral was packed. ... Promptly at 11, the Bishop & Canons met the Governor & Lady Anderson at the great door & conducted them to their seats in front of us. We had the same service as St. Paul's[4] – very simple and beautiful & a sermon from the Bishop – a funny little pinched cock robin with a big voice. After that, we had to dash to Bannerman Park, but our car would not dash. Another had backed into us and we could not reverse; half the congregation seemed to come to our help, but the lady would only gently rock to & fro. So we had to leave our carefully decorated car & accept a lift. There was an hour's wait in an icy wind while the children of the 44 schools, 8,000 of them, marched past the Governor to their stations in front of the platform. It really was a wonderful sight – 8,000 children, each carrying a Union Jack, the colours fluttering in the wind like massed anemones. I don't think the children felt the cold, they were so tightly packed. But Mr. Trentham, *very* smart city man for the occasion, was clad in thin summer trousers & frock-coat only, with his top hat & furled umbrella on his arm – just ready for a walk down Bond St.[5] on a summer Sunday. His big nose went bluer & bluer, & he was shivering visibly. I felt 'I told you so–ish' because I had begged him before we left to turn back for a coat. However, he seems none the worse, tho' he is the wiser. We had speeches which were broadcast, & the children sang a song[6] that was written & sung for the King & Queen when they visited the island as Prince & Princess of Wales in 1901. And the old man[7] who conducted them conducted the children who sang it so long ago. He was fine, with his grey locks blowing in the wind, all the force & enthusiasm of the long ago recaptured for this occasion as he swung his body to right & left & up & down to the beating of his arms & baton. It was fine – so well done.

Then the children marched back to their schools, where they received a box of chocolates with the King & Queen on it, & home to a belated meal at 3 o'c. We got our lunch about 2 & hurried off to listen in to the Empire Broadcast[8] in a friend's room. It came through very well & was very moving. In the evening, at 9 o'c., there was a reception at Government House (Fire! – Fire! – Fire! – there goes the fire engine, & there is the house with smoke streaming from the roof, the gale blowing the smoke flat across the house tops). And there go the flags up on Cabot Tower signalling the *Nova Scotia* from Boston to Halifax. – Well! that's quick work! – not five minutes & the fire is extinguished, and the men climbing back onto the engine & off again! That is one service on which the St. John's men pride themselves, & it would need to be a good one; these wooden houses are so quickly burnt down, & if one goes, half a dozen may go – it would not take long to lay the whole town in ashes again.

Government House was floodlighted, & the Colonial Building ('Sir John Hope Simpson's house,' Mrs. Alderdice says she heard it called) had its pillars & arches all outlined with 2,300 lights. This hotel too was illuminated, & lots of public buildings were well done. So it was all very gay this week. The bonfires & fireworks were to have been on Tuesday[9] night, but mist came up over the town, so this was postponed till a fine evening. Next night seemed to promise a clear fine atmosphere, & at 7 o'c. the gun announced that the show would be carried on. But at 9 o'c. mist crept over again, & the rockets were lost in dimness & we could only occasionally see the nearest bonfires as the mist broke & closed again. The whole of St. John's & many of the nearest outports had collected on the south-side heights & I should think there must have been 2,000 cars up there – almost all the cars in the island. ...

I have just had a visit from Miss Geen,[10] who came out on the ship with me; she is the new child welfare person – a very nice, tactful, highly trained woman – St. Thomas's[11] hospital–trained and welfare-trained & with years of experience. She tells me that in all the public health department there is not a single doctor or other official who has had any welfare training and she is in the difficult position of having to decide whether to tell them things they ought in their position to know! She has drawn up a paper of suggestions for her committee for their approval to place before the health department. ...

1 Heavy, slushy ice.

2 6 May 1935.

3 Anglican Cathedral of St John the Baptist.

4 London, England.

5 London, England.

6 'Hail to the Prince.'

7 Charles W. Hutton (1861–1949).

8 From the B.B.C.

9 7 May 1935.

10 Dorothy Geen arrived in St John's on 11 April 1935 to become Superin-tendent of the Child Welfare Association.

11 London, England.

J.H.S. to Ian and Sheila, St John's, 14 May 1935

... We have been having trouble with agitators of the unemployed. There is a communist deportee from Canada who has constituted himself chairman of a self-appointed unemployed committee, which consists of an ex-theo-logical student who failed to get a church, an ex-serviceman who has been convicted 12 times (once for robbery), a man who has been in jail for bigamy, and an ex-serviceman with a pension and a very bad moral reputa-tion.[1] These five demanded: 1. that they should be recognized officially as representatives of the unemployed body; 2. that they should be placed in complete charge of relief works; 3. that the relief dept. should have no say in the choice of people to work on relief works. Of course, those demands were rejected. So, last Friday, when they found their following melting away as registration for relief works went on, they held a procession & tried to force their way into my office.[2] The police prevented that and were attacked with stones. The police charged with batons, the crowd ran like rabbits and all was over in two minutes. That night, they had another meeting and then processed down Water St., the chief business street, & broke windows & looted one boot shop before the police could arrive. When they did, the crowd bolted at once. We have arrested the ringleaders, & the town has been entirely quiet ever since. It was bound to come, & it has demonstrated to the mob the extraordinary change in the efficiency of the police. They were looked upon under the last regime as beneath contempt. There was a riot in 1932[3] when the Inspector General of Police[4] was confined in the parliament building (my office) for several hours – he was in terror – and the police did not know what to do and shut themselves into the office also. I suppose that the crowd expected the same sort of thing to happen. But we have a new chief of police,[5] and the men have been properly trained and are proud of themselves. Now the whole of the mob has a very wholesome respect for the police, and the town generally feels very much happier than it did. I am, for the time being, in charge of the police, so, on Saturday[6] morning, I had a parade to thank them & tell them how proud I am that they behaved so well. ...

1 The committee of the unemployed in St John's consisted of Pierce (Pearce) Power, George Wilkinson, Herbert Saunders, John Cadwell, and Joseph Milley.
2 For an account of the disturbances in St John's see the *Daily News*, St John's, 11 May 1935, 3. Four members of the unemployed committee – Power, Wilkinson, Milley, and Saunders – were charged afterwards but acquitted. Three other men – Stephen Whelan, Denis Clancy, and James McCarthy – were tried with them and convicted.
3 5 April 1932.
4 C.H. Hutchings.
5 Patrick J. O'Neill (1883–1944), Chief of Police, 1934–44.
6 11 May 1935.

J.H.S. to Maisie, Newfoundland Hotel, 14 May 1935

... The season here is very late. The rain yesterday washed a lot of the snow away, but there are still patches on the hills across the harbour. The grass is rapidly turning from brown to green, but there are as yet no signs of leaves on the trees and our northern harbours are blocked with ice. ... We see a great many icebergs passing the entrance to the Narrows. I would not like to be captain of a steamer in these seas, with their dangerous combination of ice & fog. ...

I often wish that we could leave this place by the next boat. I am going to be 67 in July, and have worked more or less strenuously – generally more – since I was 14. From the purely selfish viewpoint, I should love to be at home and to settle down in a vegetable life in Dorset[1] or Roxburghshire,[2] or somewhere in beautiful quiet country. Yet, at present, it looks as if duty kept me busy here. I am at liberty to give three months' notice next November & to leave in February 1936. Whether I do so or not depends in some measure on the financial needs of the family. ... I am most thankful for health & strength and ability. As long as I have these, it may be my duty to continue working. Yet I miss you all very much indeed. And Quita is longing for you all the whole time. ...

1 England.   2 Scotland.

Q.H.S. to Ian and Sheila, Newfoundland Hotel, 16 May 1935

... We are starting on Saturday[1] for our tour of the south of the island. We had to put it off last week. Now the *Malakoff* is loaded up with herring bait and we should have a sweet time. I just hope the weather will keep fine. I was thankful we did not get off last week, for there was a howling gale all the weekend & bitter cold. It is not warm yet & the wind still blows – but not a gale, & the sun shines. We can have only a fortnight away – less – so we have had to cut short our tour & leave out a lot of ports & come back from Port aux Basques by train.

I had a most interesting time at the C. of E. hostel[2] for girls yesterday. I went to tea with Miss Cherrington,[3] who is in charge of the C. of E. school for girls here – about 300 girls. She is an Englishwoman & very fine woman, devoted to the work & the girls. But it is an uphill fight. She has made the hostel with the help of her friend the matron,[4] whom she brought out from England. I believe she has made the school too, but I did not hear much about that yesterday – it was the hostel's day. She told me many queer things that would interest you if I had time & you had time. Her biggest fight & her most unpopular victory was for the weekly half-holiday. The parents were furious – felt they were being defrauded; the council[5] too thought so! The teacher is to teach as many hours as possible. The Memorial College has shortened its hours, hoping to encourage the students to venture out on their own account into pastures new. But will they? No, they will not. They hang about, don't know what to do with themselves, and feel they are being defrauded. On this side of the water, in Canadian universities & schools, the students are not encouraged to read for themselves – no questions are allowed to be set in examination that cannot be answered from the set books. Miss Cherrington is trying to get the girls to do domestic science because they get no training in their homes – the mothers are so ignorant, & housekeeping is so bad. But it is 'common' to do domestic science, & the parents are jealous of their children knowing more than they do themselves. And games are unladylike. But these ladies have never learnt to wash properly, & that is one of the greatest difficulties at the hostel – with beautiful bathing & washing arrangements – to get the students to use them. They have not been used to the decencies of civilised life & don't care about them. These are young women 20–24 – rather difficult to say to them: 'You must wash properly – you smell disgusting.'

Questions of morality are a great difficulty too. 'The men have got to know we can have a child or they won't marry us.' One of the padres told Daddy the same thing – more than half the marriages have to be in a hurry. It is a most degraded condition of society – far worse, I think, than many savage tribal states; they have sanctions, brutal but cleansing to society.

I must away. ...

1 18 May 1935.
2 Spencer Lodge, Rennies Mill Rd. Later Bishop Jones Hostel. Catered to young outport women attending Bishop Spencer College and Memorial University College in St John's.

3 Violet Cherrington (1886–1956), headmistress of Bishop Spencer College, St John's, 1922–52.
4 Mabel Baudains.
5 Possibly the Council of Higher Education.

J.H.S. to Greta, on board the *Malakoff*, Port aux Basques, 25 May 1935
... Quita and I are by way of having a holiday, but it is a regular busman's holiday. We were to have left St. John's last Saturday[1] afternoon, but it was blowing a northeasterly gale, with fog, so we sent this ship, which is our bait freezer and about 160 tons, ahead to Placentia, where it should have arrived on Sunday morning. We drove out there, 84 miles, on Sunday & found no *Malakoff*, so we waited. She arrived at 6 p.m., & we went on board and started at 7. It was a nasty, rough night, and Fudge (Chief Fishery Inspector) was ill & Mother took Mothersill[2] & laid low. I was alone at breakfast on Monday. The weather cleared up, the sun came out, &, in the lee of the deckhouse, it became quite warm, so I got Quita into a deck chair & we had a lovely afternoon sail round St. Pierre and along the

south of Miquelon,³ and arrived at Cape La Hune in the evening and anchored in a little bay at the mouth of the fjord. Just like Norway.

That evening, we rowed a mile & a half across the bay to the settlement – some 30 houses & a little church in a crick in the hills – wretched houses and wretched people. We visited a lot of the houses and found one house where a child appeared to be dying of pneumonia after flu. The child was five years old and was in a wooden baby's cradle with rockers, & the mother rocking it all the time. It was a lovely sunny evening.

Next day, Tuesday,⁴ was again a magnificent day in the bay, but there was a wall of fog outside, and, as we had to call at all kinds of little outports approached by narrow channels among the rock & shoals, the captain did not dare to leave. We spent all day there, hoping for the fog to clear away, but it stayed there solidly from dawn till dark.

On Wednesday morning, we got away before five and by seven were entering Grey River. The entrance is so narrow as to be practically invisible until you are actually on it. The settlement is about 2 miles up the river and is a dismal place. Here are my notes: 'A nightmare settlement. Clothing appalling. Saw girl in school in cotton nightshirt & bare legs. Houses dilapidated. Everyone short of trawls and nets but all have dories (i.e., rowboats). No potato seed. Very little work done in gardens. People not fit to work. About 30 families. 23 children in the school. Lots of wood, but lethargy prevents any repairs – e.g., government wharf. Barter, schoolmaster, decent fellow.' It is the worst settlement I have seen. The people are dishonest, so no one will advance supplies & they are so demoralized that they are content to live on the dole rather than make an effort to work.

We went to Ramea Islands. There things are much better. We lunched with the local merchant. That was a mistake, but unavoidable. I feel that, when we consort with the merchant, we are avoided by the fishermen, who are the men we are out to meet.

We went on to Burgeo that afternoon, where conditions were said to be bad but were not obviously so. We inspected school & church & courthouse. Teaed⁵ with the local merchant & dined on board. After dinner, Quita was off to a show at the school. We are running on summer time. There they keep God's time, so she got back at 11.45 our time & I had been up since 4.50!

We laid up at Burgeo that night &, in the morning, sailed out into a lovely dawn, but there was a heavy southwesterly swell & our little boat pitched & rolled along under the sunshine. By 9, we got into Grand Bruit – a jolly little settlement placed underside of a roaring waterfall. We did our usual inspections & talked to everyone we met and came away feeling that things are not too bad there. The view from the church above the settlement, out to sea, is glorious – great reefs and rocks where the swell surged up and broke in masses of lace and between & beyond the deep blue of the ocean. As we sailed out, a beautiful schooner sailed in, & we passed cheek by jowl.

We next ran into La Poile Bay & rounded a point in the west side of the bay into Little Bay – again quite invisible till we came to the entrance. Little Bay is not a prosperous place – about 30 families – half one side of the bay, half the other. There is a retired merchant named LeSelleurs[6] – descended from Jersey people – who lives there all alone in a beautiful house. We inspected church & school, which is held in the church, and then went on board for lunch, and after lunch sailed up the La Poile Bay and then up the N.E. Arm – I suppose 10 miles from the entrance. There we found an unexpected little settlement of four houses of Stricklands and MacDonalds. Such nice people – and of them only one could read and he only a little. The old people were John & Nehemiah Strickland. The settlement had cleared quite a considerable area of woodland & had sheep – lots of them – and a cow, and, in the winter, they cut logs for sale & trap fur, and, in the summer, they fish. They are evidently very comfortable, but they are very hard-working people. We came back in the evening & anchored for the night in Little Bay.

Yesterday – Friday – morning, we left at 5.30 and got into Rose Blanche, a tortuous channel through the rocks, by 8. It was again a lovely day, with a heavy sea from the south and half a gale of wind from the N.E. Rose Blanche should be very prosperous, but the merchants have the fishermen in a state of serfdom. Prices are appallingly high and all the fishermen are in debt, permanently, to the merchants. I had a meeting of the fishermen there, and their language on the subject was lurid. It is a difficult problem which, as yet, we have not touched. I shall have to tackle it in the near future.

Our next port of call was Burnt Islands. We could not have got in there had the weather not been fine. Things there are bad – great poverty, dreadful clothing and a good deal of skin disease – dirt. There are 72 families &, of these, 48 are on the dole, though the winter fishery has been good. A great deal of the poverty is due to fecklessness and laziness, but that again is due to underfeeding for long years. It is a case of building up from the bottom.

We then went into Isle aux Morts, said to be the worst settlement on the coast, but not nearly so bad as we feared. The people were decent, cheery folk, & the children looked well on the whole. Quita had a lot of boiled sweets, & you can imagine the fun as crowds of children scrambled for handfuls thrown broadcast over the rocks. We had a meeting there in the schoolhouse – a most dilapidated wreck of a building. Then we walked back to the boat – Quita like a pied piper with all the children round her. Thence we rowed to the *Malakoff* & steamed for this place,[7] where we arrived about 7.30.

It has been a jolly and most useful trip. Now we take the railway and shall stop at Stephenville Crossing (St. George's Bay) & go out to Port au Port. We stay there a day & get back for the next express, which will contain Mr. & Mrs. Graves.[8] ...

1 18 May 1935.	5 Had tea.
2 A preventive for seasickness.	6 Thomas LeSelleurs.
3 French-owned islands.	7 Port aux Basques.
4 21 May 1935.	8 Cecil and Irene Graves.

Q.H.S. to Ian, on board S.S. *Malakoff*, Port aux Basques, 25 May 1935
... We left on our trip last Sunday. We should have started on Saturday, but it was such a wild stormy day we let the S.S. *Malakoff* do the voyage round Cape Race without us. We felt quite bad when we stood at our window in warmth & peace & comfort & watched our little ship go full steam out through the storm into such tempestuous seas – such a brave little ship she looked! We saw her rise & fall on the first great seas & then was lost in the mist & driving rain.

Next day was glorious, & we drove across the Avalon Peninsula to Placentia to await the *Malakoff*. She had a bad tossing & was 9 hours late. We got on board her in the evening. It was still very rough, but I took Mothersill and survived all right, & have not been at all seasick, tho' we have had quite big seas. It was all right, but Mr. Fudge, our companion, the chief fishery officer, was very sick.

We went straight out & across Placentia Bay & round outside St. Pierre & Miquelon, the rocky French islands, across 'the sailors' grave' to the Newfoundland coast. Such a wild, inhospitable coast it is: jagged perpendicular cliffs & solid granite – a wall with apparently no break in it. But then we came to two great humps of solid granite, & they opened two water-ways for us – like fjords. Very tricky navigation all along the coast.

It is like the Britanny coast[1] further on – great jagged rocks sticking up out of the sea, & the settlement houses perched on the rocky coasts & inlets with no means of communication except by boat.

La Hune was our first port of call up one of the fjords. We slipped in between the great guardian humps into quiet waters, & the doors closed behind us. Then, round the corner of one hump, a church on a shingle beach with about 120 houses huddled behind a low hump of rock & open to the open sea on the far side – just a low isthmus joining the great outer side to the mainland – so low that a dyke has been built to prevent the settlement being swept away in stormy high tides. Even as it is, the houses are often awash at high tide.

Up on the flat rocks above the church, but such a climb!, a tiny grave-yard, so pathetic. I can't think how they find a pocket of soil in which to bury their dead. They would be better in the sea, where they belong.

We landed before dinner and walked round the settlement. It is a most miserable place – so poor – so wretched. The children ran away like little wild animals & hid at our approach. We went into some of the houses. The people hardly stirred when we came in. The men lounged on benches with their hands in their pockets; the women went about their business, taking little notice of us at first, picking up sticks, feeding the fire or just sitting like the men. All looked dreadfully dirty, the men grey & unshaven, their clothing ragged & patched; the children many of them in a cotton nightgown with bare feet, the women often with nothing under a cotton gown & the snow still lying down to the seashore in many places. We heard of a very sick boy & went to see him. We found the rooms crowded, & the boy, a child of 5, lying in a baby's wooden cradle, the mother rocking it with her foot continually. He coughed feebly, but his eyes were sensible & I don't think he was dying. An old decent woman, the grand-mother, was feeling her way about with a stick – 'I can get about but I can't see to do a bit of sewing.' I made her try my glasses, &, as she was able to produce a Bible, she tried them & was delighted to find she could read. It is very unusual to find readers in these outports, so I left her a pair of my 1/. Woolworth glasses. There is no clergyman – the schoolmaster acts as lay reader; he is a lad of low qualifications – about 3rd standard of an elementary school. But I found when I talked to him later that he is fond of children and wants to improve himself. I gave him *How to Tell Stories to Children*[2] (Bryant's) and a pile of newspapers – *Times*[3] & *Listeners*.[4]

Grey River, another port of call, was even worse. A very difficult en-trance to the harbour but a very good harbour. The settlement was about

1 mile down a deep fjord and at the foot of a wooded gorge. Not long ago, an avalanche nearly overwhelmed the village; the waterfall was diverted & almost swept it away – the people had to take to the woods. They are a feckless lot. Despite the fact that there is wood at their doors, the wharf is broken & dangerous to walk on & the wooden houses in a state of dreadful disrepair, leaking and slatternly, while the men sit about with their hands in their pockets doing nothing. We were there very early because we are on summer time & they keep to sun time and, in many houses, the children were not up. Some of the women & children here looked terrible. I always had sweeties⁵ & papers that I have been saving up to distribute. I made friends with the children very quickly with the candies, & there is usually someone in a settlement who can read & glad of literature. I am quickly learning the science of making friends with these people.

They are queer people. Wherever we go, we get a first impression of unfriendliness, and at first I was terribly daunted & felt almost afraid – shy of entering a house, fearful of intruding – almost afraid the men might attack us, and more afraid that the children would hate us. But it has been our experience everywhere that all this apparent unfriendliness is a sort of smokescreen of shyness, almost indeed a custom of the country. Very quickly it goes down before an assault, and before we leave the people are responsive & friendly, following us in crowds, & we depart in an atmosphere of kindliness & friendliness.

The most marked case was yesterday at Isle aux Morts. We had heard of the place ever since we came – that the people were a hopeless lot – degenerates mostly & past hope from the human point of view. We made a skilful entrance into a difficult rock-strewn harbour. We were greeted as a salute (as we are in many of these little settlements) by the sounding of the foghorn (so weird on an exquisite clear sunny day), and our ship responds with three blasts of her siren. In addition, at Isle aux Morts, we were welcomed with rifle shots. All very cheering. Also, the settlement did not look nearly as bad as Grey River or La Hune. We anchored about a mile from the wharf, as we have to do in most places. On the wharf lounged about a dozen men, lying on a pile of planks. They let us approach without moving to greet us, as usual. I had a little difficulty in climbing up the wharf & asked for help to get over the edge. At once, two men leapt to my help – so kindly – & pulled me up. They all subsided again on the logs. 'Well, how are things with you here?' 'Worse than ever before. Isn't that so, lads? Worse than ever before they are; and that's so.' 'But you've had good fishing this winter, haven't you?' 'Yes, that's so, plenty of fish there be.' 'Yes, plenty fish,' corroborated the crowd; then silence. We know what that means – low prices for their fish & high prices for their supplier & the merchant getting all the profits. The truck system is the ruin of the people.

'Well, have you got a school?' 'It's called a school; it's a ruin – if you go in you'll come out pretty smart, I reckon. I suppose you've come to see what's to be seen?' So we started off over the rocks. A few children were standing about – I gave them 'candies.' More gathered, till presently we had a crowd, growing as we went, & by the time we got to the school, they were all chattering & laughing.

The school was truly a dreadful place, great holes in the floor & a broken roof. But the crowd pushed in after us, & I suggested that the children make room for the men & they were sent out, & the men crowded in & Daddy talked to them, asking them questions & making notes of their difficulties & telling them what the government is doing & suggesting what they could do to get the benefit of opportunities that are being offered to fishermen. The men warmed to it & talked more freely than anywhere we had been. As the crowd of men went out, children poured in again, & while John talked to some of the men who had waited behind for further questions, I talked to the children & told them a story – *The Three Little Pigs*. It was a most inspiring audience – I don't think anyone can ever have told them a story before; they gaped, and waves of laughter rippled to & fro. There was a group of men lounging round the door & they bent forward to listen, & I became conscious of a big, fat merchant with only one leg who had subsided into one of the children's desks beside me – his rubicund face & staring blue eyes were fixed in attention & appreciation as keen as the children. It was a delight to be able to give so much pleasure with such a little thing. Outside again, the hillside was crowded with children, so I gave them a scramble for candies – luckily, I had lots with me because I [had] heard this was a place where the children never have anything. They did enjoy it, and so did the men watching them & the women in the doorways. It was a very different crowd that followed us to the boat when we returned, & I did not need to ask for help to climb down the wharf edge to John's helping hands below.

It always comes as a surprise to me when these children talk English – they seem such little foreigners – so wild & furtive. One little figure specially stands out in my memory – a girl child of about six with straight fair hair & delicate features, standing on the edge of a wharf seeing us off from Grey River – barelegged & barefooted in a grimy white nightgown, snow on the hillside behind her. I wanted to go back & wrap her in my coat & carry her into her house.

In these small places, very few of the people can read. 'I've no learnin',' they say. At Isle aux Morts, the fat, one-legged merchant was the only man who could read & the only fat man, & there were from 80 to 100 of them. I am sending him some papers. Even when there are men who can read, like the schoolmasters, they get no books. There are travelling libraries started, so I hope these people will get the use of them. Salaries are so low the schoolmasters can't afford to buy books or get newspapers. I am going to send *The Children's Newspaper*[6] to the man at Grey River; then he can read it to the children.

Here[7] there are 2 big schools, 300 in the Anglican, which is under a fine young fellow who has been under Dr. Paton's influence for 5 years & is keen as he can be; the other, with 150 children, is a United Church school. But this is a big, fairly prosperous settlement.

But the roads through the settlement are just mud and rock. It is a lovely spot really – it reminds me of Mallaig[8] on the Scotch coast. The sea is deep right up to the shore – you see the shore fall away in a precipice at the water's edge, so that big ships come right up to the wharf. The Corner Brook paper mills (the International Power & Paper Company) have a huge storing & packing shed here – the finest in the world, we are told, built last year by the Commission. The I.P.P. will pay for it over 10 years. That is a great benefit to the place.

We have seen 11 settlements since we left a week ago, all along the south coast – all most interesting. In two, there were Nonia nurses – government nurses they are now. There has not been a single doctor along until we got here – about 200 miles without a doctor. The hospital ship,[9] with doctor, 2 nurses & 4 beds, is going to be a tremendous boon to these forsaken people.

I could go on and on telling you of our experiences, but you are busy people. We are in our carriage in the railway now and this will be our home for the next 5 days, till we get back to St. John's. We go on tonight to Stephenville Crossing, where we leave the coach for one night to do two out-of-the-way settlements on the west coast. ...

1 France.
2 By Sara Cone Bryant (b. 1873). The book was published in Boston in 1905.
3 Of London, England.
4 Published by the B.B.C.
5 Candy.
6 Published in London, England, 1919–65.
7 At Port aux Basques.
8 At entrance to Loch Nevis, West Inverness-shire, Scotland.
9 The M.V. *Lady Anderson*.

Q.H.S. to Maisie and Blair, c/o Mr & Mrs House, Aguathuna, 27 May 1935
... From Port aux Basques by train to Stephenville Crossing, we found
conditions very different. Instead of bare rock, lovely land & plough &
decent houses.

We were met by a car, the doctor's,[1] & driven 20 miles by the doctor's
son (whom we tipped) to Aguathuna, where we stayed with the Houses.[2]
The place is really created by the limestone quarry company, Aguathuna
being the Indian name for limestone. The name of the town used to be Jack of
Clubs because of a rock there, but the company changed it. ... They gave
us a great welcome – arches of spruce branches & flags everywhere & cheers.

We also went on from there by boat to Piccadilly! (Pic à Dennis[3] originally), where Mr. House has a beautiful hygienic clam factory.[4] We saw it
all, & the employees here gave us a great welcome & we lunched off fresh
lobster in the staff house & then went on to West Bay. Here we had to
disembark first into a small motorboat & then into a dory, the fisherman's
little boat – a most wobbly affair. I nearly tipped it over when I turned to
speak to Daddy. When we got near the shore, a lot of men waded out to
meet us and dragged us in & rushed us few up the shore through the
crowd of people, some of whom had walked 10 miles to greet us. They
fired off guns, and there was an arch of welcome to us as at Aguathuna, &
Father O'Reilly,[5] the priest, & Father Curwen,[6] the priest from Aguathuna,
were there to greet us. Then we had to get into a sort of buggy all beflagged,
and next thing we knew we were back in Somerset in the after-election
excitement[7] & about 30 men had harnessed themselves to our buggy. The
fat jolly priest & I sat in front, & Daddy stood up behind, & away we
went careening over the most appalling road, the crowd running alongside
laughing & chattering. It was 1½ miles to Lourdes & a very heavy road,
but the men kept changing places and we never stopped or were thrown
out. At Lourdes, there was another great triumphant arch of spruce, and
the women & children were lined up waving flags & they threw bunches
of mayflowers in front of us. It was such a pretty scene & really very
touching. Then one of the new settlers (another Markland is being founded
here) read an address of welcome, & then we got out of our chariot and
gave the children scrambles for candies and there was much laughter &
everyone was very happy.

We spent that night with the priest and had much interesting talk.
Father O'Reilly is really a splendid fellow – an Irishman. Father Curwen
talks Irish too, but he is a Newfoundlander. It was Father O's suggestion
that another Markland be formed at Lourdes. The land is the best in the
island, but the people are demoralised by the dole & they are not of the

best stock – deserters from the French ships, many of them, and very disloyal. The new men are fishermen from the south coast and they think they have come to a paradise – they could not believe there was such land in the world, & they are working magnificently and have influenced the original settlers already, so that they are working too. And they have all changed their names – these French people; Le Roi is King – Le Jeune is Young – Benoit is Bennett & so on. It is most amusing. The priest is so delighted. And the new women are a fine lot – so grateful for what is being done to help them & so happy & hard-working. The women & children had a bad time coming from their houses. The ice was in West Bay, & the captain of their ship turned back & landed them all at Port au Port after a very hard trip & kept their gear to bring on later. Father Curwen took them all in & looked after them, & everyone was good to them. Two people had pleurisy. Then they were all brought on in an open motorboat on a cold rough day, so it was a hard beginning for them. But they don't think of anything but how good everyone has been to them and how happy they are to have got to such a land of promise. I went round next day & visited them all in the makeshift houses that Father O'Reilly has rigged up for them. Their own gear can't get to them for another two months.

I had a long talk with Dr. MacDonald of Aguathuna, who came on with us just for the trip. He is a Newfoundlander. I called on his wife & found the house full of trophies, as he is a marathon champion. ... He is a rough-looking fellow but seems kindly. He told us that he has brought 2,600 babies into the world since he came to Aguathuna 24 years ago and never lost a mother! 'I've been very lucky. For sure it's not much ye can do in the way of sterilizing your instruments when there is not a drop of hot water to be had, let alone filin'.'[8] One of his patients has had 20 children. 'I've been thinkin', doctor, will the governmint give me a bounty if I have another do ya think?' 'The courage of her!' I said: 'If the government does not give ya a bounty, I'll be givin' ye one meself. ... But ye know these poor women, they get no sympathy – the men's hard.' I asked him what he felt about birth control. 'No man that seen what these poor women suffer can have any heart in him if he does not think it right.' He is a Catholic. But they dare not go against their priests. ...

1 R.J. MacDonald. Born in Canada. Arrived in Newfoundland in 1908.
2 Arthur and Anna House. Arthur House was manager of the

Dominion Iron and Steel Company's mine at Aguathuna. He was born in England.
3 Usually Pic Denis.
4 North-West Products Co. Ltd.

5 Michael O'Reilly (1894–1973),
   Bishop of St George's, 1941–70.
   Born in Ireland.
6 John Francis Curwen (1886–1969).
   Ordained 3 September 1914.

7 Refers to Sir John's election as
   member of Parliament for Taunton,
   Somerset, in 1922.
8 Filling.

Q.H.S. to Greta, Newfoundland Hotel, 3 June 1935, the King's birthday
... I sent you a miserable scrap from the train. It was almost impossible to
write while we were on our trip. I am going to begin at the end of it because I
know you will be specially interested to hear about the Graveses. ...

Well, we got on the train – or rather, into our carriage, the *Terra Nova*
– on Thursday[1] night, having sent a telegram to Port aux Basques to welcome the Graveses & a note to their carriage to ask them to join us in our
observation car in the morning for breakfast. ... Our carriage was shunted
onto the mail in the middle of the night.

June 5. ...

Well, we had a very jolly day together in the train. I did wish you could
have shared it. N.F.L. was not looking its best, except at dawn, when I think
they were not seeing much of it & not having a very comfortable night. But
Mrs. Graves just sat & looked out of the windows & said quietly, 'I've
enjoyed today more than any day since we left England. I *like* this sort of
country. It's like Scotland. Nova Scotia is too closed in with trees.' ...

We crossed the outward mail & we stopped for a few minutes, & friends
who were outward bound came in to see us for a minute or two, which
amused Mrs. Graves greatly. Another thing that amused her was that the
captain[2] of the S.S. *Caribou* (such a simple, capable fellow), when she said
she must get a photo of something, said: 'I'll take her nearer to the land for
you,' & proceeded to do it. There is something very friendly & attractive
about a country where officials take a personal interest in you. The captain
had been in to see us on the train before we left Port aux Basques for
Stephenville Crossing & before he went back to Sydney – in fact, the
Caribou did another crossing before she brought the Graveses over. I told
him the Graveses were coming & asked him to look after them, but he
would have done so in any case, I expect. These N.F.L. people are like that
– so hospitable. After lunch, we made them both lie down in our cabins,
which had beds & lovely windows, & they had a good rest. After tea, we
played bridge & then sevens.[3] ... We all rested after dinner again, as we did
not get in[4] till midnight.

They have a very nice suite – the one we had at first, and Mr. Trentham had put flowers to welcome them. He had filled our room with flowers too, which was kind.

Next day was Saturday[5] & we all lunched with Mr. Trentham.[6] It was a lovely day. The Graveses walked up Signal Hill & were thrilled to see a huge iceberg. We had to go to tea at Government House to tell the Governor & Lady Anderson about our travels. Then Daddy had to broadcast about the forests. ...

Sunday, they went to the Catholic cathedral,[7] & (another instance of the kindliness of the people), as they came out, a man who had been a steward on the *Caribou* & had seen them there came up to them as they were walking away & said: 'Next Sunday go to the 4th pew on the right. I shall not be there but you'll be welcome there.' We went to our own St. Thomas's. ... I should have loved them to see the wildflowers; they have not even begun yet. Everything is a month later than usual here.

Monday[8] was King's birthday & a holiday for offices (but not for the poor shopkeeper). ... Daddy was busy all day & we had to meet the *Newfoundland*, which came in at 3 o'c. Mr. Howley[9] was on board. ... At night, we went to the official birthday dinner at Government House & we wore our new medals for the first time.

Yesterday, Mr. Graves was busy & much entertained by his business all day. I took Mrs. Graves & David[10] for a trip round the country north of St. John's, or rather she took me. She drives beautifully, & the car loves her hand & runs so sweetly for her. She loved Logy Bay. We walked out over the grassy cliff tops & sat on the tussocks looking down into deep green water pouring over seaweed-covered rocks. We saw 5 schooners lying out in the open sea & watched some curious wildfowl floating on the gently heaving waves. It was a lovely day. We did not get back till 6 & then we made tea & Mr. Graves joined us. ...

1 30 May 1935.
2 Benjamin Taverner.
3 Another card-game.
4 To St John's.
5 1 June 1935.
6 The Commissioner for Finance.

7 Cathedral (now Basilica) of St John the Baptist, Military Rd, St John's.
8 3 June 1935.
9 The Commissioner for Justice.
10 David Hope Simpson, Sir John's nephew, who was working at Lomond.

J.H.S. to Maisie, Newfoundland Hotel, 8 June 1935
... Today is Tuesday, and the time is before breakfast. I am having a

difficult time, and major questions, many of them contentious, are pressing upon me. On each one of them, opinions differ. That does not so much affect the decision of the problems, but it does give an infinity of work in reconciling the decision to the criticisms. I want and need some leave, and see no prospect of it for a long time. My staff is also getting stale and overworked, & the Secretary[1] of the Dept. has gone into retreat for a week, whence he emerges on the telephone when anyone gets tied up.

One of the many difficulties of this country is its low level of morale and of morals. The people have been demoralized by the dole. They have learnt not to work, indeed to dodge work in every way they can. A large number have thus become incapable of work, & the vicious circle is complete. The dole has nominally ceased for the summer. I have heard from two of the magistrates within the last two days that, in each case, there are over 300 families who will starve unless we supply them either with goods to enable them to go fishing or with dole to keep life in their bodies. Last year, we advanced $230,000 in supplies and lost $80,000 of it. We decided to give up making advances. The people must be taught somehow that they have to rely on themselves.

We are attempting to organize the codfish industry and have constituted a statutory association,[2] with a board as its executive. It was difficult enough to push that through, but we were successful. Now we have the appointment of a chairman, and that is giving every kind of trouble. Whoever is appointed, there will be trouble. I shall just have to take the bull by the horns, make my appointment as seems to me best, and stand the racket. I should have done better had I not consulted anyone. As it is, the advice of one side or the other must be rejected.

Then I have my Ranger force, starting as from 1st July. We have as yet no quarters for it, and I have to fix a H.Q. – appoint the Chief Ranger, the Sergeant-Major, & the Inspector, & 20 men – build quarters – have the men trained – arrange for quarters for them where they are to be stationed – [and] frame the law to govern the force (that I have drafted).

Again, we have to start three or four more land settlements. We have already got two started. That means surveys and land clearing & moving of families – a thousand and one details.

Yet again, we are reorganizing the magistracy. I had the whole thing cut & dried before Howley came back, and now he is altering it in the interests of the lawyers, to get them more pay. Lawyers are dreadful locusts. I do not think that he will get away with it this time, however.

I am being worried by enthusiasts of every kind, each one of whom has a pet idea to save the country, and each of these ideas implies either money or concessions from the government: e.g., Thomson,[3] 'fog-free' Thomson, wants a concession of a hundred square miles of territory and a monopoly for a free port and settlement at Mortier Bay on the Burin Peninsula, which he has always described as 'fog-free.' He is backed by Murdoch MacDonald,[4] the big engineer, & they talk of spending £1,000,000 on the project, which I shall turn down flat. It is just as much wildcat as Mr. Christian's[5] application for a monopoly of the shark fishing industry! Then there is one Hawkin, who has a mad idea of roads from Battle Harbour[6] to Quebec, and railways on the Labrador. And so *ad infinitum*. But each of these projects means hours of wasted time & wasted patience for J.H.S.

It is all interesting & good work, and our present embarrassment lies (*entre nous*) in the influx of revenue well above our estimates. Though we have spent freely on various schemes of development, our balances have increased by half a million dollars in the year. And this though we have sacrificed a million in reduction of taxation. That is as if in England you had reduced taxation by £70 million and then ended up with a surplus of £35! You will say that we should have no trouble in disposing of the money. That is true. But our grants-in-aid cease at the end of June 1937 and we have to face an additional expense in the sinking fund of $ one million a year thereafter. So we cannot just think of the present. ...

1 Claude Fraser.
2 By the Salt Codfish Act, 1935, of 13
   June 1935.
3 Harry Craufuird Thomson.

4 Sir Murdoch MacDonald (1866–
   1957). Founded the firm of
   Sir Murdoch MacDonald &
   Partners, 1921.
5 W.G. Christian.
6 Labrador.

Q.H.S. to Greta, Newfoundland Hotel, 13 June 1935

How you would love the great bunch of lily of the valley that has just come in for us! – a gift from Mrs. Andrew Murray – the very first from her garden out at Salmonier. They are only just out – all the top blooms are still palest green. And the sweetness of them – piercingly sweet they are. The fragrance brings out such memories of my girlhood when we picked them growing wild in the spinnies at Sedgley. The wild ones have this piercing sweetness that the hothouse-grown blooms lack. Is it fancy, I wonder? I don't think so. These grow like our wild ones, hale, delicately vigorous, & so green. Mrs. Murray sent me her first gathering last year, & her last precious posy too. I love having a gift like this from her; she is like a flower herself, with her lovely shy blue eyes fringed with dark lashes and her shining snow-white wavy hair & young face. ...

O it is so lovely today! And I am so tired. We were out all day yesterday driving round 'The Bay' – that is, Conception Bay – with Lady Crosbie[1] & her son 'Ches' – seeing a new business he is starting at Harbour Grace, which is to be of great importance, J.H.S. thinks. We started at 10.30 & got back about 10.30 at night – a very lovely drive and most interesting but most exhausting. A whole day with someone you don't know except casually &, in the middle of it, when you are exhausted after the first lap, at 1.45, an enormous lunch with people you have never met before, & then a séance – ladies in one room, men in another, your eyes weighed down with sleep & a hot room & that enormous lunch. Then, at about 3.30, on again – on & on & on – seeing things – on again – dinner at Brigus & then on again – on & on & on – about 160 miles altogether. Lady Crosbie is a sweet woman & I like her, but she is a delicate woman & I am sure she was just about done before we got back.

She has about 12 children – 13 & 11 living;[2] & she is so young-looking – she has 12 grandchildren. I believe she was fighting tubercular trouble all her life & she lost her eldest daughter[3] with it, so it is a constant anxiety for her about her family. They look most robust. Ches is a great strong fellow of 29 – the eldest son. ... He is full of energy & initiative & very good to his men. We stopped to see the younger brother's[4] business – a butterine factory – most efficient & hygienic & economical. Another brother, a very handsome young fellow,[5] does the office work there, & all is really marvellously well done. Outside the factory, runned along the main road, they have a beautiful garden, gay now with tulips & forget-me-nots – a joy to the whole town. At night, a neon-lighted cow (the only neon light in St. John's) wags his head up & down to the great delight of children – including me. The butterine factory brother is fat, tho' he is only 28; he looks as tho' the business has filled him out. But he is as keen a young fellow as any of them, & the factory is a model of efficiency & cleanliness, & the employees are well looked after & well paid. Efficiency is not the first consideration either; they burn nothing but wood because of the employment this gives, and they use machinery that employs 60 men instead of one that would take only 6 men: 'We'll do that as long as we can make a reasonable profit.' They are a decent family – decent employers. Ches Crosbie is a fish merchant; he inherited the father's business, & this year he hired the *Caribou* (the government ship that is used for the passage from Sydney to Port aux Basques) to send a crew to the sealing. John was chaffing him about something one day, & he (Ches C.) said: 'Well, I'll send 1 cent a seal to Lady Anderson's Service League.' He had £70 to send her on his catch. And he paid the men a decent wage & did not charge them for spoilt seal pelts, as the other owners do. So think of Lady Crosbie, a refined-looking young 50-odd, with her 5 big sons & 6 daughters & 12 grandchildren, & think of Ches, the eldest son, 29, dark, square, forthright & downright, talking a brogue I can hardly understand; & Jack, short & fat & buttery; & George, very smart & handsome (Regent society); & the 4th boy,[6] being broken in to the fish business to help his eldest brother – out on one of the trawlers now, while the youngest,[7] 17, is to be the lawyer of the family – all these lads keen & go ahead & no nonsense or false pride in their make-up – the three eldest married & with families already – a Presbyterian[8] family this – a real asset to the country. Would there were more like them here! The only dark cloud on that horizon is the tubercular tendency.

It was such a lovely drive to Carbonear – in & out and along the most lovely bays. As I told you, we lunched at Carbonear & came back later to Harbour Grace to see the new fish trawling drying plant that 'Ches' has started. He has bought about 7 acres of land on the shore, with old buildings (which he is adapting) in the background. And he has covered the land with fishing 'flakes,' the stages on which fish are dried and salted. He is building a wharf where the fish will be landed & washed & from which they will be dispatched to Greece & Brazil etc.

On the way back, they threw in a special little treat for me. I chanced to ask if we passed through Cupids. So we were taken a most lovely round – up North Arm[9] which reminded me of the Lake District ... & away out to Cupids, which is the place where John Guy landed as the first Governor in 1610 & made the first settlement. It is a bleak-looking place now, but I expect the woods have been cut & burnt since those days; with wooded slopes & gullies, it must have been a lovely spot. Now the great rock that guards the entrance is fine, but bare & seared where the earth has been swept away by rushing streams. We found the memorial that was erected to ... Guy a few years ago.[10] Already the inscription is illegible, and the bronze inset is falling out. One result of our visit is that that will be repaired. We saw an unexpected inhabitant – a green & red parrot sitting on a ladder watching all our proceedings; he talked a lot to himself – probably Elizabethan English. He probably came out with the first Governor – he looked like it anyway.

Friday. 14 June. Long days again & so hot that we sleep with all the doors & windows open & one blanket. We have got the fly protectors in the windows too – it spoils the view a bit. The wild azaleas & the wild cherry blossom are out, so the country is lovely. I saw sheets of blue violets too, & white violets are everywhere. The irises are coming out fast; they are about 18 inches high.

The Graveses are due back at midnight today. They have been away salmon fishing on the other side of the island – the west. It is early for the salmon anywhere, but they come to the west first. Baden-Powell[11] & his family are here too fishing, & they are due today too. He is thrilled with the fishing & wants to cut his stay in St. John's short by one week to get back to it. ...

1 Mitchie Anne (Manuel) Crosbie (1876–1953), widow of Sir John Chalker Crosbie (1876–1932).
2 Sir John and Lady Crosbie had thirteen children, of whom eleven were living in 1935.
3 Jean Crosbie (1901–1918).
4 George Crosbie. Known as 'Gentleman George.'
5 John Chalker Crosbie (1908–1960). Known as 'Jack.'
6 Percy Manuel Crosbie (1913–1975).
7 Alexander Harris Crosbie (b. 1919). Known as 'Bill' or 'Bing.'
8 They were United Church but of Methodist background.
9 Probably North River.
10 The monument of John Guy was erected at Cupids in 1910.
11 Robert Stephenson Smyth Baden-Powell (1857–1941), founder of the Boy Scouts and Girl Guides.

J.H.S. to Betty, St John's, 16 June 1935
... Monday. 17 June. 6.15 a.m.

I am up early and have a heavy day in front of me. We are having busy and difficult times. 'People' in general are so unreasonable. At least it appears so, possibly because what I decide or approve is 'reasonable' and they think differently. 1. We have just constituted a codfish board, and there has been trouble over the appointment of the chairman. 2. There is trouble between the herring board and its chairman.[1] 3. My chief fishery officer is upset because he gets less pay than the forest officer or the agriculturalist.[2] 4. Mr. Alderdice hates Markland. 5. Mr. Howley thinks that there is not sufficient cooperation between members of the Commission, and so on & so on, and our enemies love all these difficulties. It will all be right in the end. Like yourself, I am asking for guidance in all difficulties and am getting it, and that removes all worry, though of course not all hard work. It does mean peace of mind, *mens aequa in arduis*.[3] It does not mean that one does not get tired – I am tired frequently – I almost said 'generally,' and that would be true at the end of the day.

Summer has come with a rush in the last fortnight, and the cows are revelling in grass. All the farm animals are swelling visibly. The leaves have rushed out, and I got into my summer clothes a week ago – and yesterday had to revert to cardigan and overcoat. ...

1 The Newfoundland Herring Board was created by the Newfoundland (Scotch and Norwegian Cure) Herring Act, 1934. This act became law on 11 December 1934. The chairman of the board was John T. Cheeseman (1892–1968).

2 Anthony B. Banks.

3 An even mind in difficulties.

Q.H.S. to Maisie and Blair, Newfoundland Hotel, 16 June 1935
... I am very much afraid we shall not be able to get home this year. John feels he must see more of this country than he can in the ordinary way of his work, so he will have to combine work & play. I am sorry indeed. It would be such a joy for him & me to get home to see you all. But if he came, the Dominions Office would keep him busy, as they did last time, & he would not get the holiday he so badly needs.

Sunday – later. He has had a real rest today. He has a touch of lumbago, so he lay late & we breakfasted in our sitting-room. After he dressed, he lay in his chair with his feet up & we did not go to church, and he slept till nearly 3. I was so glad – sleep is his great restorer. Then we took Walter & Andrew Grieve[1] with us & drove out into the country to Holyrood & had tea there. We have leapt into full summer – the leaves are almost in full leaf – the wild azaleas are in flower all over the country – carpets of rose – there are sheets of blue violets, sweet ones & as large as wild pansies – & today the buttercups are out – the dandelions are in clock & the irises are so high they will be in flower in another few days. Mixed with the wild azaleas are the flowering fruit trees, cherry & plum, & lots I do not know. The cottage gardens are a lovely sight with cherry blossom too. Another two days & the lilac will be in flower everywhere – it is just bursting. Everyone is getting out into the country – the roads are busy with cars. One day it is warm & we sleep with one blanket & all the windows wide open; next day it is cold. Today has been grey & misty, & the wind is so cold that the heat has been turned on again & we are glad of it. It is a queer year. My room is gay with flowers, gifts from friends – tulips from the Frasers' (John's secretary) garden – & sweetest of sweet things – piercingly sweet – lily of the valley – a great bunch – the first from the Murrays' garden at Salmonier. Mrs. Murray sent me the first gathering last year &

the very last too. I do love them; they are so different from the hothouse delicate fronds – so strong & fine. David[2] gave me a lily – I don't know what sort it is; it is pink & white – four great blooms on one very strong stalk. There is another coming out too – the four are now all out together – quite a show. ...

We are much enjoying having the Graveses here. They are so jolly & friendly – loving doing things with us – simple things like having tea together in our room & washing up and not going to parties and playing friendly bridge together. As soon as they come in from anywhere else, they ring up to know, 'Can we come along to you and tell you about it?' They have been away on the west coast for 4 days salmon fishing. ...

1 Son and father.   2 David Hope Simpson.

J.H.S. to Greta, Newfoundland Hotel, 16 June 1935

... The Graveses had a busy week before leaving for the west coast for fishing. We got them a private car – the 'Business Car' – which has two bedrooms, dining room, kitchen and observation compartment. There was a cook attached, and they were fed in their car. It was cut off at South Branch within a couple of hundred yards of the pool. They had an excellent time. She caught a 10-lb. salmon & lost another, and he lost two. They got back yesterday, & I met them at the station. He looks splendid. I have never seen a man look better, and they say that they have enjoyed every minute of their time.

We have been playing a good deal of domestic bridge with them & they seem to enjoy it. ...

J.H.S. to Ian and Sheila, St John's, 18 June 1935

... I am wrestling with difficulties, sometimes due ... to perverted personality. I have just circumvented one, which threatened to wreck efforts to create a machinery for the codfish industry. That industry was archaic in organization; ABC, &c., down to XYZ have been producing comparatively small quantities of codfish of a multitude of standards of cure – each racing it off to the market to get ahead of the other fellow – and accepting a cent a pound less than all rivals to induce a sale. The results were quite inevitable. For the last 300 years, there has been inferior quality, and directly competition emerged in Iceland & Norway, our trade fell away – as it deserved to do. That resulted in fiercer competition among ABC, &c.,

down to XYZ, and I was faced with the problem – not because of the firms, but because of the producing fishermen on whom the loss of price ultimately falls.

So I have got legislation[1] through the Commission constituting a statutory salt codfish board with nine members, of whom I nominate the chairman & two others. I have had infinite trouble over this, and have had to exercise my great tact. The exporters' association nominated a man for chairman whom I could not accept, with the result that the chairman of that association threatened to refuse nomination as a member of the board. That would have been fatal at the start. Last night, on coming back from a party at midnight, I found a note from him agreeing to serve. So all is well. But it has meant a fortnight of careful negotiation to reach that result, and at the same time to secure as chairman the man[2] I want.

We have had Graves of the B.B.C. & his wife here for the last three weeks and have much enjoyed their company. They are both nice, each in a special way. He has helped us with advice as to broadcasting here, and I think that eventually we shall have an independent corporation under government control, but that is a long way ahead. Our first step is to get efficient distribution. We have now two companies & three private broadcasting stations, and the first step is some form of compulsory amalgamation. The next will be, some day, to acquire the amalgamated organization & then to initiate the new scheme. ...

I am getting tired and am looking forward to some leave at the end of July & in August. That will include inspection of two of the bays on the south coast, and then, I hope, three weeks fishing. ...

1 The Salt Codfish Act, 1935, of   2 Raymond Gushue (1900–1980).
13 June 1935.

Q.H.S. to Ian, Newfoundland Hotel, 20 June 1935

As I write the date, I realize that tomorrow will be the longest day! And yesterday we had little icebergs in the harbour, to the great delight of young boys who rowed out & scrambled about them. It was a glorious day too, but the wind was keen. We have had a lot of icebergs passing, blown down by the north wind. One that nearly entered the harbour was just like the pottery baking kilns, or perhaps more like an igloo, with two tall chimneys beyond all on an iceberg platform. The chimneys must have been about 50 feet high. Today is glorious again, and I fancy it is much warmer. Yesterday, I had to turn on the electric iron stove, I was so chilly.

Today, all my windows are wide & the sun streaming in, & I am very happy & comfortable. ...

The Baden-Powells[1] are here now. We dined quietly at Government House to meet them two nights ago – just ourselves. They are wonderful people really. He at – what age? – 78 – is so brimful of interest in his work still. She is so much younger that she is in her prime, & they have two young daughters, about 18 & 20, who are delightfully fresh & unspoilt. ... I had a long talk with him after dinner. He told me that he was rather worried because his son's reports from school, Charterhouse,[2] were not as good as he expected, so he turned up his own of long ago to show as a pattern & very hastily had to put first one & then another aside. 'Not this one!' 'Not that one!' The remarks were not exactly laudatory. 'This boy sleeps steadily through my class,' etc. He told me about his boyhood – his mother left a widow by a poor parson when he was about 3 – with, I think, 5 sons & some daughters to educate. I think most of them have risen to distinguished positions. He began his scouting by hiding from his masters, apparently! Then, last night, I went to a rally of the guide leaders to hear Lady Baden-Powell speak to them. ... I was interested in watching her own girls as she talked. They sat on the ground among the rest & kept their eyes fixed on their mother – drinking in every word as tho' they had never heard it before – such charming fresh young faces. ...

1 Robert Stephenson Smyth and Olave St Clair (Soames) Baden-Powell (1889–1977).

2 English public school.

J.H.S. to Maisie, Newfoundland Hotel, 26 June 1935

It is a dull foggy morning with rain, and we have had very unsettled weather for the last few days. There is still a great deal of heavy ice on the Labrador coast – so much so that ships are being held up, and they have not yet been able to start loading timber. There are about 35,000 tons waiting to load, & steamers have been chartered on time charter and a whole month has been lost. Meanwhile, the fishery has commenced and prospects are remarkably good – better than they have been for years. Markets, however, are very difficult. What with 'economic nationalism' and quotas and disorganized exchange, the merchant's life is not a happy one at the moment.

On Sunday, Quita and I drove ... Mr. & Mrs. Banks,[1] our Director of Agriculture & his wife, to Markland. While we were inspecting the settlement after lunch, a thunderstorm began & the rain came down in torrents. It continued for two hours – rain of the kind you get in India. On Monday, we drove ... to the forestry operations for the unemployed young men. They are both interesting & successful. We have taken so far 130 single men from 18 to 25 years of age, and have clothed them. We feed them well, giving them as much as they can eat, and pay them 20 cents a day for 10 hours' work. We are opening out a lovely stretch of forest country – full of lakes – for a holiday ground for St. John's. It is called 'The Salmonier Line' – and is 50 miles from St. John's. When the plan is complete, we shall have an ideal tourist area. We are putting up scores of 3-room huts, for week-enders, in chosen spots overlooking the lakes. There are hundreds of choice sites. We shall let them to week-enders for two or three dollars a time. We are catering for the poorer class – the shop assistant & clerk.

Friday – 28th June. ...

We did rather a dreadful thing on Wednesday.[2] The directors of the Grenfell Association[3] are here from New York – not including Sir Wilfred, who is I fear not much longer for this world – and, among other festivities, the Y.M.C.A. gave them a lunch, to which we were invited. The Governor and Lady Anderson were also invited, and a lot of the elite of St. John's. Quita & I, through some misunderstanding, forgot the lunch! A dreadful gaffe.

The Grenfell people are a fine lot. They are businessmen (which Wilfred is not) and understand our difficulties. Wilfred does not, and loses his wool when we cannot fall in with all his plans and accept all his recommendations. The directors are very anxious to work with us in every way, and I think there will be little difficulty, though there is serious antagonism in one department, under one of our N.F.L. colleagues.

My own dept. is full of interesting, difficult and sometimes anxious problems, and I, personally, am getting tired and need some rest. By the time you get this, we shall be on the verge of starting for some leave. On July 20th, we hope to get to Placentia & thence tour the Fortune Bay & Hermitage Bay areas, probably by motorboat. We shall then take the local steamer to Port aux Basques, come up the railway as far as Corner Brook, and thence I hope to go to the upper Humber, leaving Quita at Corner Brook for a few days. I shall come back & we shall then come on to Glenwood & have a quiet fortnight. That will mean being back at St. John's in good time on 1st September.

1 Anthony B. (1901–1960) and Belle Banks.

2 26 June 1935.

3 The International Grenfell Association.

Q.H.S. to Maisie and Blair, Newfoundland Hotel, 27 June 1935
... Now, before I forget, do you think it would be possible to get a second-hand wheeling-chair[1] given to us? There are a great many N.F.L. people in Liverpool – people who have connections with N.F.L. We want things like that so badly – for use of the nurses in the outports. There are none to be had here. Could you advertise for us? I will write out the advertisement & enclose it, & of course we pay for it. The Furness Withy people would ship it free of charge for the Service League, and if it were second-hand, there would be no customs duty. I am on the committee for the 'Nurses Special Needs Association.' Old linen it is no use asking for; every hospital & every nurse in England is crying out for that. It is dreadful to hear of the lack of the commonest necessities here. The nurses are thankful even for old newspapers for pads. And the nurses seem to spend their own small salaries on food & comforts for their patients; the houses are so terribly empty of everything we in England consider necessities of life. If you could hear of a wheeling invalid chair, we would gladly pay [the] expense of getting it to the dock, etc. ...

The district nurse who is appealing for a Bath chair[2] is at Port Saunders & she has turned an old disused lighthouse into a tiny hospital, with four beds for adults & two for children. She is an Englishwoman – came out as a Nonia nurse. All these nurses are doing magnificent work under incredibly hard conditions. ...

... We have been to a huge garden party at Government House – about 400 Orangemen[3] & women from all parts of Canada & Newfoundland. It is a society that has for its object to uphold British tradition & customs. Lots of them are staying in this hotel. The women float about in diaphanous white frocks. They are mostly white-haired and very plain – some fat, some lean – 'The Priestesses,' we call them. They were all tremendously pleased at being invited to Government House. 'This is the treat of a lifetime,' I heard one old man say. And another, when John handed him cakes: 'To be served by a Commissioner!' ... Sunday we ... went to Markland & spent some hours there. It is a lovely bit of country & the people are doing so well. There are about 150 families out there now. You would not know it was a 'settlement.' You drive along through woods, & all you see is a winding path leading up to a charming little wooden bungalow set on a hill – often hidden from the road by the trees. If you go up the path, you find the house with a nice little verandah & a patch of well-cleared land under cultivation & a little garden & a few hens. The homes are scattered about on suitable land, none of them close together & all very private from

the road. The first schoolhouse is up on a knoll, with terraced steps leading up to it at an angle from the road, & it looks down the road and over
a valley through which the Rocky River runs. Some of the houses are
2 miles from the school, and at first the children, being townees,[4] were
brought in a truck. But now they all walk. Miss Cochius,[5] the charming
schoolmistress, a girl of about 21, thought the truck too dangerous and
now the children are so much stronger it is not only safer but better for
them to have the walk. They always arrive one hour before school begins,
& the school is open for them: 'We like them to come early; they have a
rest & some read & some play the gramophone & some play games.' ...
There are all sorts of interesting experiments going on & it is a most happy
colony. A tremendous tropical storm of rain burst on us while we were
there, so Mrs. Banks & I took refuge in the schoolhouse. Miss Cochius
was delighted with the pipes, etc. She says she will take them to camp next
week (she is taking 50 of the children for a fortnight), & they will be a
great source of delight, copying them & playing them. I took her lots of
books too. ... On Monday ... we ... [went] out to see the unemployed who are
at work in the woods about 60 miles away. There are 200 of them. They get
10d. a day and are under a semi-military organization, their officers being
chosen from among themselves and ex-servicemen who were on the dole.
It is entirely voluntary, but there is great competition to be in these camps,
& the men's one anxiety is ... to be found [unfit] in any way. At first, there
was a lot of opposition to the scheme in the town – talk of preparing for war
& cannon fodder. But the men themselves have changed that; they can go
back to town once a fortnight for the weekend but must be on the return
lorry at 6 o'c. on Monday morning. Not a man has been late yet. There are
two camps – one for newcomers, where they are taught the first essentials of
woodcraft. ... We had our lunch on a trout stream, out in the open, where the
flies did not bother us. It was just like a Scotch salmon river. ...

This weekend, we are going to Whitbourne to stay with Prof. Fraser
Bond, whose property John has been trying to buy as a headquarters for
agricultural work & his Ranger force & [as] a colony for a sort of Borstal
institution.[6] ...

1 Wheelchair.
2 Hooded wheelchair as used in Bath,
   England.
3 Members of the Orange Order.

4 Townies, i.e., natives of St John's,
   especially males. By contrast, outport
   inhabitants are called 'baymen.'
5 Clare Cochius.
6 Reformatory for young male
   offenders.

Q.H.S. to Greta, Newfoundland Hotel, 28 June 1935
I wonder whether you have seen the Graves yet. I do hope they arrived
home feeling really well. ... We watched until the *Nova Scotia* turned the
corner, our hearts going out with her in longing to be on our way to you
all too.

But where we are, there must we be. And we are really enjoying the life
& the work here. Daddy is very tired – he does need a holiday badly. But
he is sleeping very well. ... There is so much being started, & all the detail
has to be thought out and so many people have to be seen. But it is
remarkable how people are rallying round now – unexpected people re-
sponding to demands upon their services. The way the dole people are
working when they get the chance is very remarkable – the Markland &
similar experiments in agricultural settlement, the 200 young unemployed
in camps on 1od. a day clearing trails & building bungalows out in the
woods for summer holidaymakers – all keen & happy & only afraid of
being outed. But if Daddy had not learnt patience, where should we all be!
I told you about the new settlement at 'Lourdes' and what splendid work
Father O'Reilly is doing there away on the furthest corner of the island.
He needed & wanted help with the layout of the settlement, & Daddy
arranged to send the Markland manager, Cochius, who has done magnificent work at Markland, & 2 young agricultural experts who have also had
special training under him. This week came a telegram from Father O'Reilly:
'*One Cochius* interfering our work. Kindly instruct him to desist,' or words
to that effect; but 'One Cochius' was the beginning. Daddy wired something [in] reply & wrote fully & carefully, & yesterday came a long
telegram: 'Most grateful for all your help. Work going splendidly. Cor-
dially invite Mr. Cochius & helpers to stay at my house,' or words to *that*
effect. ...

Tuesday, July 2. We have come back last night from a delightful visit to
Prof. Fraser Bond at Whitbourne. He owns one of the few real country
houses. Whitbourne was created as a railway junction, but the most coun-
trified of junctions – just a collection of little wooden houses with a church
& churchyard perched up on a knoll about 6 miles from the sea, on the
most lovely succession of lakes embedded in gently rolling hills & wood-
lands. 'The Grange' stands above one of these lakes, an old white-towered,
long wooden house with the loveliest garden – a wonderful sight just now,
with lilacs & rhododendrons & laburnum & lupins in masses everywhere
– a half-wild garden with avenues of arched-over trees leading in all directions – the loveliest being those thro' which you look straight down into
the blue of the lake. One such starts from the terrace, which is hedged

with hawthorns in flower – the flights of steps too hedged by it till it melts into the avenue. There is a lovely farm too, & he owns all the land & miles & miles of lakes. He inherited it from an uncle who was a very fine man & prime minister.[1] He was a scholar too & built this house & bought the property to make a centre of culture inland. Fraser Bond, this man, is only 40,[2] & he is almost blind. He is such a nice fellow – a charming host. He is waiting for an operation for cataract & meanwhile has had to give up his teaching & devote himself to writing. He is Professor at Columbia University.[3] We have had two lovely days with him. He is a bachelor, & it seemed sad to see him so handicapped. But he lived & played in this place as a boy & knows every stone & every corner & needs no guidance – dashes in among the trees to guide you to the secret garden of lilacs & rhododendrons that are marvellously lovely just now, & warns you to beware of extra depth in stone steps & points out the distant loveliness of the narrows. He is such a nice-looking fellow too, with hair that is pale golden white – I can't be sure whether it is very golden fair or white – & it curls a bit, & he has a nice squareness of head & make & grey-blue eyes that are only a little shadowed by his blindness. He usually has a friend[4] as secretary with him, & lots of friends & relations come to fill the big roomy house.

But O I have been so bitten – eaten up by sandflies & mosquitoes – Daddy too. We stupidly forgot our mosquitol[5] & we lunched on a grassy bank among blue irises down by the Salmonier River & were besieged. I was awake for hours last night. My face & neck are a sight, & I am lunching & dining out today. ...

I just longed for you to share our drive back yesterday. The country is glorious – buttercups – a golden dream, & blue irises & moon daisies floating on green depths, and every village buried in lilac & apple blossom, & all the lakes & the sea intensest royal blue. Coming down from the Brigus barrens was marvellous – you look down as from a high mountain top over 50 miles of knobbly peaks & rose-red precipices & blue inlets & lovely valleys. ...

An exquisite morning & the *Newfoundland* lying below ready to start. ...

1 Sir Robert Bond, Prime Minister of
   Newfoundland, 1900–9.
2 He was born in 1891 and so was
   older than forty.
3 New York.

4 Possibly the lawyer Donald Fraser,
   a boyhood friend and fellow New
   Yorker. They were both sons of
   United Church ministers.
5 A repellant.

Q.H.S. to Betty, Newfoundland Hotel, 2 July 1935
... I think things are *really* improving here. The railway has paid its expenses for the first time in its life; the customs have been brought down
from 75% to 15%; & the income is far in excess of what it has been before.
Houses are actually being painted here & there – ground is being broken
up – the settlements are doing marvellously well – there is a new spirit of
enterprise & hope abroad. ...

Q.H.S. to Ian and Sheila, Newfoundland Hotel, 6 July 1935
... Here I have been immensely impressed lately by the results of John's
patient handling of men & difficulties. I noticed it first in India. I think it
is one of the secrets of his success in these big difficult jobs. He is not
naturally a patient man, as you know – so quick himself, the stupidities &
hesitations & mistakes of other men must grudge him dreadfully. It astonished me in India to watch him as he listened to interminable tales, helping
with a word here, a suggestion there, until a tangle was straightened out
and the petitioner or subordinate satisfied that his case had been heard and
understood and, whatever the decision, the Sahib would deal justly according to his knowledge. There have been three cases here last week. One
in connection with Markland – the big experiment – not only the settlement there of 150 men but the five others like it. The trustees all resigned
on a question of control – as from July 1st! They are fine men doing most
devoted & excellent work, & it would be a disaster that they should withdraw. But they can't be allowed to establish a unit independent of government. He got them together – made them realize that government appreci-
ates & understands their work (he has done this all along, of course), and
together they worked out a plan of control that made the work of the
trustees easier. Then one of the most respected of the fish merchants wanted
to insist upon a certain nominee of their own being appointed as secretary
of the new council[1] – if not, he would retire from it. It was a case of
wheels-within-wheels nepotism – the man was not the best qualified in
any sense. Patient & courteous handling of the situation got the right
secretary[2] appointed, & the merchant won over to whole-hearted support
– such a nice letter. Over & over again, this is what happens.
    But – it is all very wearing! Daddy is quite definitely tired. He has had
much bigger jobs, but none in which the personal element is so important,
I think. ...
    It is so cold today, & yesterday we had to have the heat on; the wind is
icy. There must be another bunch of icebergs about. The conditions on the

Labrador are very anxious; the fishery has not begun there yet. It is very late, but the ice is still in along the coast and the schooners can't get in.

We had lovely days at the beginning of the week. The country is simply lovely – the green so fresh, untarnished by the heat & dust we usually have long before this. And the buttercups make a golden glory of the pastures, & there are moon daisies swimming on the deep green of the hay fields, & everywhere there are blue irises. The villages (or rather 'settlements' we call them here) are smothered in lilac & apple blossom now; the cherry & plum & pea are over. I had almost forgotten how lovely this country is; at least I thought I had exaggerated it. ...

I wish you had been with us one day up on the marshes. We had to stop for something, & I heard sandpipers making a great to-do. I got out & they swooped to & fro over my head as tho' they might attack me. I looked all about for the nest but could not find it. It must have been almost under my feet. The marshes are lovely – the marsh laurel is in flower – a little rose-like parasol in clusters; & the arethusa, a dainty little rose-coloured orchid; & the pitcher plant, with its pitchers lifting their lips from the ground & their wine-red flowers like Christmas roses but standing up boldly on a 6-inch stalk – so beautiful when the sun is setting over the marsh & turns it to a table set with wine-filled cups. ...

1 Chairman of the Salt Codfish Board.   2 Chairman.

J.H.S. to Ian and Sheila, St John's, 7 July 1935

... Our first complete financial year ended up on 30th June and marks a good showing. Even after returning £90,000 ($450,000) of the grant-in-aid from England, we are $900,000 up on our estimates of income. Thus, in fact our income was $1,350,000 more than the estimates. Our expenditure was $400,000 more than the estimates. We ended the year with a balance of about $900,000, as against an expected balance of $400,000 and an estimated balance of nil. And this though we reduced tariffs on January 1st, which anticipated a loss of $650,000 in a full year. As from 1st July, we have again made reductions, anticipating a further loss of $250,000. This is the first time for very many years since there has been any reduction in taxation.

It can, I think, be said with perfect truth that the economic position of N.F.L. shows enormous improvement as a result of the Commission's existence & the Commission's work. Yet there is still an Augean stable to be tackled. The whole mass of the fishermen are in a state of serfdom. The truck system is rampant, and over large areas there is not a single cash transaction. The merchant 'supplies' for the fishery – i.e., he advances the necessaries for the fishery and for the maintenance of the man and his family during the fishing season – in kind and in many cases at exorbitant prices. These are debited to the a/c of the fisherman. He, in his turn, turns his catch in to the merchant, and is credited with the price the merchant fixes for that fish. Incidentally, almost every fisherman who is forced to this method – and it is universal – is in debt to the merchant, never has his a/c in funds, never sees a penny in cash, and after settlement of accounts at the end of his voyage, is compelled to go on the dole. It is an appalling system of exploitation, and we shall not justify our existence till we get rid of it.

Another form of exploitation is the lawyers. They are on top. Of course, in the past they have made the laws. Now they are having a bad time, for we avoid government litigation as far as that is at all possible, and we make the laws and in doing so avoid, as far as possible, any obligation to litigate. I have a constant struggle with the Justice Department in this matter. Take the case of landed property. In this island, there are tens of thousands of grants of crown land. There has never been a survey. The result is that boundaries are nebulous & constantly overlap. This must be straightened out &, as the enormous majority of cases are of very small areas & of very little value, we want a summary method of settling them on the spot (as is done in India). We have arranged in principle that this should be done by the stipendiary magistrates. The Justice Dept. drafted an act to carry out the decision. It applies to those cases all the rules & regulations of procedure of the Supreme Court! That would mean that no case could be run without expert lawyers for plaintiff & defendant & a harvest for the bar. I am fighting that tooth and nail &, if it goes through, I shall recommend the whole attempt be dropped.

Monday morning. 8th July. A perfect day of brilliant sunshine. It is now 6.40 and I have had my quiet time. One could not carry the burden of government of this island without the quiet time.

Yesterday was Remembrance Day – celebration of the anniversary of Beaumont Hamel, when the N.F.L. Regiment made its heroic attack and was practically wiped out.[1] It was a cold misty morning, but by the time of the celebration at the war memorial,[2] the weather had cleared and we had brilliant sunshine. The war memorial is a very fine open space in the city, sloping down to the harbour – a semicircular site – like a Greek amphitheatre. In the centre at the top, there is the memorial proper – a bronze group – with fisherman and woodsman in the centre and soldier and marine in action on either side. A fine bronze group. The whole town turned out, and there were detachments of the old regiment,[1] of the marines from the *Scarborough* now in port, of Boy Scouts and Church Lads' Brigade[4] and various semi-philanthropic organizations. All the chief officials were there, including Governor & staff in full uniform. It was a well-run show – 'O God our Help' sung by the crowd & led by the bands – wreaths laid – 2 minutes' silence – 3 volleys – last post. The Newfoundlander loves to have his feelings harrowed and harrows them right well. ...

Officially, the most important items at the moment are the beginning of the Ranger force, and the land settlement scheme. For the former, we have a sergeant instructor from Canada, from the R.C.M.P. – that model of police administration. We are recruiting 25 to begin with. If the experiment succeeds, we shall go on to recruit another 25. For the latter, we have £100,000. Markland continues & we are hoping to multiply it by five. We are finding little difficulty in inducing people to come off the rocks of the south coast into places where they can combine fishing & farming. But it will be a long job.

I wish I could get home. ... However, God's in His heaven. ...

1 On 1 July 1916, the first day of the   3 Royal Newfoundland Regiment.
   Battle of the Somme.   4 An Anglican organization.
2 St John's.

J.H.S. to Ian and Sheila, St John's, 16 July 1935

A lovely morning of sunshine. I have just finished a letter to Greta, and it is 7.30 and I have half an hour before breakfast. I have the habit of early rising, and it is valuable. One can get through far more in the two hours before breakfast than in any other two hours of the day. My study looks out on the harbour, and the fishing boats go out in their twos & threes to the cod traps. They are motorboats and are coming back full just now – sometimes towing another boat also full of codfish. The fishing is patchy – in many places excellent, in others very poor. And the European & Brazilian markets are rotten. This means a low price to the fisherman, for the merchant, the broker, and the agent all secure their profit, and the loss comes in the price fixed by the merchant in buying from the fisherman.

I heard a professor[1] of the (R.C.) university, Antigonish, speaking at a Rotary luncheon here. It was attended by all the leading merchants and businessmen of the place. He began: 'A state of society in which the great mass of the people have no say whatever in fixation of the price of what they buy, and equally no say whatever in fixation of the price of what they sell, is fundamentally immoral.' That is the case in N.F.L. And he might have pointed his finger at any individual in the audience (except myself) and have truly said: 'Thou art the man.' That is the most important and radical problem for the government, and we have not yet tackled it. We are making our enquiries and thinking out a scheme, but it is intensely difficult and the existing system of fishery supply, which has been in operation for 300 years, cannot be changed in a moment. We have a cooperative expert[2] just arrived who may help. ...

Here things go along in the normal way. Work does not diminish, but my office has become infinitely more efficient, which, of course, means that my personal work has become less burdensome. Some individual matters give rise to great anxiety. I am having recourse to consummate tact in dealing (for instance) with the Markland trustees. Also with the new cooperative expert. And with some of my N.F.L. colleagues. But, taking things by and large, official work is much more comfortable. I wish I saw a chance of getting away from this island next year. I shall (D.V.) take leave home next year if I am still alive, but I cannot see retirement before 1937.

Andrew Grieve ... went out jigging codfish last night. They got 45 big fish in two hours. The boats did very well, and people were splitting the fish till after midnight.

Quita and I leave on the 20th for Placentia, where we pick up the *Malakoff* and start on a fortnight's tour of the south coast – Placentia Bay, Fortune Bay and Hermitage Bay. When that is done, we shall have been round the whole of the island, and shall know more about the coast of N.F.L. than 99% of the population. We end up at Port aux Basques about the 31st, and then Quita returns here while I go up the upper Humber, and we meet again about the 10th August at Glenwood (Gleneagles Hotel) for three weeks absolute loaf. I shall come back at the end of August like a giant refreshed. I feel rather guilty in leaving a lot of work to be done by my colleagues, but I *must* have leave for I am getting stale. Quita keeps very well. ...

1   A.B. MacDonald.   2   W.D. Beveridge.

Q.H.S. to Greta, Newfoundland Hotel, 16 July 1935

... We had two mails together last week – one overland in the morning and one by the mail.[1] The Lodges returned by it, and we were very glad to have them back.

You asked about collecting surplus toys for us for the outports; I should be thankful for anything. If they could be sent to Messrs. Furness Withy addressed to me for Service League, I should not have to pay duty on them, & Messrs. Furness Withy would carry them free. I would gladly pay postage or freight to Liverpool. You know I brought out five cases of toys and books and they are invaluable. I sent 3 up to the Labrador to 'Hope Simpson.'² ... I also sent a tremendous bundle of newspapers & magazines I had collected for the purpose. I took a lot of books & magazines round the coast too, & took books & all the necessities for musical pipe-making & playing, with tools & music & extra made pipes, etc., & the school-mistresses were delighted. ... We shall want every toy & book we can lay hands on to sent round to the nurses in the outports for Christmas, & these have to be despatched not later than the beginning of November or end of October because many of them are cut off as soon as the snow comes. So if anything can be done in the matter, the sooner the better. Lady Anderson has started a new society for collecting & sending extra comforts and help for the nurses in these outports to use in their work. It used to be done by Nonia, but Nonia has been merged in the district nursing service now. We all have to give a present to this society on our birthday. Of course, we can & do give at other times. I gave £1 worth of flannelette, as that was urgently needed for the babies' layettes. I must send something for Daddy's birthday, as I put his name & birthday down. All the children have to send something, & they like the idea, and the central cupboards are doing well at present – tho', when you come to think of it, it amounts to very little. I helped to pack 10 boxes for outports last week – cans of milk, cereals, fruit, jelly squares – a few little garments, a few magazines – so little really when you think of the numbers the nurse is serving. Still it is something – a great help, and before the nurses were providing these things out of their own salaries. ...

We are having a hot spell here at last. Yesterday & today have been torrid. I should be at the hospital this afternoon but did not dare go. I am afraid it will dry up the buttercups & blue irises & dim the freshness of forest & field. That has been one of the advantages of this late cold season – such wealth of exquisite fresh loveliness everywhere.

We have had some long expeditions. One day, we went to Heart's Content – spent the night there and the next morning at Heart's Desire & came back down Trinity Bay by Heart's Delight. Are not the names lovely? – so are the places – well named. I have never been so far by car to the north of the peninsula before. You will have to come & see this island. You would so love it. That drive [is] in & out of the loveliest bays – up over mountains looking down over a world of mountain tops & lovely valleys & marvellous blue sea & lakes & inlets, and everywhere flowers – buttercups & irises & moon daisies, &, on the marshes, the rose-red marsh laurel, & all the berry flowers, & the dainty arethusa & the pitcher plant like a ruby-red fritillary. ...

We took Mrs. Harold Mitchell with us, & Mr. H.M.[3] followed later with another of the trustees of the Heart's Desire experiment. We spent the night at Heart's Content because there are decent houses where you can stay there. It is the N.F.L. station of the Atlantic Cable. I had a great thrill. We met the manager[4] in the morning, when Mrs. M. & I were having a walk round, & he invited us in. It gives one a queer feeling to see the cable when it comes up out of the sea after its 2,000-mile journey across the Atlantic. It is only about as thick as the wrist of a child of ten, but it carries 7 messages at once, I believe. There used to be 280 men (roughly) employed – now the machinery is so uncannily efficient that only about 28 are required. When anything goes wrong, the detector can indicate exactly where the fault is, & you can imagine how exact it must be when such a comparatively tiny thing has to be found perhaps 3 miles down on the west floor of the Atlantic. Grapplers find it, hold it, & sever it, because the great weight of the whole cable would be an unnecessary strain on the ship; first one end, then the other, is lifted onto the ship, the fault repaired, the cable joined again & sunk into place.

The manager asked if I was in a hurry, & I thought he had to attend to some business, so I strolled on looking at things. Presently, he called me over to the table where typed messages were reeling off a machine: 'Now look,' he said. There was a message from London to me: 'Lady Hope Simpson at Heart's Content. Hope trust you are enjoying your visit to Heart's Content.' It had not been more than 4 minutes from the time he asked me to excuse him. The message asking for a message to me personally had gone via New York to London &, I suppose, back the same way (I don't know) – he said 6,000 miles – in 4 minutes. He cut it off the reel with the corresponding squiggles, both the direct & the corrected ones; the messages get distorted in transmission and one of the machines corrects the distortion. ...

Heart's Desire was one of the worst places on the coast – the fishermen down & out & heartbroken. Mr. H. Mitchell has been working to improve things along that coast. Last year, as a result, he instituted a fair at Heart's Content & it was a huge success. People came from up & down the coast to see the pigs & the sheep & the weaving & the fruit & vegetables. Last year, government backed him in his work, & a committee was formed &

government money backed the work. Now, at Heart's Desire, the people
are working under a 'captain' – a hard, capable fisherman – & he is making
them cooperate. They have built a fish-making shed, &, as luck would so
kindly have it, the fishermen had a big haul of fish the day before – the
first for the year if not for several years – & there were all the people hard
at work, men & women & children, washing the fish, splitting it, cleaning
it, washing it again, salting it, laying it out to dry, washing down the heads
& offals into a big open case on the shore below from which the water
drained away, two men being detailed to cart the offals, etc., up to the
experimental hundred-acre plot half a mile away up on the hill, then to be
sunk in a pit & mixed with the loose peat of this country & with seaweed
for use as a very fine manure next year. We had to see the pigs here too –
large blacks like ours, & the sheep & hens, & the school & the children's
plot of land. It was most thrilling and, as we had 4 lovely days for the
expedition, it was really delightful. And it was lovely to see the happiness
& eagerness of those people. There are great difficulties, of course. These
N.F.L. people will not cooperate unless they are dragooned into it. They
have to learn the value of it – they have always worked to have everything
they can for themselves – one family settling in a cove to keep all the
fishing there to itself – two men in a boat, one gets his line entangled, the
other will not help him. And they have to be dragooned into taking thought
for the future. They will catch fish to sell it, but not to pickle it for
themselves for the winter. Money in the bank is their only idea of well-
being. And money in the bank must never, on any consideration, never, in
any need, be touched. Thousands of people on the dole have money buried in a bank or in a stocking. They are queer, these people. They need
understanding, just as foreigners need understanding by those who are not
of their race & education.

Another day, Saturday afternoon,[5] we went down to Salmonier & spent
the night with the Andrew Murrays (it is she who sends me the first lilies
of the valley & the last). It is an exquisite spot – a bungalow with wide
plate glass windows, looking over a great pool & meadows to the forest.
The water lilies are in flower, & the pool is full of salmon, & we could see
them shouldering each other up the river[6] below our bedroom window – a
wide, shallow river with bright, emerald weeds & yellow rocks shining
through the water. They were leaping in the pool & in the river, but tho'
John fished till dark, & was in the water by 4 o'c. next morning, he did not
get even a rise.

We had to leave at 11 o'c., as John had to speak at a meeting of the
Salvation Army. He had spoken for all the other denominations, so he felt

he must respond to the Salvationists, tho' he does not approve of their methods here – too sectarian. But they are decent people, hard-working & touching a class that others do not.

Such a lovely breeze! I have all the doors & windows open, and I have the room full of sweet peas. The Governor is dining with us tonight – just him and his secretary, Captain Robinson,[7] whom you met, & ourselves. Lady Anderson is away at Black Duck[8] for a rest with Capt. & Mrs. Campbell[9] (the man who was with Scott at the South Pole at one time & brought a party safely through a terrible winter in a low igloo, when they could not even stand upright). ...

How I do want thee, my beloved child. I want you to see the good things I enjoy. I feel as selfish having this easy life, while my children are working so hard – my husband too. All I do is to be here when he comes home & make tea for him at all hours & play patience or bridge with him & go [on] lovely trips. Sometimes I think I will launch out & do something myself. But then anything I think of is unsuitable to be done by a Commissioner's wife – clothing the poor just makes the poor more dependent, and the work of the Commission is made more difficult by amateur attempts at helping – etc., etc. So I just sit & am a wife & nothing more helpful.

We are due to start off next Saturday on another trip round the coast, starting as before at Placentia by the *Malakoff* & doing Placentia Bay & Fortune Bay & Hermitage Bay. They say Fortune Bay is almost unbearably lovely. Let's hope we don't get fog & storms. You never know from hour to hour in this country. ...

1 The *Nova Scotia* arrived from Liverpool on Monday, 8 July.
2 Port Hope Simpson, Labrador.
3 Harold and Frances Mitchell. Harold Mitchell (1891?–1952) was manager of J.B. Mitchell and Son, brokers and customs agents. First president of the Great War Veterans' Association. Member of the House of Assembly for Trinity South, 1932–4. Defeated Sir Richard Squires in the election of 1932.
4 William J. Stentaford was superintendent for the Western Union Telegraph Co.
5 13 July 1935.
6 Salmonier River.
7 H.B. Robinson.
8 On the west coast of the island.
9 Victor and Marit (Fabritius) Campbell. Victor Campbell (1876–1956) was a mate on the *Terra Nova* when that vessel was a supply ship for the ill-fated Antarctic expedition of the British explorer Robert Falcon Scott (1868–1912).

J.H.S. to Betty, Newfoundland Hotel, 19 July 1935

A lovely morning. Cool south breeze and a pearly horizon. The sun is not yet up over Signal Hill. I am up because we are leaving for the south coast early tomorrow morning, and I want to make sure that each one of you children gets a letter by the direct mail.

I wish you were here. You would so enjoy the beauty of the harbour in the early morning – specially a day like this with the fishing boats running out – each making its V-shaped wake in the calmness of the water. They are having great fishing here. ... And people are pestering you to buy fresh fish on Water Street, and Job's have got so much that they do not know what to do with it all. And with all that, the foreign markets are so bad that the merchants say they cannot sell the fish, and are giving very little to the fishermen. It is indeed a mad world, and maddest in it is Mussolini.[1]

The Newfoundlander is pretty mad too in some ways (I suppose we all are). At Alexis River,[2] the people have been earning great wages – the men about $3 a day. Yet, directly the fishing season began, a lot of them left work to go fishing, though they know quite well, even were they lucky, they might possibly clear $50 in the whole season. But it is the sport of the thing, I suppose, and the gamble, that appeal to them.

We are pegging along. We have organized the first of the Ranger force and are having H.Q. at Whitbourne. We have a Sergeant-Major[3] from Canada as instructor, and a first-class Newfoundlander[4] as Chief Ranger. Our second in command[5] is a man who was with the Black and Tans[6] in Ireland. I expect that he is sorry for that episode, as we all are except General Tudor,[7] who was in command. He, by the way, lives in N.F.L., but we never see him. The fact that we do not belong to Bally Haly Golf Club[8] means that there are many people we do not know. That is the society centre in summer. Nor do I belong to the City Club, which is the men's meeting (and drinking) centre in the winter. Indeed, Quita and I are rather aloof from the ordinary society of St. John's. I am not convinced that we are doing wrong in this. It is well for the government not to be on Tom, Dick & Harry terms with the people with whom they are bound to deal officially. ...

Last night, I spoke to the summer school on China. The summer school is a wonderful institution. There are 450 teachers here for study – of them about 130 are nuns. Professor Shaw[9] (a Presbyterian) is taking the nuns in a course of teaching. That is a very hopeful sign. Another hopeful sign is the keenness of these teachers to learn more themselves. As you know, they are very poorly paid, but we are improving the scales, and they are looking forward to a better future. ...

1 The Italian dictator.
2 Labrador. The Labrador Development Company was running a
   logging operation there.
3 Fred Anderton (1889–1974). Born at
   Claybrook, Leicestershire, England.
   Pensioned from the R.C.M.P.
   8 August 1937.
4 Leonard T. Stick (1892–1979).

5 Raymond D. Fraser.
6 The British force sent to Ireland in
   1920 to suppress insurrection.
7 Major-General Sir Henry Hugh
   Tudor (1871–1965).
8 St John's. The Bally Haly Golf and
   Country Club Ltd was founded in
   1908.
9 Lloyd W. Shaw.

Q.H.S. to Ian and Sheila, Newfoundland Hotel, 19 July 1935

... Here ... we are in midsummer weather at last. It is such a joy to see everyone in summer suits, and to be able to wear our tropic suits ourselves. We have had a whole week of this gorgeous weather. As a matter of fact, the population is panting under the changed conditions. Usually, summer comes on us gradually, but last week we had icy blasts. ...

I have one or two stories for you, Ian. I expect you have this one, but just in case you have not. A man had got out of his car, & when he tried to get in again, the door stuck. He pulled & pulled & swore & swore. A kindly bishop chanced along &, hearing the language, was shocked. 'My good fellow, how can you expect a response to such oaths? You should be praying about it – not swearing.' Rather to the astonishment of the bishop, the man fell on his knees & prayed. Then he leapt to his feet, seized the handle & pulled, & the door opened at once. 'Well I'm damned,' said the bishop.

This is something of another sort, tho' clerical, & it happened here a few days ago. A poor woman went into a grocer's shop & was complaining bitterly that she had not a cent to buy anything. 'You should go to the Rev. Godfrey;¹ he is very kind & he may be able to tell you what you can do.' She went to Mr. Godfrey, who is a poor Anglican curate with a large family and a large heart, & she poured out her troubles to him. He gave her a dollar (4/.) he could not spare. A day or two later, he was in the grocer's shop, & the manager said to him, 'Did you give Mrs. O'Brien a dollar the other day?' 'Yes, I did. What of it?' 'Well she came down here next day, and "Glory be!" she said, "I've been able to pay me dues to Father O'Mara² with the dollar the Rev. Godfrey gave me."'

These Catholics really do make me mad. There's about a mile of the

Topsail Road under repairs, and for a week now the traffic has been diverted two miles round. Last Sunday, on our way back from Salmonier, out along the same way, we were astonished to find the road open, & more astonished still to find that we had to travel on a mass of loose metal quite untamped. It seems that the R.C.s were having a fête on a lake about two miles beyond the closed road, & the R.C.s went to the head of the roads repairing office (who chances to be an R.C.) & asked him to have the road opened for the Archbishop to come along to the fête (there was no reason why he should not go round like everyone else). The official refused to disobey the orders of his superior officer. But the priest went to the man actually on duty & ordered him to open the road, & he did it. The result was that all the traffic passed that way on Sunday afternoon, & the earth was worked up into the metal, and about 1 mile of metal has to be taken up and *washed* because, if there is any dirt in it, it will not set for tarmac. The man was dismissed on the spot. But how unfair – Can you imagine the poor man's quandary? The *Archbishop's* orders against a mere road official's. That is the sort of thing that happens in this country. The Archbishop is now working and *preaching* against the Commission. And yet many of them seem so friendly. But incidents like the road business make one realize a little how intense feeling may become. The annoyance of it. And the selfishness. And no matter how poor people are, the priest's dues must come before anything else.

I wonder whether you are enjoying these lovely moonlight nights. Here we have gorgeous eastern skies after sunset, & then the moon comes up an immense ball of fire, such a blaze that one night, as I turned out the light in my bedroom, I was startled by what at first thought was a terrible fire at sea. But then, when it rides high over the harbour & the water glimmers in silver iridescence or still as a mirrored world, the shadows are black as ink, and the light in Cabot Tower shines dimly, & the beacon light blazes & dims, & the lighthouse blazes & dims, & they throw a streak of golden light across the silver of the harbour. Every night, we stand at one window and watch the beauty for a time.

I must dress for dinner. Andrew Grieve has a party tonight. ...

1 William Ewart Godfrey (1880–1935).   2 John O'Mara (1901–1962). Ordained
20 June 1926.

J.H.S. to Maisie and Blair, on board the *Malakoff*, lying off Rencontre, Fortune Bay, 24 July 1935
Blowing hard & terrific rain, like Indian. I have told the skipper to lie here

till early morning, & then, if it is not too rough, to get across to Pool's Cove. We have had bad weather the last couple of days, with a lot of fog and very heavy rain – so heavy that one does not think that it can last much longer.

We left St. John's on Saturday[1] morning. The *Malakoff* started at 5 on Friday & should have been at Placentia by early morning Saturday. We drove out in a taxi 86 miles, getting there about one, and found no *Malakoff*. She arrived about half past seven, having had a lot of fog, while we were enjoying glorious sunshine. We went on board at once and found that the ship was aground on the mud, & we did not get off for an hour. We got to Harbour Buffett at midnight & had gone to bed. But they had organized an official reception, with rockets & guns and foghorns & church bells. It is a lovely little harbour. We went to early service there next morning and saw a very high church young man go through his ritual performance with an acolyte in attendance. It always to me seems disconcerting, and inappropriate for the spiritual intimacy of the service. And it was peculiarly so in the wooden church of that little outport, with some twelve communicants.

After the service, we started off in brilliant sunshine and ran straight into mist, & steamed through it about seven hours. Then it lifted just in time to allow us to enjoy the entrance to Mortier Bay. That is an enormous bay, land-locked, on the east of the Burin Peninsula. It has a lot of small settlements along its shores – Spanish Room, Creston, and others – but the chief settlement is Marystown, which used to be an important place but is now decayed and miserable. The war[2] ruined these places. The price of fish went up to 300% of today's prices, & there was no question of quality. So people made bad fish & much money & thought those times would last forever. The change came gradually but inevitably and completely, and now these fishing settlements all round this peninsula are in abject poverty. It is an appalling problem, for they are dyed-in-the-wool fishermen. ... We are trying hard to make agriculture at least a subsidiary, for the bottom is rapidly falling out of the fishery. And, of course, we are pushing other developments – forests – mines – game, &c., for all we are worth. The codfishery this year has been very patchy. In some places, it has been excellent. In others, it has been almost a complete failure.

I was at Mortier Bay – Marystown. We got there on Sunday evening & had a warm welcome from the doctor and the constable and the customs officer and a few men & their ladies. After supper, we were taken in the customs boat a few miles up the river[3] – a lovely sail on a lovely evening.

The settlement is built – as all are – along the sea front. The houses are of wood and they look bare, for they are planted right in the middle of a small field, as a rule. They have no flower gardens except in a few places.

On Monday, we drove across the peninsula from Marystown to Garnish. That is a most self-respecting place – no one on the dole – hardworking people with nice houses and gardens. The women were all wearing sunbonnets & looked so Somerset. I wish there were more Garnishes in the island. From Garnish, we drove back across the peninsula to Burin, where we had arranged to meet the travelling clinic, the hospital ship *Lady Anderson*. It had the Commissioner for Public Health on board, and we had to meet the local people to arrange for a cottage hospital. We settled it, and there will be one of 16 to 20 beds. That will be of great value. There is a similar hospital at Grand Bank on the other side of the Burin Peninsula. We spent a couple of hours at Burin & got on board the *Malakoff* (which had come on from Marystown) and sailed to St. Lawrence – another depressing settlement. It is mainly Catholic-Irish – a bad combination in a country where sturdy hard work and thrift are essential to comfort. They have a struggling fluorspar mine there, which would be a great thing for the place if it had sufficient capital. We went to see it. It is a cleft dug in the ground four feet wide, 85 feet deep, and without hoists, except for the mineral. The men go down a complicated arrangement of ladders. I would not like to work down there. And the men are paid irregularly, as the management can raise the money. Altogether, it is unsatisfactory.

From St. Lawrence, yesterday, the parish priest[4] drove us 27 miles over an appalling track in 2$\frac{1}{2}$ hours to Lamaline, another most depressing place, but blest with a Napoleonic nurse,[5] who is compelling the people to take to agriculture. She started a show last year, & they had 124 exhibits altogether, but its influence has resulted in improved attempts at gardening all up the coast for fifty miles. It is a great stock-raising country, but the people do not raise what they could. They look upon stock as for sale, not for consumption, which is typical.

Rain came down in sheets there, & I got properly wet, as I had no waterproof. It was a lovely morning when we started. We lunched on our sandwiches at Nurse McKeague's cottage, and then drove 26 miles through the rain & mist to Fortune, where I had to inspect a breakwater and harbour, and to look into relief matters. We had tea in the house of a merchant called Dixon[6] – nice people – and then drove to Grand Bank to find our *Malakoff*. At Grand Bank, there were the magistrate and the doctor & the relieving officer & the harbour with a breakwater, part of which has been undermined by the sea and will assuredly be washed away, if it is not repaired. They want the government to do it. It belongs to the local harbour board. We shall offer them part, if they do the rest.

I inspected the hospital, and went to visit the local J.P., who was in bed with heart and oedematous[7] legs, and then came on board and was interviewed by one after another till 10.30. We sailed about 3 o'clock, & I was up on deck & again at 5, when we came up to the foghorn at St. Jacques. A lot of the navigation consists in identifying foghorns & setting your course according.

We arrived at Anderson's Cove early in the morning, & were going to have a holiday fishing in Long Harbour River, but the rain came down in sheets, and, as we sailed up Long Harbour, we found the telegraph wire across it so low that we could not pass. So we came on here,[8] & found another poverty-stricken settlement. No fish. I tried to get a sea trout in the local river this afternoon, but only got drenched in the process. I did not get a rise.

The wind is blowing hard. If it moderates, we shall start at 6 tomorrow morning. Otherwise, we shall spend tomorrow here. Our next fixed point is Port aux Basques, on the 30th, so we have some spare time. ...

1 20 July 1935.
2 The Great War of 1914–18.
3 Through Creston Inlet.
4 Augustine Thorne (1890–1951).
   Ordained 18 January 1920.
5 (Clara) Beatrice McKeague.
6 George T. Dixon (1873–1952) or his
   son John R. Dixon.
7 Swollen.
8 Rencontre.

Q.H.S. to Greta, S.S. *Malakoff*, off Rencontre, 24 July 1935

... Picture us in the little saloon of the *Malakoff* – outside rain is pouring down with a swish on the water, and mist blots out this very lovely harbour. Inside, we are quite cosy – J.H.S. is playing his new patience, & we have just finished our piquet; he has won 4 games out of 5 – to his great satisfaction, as I have been holding unholily good hands for months. Now he has finished his patience & is reading *Victoria Regina* by Laurence Housman.[1] Do you know it? It is extraordinarily clever & most amusing. I wonder what the royal family think of it? I can quite believe they 'are not amused.' I gave it to Mrs. Lodge some time ago, but have only just got hold of it to read it myself; it was in great demand. This was to have been a holiday for fishing in a very fine salmon river. But the fates are against us. After 12 days of glorious weather, yesterday (J.H.S. birthday), the skies clouded over at midday, & we had a thunderstorm with torrential rain which has gone on for more than 24 hours. The result was that this morning, when we sailed up a marvellous fjord called Long Harbour, we found the river in which the salmon are to be caught so flooded that the fishermen would have had to walk 12 miles up to catch them. And it would have been a tremendous walk apart from the distance, & in such weather impossible. So we turned back down the fjord and came to Rencontre. This too is a wonderfully beautiful spot – not so wild as Long Harbour – but more lovely. Here too the fjord is set about with individual rocks – mountains almost – 300 to 400 ft. high almost sheer from the sea, with magnificent waterfalls cascading down them, often right from the summit. Here there are lovely wooded ledges, & the houses are set on the rocks just wherever there is a foothold for them, a lovely little church on a point with woods & houses just below, and a long barachois of red cliff from one island almost to another &, on the top of it, a big R.C. church with a cluster of houses below it on the sheltered side. It looks such a neat, well-kept settlement from the ship about ¼ mile out that it was a surprise to hear of the terrible distress here as elsewhere all along this coast. I landed with J.H.S. this afternoon when the rain held off for a little while, & I went and visited some of the houses, especially two blind old women. I went first to the schoolmaster's house & found his wife – a girl with her hair about her shoulders, just 18 – living with her mother & family. I asked her to take me to see these women, & we had a wild rough walk scrambling on over the shoulder of the rock & down to a group of miserable shacks in a cove further up the fjord. I found the poor old lady stone-blind, living with a son & his wife & two children – all so dreadfully poor. 'The government allows me $16 a quarter, but the money's not come this quarter, & it's five weeks now since it should have come and there's no fish at all this season. If you could just leave something for me with the merchant that he'll give me just a pick of sugar – I haven't had a pick of sugar for weeks – no sweetness in anything.' I went next door to see another daughter – two other daughters, with husbands & children. One husband with only one leg, & crowds of little children – all so terribly poor. I have never seen such patched clothing except in China, & there the patching was so neat; here it seems as tho' they had not even decent needles & thread, & the patches are of all sorts of stuff & patterns.

Then we went back on that path – the rain beating down again just like tropical rain, & the wind rising so that I looked down anxiously to the sea. And we climbed another path up to another miserable shack, where the other blind woman lives with her old husband. ... She broke her hip

8 years ago and is so crippled she has to be carried from her bed to her chair & can do nothing for herself. The little place was bare but spotlessly clean, & the old lady almost daintily clean, & such a sweet old thing. And they have only the $16 a quarter, & this quarter's money is 5 weeks over-due, and the old man, when he came to see us this morning, told us he had not had 'a pick' today, 'me & the missus.' He does everything for her & the house. She is 77 & he 67, & he just a little bit wanting – a wild helpless look, but so gentle. And he is a good housekeeper & nurse. 'He is so tenderful,' the old lady told me.

I have just looked out – the mist has lifted. There are only 4 lights among the houses – 300 people. That is an indication of the poverty.

Yesterday,[2] we drove about 14 miles over a rough track with the priest from St. Lawrence to Lamaline – such wild moorlands & such hills. He told me that, in many of these houses in the winter, the family take it in turn to creep under an old sail to sleep, while others keep the little peep of fire going. 'How they exist I don't know. The animals could not survive such conditions.' It is terrible. And what can be the solution of the prob-lem! Only moving the people from the rock of coasts to places where they can find some means of livelihood besides the fishing. In the old days, there must have been more fish and less competition from other nations, but it must always have been a most precarious livelihood.

We have seen the results of a terrible catastrophe that happened along the coast in 1929, as we came along. Everywhere, they tell us about it. There was a tremor one November afternoon[3] about 5 o'c., the priest told us; he thought there must have been an explosion in a mine & forgot about it. Then, about 7 o'c., there was a great shouting, & the people came rushing up to tell him of a great wave that had swept up on the shore & the houses & then withdrawn the sea half a mile & was coming up again. They say that in some places the wave rose to 70 ft. This went on for about two hours. At Burin, 18 people were drowned at once – many were swept out to sea on their houses & swept in again on the returning wave. Have you read *A High Wind in Jamaica*[4] that describes the same thing? It must have been horrible. At Burin, John saw the board plastered with telegrams of condolence – one from the King. Yesterday, we passed the remains of a settlement that was completely wiped out. The people who escaped never returned. The priest said it was most pitiful because the calamity came upon years of misfortunes, & men who had struggled in keeping them-selves & their families off the dole were left with nothing – no homes, no implements, no tools – nothing with which to start to work again. It seems as tho' the whole of the coast had suffered in this way – misfortune treading on the heels of misfortune, treading them down & down. The atmosphere of depression and hopelessness is terrible. I had never realized how bad things are.

And it is a marvellously beautiful country – quite as fine as Norway, John says. Such a country for tourists & sportsmen, if it could be sufficiently developed. The difficulty is that the need is terrible & so unjust, and schemes of development take long to mature, & meanwhile a people are deteriorating & dying by inches, & there is not money to rescue them in the big way that is necessary. ...

1 British writer (1865–1959). *Victoria*
   Regina was published in 1934.
2 23 July 1935.

3 18 November 1929.
4 By Richard Arthur Warren Hughes
   (1900–1976). Published in 1929.

J.H.S. to Ian and Sheila, in a fog somewhere near the entrance to Harbour Breton, 25 July 1935

... Early on Thursday, we sailed to Pool's Cove – a lovely little spot where the Colonial Missionary Society[1] has a station. They are Congregationalists. There was a man of parts here, one MacDermott, but he has gone, and the people are slacking off. Still, they have beautiful gardens & a lot of cattle & sheep, and there should be no dole. But they have no shame, and would take dole if they could get it.

We went to Belleoram. BELLEORAM – what does it mean? ... Here again, there are bankers (i.e., banking schooners) and prosperity. The weather cleared up, & we had lovely sunshine for our visit. It was so warm that small boys were diving off the pier alongside of which we lay. We got away early in the afternoon, with slight mist driving up. It got thicker, and, by the time we got to the entrance of Harbour Breton, it was so thick that we missed it, & went on two or three miles, until we saw breakers, & stopped & anchored. ...

1 A Congregationalist society formed
   in 1836, later the Commonwealth
   Missionary Society. In 1966 the latter
   body joined with the London

Missionary Society to form the
Congregational Council for World
Mission.

Q.H.S. to Betty, S.S. *Malakoff*, off Harbour Breton, in a fog, 25 July 1935

Here we are, as you see if you read my address, in a dense fog, lying off a terribly rocky coast. Luckily, we have been able to drop anchor, and, luckily too, there is only a swell, but we can hear the swell dashing up on the rocks, & a little while ago we could see it. We have been riding at anchor for the last two hours, hoping the fog would lift. We had such a glorious morning and afternoon till about 4, when we ran into this mist. This south coast is terribly fog-bound – the fog lies along the shore, withdraws to the banks, & creeps in again, but seldom goes over the land.

We have had a spell of really hot weather till three days ago. Then we had torrential rain for a day & a half, & it was so raw & chilly.

We are having a most interesting trip again. I wish you could have shared it. I am getting quite expert at hopping up & down wobbly ladders & in & out of boats, & climbing slippery seaweedy wharf walls. ...

There! We are in! The fog thinned for a few minutes and the captain recognized the land, & found that we were a mile beyond the landfall we wanted. Lucky he is such a careful navigator! So we turned & slipped along as fast as we could, with the mist threatening to enfold us again. And then a light gleamed out, and still we held on past the lighthouse, apparently into the mist again – then the sound of sheep baaing – & a little white church on the shore and great 3-masted schooners like phantom ships, riding at anchor in the harbour. So now we are safe alongside the wharf in Jersey Harbour. Very thankful we all are.

It is a curious thing that the settlements that are really well-off are those that practise the banking fishery – that is, the schooner goes out where the fish are likely to be and lets down a line of hooks. The fishermen who put down traps have done nothing this year. Some of the bankers have gone to Greenland. There is a man who has just come on board, & he is talking to Daddy, & he has just said, 'I've got three bankers in Greenland just now' – 2,000 miles away!

This is a beautiful coast. ... Yesterday, we went up & down real fjords, as beautiful as anything in Norway – great rocks of mountains rising to 1,000 ft. – and covered with woods sometimes, sometimes bare, running back to lovely green sward with buttercup meadows; sometimes marvellous rose-red – sometimes harsh rust-red – sometimes taking queer shapes like monstrous animals crouching on the sea, sometimes like great sphinxes.

Saturday 27. We have passed through such beautiful waters the last two days – it has been like sailing among the lochs & islands on the west coast of Scotland. As a matter of fact, we passed a place called 'Pushthrough,' coming into Bay Despair (which is really Bay d'Espoir), and it certainly was difficult navigation between rocky islands. As we came up to the entrance, we passed a schooner about 1/2 mile away, and were much touched to see a man right at the top of the mast holding up the Union Jack to greet us. The siren blew an acknowledgement, & we waved handkerchiefs & my white hat. All the lighthouse fog signals boom a greeting to us, & we siren back. Pushthrough was decked with flags, & a little crowd was gathered on the wharf to wave to us as we passed. Wherever we go, the people give us such kind welcome.

Bay Despair is perfectly lovely. I don't know how the captain finds his way, for lovely lochs open up on every side & great islands & rocks stud the bay. I think Gaultois is one of the most picturesque settlements we have touched. The entrance is almost hidden, and you turn in from the south of the wide-open bay into a harbour tucked into a curb of land. High rocks guard the entrance on both sides, but well apart, so that you look north from the little harbour right up the open bay. Daddy says it is just like a Japanese village. As you come in under the great rock that guards the entrance to the south, there is a stairway on the rock, down to a little lookout. High on the rock is a pocket of earth with a garden & a shack on it & a man & woman leaning on a fence to look down & wave to us as we passed in. Right in the middle of the harbour is a beautiful little white church perched on the rock about 100 ft. up, and below it and beyond it, unseen, of course, from our ship, a great lake, & beyond that, high mountains. The lake water spills over beside the church & comes tumbling & foaming down in a cascade to the sea. Higher still, & quite apart, a tiny white R.C. chapel stands on a high rock. It is all well wooded, &, in the deep curl of the harbour, there are neat & pretty merchants' houses with trees & gardens & good wharfs & great fish rooms, some of them 150 years old. The centre of the curl of land is so steep there is no foothold for houses – only shrubs & creepers; and a wooden roadway is built right round over the water to the fishermen's village. A stairway leads over the rock to the church & to the brightly painted little houses sprinkled over the rocks; then again, beautiful red rock covered with pine & birch trees. A sweet old lady in a blue sunbonnet was making hay on the strip of land between some houses – about 3 yards by 20 – good hay too – 'for me goat.' And I invited [myself into] many of the houses, so clean, with lovely geraniums & begonias ... [in] the windows & little verandahs here & there. I found no big families there. One pathetic little group – an old man of 85, very white & still, lying on a couch by the window, looking out to sea, & his old wife, a crumpled cripple in a chair bedside him, and, coming in at the gate with heavy pails of water from the well, a lovely girl, their daughter-in-law, her voice gone to a whispered croak with consumption – 'and the cough so bad there's no sleep.' There is often very sad, empty old age, & sickness that gets no relief from doctor or nurse in these distant outports.

Sunday morning. I will just finish this letter before I get up. We had such an interesting day yesterday. St. Alban's, which we expected to find on the rocks in every sense, is really a lovely country with beautiful farm-ing land & good gardens. The priest[1] is, I think, partly responsible; he is well-meaning, but so stupid & foolish, telling the people they ought to take 'goons[2] & blow the loggers out of the woods' at the head of Bay Despair[3] – men who have as much right as St. Alban's men to those woods; 'the woods that God has given to *you* St. Alban's men,' he says. John spoke very straight in answer, but avoided crossing or rebuking the priest before his own people. But really, he talked for ¾ hour as chairman, & told the people what he *thought* John was going to say, including that he had not any help to give them, & that the government was 'held by the nose' by the big paper companies and could not help themselves. Really, it was difficult to sit through it. But evidently he can't lead the people; they won't follow.

Then, in the afternoon, we came to Conne River to look for salmon to fish, but the book[4] about the N.F.L. salmon rivers gives the wrong season for the fishing here, and we are too late – the salmon have gone up the river to spawn. There is a settlement of Micmac Indians at the mouth of the river – another lovely spot. A spit of land runs out from under the cliffs, & in the woods above is a little church with pepper-pot towers that the Indians built themselves. On a little lawn in front of the church, half-veiled by poplars, a group [of] Indian girls in bright feast-day frocks, red, yellow, rosy, & blue satins (St. Anne's Feast),[5] came running down to the edge of the lawn, and made such a pretty picture in the sunshine with the church up above them and the forest around & below. We climbed up to the church – having first been welcomed by some very pretty old men & women Micmacs – and found the party in the schoolroom, with a Sunday school feast all arranged on one side, just as in a village party in England, & the rest of the hall cleared for dancing. They danced a Micmac dance for us – very much like the lancers,[6] but with a good deal of heel & toe work by the men, & far more twirling around of the couples – all very fast, to the accompaniment of a concertina, but very dignified. We shook hands all round, & everyone pressed forward to greet us & to say farewell, & much of the party accompanied us down to the river. They are not pure Indians, & they live in houses. They do some wood logging in the summer, & go into the forest for trapping in winter, but they can't make a living now, and are all on the dole. How they manage to rise to these cheap satins & silks I can't think; they evidently made them themselves. But I noticed that their boots & shoes were good. They are very mixed-looking people – some very Indian with the high cheekbone & flat faces, rather like Mongols; others you could not tell had any Indian blood in them. The Indians are all Catholics. ...

1 Stanislaus St Croix (1882–1968). Parish priest at St Alban's, 1916–46.
2 Guns.
3 Bay d'Espoir.
4 C.H. Palmer, *The Salmon Rivers of*

Newfoundland: A Descriptive Account of the Various Rivers of the Island (Boston 1928).
5 26 July.
6 A square dance or quadrille.

J.H.S. to Betty, at Port aux Basques, 30 July 1935

Our inspection trip is over. I expect Mother has written you long accounts of it. We have been fortunate all through and not least so last night. We were coming along the coast in fog and with heavy fog over the land, and the captain told me he would go slow, so as to get in at daylight. Then the wind sprang up from the S.E. and the fog cleared away, so that we got in at midnight. The wind increased, and by morning there was a tearing gale. The sea also got up, and great breakers were surging over the rocks this morning. We should have had a really bad time, had we not got in, for our steamer is very light. She has burnt all her coal and used all her water, and is consequently very lively in a sea. ... Tonight, we go on by train. Mother goes to St. John's to meet me again, on the 9th, at Gleneagles. I go to Deer Lake & up the upper Humber. It should be good fun. There is an awful lot of poverty here – dreadful. The fishery is poor, & the markets have gone to pot. The people are only getting about 55 cents for 100 lbs. of fresh fish. They cannot live on it. Frankly, it is exceedingly difficult to know what to do. ...

Q.H.S. to Maisie and Blair, S.S. *Malakoff*, Port aux Basques, 30 July 1935

... We have had a mixed bag of weather on the south coast trip – storm & sunshine & mist & clear weather. It is a wonderfully beautiful coast and all so interesting, tho' often terribly distressing. One can't see any future for the fishermen as fishermen, and they know no other way of life and are not suited for it – the sea is in their blood. ...

Q.H.S. to Bel, Newfoundland Hotel, 1 August 1935

... Here it is very warm, but very unsettled. Today has been glorious after a night of wild thunderstorms & torrential rain. Lucky too, because some friends had a fête – they thought the storm would wash it out. But you would never dream that anything had happened to make them anxious; the ground was dry, & the day was perfect for summer garden-party frocks. It was such a pretty scene. The house is built in the old colonial style, and the garden is terraced & well set among trees & runs down to a little river.

John is away just now. ... I rejoin [him] ... at 'Gleneagles,' the lovely log cabin where we spent a few days last year. ...

There! I have, I hope, got a companion for Mrs. Levick[1] for camping. You know the Captain Levick who brings a party of schoolboys over.[2] Mrs. Levick comes ahead & prepares everything for them, & then camps herself, with her own small boy & a friend. Her own little party is belated, so she asked me if I could find a friend who would enjoy that sort of holiday with her. I have got just the girl – such luck – a very nice young married woman who will love it, if her husband will let her go. It is such a chance. A real camp in the wild with fishing.

It is a remarkable thing about this country. No one is afraid to go anywhere alone. There is no crime. Lots of petty theft and swindling, but no murders or horrors. I suppose it is partly because the population is so small, & a criminal could not hide in the settlement, & could not survive in the woods, & he could not escape by sea; everyone who comes & goes at a port is noticed.

We saw some wonderfully beautiful scenery again on this last trip. The south coast is just a wall of jagged rocks that looks as tho' there were no entrances to the land. But you turn in among the rocks & find yourself in the loveliest lochs. Of course, the entrance to the big bays is wide – like Placentia Bay & Fortune & Conception & Trinity, etc., etc. Placentia Bay must be 100 miles deep, & Fortune & Trinity too; Conception, the one I know best, always called 'The Bay' in St. John's, is about 50 miles deep. ...

1 Audrey (Beeton) Levick.   2 From the United Kindgom.

Q.H.S. to Ian and Sheila, Newfoundland Hotel, 4 August 1935

... We had an extraordinarily interesting trip ... on the south coast. ... I think it is about 300 miles from Cape Race to Cape Ray – about the same as the south coast of England – as the crow flies. But the coastline here must be, I should think, about 8 times as long as the English south coast-line. Placentia Bay is about 100 miles deep, & Fortune not much less. They are lovely – very like the Scottish coast, with lovely lochs opening off them. But, in some parts, it is more like Norway – Long Harbour is just as fine a fjord as you will find in Norway, tho' John says it is on a smaller scale. It is difficult to realize scale here; the impression is of grandeur on a big scale. I am sure it must be because we are really living on the tops of high mountains that have been submerged, all but their highest peaks. It is a wonderful country for geologists. If you know of an easy primer on the subject, you might give me the name. The extraordinary formations here mock one's gross ignorance. At a place called English Harbour, the coast was of red sandstone cliffs – a glorious colour and taking shapes like immense grotesque animals kneeling along the coast.

The fishing along the coast has been very bad this year, and conditions are frightening. Some years ago, there was marvellous trap fishing, & the fishermen gave up going out to the banks, following the fish, & got an easier living nearer their homes. But whether trap fishing has destroyed this fishery or whether the earthquake of 1929 drove the fish away, no one knows, but the trap fishermen & the shore fishermen have done badly ever since. Only the bankers – the ships that follow the fish – have done well, and wherever there is a banker settlement, you see the difference at once in an air of greater comfort – decent houses, good wharfs.

But wherever we went, we were so kindly greeted – flags flying, people gathered to welcome us, the foghorns at the lighthouses moaning a greeting to us, every gun in the place fired in our honour. At one place, Pushthrough, where we could not stop, it was pathetic to see the people gathered on the wharf waving to us, and flags & guns being fired. We always sirened our response. Once, we saw a schooner half a mile away with a man at his masthead waving a Union Jack. We sirened him in response, & weren't we glad we chanced to notice him!

I invested in £1 worth of boiled & sugared candies to take with me as before and, as before, the maker doubled my order and did up the candies in half-pound bags so that they are not sticky, and when there were too many children to give a handful to everyone, I gave scrambles – girls on one side, boys on the other, & tinies by themselves. It gave great delight. I gave them to the old people too who relish 'a pick' of sweetness. We took all the old papers & magazines I had collected too, & distributed them. I gave away a pair of my spectacles too, to a paralyzed woman who could read & could do nothing with her poor crippled hands. She had not been able to see to read for a long time so I made her try my Woolworth specs[1] & we gave her a book: 'But it's lovely – I can see – quite plain – listen!,' & she read to us proudly. In another place, I gave away all my cascara tablets[2] to the lighthouse keeper's old father! 'Twelve days it be,' his kind son told us anxiously. No doctor within 100 miles. But the hospital ship, the *Lady Anderson*, is going round part of the coast now, & will deal with some of their cases.

I got a nasty bite from some poisonous fly on the fish stages at one place a week ago, & have been having a nasty time with it the last four days. ... There is a nice English nurse here, Miss Geen, who has come out to take charge of the infant welfare organization, & she has been advising me. She is a St. Thomas's nurse ... & has had an interesting career ... in London organising welfare in Islington, till it was as perfect as she could get it; in Kenya, in charge of a nursing home for three years; & now here. The condition of things in St. John's is beyond all belief, she tells me. I thought infant welfare was a simple affair & pleasant work. But she has enlightened me. In this little town, there are about 600 girls on the streets, many of them girls of 14 & 15. And the fathers of the babies are often boys of respectable families, still at secondary schools in the town – and the father pays & the boy still continues at his school – all is hushed up, so far as the boy is concerned. The laws here are made by the men for the men. The women are of no account – nothing but drudges & child bearers – and there is not even the morality of the tribal system to protect society. There has been no enforcement of registration of births. Everyone was afraid of the revelations that would have to be faced. The work of a Josephine Butler[3] and an Elizabeth Fry[4] and every other sort of social reformer is needed here in this town alone. It makes one feel Bolshevistic too – the well-to-do so scornful of the possibility of any improvement in the poor. Indeed, there are many things that happen that are most discouraging to the reformer, but I expect that is not unusual anywhere. For instance, there is lots of driftwood or burntwood near one of the settlements. The children could be organised to collect it. But the people pull up & burn garden or, rather, field fences rather than bother to collect the driftwood. ... It is as tho' they had missed the stiffening of moral texture that was the Victorian contribution to private & public standards of living. ...

I found harebells up on Signal Hill. I do love them. Today, my room is full of wild roses. They are larger flowers and deeper pink than in Wales &, as in Scotland, they come in August. They are much stronger-scented – delicious too. But they grow in dwarf bushes or climb up the shrubs.

We have had lovely days for a whole week now, but we have had tremendous thunderstorms & heavy rain two nights. There was a fête on Friday, the day after the worst night, but the garden where the fête was held was quite dry & you could not have had a lovelier day for party frocks. Today, the tennis tournament begins on the grounds below the hotel. Mr. Lodge has turned the waste lands there into tennis grounds & park. This week too there is the great regatta[5] on Quidi Vidi Lake.[6] So we are quite gay in spite of all the misery & problems of this most distressed island. ...

1 Spectacles.
2 For the relief of constipation.
3 1828–1906. British advocate of women's rights.
4 1780–1845. British prison reformer.
5 An annual event, said to mark the end of summer.
6 St John's.

J.H.S. to Maisie and Blair, in Camp at Birchy Lake, 6 August 1935[1]

You will have to forgive handwriting on this occasion, for I am writing on my knee, with fishing gauntlets on my hands to prevent mosquito bites, and, as you will notice, I am writing in the rain. Yet we have had wonderful weather this first week of our holiday – only one wet day; that day it did rain, and the following night – with terrific thunderstorms. The balance of the week has been glorious sunshine.

Quita is in St. John's. I wanted to see the country of the upper Humber, and especially to gauge its suitability for a game preserve. I only intended to go as far as Aldery Lake,[2] where the true moose country begins, but have been induced to go on to Eddy's Lake,[3] at the base of the foothills of the Long Range (the mountain backbone of the island), & on the way back to diverge to see the Birchy Lake area. It has been a marvellous trip – I parted from Quita (who was sleeping the sleep of a cherub) at Deer Lake in the express on Wednesday[4] morning last at 3 a.m. I had had one hour's sleep, & was horrified to find that my friend Ken Goodyear[5] and my guide & the party proposed to start at once. So we started for the jetty and travelled across the lake and, as far as the boat would go, in a motorboat, up the river. I suppose we went in all about six miles. Then we had breakfast at 5 a.m. (summer time), just as a marvellous dawn was breaking. It was too marvellous for a prospect of fine weather, but the day was none too bad.

Goodyear & I walked the first two or three miles, as the rapids were very heavy and the three men had quite enough to do to pole up the canoes – three of them – laden with tents & gear, without the additional weight of Goodyear, who weighs 260 lbs., & myself, who weigh 202. The path was very wet, and, in avoiding one pool, I slipped on a rotten log and fell on a stump, which got me fair in the right ribs. It was exceedingly painful, & I was afraid of fracture, but that has evidently not occurred.

Today, a week later, the rib is very tender to the touch, & I cannot lie on my back (!), owing to the pain in the rib if I do so.

That day, we poled & paddled up the river to the Small Falls,[6] about 18 miles from the river's mouth. The river is very beautiful, though the sameness of the jungle on both sides for mile after mile tends to become monotonous. Small Falls are lovely, but on that occasion were devoid of salmon unwily enough to take a fly.

Next day, Thursday, we had a long trek of river, with rapid after rapid, for 18 miles to Big Falls. Just above Small Falls, while the men were portaging canoes & gear round the falls, I caught a beautiful salmon, about 8 lbs. in weight & fresh run from the sea.

Grand Falls[7] is magnificent. The river is confined in a gorge of red sandstone, tree-clad to its edge, and comes down, I suppose, 30 feet in a roaring, raging torrent. At the bottom of the falls, hundreds – no thousands – of salmon are leaping, leaping all the time in the hope of getting up to their spawning grounds. It is a marvellous sight, & goes on without intermission from dawn to dark. I should say that of 50 leaps, one is successful. You can see, from above, the successful salmon clinging like a limpet to the edge of the fall & gradually wriggling himself to safety and a further voyage up the river. I should have expected to find many dead salmon below the falls, for the unsuccessful are swept back into a boiling, foamy cauldron. We did not see one, except the salmon we killed ourselves.

We had a great day's salmon fishing there. I brought eleven back, having returned a further five to the water and deliberately shaken off four – total 20. Goodyear brought home 22. We salted them down to take home with us.

Next day, we went on up the river another 16 or 18 miles, with a lot of heavy work in the rapids. We stopped at a place called 'The Forks,' which is marked on no map, but where an island splits the river into two channels – a beautiful camping site, with lovely views up & down the river. Just before we got there, we saw a cow moose grazing on the alder buds by the river's brink. We did a most successful stalk and got within 15 yards, & I took a snapshot – but, alas & alas, there was no film exposed. I had put in a new film in a hurry & forgotten to turn to number one.

Next day was Sunday, & we went up the Humber to where it emerges from Eddy's Lake, and across it, some two miles, to the mouth of the White Brook. On the way, we saw two cow moose feeding, and again did a successful stalk, & this time I got my picture. When we got into camp, we each caught a couple of salmon. Next day, I fished in the morning without success and in the afternoon went exploring the western end of the lake. On the way there, on a little green island, I saw a pair of antlers sticking up out of the grass – we stalked, & a great bull moose stood up & looked at me, and I took his photograph. That evening, we saw another moose cross the river above our camp.

On Tuesday,[8] we returned on our tracks, down some fearsome rapids, and turned off north to Birchy Lake, a mile before we got to 'The Forks.' We had a glorious time there. We saw two moose, a bull & a cow, feeding the other side of the lake when we arrived, and in the afternoon my guide, Matt Burton, took me in a canoe and we went some four or five miles up the Birchy Brook, between alder beds at first, & the last mile or two through forest. We had a marvellous time. First, we saw a beaver house. Then, two bull moose swam across the river in front of our canoe & I got snaps of them swimming and then one of them standing on the bank. Then, we saw a cow moose swim the river & higher up another cow moose crossing. On the way back, we came across a pair of otters, evidently with young, for one of them followed us in the water & every now & then stood up in the water & cursed us.

In the evening, Goodyear & Bruce Dennis, his canoe man, and Henry Cross, our cook, had an extraordinary experience. They stalked a cow moose and, going round the corner of an island, Goodyear got out & walked along the bank, the canoe being alongside of him. They came upon a calf feeding, & got right up to it before the calf saw them. Then it roared out a bleat and jumped right over the canoe into the water & swam. The cow heard the call & bellowed and charged straight at Goodyear, who leaped into the canoe & escaped – the cow following its calf into the river. There is an adventure for you. But another thing happened that is difficult to believe. I caught a freshwater clam with a fly! I was fishing for salmon & thought I had got caught up in a stick. I hauled in and it was a large clam, which had taken the fly. I have the shells as [a] memento of what must be a very rare experience.

It is now Thursday[9] & we are back at Big Falls after quite an exciting journey. We came down rapids which were too heavy to take us through on the way up – and we saw beaver & quite a number of moose. Matt & I stalked one young bull up to within ten yards, and he went on feeding though he saw us. I was just getting my camera ready when Henry clicked his pole in the other canoe and the bull bolted. Goodyear got within a few yards of an enormous bull, who showed distinct signs of animosity, so Goodyear hastily retired.

In four days, we have between us seen 28 moose & 3 moose calves. Some game country. And moose were only introduced in 1905.

This has been a gorgeous trip. Of course, there are drawbacks, & in this case they have been mosquitoes – and, *much* worse, black flies. They bite me unmercifully, notwithstanding my kind of oil & dope. They are the worst kind of affliction. ...

1 This letter is dated 'Wednesday 6th. August.' The Wednesday in question, however, fell on 7 August.
2 Alder Pond.
3 Adies Pond.
4 31 July 1935.

5 Harold Kenneth Goodyear (1896– 1977), a businessman in central and western Newfoundland.
6 Little Falls.
7 Big Falls, Sir Richard Squires Provincial Park.
8 6 August 1935.
9 8 August 1935.

J.H.S. to Greta, Gleneagles, Glenwood, 14 August 1935

... I got to Gleneagles about one o'clock on Monday morning & found that Quita had arrived the previous evening. We told you all about Gleneagles last year, though I expect that you will have forgotten. It is a log cabin inn on the border of the Gander Lake. The bedrooms are separate little log cabins, each with two beds. It is very homely and well run, by a Mr. & Mrs. Reid. The fly in the ointment at the moment is Mrs. Murray Levick, wife of Surgeon-Commander Murray Levick, who runs the Public Schools Exploring Society, of which Mrs. M.L. is Honorary Secretary. The exploring party went up from Gleneagles to the wilder parts of N.F.L., & Mrs. M.L. is stopping in her own tent close to the hotel & using it as a convenience, for which she pays nothing. It is specially mean, as the Reids have nothing except what they can earn during a very short season at the hotel, and they have told her so. Last year, they went in from Grand Falls, H.Q. of the Anglo-Newfoundland Development Company (Lord Rothermere). Her father,[1] in olden days, was manager of the concern, and on the strength of that she ordered everyone about as if she were boss. The staff were much annoyed, but made no kick, as Lord Rothermere told them to give all the help they could.

I cannot think why I waste your time and my own in writing this kind of tittle-tattle. ...

1 Sir Mayson M. Beeton (d. 24 June 1947). Organized and administered the Newfoundland Forestry Corps, 1915–18.

Q.H.S. to Greta, on the Gander River, 15 August 1935
Here we are in canoes going down the Gander River. We have just passed
our first rapids, so I thought I would share my experience with you. We
left Gleneagles – log cabin inn – at 10 o'c. Robin Reid took us in his
motorboat as far as Glenwood, towing our canoes with all our gear – pots
& pans, etc. – as we are off for 5 days in the woods. At Glenwood, we
came through our first rapids – quite mild excitement – then under the
railway bridge in among the rocks to take in a camp-chair for my greater
comfort. The luggage train was crossing the bridge as we passed under, &
the men shouted to us below. Also some men perched up on one of the
piers. Three ragged little girls came rushing down with axe & waterpot. ...
    My it is hot! But it is glorious – the river intensely blue, the woods
living green, the firs swaying in the wind, the birch leaves all atremble, the
rocks in midstream & along the shore grey & gold.
    Then we had to get out and walk for about ½ mile over great rocks set
about with late blue irises & harebells & long-stalked large violets. ...
    Now we are on a wide, long stretch with a wooded hill beyond it.
There is a strong breeze now, and the river is broken with sapphire waves.
John calls: 'Don't write – look out for bear & moose.' The guide has just
swung the canoe round for me to see Mount Peyton, lifting his great cone
above the river, inset in the gap. On again. Here is a lovely little wooded
peninsula jutting out into the river. Tempting little beaches too. I have had
to put on gloves to protect my hands from the sun, & I have a muslin
puggaree[1] hanging from my big felt hat. How you would love basking in
the sunshine & paddling quietly up the river. John & I each have a deck-
chair in the bow of the canoes, & we lie at ease facing our way of progres-
sion. John has his feet in white tennis shoes stuck out on each side of the
bow. I am thankful I put on my coolest garments this morning – that blue
silk check you chose for me. White cirrus clouds are floating low driven
by the wind. Luckily, I brought a mackintosh – such a pretty one – apple
green & white check. ...

1   Thin scarf of muslin, etc.

J.H.S. to Ian and Sheila, in camp at Third Pond, 19 August 1935
... Quita will tell you of the loveliness of the river and all the details of the
journey. Her 'guide,' Sandy Parsons,[1] is cook/parlour maid. An excellent
'general.' Mine, Cecil Pelley,[2] is a one-armed man, and it is a revelation to

see him manage his canoe – which he built himself – in a rapid. He also makes his own boots! He has invented quite a number of gadgets to play the part of the missing arm, which he shot off when a boy of twelve. ...

We are having very great heat. There is a large forest fire in progress somewhere. We do not know where, but we can smell it all the time. It is certainly not less than 50 miles away. Forest fire is the appalling danger of this country. We have an excellent fire-fighting organization, but in this dry hot weather, with a high wind, it is almost impossible to subdue a fire that gets fairly started.

I must to bed. I was up at 5.30 this morning & it is now 10 p.m.

We wish so much that you could have the chance of a holiday like this one. It is superb. ...

1 15 January 1911 – 17 April 1991.   2 8 June 1910 – 8 February 1951.

Q.H.S. to Maisie, in camp, on the Gander River, 19 August 1935

Here we are having a marvellous holiday – the sort of holiday I feel ought to be yours – it is so essentially a young folks' holiday. We really ought to be at Bournemouth being wheeled about in Bath chairs. Instead of that, in canoes, sliding down a lovely uninhabited reach of river, camping at night in log cabins perched on the bank at intervals of about 5 miles. I never thought this would be possible for me, but it is really quite easy & not uncomfortable. ... The first part through the worst rapids was most exciting. My guide, 'Sandy,' & I stuck on a wedge of rock above a drop into deep water. John's guide, Cecil, a one-armed marvel, had to come to our help. He tied his canoe to a rock (with one hand) & climbed over the rocks, leaving John helpless in a camp-chair in front of the canoe, not daring to move in case his canoe broke loose & went careening down the rapids without any hand to steer it. We have had lots of rapids since then but nothing exciting because the river is so low – 'never seen it as low.' We often stick, Sandy & I, but Cecil & John never stick. Cecil is a wonderful guide. To see him rig a sail to help us across a 3-mile lake! He cut down two trees for 'matches' (masts), tied his blanket to it using teeth & feet to help him, & he paddled or poled or rowed as he sailed: a nice fellow – always happy & courteous. Sandy is his stepbrother – a year younger, 24 & 25 – he is a rough type, & much more difficult to understand – a flaxen curly head & sunburnt, rather puzzled face. Sandy does the kitchen boy & handmaid while Cecil is out in the pools with John fishing. 'Do you like cooking, Sandy?' I asked him. 'I like every kind of work,' he declared passionately. They are so nice to each other there too – deferring to each other & affectionate one can see. 'That's where the bear visited you three years ago, Sandy.' 'Tell me about it,' I said. 'O he just stayed around our camp sniffing about for 3 hours.' That was today, as we crossed a big lake. They are real gentlefolk these outport N.F.L.ers. As a rule. I wonder if that is why there is no crime in this island. ...

J.H.S. to Betty, in camp at Joe Batts, Gander River, 23 August 1935
We are sitting in a log cabin with a birch-bark roof, and writing at a little collapsible table, and the rain is coming down in sheets. We are very glad of this, as an enormous forest fire has been raging near Grand Falls for a fortnight. It is about 40 miles from where we are, but yesterday afternoon the wind was blowing in our direction, and at half past four the sun disappeared with smoke cloud from the fire. It was within three miles of Bishop's Falls yesterday morning. The mill there & the Buchans mine both had to stop working. And now all danger must be over. It rained a little off and on all night, & for the last two hours it has been coming down a regular soaker. I fished until it became too heavy even for the fish.

We are getting near the end of our holiday – just another week but it has been a very spot holiday. ...

I met mother at Gleneagles on the 11th, & for the last ten days we have been camping on the Gander. I was afraid that it would be slow for her, but she says it is the finest holiday she has ever had. We have had tremendous heat but yesterday, when we came up here from Third Pond in a gale of wind. The sun was shining brilliantly, &, as the wind was from the west, & we travelling east, the water was not too bad on the lake. When we started, the men were not certain that we could get through. We have two guides, each of whom has his canoe. Quita's man is Sandy Parsons, who also does our cooking. Everything is fried, but that cannot be avoided. It is the easiest way to cook. My man is Cecil Pelley, a one-armed man. It is a marvellous triumph of intellect over disability. He manages his canoe in the rapids just as well as any man with both arms. He built the canoe himself, & makes his own boots, and traps in the winter-time, and bakes his own bread, – all with one hand. He is my guide, & goes fishing with me. So far, I have caught 8 salmon on this trip & I suppose 100 trout, and have lost five salmon.

Tuesday – 27th August – and we are back at Gleneagles. I am sitting in the dining-room, looking down Gander Lake – facing S.W. The wind is blowing straight towards me, and the lake is touched everywhere with

white flecks where the waves are breaking. It is a day of sunshine, but the
wind is cold. Quita & I have both had warm baths, a great treat after 10
days without a bath, though I bathed in the lakes on three occasions, and,
of course, there was ample water for ablutions everywhere. ...

J.H.S. to Betty, Newfoundland Hotel, 4 September 1935
... I have just been trying to work out what we shall have to live upon if I
give up my present job. Our total income would be about £1,500. Out of
this, we have to pay allowances ... [in] total, say, £650, leaving about £850
for our house at home and all other expenses. That is less than half what
Dolguog used to cost us – or rather, less than half we used to spend when
at Dolguog. It will mean living in a cottage somewhere, and no motor. But
both Quita and I will be perfectly happy in a cottage with no motor! We
shall have it somewhere within reach of a holiday centre for the family. ...

Today is Labour Day, and, by way of being a holiday, I spent an hour
& a half this morning in conversation with the Governor, & this afternoon
I am going out to inspect Mount Pearl farm, which we have bought as an
experimental farm for the government. ...

Q.H.S. to Greta, Newfoundland Hotel, 8 September 1935
... I must tell you something of our holiday.

We had a marvellous time – such fun. We had two canoes with two
guides – Cecil, or 'Ceecil,' & Sandy. 'Ceecil' had only one arm, but he was
wonderful, using teeth, knees & feet to help as an extra three hands. His
arm had been blown off by a gun when he was 11 years old. He told me
about it so mildly: 'I was never a bit frightened – My heart never beat a bit
faster – That's what saved me the doctor said.' He & another boy of 15
were duck shooting and were 15 miles from home by boat across Gander
Lake. 'The blood spurted as far as to that tree (about 15 yds.), & the bones
were all splinters, so that I had just to take them in my hand & throw them
away before I did anything else. I just lay in the bottom of the boat, & Jim
Shea,[1] he could do nothing but cry all the way back: "Don't die, Cecil;
don't die or they'll all think I killed you." "Well you get me home quickly
before I die on you, & then they'll know you did not kill me."' And when
they got to the end of their 15 miles across the lake, he walked home a mile.
But that night, when he was lying on the bed & they brought him some
tea, he felt all right, but, when he tried to sit up, he could not even lift his
head. Luckily, it was the mail day, & when the train came along, they took

him to the Grand Falls hospital; & when they arrived at 3 in the morning, they got the doctor out of bed to him & he operated at once. 'Another half hour & I'd have been done for,' he said. 'For why? – the blood poisoning had set in.' He is such a nice-looking boy, tall & lithe with nice blue eyes & straight brown hair that he is always throwing out of his eyes. It is a beautiful sight to see him poling with that one arm so strong '& me stomach like iron with the muscles of it.' Sandy, my guide, often got stuck on rapids & shallows, & 'Cecil' was the one to come to his help. Sandy never had to help Cecil; he seemed to have a special river sense & knew every rock & every turn. The only time he got into trouble was once in the hurricane, when we were fighting our way across one of the lakes & the wind caught his canoe on the shallows when there was no bottom to the mud. 'I'll get out & push,' John said. Cecil leapt at him: 'No – no – you'll never get in again if you did.' Somehow they pulled round, & we got across safely.

But that first week was heavenly – a gorgeous week. I sat on the bedding facing the bow, & Sandy poled & paddled behind. The river opened up before us, every reach more lovely & more interesting than the last. There were lots of rapids, & some of them were quite exciting & good fun. Sometimes we had to get out & clamber over the boulders & rocks for ¼ mile, & that was really the only thing I found dangerous – a slip would probably mean a broken ankle or leg. In most places, the river is about ¼ to ½ mile wide & strewn with golden boulders & rocks, & with lovely islands dividing the river into many streams & deep pools, where you could see the salmon lying. There was a lovely weed streaming under the water from the depths, red-gold like Maisie's hair as a child, with vivid green, & when the sun shone through the water, it glowed blood red & emerald. And every mile or two of river there is a lake about 4 x 2 miles – ponds they call them here. Once the wind was favourable, so Sandy & 'Cecil' cut down poles & tied their blankets up as masts. John got quite a good photo of me. I think I will enclose it. Most of the photos are not of much interest unless you know the places. I think we ought to have one of those lenses that bring out the comparative heights. Our photos are excellent, but they always seem to me so dull, & give no idea of the country.

Crossing the lakes was always interesting too – there were lovely bays with yellow water–lilies lifting their cups above the water, and river mouths with dim rides up into the forest, where you watched for bear & moose. And the shallows were covered with that white lobelia that I think grows in Welsh pools in a sparser & less interesting way than here. John would fish for an hour here and there among rapids or on pools, & I would have

my book and my writing and my knitting in a bag at my side, so that I was
quite happy to rest for a bit from watching.

We camped in shacks that the Reids (of Gleneagles) put up last winter
at intervals of about 4 miles down the river for the convenience of their
guests, & the guides had their tent, which they pitched at a little distance.
In the shack just two beds – rough log-steads with a canvas stretched
across. I had a sleeping bag, but I simply could not bear it, nor the scratchi-
ness, nor the memories that haunted my dreams, so after a week we ex-
changed. But next time (!) I shall take sheets when I go to the North Pole.
I used to spread that beastly bed bag on the rocks in the sunshine every
day, but every night things seemed to crawl all over me, & make my hair
stand on end, & my flesh creep with horror. And I ached with the hard-
ness of the canvas, & when I was warm on top, I was cold underneath, &
spent the night turning on a spit. But I loved it all! And, gradually, I learnt
how to be more comfortable – giving John the sleeping bag, for one thing.
I had had a delicacy about that because it had been lent specially for me. I
managed the blankets much better than he did – rolled myself round &
round in a cocoon. Then there was a 'cabinet'² along a little path behind –
convenient, & a real comfort in bad weather, but at night – no! Nothing
could induce me to face the horrors of that black hole at night. ... There
was also in the cabin a very simple stove – just a sheet of iron bent over on
a stone with a pipe leading outside. We thought we should never dare to
use [it], & we did not need it the first week; we built our fire on the shore.
But the last week, in the days of the great storm, we were thankful for it,
& not only dried our clothes & our bedding at it but managed our cooking
on it too – a kettle, & a pan of frying salmon steaks, or porridge. I don't
know how we avoided an accident for the balance of frying-pan & kettle
was most precarious.

The camp I liked best of all was on an island at the end of Third Pond.
We spent 4 days there because we had to send Sandy back to have a tooth
pulled out. He was away 3 days, travelling fast all the time, but he came
back a happier man. I spent those days on the rock above the river, or
sitting on a bed of spruce boughs in the shade with birds & animals so
friendly round me. I could watch John fishing up & down the river below.
All the time we were out, we had smelt fire & we could see the smoke, but
Sandy brought back word that 100 square miles of Grand Falls forest was
burning and St. John's had rushed up 400 extra men & a trainload of extra
forest fire–fighting equipment to as near the scene of the fire as they could
get, & warnings had been sent out to the Levick schoolboy expedition,

whose base camp would be in danger if the wind veered a little. That day, the sky was darkened with the smoke clouds, & early in the afternoon, the river was lighted up as tho' with sunset by the reflection from the fire on the clouds. John got anxious to get back to the railway to find out what was being done. He said we were safe because we could always get out onto a lake (we heard afterwards that the fires will leap a lake even). It was terribly hot still, but there was a tearing wind. Next day, we had a terrible battle across the lake against the wind – John & I helping with the paddles while the guides poled. We did the 4 miles to the next cabin with the greatest difficulty. John had wanted to get another stage because we were getting short of food. That afternoon, the air was thick with smoke & flying ash. But, that night, the storm broke, & we lay & listened thankfully to the rain, knowing it was better than 1,000 more men to fight the fire. We could not move next day. Our roof leaked all over, but Cecil mended it with birch-bark, & we were quite comfortable, & John blissfully happy on the river. I think he got about 70 salmon altogether & masses of trout. We salted it. Now & then, a canoe passed – men going up to the railway from Gander Bay, 34 miles down the river – & we sent in fish by them or gave it to them. The hurricane was still raging next day, but we had to get on: 'Never known a storm like this on the river before.' But we got on better because there was more shelter on that reach. Next day, crossing 4th Pond was worse than ever; we had hoped to get right on to Gleneagles, but the guides were done by the time we got to Nut Brook, & we were thankful to climb up to shelter, & we all sat & rested in the cabin before we could get to work on fire & food. The guides soon recovered; I heard them late that night laughing & singing in the distance. 'We've a lovely pitch – like birds in a nest,' Cecil said. They are great lads for laughing, & Cecil had a store of lugubrious hymns that accompanied all his jobs. Our beds at that camp were pools, so the first thing we had to do was to get the stove going & make the cabin roasting hot, while Cecil mended the roof. Being so new, the bark had shrunk. The flies had been rather troublesome, but the smoke from the stove, tho' it made our eyes stream, cleared off the flies – mosquitoes & sandflies – & we had no bother with them there. Indeed, the flies bothered us very little at all on the trip; they were "ome.'[3] Next day, the storm was still raging, & the rapids were very difficult against the wind, & we had to take to the shore many times, scrambling on rocks & boulders while Sandy & Cecil battled with the river. But we got up to Gleneagles that evening, having finished the last of our rations at lunch-time.

I never enjoyed a holiday so much. But I certainly did enjoy a hot bath up in the woods next morning, & my bed in 'Birchy Cabin' was wonderfully comfortable. ...

One camp of loggers got caught by the fire in the night & had to fly for their lives, & the fire flew faster & they had to take refuge in a lake up to their necks in water, cooling their heads & faces all the time. Two had to be taken to hospital, but all escaped with their lives.

1 This should read Larry Shea (son of   2 Toilet.
  Jim Shea).   3 Home.

Q.H.S. to Maisie and Blair, [St John's], 10 September 1935

... The Murray Levick of the schoolboy expedition dined with us last night. The party all go off by the boat. Very thankful the Reids at Gleneagles were to see them go, I think. They have given them endless trouble & very little in return for all the advantage they had from having the Gleneagles settlement behind them. They were so thoughtless & discourteous. Mrs. Reid stood for $1^1/_2$ hours on the shore one night in the mist, holding a lantern to guide her husband's motorboat back, & not a lad or a leader offered to relieve her, tho' it was their work Mr. Reid was busy about. All winter, Mrs. Levick was writing letters to them for information & advice & it took hours to answer them. And they had their tents pitched on the Reids' ground. But Mrs. Levick's one idea seemed to be to avoid paying for anything she could help. Meals were the only things occasionally, & eventually some of the party were forced to be guests of the house. But that night they arrived, they had no tents pitched, and half the party could not get on across the lake on account of the mist, & so Mr. Reid said they could come into the house & lie on the floor. They took possession, & Mr. & Mrs. Reid spent their night in the big kitchen feeling that their house was not their own. No thanks! The boys, of course, think everything is paid for & take it as a matter of course. And when you think how the Reids toil to make a living by making this guest–house settlement in the jungle. It makes one so mad to see these people so self-assertive and bursting with self-satisfaction. You would think no one had ever been in that country before, whereas trappers are all over it every year & it is well known to the people. It is a jolly holiday for the boys & very good for them to rough it. And it is so important to get a good account in the *Times*.[1] I think we gave them an idea last night that the N.F.L.ers are not too pleased with the impression they are giving of conditions here & don't like it. So, Commander Murray Levick was a bit more careful what he said to the reporters.

Summer is nearly over. One day is still hot; the next we have to have the heat on. ...

1 Of London, England.

J.H.S. to Maisie, St John's, 13 September 1935

... I agree entirely with your hatred of Mussolini's Abyssinian adventure.[1] There is a little ray of sunshine today in the news that France is going to support Great Britain in proposals for financial and economic boycott. That is now the only hope. The fear, of course, is that Germany & Italy will be driven together. Italy will almost certainly leave the League,[2] but she has never been anything but a lukewarm and somewhat contemptuous member.

Here we are having our anxieties also. The fishery has been unsatisfactory and prices are dreadful. The custom of the country is that [a] fall in price abroad does not affect exporters' profits but is passed on to the fishermen. The result this year is that few fishermen will get anything. So we are anticipating a bad winter, and our political enemies are using the opportunity to start hostile organization. They have called themselves the Newfoundland Crusaders,[3] and are having a public meeting tonight. *Voyons à qu'arrivera.*[4]

I personally am back in the thick of it all. My department is too heavy for one man. They have kindly transferred land settlement to Lodge, which relieves me somewhat. I am left with fisheries & forests & mines & agriculture & game & fur. Each of these is providing a great deal of work. And now I have the Ranger force in addition. That is going to be a very valuable item in the administration, but is at present in embryo. They will replace the police in the outports, and will in addition be used by customs & relief and game & fur administrations. I went out to see the force (there are so far only 30) in their training camp at Whitbourne last Saturday. They were *excellent*, and have made a very good beginning. We shall recruit another 20 in the spring, & by this time next year we should have the whole of the policing arrangements of the island & of the Labrador, except the Avalon Peninsula & the larger towns.

Private

Quita & I are considering very seriously the question of whether I should resign my appointment here and return to England in February next. I can do this under my contract by giving notice in November. This is an ungrateful country, and the people are very fickle. No one can have any conception of the fundamental dishonesty in this country who had not seen it. Everybody seems to grasp at the immediate advantage, no matter how obtained, without thought of the future. That is very marked in the fish trade, where they will pack firsts top & bottom of a cask & thirds in the middle. It is not fair to say that everyone does this. There are a few firms whose marks are accepted as reputable. But it is a common practice.

Socially, people are very hospitable, but social life here is unattractive. Interests are very circumscribed & narrow. Gossip and rumour are universal, and believed by everybody. The chief feature, however, is that they are ephemeral. The rumour lasts for a few days & is then replaced by a new one and forgotten. This is an instance of the fickleness of the people.

Of course, if we resign, we shall have to live very quietly in England. We are talking of possible locations: Dorset, Surrey, the Lakes, Scotland. It would depend to some extent on whether I could get any kind of employment. I shall be 68 next year! I might possibly get some directorships through the Bank of England, in which case we should have to be within reach of London. But perhaps the time has come for quiet contemplation of my latter end. ...

1 On 5 December 1934 Italian and Ethiopian troops had clashed on the disputed Ethiopia–Somaliland border. On 2 October 1935 an Italian expeditionary army invaded Ethiopia.

2 League of Nations.

3 The Crusaders pledged themselves 'to work assiduously for the return of Representative and Responsible Government, and the administration of our own affairs.'

4 Let's see what happens.

J.H.S. to Ian and Sheila, St John's, 17 September 1935

... Here things go much as usual, but we are being attacked rather viciously at the moment by disgruntled ex-politicians. They have organized a movement called the 'Newfoundland Crusaders,' and, while disclaiming any hostility to the Commission, they suggest that they will act as 'intermediaries' between the Commission & the people. They may not think themselves hostile, but judging by the tone of their criticism, they are not exactly in favour of us. ... The fact is that the fishing industry is in the dumps. The Italian market has just disappeared. The Portuguese market is very difficult, and you cannot get your money from Brazil. Prices have dropped rapidly, and this means that the fisherman is not getting enough to keep him off the dole in the winter. And there are 30,000 families of them – half the population. So, naturally, there is unrest and discontent. And the people all believed that the Commission would ensure immediate meteoric prosperity generally. Which is impossible. Our policy will ensure ultimate prosperity, but not the Archangel himself could convert a poverty-stricken into a well-to-do community in a year & a half. Things are unquestionably better than they were two years ago. St. John's has not been so comfortable for many years, but there is a long row to hoe before conditions can be satisfactory, and all possible resources of every kind must be developed. We have adequate policies for agriculture & game & inland fisheries & forests & mines. We are at the moment engaged on the most difficult problem of all – the codfishery. Whatever we do there is certain to be unpopular. The first point of attack is the profits of the merchant. He gets the same profit, apparently, whether the price in the markets is low or high. Every fall is pushed onto the fisherman. You may imagine that I am having a difficult & an anxious time.

Socially, we are very busy. We have a Catholic priest, Father O'Reilly (from Lourdes on the Port au Port Peninsula), as our guest for a week at the hotel. He is a very fine public-spirited fellow & has managed for me the settlement of some 20 families from the south coast. They were literally on the rocks in a locality with no soil & no wood, and dependent entirely on fish. At Lourdes, there is ample fine agricultural land, and lots of forest, in addition to fish & lobster. The people from the rocks regard it as an earthly paradise, & I hope that ultimately we shall have a thousand families moved. On Sunday evening, we went to a lecture in one of the theatres by the Prefect Apostolic¹ of Chekiang (China). We were on the platform. He spoke very well, & I said a few words in supporting the vote of thanks. So you may realize that we have been moving in R.C. circles this last week. ...

I am having quite an interesting time with game. We are starting four beaver farms – protected beaver areas – and are planting beavers there. That is a difficult job. We took them from one of our protected areas. These have been protected for about 15 months, but the muskrats have increased so rapidly that we are always finding them in the traps instead of the beaver. So far, I think we have caught & transported about 40 beaver. We want to transport 400. I am also going to introduce the Nova Scotian

red deer – a little, very active animal which spreads with great rapidity –
and the mink – the most valuable of the fur animals. ...

1 Monsignor William C. McGrath.
   The lecture was given at the Nickel
   Theatre on Military Rd.

Q.H.S. to Betty, Newfoundland Hotel, 24 September 1935
... We are having a busy time socially as well as officially since we returned. This week is dreadful. We decline such a lot of invitations, but,
even so, here is the week. Yesterday, I went to a lunch party – 23 ladies –
given by the American Consul's wife, Mrs. Quarton.[1] And we both dined
with the Harveys,[2] a longstanding invitation to his 74th birthday dinner. It
was a great feast, & the table was so pretty & he so happy. Sir Edgar
Bowring[3] made a speech, & Mr. Harvey replied. Afterwards, we played
bridge – I was with Mrs. Herbert Outerbridge[4] against Sir Edgar Bowring
& Mr. Harvey, & we had great fun. Today, we dine at Government House,
a big official dinner. Tomorrow, Wednesday, I have a meeting at Government House at 11.30, & J.H.S. calls for me at 12.00 & we go to Topsail for
lunch with the Bowrings[5] (you remember going to tea there?). At night,
we have [to] give [a] dinner party for some ... men from England (Post
Office people) who have an introduction. ... Friday, I am going to a ladies'
at-home here – tea & bridge (about 40 people). Saturday,[6] we go out to
Whitbourne to be hosts at the laying of the foundation stone of Daddy's
new Ranger force buildings. So there's a week for you! ...
   Private. It does seem as tho' nothing but a change of heart & mind
could dynamite this country out of its complacency with things as they are
& should not be. Conditions are really medieval, & it is doing the Middle
Ages a wrong probably to say so. The mass of the people are serfs &
helpless to help themselves. Here are the fishermen bound to the merchant, helpless in his toils. And the shop assistants – they dare not combine or complain or they would lose what little they are getting. How can
a man with a family risk losing even a pittance? It is truly horrible – more
horrible the more one knows about it. Daddy is disheartened & dispirited.
Many of the people who ought to back up the Commission are working
against it – behind its back. It is no good simply feeding & housing &
clothing the poor – that gets you no further towards the solution of the
problem; it only really strengthens the hands of the oppressor. The foundations of well-being are being well & truly laid but what in – ? Isn't it

sand? It is the spiritual aspect of the condition of the country that is the most menacing. Last night, after dinner, some of the leading men were talking to Daddy of what he is doing – they think him a dangerous revolutionary. 'What's the good of giving the people better education? What's the good of giving them better food? You only make them discontented.' That is their attitude. The people are quite happy with the lowest possible levels of life – leave them alone. How would these wealthy men like to live on tea & molasses & flour & not much of that? How would they like to see their wives & children practically naked in the bitter cold of winter here? How would they feel if their son married their own sister & produced idiot children? It makes one's blood boil to hear them. The condition of the poor here is worse than the condition of savage tribes, I believe. Daddy said: 'Contented! Well they ought not to be! if they are!' And they are not. Claude Fraser[7] said today that it is only the knowledge that Daddy's Dept. of Natural Resources is trying to help the people that gives any courage to the poor. All the time I am feeling, 'What can I do! What can I do!' It seems as tho' the only thing I personally can do is to stand by Daddy & hold up his arms. ...

1 The U.S. consul general in St John's was Harold B. Quarton. His wife was Helene Quarton.
2 Charles and Ethel Harvey. Charles Harvey was with Harvey & Co.
3 1858–1943. Businessman. Newfoundland high commissioner in London, 1918–22, 1933–4.
4 Alice Margaret (Hutton) Outerbridge. Herbert Outerbridge (b. 1883) was a director of Harvey & Co. and other companies.
5 Edgar and Flora (Munn) Bowring.
6 28 September 1935.
7 Secretary, Department of Natural Resources.

J.H.S. to Betty, St John's, 25 September 1935

This is a holiday Wednesday – and an unsettled day, after several days of really bad weather. Masses of rain. The sun at the moment is brilliant, watery and hot. Quita is finishing her toilet and making tea, and we have had breakfast. Presently, we have to drive to Topsail to lunch with the Edgar Bowrings. 'S'Edgar', not 'Sirrredgar,' as everyone impresses [upon] you. ...

I am having a very difficult and anxious time officially. The fishery has been in large areas a failure. In others, there has been too much fish. Weather has been very bad for curing, and the quality is thus inferior. Then markets are dreadfully difficult. The Italians have ceased to buy our fish. We usually sell 9,000 tons in Italy. That has meant diversion to other markets – especially to Portugal, and a heavy fall in the price there. That fall has been pushed onto the fisherman by the merchants, and even those fishermen who have caught a lot of fish are getting insufficient for it to cover the cost of the voyage and leave something over for the winter. We are going to have a bad winter, I fear.

I was at dinner at the Charles Harveys on Monday. After dinner, Sir Edgar Bowring, Herbert Outerbridge, Alderdice, Harvey and I sat talking. I raised the question of the appalling conditions in some parts of the island, and pointed out that decent life is impossible with the present system. The whole of the loss is borne by the fishermen. The merchants at once piped up: 'They are used to nothing else. They are perfectly happy. They have blueberries and pay nothing for their firewood. In winter, they can snare rabbits.' And Alderdice warned me that we, United Kingdom Commissioners, should give up trying to raise the standard of life. We only made the people discontented. It is a dreadful state of affairs really. The merchants are living in luxury on the proceeds of risk from which the fisherman cannot make a living of any kind – much less a decent living. I have been taking action in the matter. I have worked out what the merchants get for the fish they send to each market & what they pay the fisherman for that fish & have written to the Salt Codfish Board[1] for an explanation of the wide spread between these two prices. They have not yet replied. But in one case the spread amounted to 80% of the price they paid for the fish.

The whole economic condition of this country is a nightmare. We have at the top a layer of well-paid, well-fed people, who drive in motorcars and have all they want (like you & myself). Then a slightly thicker layer of middle-class people, who live comfortably. Then, below them, the mass of the population, who live in miserable conditions and of whom about half are compelled to go on the entirely inadequate 'dole' during the winter. We have adopted a long-range policy, which will improve matters for the next generation. But the people who are suffering, very naturally, want things put right now, which is impossible. Improvement is bound to be a slow process. ...

We are having lots of social engagements, which I do not much like. They throw us out of our domestic stride. Last night, we were at Government House. On Friday, we were at the Reids.[2] In each case – and at the Harveys – it was white tie and tails. A nuisance. ...

1 Established by the Salt Codfish Act, 1935, of 13 June 1935.
2 Probably Robert Gillespie and Edythe (Linton) Reid. Robert

Gillespie Reid Jr (1875–1947) was president of the Reid Newfoundland Company, 1929–47.

J.H.S. to Maisie, St John's, 26 September 1935
... Here we have our own anxieties, entirely official. Domestically, our one drawback is absence from home and all of you. Quita is very well, I am thankful to say, and dizzy attacks (touch wood) are gradually fading out of the picture. We have lots of social engagements – far too many – but they are not sufficiently important or serious to be a nuisance. Now & then, we grumble & grouse. That is a privilege accorded to everyone.

Official matters are frequently difficult. Just now, we are having a great deal of trouble in the foreign fish markets. ... I am dealing with the merchants – asking them inconvenient questions – and am looked upon as 'radical' – which here means communist – in consequence. But I am going to follow the thing through to the end. There are 30,000 families of fishermen & 100 exporting firms. If this 100 disappeared, it would be regrettable but bearable. If 30,000 families are on our hands, it means disaster. We have to take drastic steps to limit the freedom of action by the merchants on the Oporto market. No one can now sell fish there without a licence, which can be refused for any reason – e.g., that the price is too low. That has already had an effect. And the effect has gone a deal further than the particular market & the particular industry. The other markets are watching their step and the logging industry is taking notice. But, in every direction, we have problems, and they all seem to come back to the Commissioner for Natural Resources.

The merchants are incorrigible ... living in luxury & driving motorcars, because the fisherman is starving & has no decent clothes. 'Starving' is an exaggeration, but the standard of life is lower than anything you can find in Europe. It makes one realize how the love of money is the root of evil. I do not believe that the merchants can know what conditions actually are. If they did, they could not bear that they should continue.

Things are gradually getting better. I have just been phoned up by a merchant who tells me that the price of Labrador fish has gone up to $3 per cwt. It was less than $2. This means a very great difference to the fishermen – the difference between the possibility of self-support and the necessity for the dole. And, in other directions, we are making progress. Agriculture, game & inland fishery – forests – mines. The combination is important. But fishing at present is all-important. ...

Q.H.S. to Maisie, Newfoundland Hotel, 26 September 1935
... Here we are in the thick of work & social duties & pleasures again. Work is rather depressing at the moment because the Commission is not backed as it ought to be. The home people allow agitators & disgruntled

politicians to appeal to them against the Commission &, instead of trust-
ing the men on the spot, to whom they have entrusted the job & whom
they know to be efficient for it & absolutely trustworthy, they call for
reports & add to work & worry & encourage the opposition by doing so.
It is stupid. ...

We are having such a lot of social business again. I decline every engagement I can, but we can't keep out of friendliness. But I decline to go
to bridge afternoons – if I did not, I should never be in till 7. And we
decline all Sunday invitations. Mrs. Keegan, the wife of the principal doctor here, said to me when she dined with us last week: 'Tell me now, are ye
still so bigoted ye won't go out to supper on Sunday night.' I said: 'It's not
a question of principle, but of rest for my husband.' 'Tchut! he could rest
with us.' If you knew her! She talks 19 to the dozen, not only with her
tongue but with her head & her body. Poor soul! She is like one of those
women who knitted & watched the heads fall from the guillotine. She
gives me the creeps. She is so bigoted herself – an R.C. and a virulent one.
... Yesterday ... we had to go out to Topsail for lunch with Sir Edgar
Bowring. Topsail was heavenly – I have never seen it lovelier – the sea
royal blue & the islands clear-cut, rose-red cliffs, & the far side of the bay
stretching out 50 miles into the Atlantic. But we sat indoors & ate an
exquisite lunch, but so rich that Daddy was ill after it (I skipped most of it
& did not suffer). On the way back, I made Daddy drive up the hill to
Paradise. I had always wanted to explore this road, but it is steep & rough,
& always when we pass we are on our way somewhere. But yesterday we
went. Paradise is a ramshackle settlement, but I don't wonder someone
christened the spot Paradise; the road is truly lovely with views over the
hills to the ocean north & south & west. I gathered branches of wild pear –
a glorious colour like Virginian creeper but sunnier, & golden ferns.

As I wrote, a bellboy brought in a huge sheaf of purple & pink asters
from Mrs. Andrew Murray, so my room is gay. ...

I have just rung up to ask about a small boy here who is down with
tetanus. Isn't it dreadful. There are 7 cases. The spasms seem to be less
acute today, so the parents are hopeful. The nurse who has charge of our
friend's child has had it herself. Just stabbed [a] toe last Thursday, a week
ago – they doctored it & thought nothing of it till Friday night.

I must put the kettle on & get Daddy's tea. ...

J.H.S. to Greta, St John's, 29 September 1935
Here is our 35th wedding anniversary – outside a day of gloom. The fog-

horn is mooing like a distressed cow. Rain is coming down in streams. It is now 10 a.m. We were up early and went to early service. There is no gloom either in our temporary home or in our hearts. You have a wonderful mother and I a very wonderful wife, as I have realized all through these 35 years. I think one of Quita's most endearing qualities is the way she enjoys a joke against herself. ... You know the way she always tells stories against herself with great gusto.

She is a delightful person with whom to live – so unselfish, so kind, so thoughtful, so uncomplaining and hard-working. And all the time doing nice things for other people. I shall never forget how she gave her spare woollies – not really 'spare' – to underclad women on the south coast during our inspection tour last May. She has acute sympathy for every kind of suffering. All the maids in the hotel love her because she is interested in their family affairs. She is very welcome at the hospital here also, and whenever we drive round the country, she takes with her bags of simple boiled sweets for the children. On our inspection tours, she has great bundles of old magazines & papers for the outports that never have any literature. It is not a question of 'Lady Bountiful' distributing of her superfluity. It is the human instinct that thinks beforehand of what the people will be lacking and takes the trouble to collect the material necessary to fill the lack. ...

There has been no letter from you now for some time. A direct mail is due on Tuesday[1] and we expect to get letters by that. This place is really more out of the way than India. There we got our regular weekly mail that took a fortnight from England. Here, once in three weeks we have the direct mail, and any mails between are via Canada or the U.S.A., and take at least a fortnight to get here. ... On Friday,[2] I presided at the annual meeting of the Y.M.C.A. & Y.W.C.A., and yesterday[3] we went out to Whitbourne, 75 miles by car, to see the Governor lay the foundation stone of the barracks for my new Ranger force. ... The Rangers have been regarded as one of the strange expensive experiments which J.H.S. invented, so we asked all the Commissioners & the editors of the local papers & their wives & two or three special guests such as the Chief of Police[4] to the show, & they were all delighted. The Chief of Police is rather anxious as, if the Rangers are a success (and I shall see to it that they are), it is certain that in time they will replace the police force, in which case the Chief of Police will have no force to command. However, that is for the future, & can be left for the moment. The Rangers are going to take charge of police and general administration in the wilder parts of the island & on the Labrador. Twenty-three of them are going out next month. Then we shall recruit another 20 for training in the early spring, and by this time next year the whole of the island, with the exception of the large towns & the Avalon Peninsula, will be administered by the force. I expect that in 1937 we shall take over the outlying towns, and in 1938 the Avalon, except St. John's. By 1940, the Rangers should be the only police in the island.[5] How we shall fit in the present Chief of Police I do not know. The disciplinary standard demanded from the Rangers is infinitely more severe than anything that the police have so far contemplated. ...

1 1 October 1935.
2 20 September 1935.
3 28 September 1935.
4 Patrick J. O'Neill.

5 When Newfoundland became a province of Canada in 1949, the Ranger force was absorbed into the R.C.M.P.

J.H.S. to Ian and Sheila, St John's, 5 October 1935
... Here we are having a busy time also – both officially and socially. I do not so much object to the former as to the latter. The pleasantest evenings are those we spend quietly at home. Officially, there is a lot of anxiety. As you know, this country depends largely on codfish – indeed, some 30,000 families are supposed to get their livelihood from it. The total value of the fish produced is not more than £1 million to £1,200,000, of which half represents 'cost of production,' leaving £500,000 to £600,000 as the net value. Of this, a large percentage goes to the merchant in overhead, packing, freight, profits, &c., and a calculation which I have just made proves that in the best of circumstances the average income of the fisherman does not exceed £20 per annum. Even in N.F.L., that is a wage entirely inadequate. This year, prices are £4 a ton less to the fishermen than they were last year, and the average income will not be more than £13. As a result, we expect to have a very difficult winter, and it is an anxious outlook. ...

Private. I am thinking very seriously of resigning this appointment, as from 16th February next, when my two years will be up. In a sense, I shall be sorry to leave, for a great deal has been started which I should like to see completed. But it is certain that both Lodge and I cannot leave at the same time, and he will not bind himself to stay till 1938, though he is willing to stay till 1937. And in any case, from the point of view of results, we shall not see any to speak of by 1937. The things we have started will not have their effect for several years. So, all things considered, it seems advisable that we should be the first to go, and that means giving notice by

16th November. The Ranger force has been constituted, and the first batch of men – those for the Labrador – leave on October 18th. ...

J.H.S. to Betty, St John's, 8 October 1935

... I began last Wednesday.[1] Now it is Sunday the 13th and 9.20 a.m. At communion service, all of you dear ones are remembered, and seem to be particularly close to us. We have had a couple of lovely days since last I wrote. Today, we had a silver sunrise, after heavy rain in the night. ...

I am having anxious days. They present small anxieties when compared with the enormous problems of Europe and specially of the League, but they are locally of great importance. The fishery has been, in many parts, a failure. In others, there has been an excess of fish. The weather has been very bad for fish making, and there is a lot of poor fish on the market. Then Italy is entirely closed, and the fish that usually goes there has to be exported to other markets, which brings down prices. The merchants must still make their profits. So the fall in price is passed on to the fisherman. This means that they in their turn do not get enough to settle their a/cs, let alone have anything over to meet their expenses and those of their families. So they come straight back onto the dole. They are thoroughly discouraged. So am I.

Human wickedness is a strange phenomenon. Here it is evident in every direction. The supplier and employer grind their clients. The fisherman retaliates by selling his fish away from his supplier, and then failing to pay him. Or by foisting bad fish on him for good. Some merchants sell 2nd-grade fish as first-grade, and are proud when they get away with it. The shopkeepers underpay their shop assistants, and the shop assistant does not dare to protest. There are so many waiting to take the job. Love of money is the root of all evil. It is at the bottom of the supply system, of the grinding-down of the fisherman and of the shop assistant, of the dishonesty of the fisherman and of certain of the merchants. They all need the change of heart which we also need.

We have been having occasional social engagements, which I do not enjoy. Also certain official ones. I opened the fair at Brigus the other day, and am opening that at Heart's Content next Wednesday. On Tuesday, I go over to Bell Island, where the Governor is opening the fair.

I received a mysterious telegram from one of the Chinese ministers at Shanghai yesterday: 'Please accept my sincere congratulations on the occasion of your well-merited decoration by our government – Kung.' So I suppose they have made me a mandarin, or given me the 'Order of the Excellent Crop' or some other quaint distinction. It is just what the Chinese would do – decorate you 2½ years after your work is finished.² ...

1 2 October 1935.
2 Sir John had been in China, 1931–3,   as director general of the National
                                              Flood Relief Commission.

Q.H.S. to Greta, Newfoundland Hotel, 10 October 1935
... I have been thinking so much about you – a sort of singing thought in my heart as I go along. The clang of the tram bell below my bedroom window reminds me of Greece & our days together there. ...

This is such a glorious day. ... It is lovely to have a bit of summer again. ...

Daddy & I are getting in a lot of flying about while the roads are still open, and we have been doing a lot of entertaining & being entertained. I had a very jolly at-home for ladies. We had it in the mezzanine here, & used the gallery round the main hall for bridge & other games, & those who did not want to play sat out & watched. The cook here made all the cakes, which were most professional & so good, & everyone seemed to enjoy themselves. They shouted a lot, which is apparently a sign that a party is a success here. I have never heard anything like it in England. Two nights ago we were at a *very* swell dinner – all the 'elity' & a lovely, most tasteful house & exquisite food – & the noise was terrific, tho' we were only a party of 10! You simply could not talk to your neighbours; you were shouted down. That is quite a feature of society here. A bridge party is a maddening affair because one table shouts its remarks to another all the time, quite irrespective of the play. So I reckon my party was a real success.

The next day, Saturday,¹ we went out to Whitbourne, 76 miles, for the laying of the foundation stone of Daddy's new Ranger force barracks. The first 30 men have had 6 weeks intensive training & are now going out to their posts. Canada has lent a first-class Sergeant-Major² for a year, & he is a fair person, & the men look so fit & well turned out, & their drilling is remarkable. The Governor was delighted with them, & the Chief of Police was racked with the pains of envy because the Rangers are so much smarter & better drilled than his police. He wanted the sergeant to drill his police, & he wanted his men to have a uniform like theirs. The police uniform here is so very un-smart. They wear a long coat down to their heels in winter and a sort of high bearskin cap like a Russian in the winter – a thing that pulls down over the ears. ... But to continue, this Sergeant-Major

Anderton is an Englishman from Leicester, but he has spent 11 years as a N.W. mounted policeman in the Arctic. His wife[3] was a nurse in the Arctic too, & both are such kind helpful people to the folk at Whitbourne – not only to the Rangers. She nurses the poor, who cannot afford doctors, & has brought 3 babies into the world, & he will go out at any time of the day or night to doctor a poor man's cow. She takes poor children berry picking, sells the berries for them, & when the fathers say, 'Now I can get a lb. of tobacco,' she says, 'Now you must get your children new shoes for the winter.'

Nine of these Rangers are leaving for their posts on the Labrador in a few days now, & another day last week we went out again & Daddy talked to all the Rangers about their duties & responsibilities, making them realize that they are not just a body by themselves but important cogs in the wheel of government & that the government will depend upon them to do & be in their posts something that will be an example of right living and official efficiency in their own work & cooperation in the work of other officials. This last point has to be emphasized because hitherto there has been so much jealousy between one department and another, and cooperative effort is so alien to their experience that the spirit of it has to be created. But they are a fine body of men – magnificent material – far finer than anything Sergeant-Major Anderton has had to handle in Canada, he tells us. He is tremendously pleased with them. Of course, he has men who in ordinary times would have gone into professions – college-trained lads. And tho' he is a very strict disciplinarian, they all love him & admire him enormously.

We gave the men all testaments or R.C. prayer-books, with their initials stamped on them – little ones to go in their packs, & they were so pleased. One article of their uniform, which they will need in the winter, is a garment in shape like the Esquimaux wear[4] – a coat made of two thicknesses of scarlet English blanket with a peeled hood to pull over the head. When they get further north, they will get fur linings, and they have, in addition, a thick, closely woven, waterproofed cotton coat to fit over this. So they ought to be warm. ...

We spent that Saturday night & Sunday (after our meeting with the Rangers) at Whitbourne with Prof. Fraser Bond. ... We walked over the fields with him, & loved the wide views over fields & lakes & forests to the distant hills – such a glorious Sunday we had. He wanted us very much to stay on & to take us down his lakes, but we had to get back.

I must tell you of an incident on the way back. Near Ocean Pond, we passed an old man walking. We knew it was far from any houses, so we backed & offered him a lift. He accepted gladly: 'I'm that bad with the rheumatism. Never a pain in me stomach – its just me legs' – & we took him along about 10 miles to Brigus. When he got out, he said, 'God bless you, sir.' 'Not at all! Not at all!' was the absent-minded reply. I tried to grab it back. 'O no!' I cried. I was dreadfully afraid of losing the blessing.

I got Daddy to gather branches of golden birch and ash – such gorgeous colours with its red & rose-gold leaves & scarlet berries (there are such masses of them here) – & long sprays of ruby-red bramble, & rose-red wild pear & cherry. But all except the bramble were crumpled & useless by morning. I want to keep something for the winter, when we have no flowers. ...

We had some glorious days lately, & Mrs. Lodge & I are taking advantage of them to get some exercise & joy in the air & views while we can. So soon now we may be shut in. Two mornings ago, we woke to white frost. But winter seems far away again today. If we can't go for a walk or are too busy, she usually comes in to smoke her morning cigarette at 11 o'c. with me, which is pleasant & friendly. One day we walked down to Quidi Vidi,[5] a beautiful little harbour, & we sat up on the rocky hillside & felt as tho' we were in Wales. Today, we walked right down the town & did some shopping, & then climbed the hill up past the English cathedral & the R.C. cathedral (which dominates the town & harbour) & rested on a bench on a little green, which has just been evolved from a horrible rubbish heap. Old men & women come & rest there now & watch the schooners coming & going. The reclamation of bits of waste land all over the town is improving it greatly. The land round the hotel was just a waste & dumping ground. Now, we have a formal garden on one side, & behind we have 3 tennis courts & a clubhouse (the courts were used last winter for a rink) & more gardens, & now beyond that they are filling up a horrible midden heap and are levelling it and making a bowling green with a bank & a line of trees beside it – all Mr. Lodge – with Mrs. Lodge encouraging & praising his work! But she really is helping too. She does the hotel for him, & he has improved things vastly here. The maids have a rest-room & baths, & so have the men.

We spent another day this week at Brigus. It was a glorious day. Daddy was opening an agricultural exhibition there. Monsignor Murphy[6] & Mr. Broughton[7] (Wesleyan) were the moving spirits in the enterprise. They are brothers in arms, both so devoted to their work & their people & each other. It was really very touching to see their oneness of heart – real Christians both of them, Mr. Broughton such a rough Lancashire man & the Monsignor such a gentle enthusiast. They were discouraged & disheartened because the people had needed so much stimulation. Last year, the exhibition was a novelty, & everyone worked hard & came in hundreds. I think John's speech heartened them. The old monsignor (probably 10 years younger than I) patted my shoulder & called me 'my child,' & plucked Mrs. Lodge & me flowers in Mr. Broughton's garden. We called on old Mrs. Bartlett,[8] mother of the famous Bob Bartlett[9] (I dare say you never heard of him but he is a hero here – he went to the Pole[10] with Peary, or rather towards the Pole[11] – Peary left him & everyone else behind). Mrs. B., his mother, is 84 & a scrap of fragility she looks, but she is like steel they say. She made a wedding cake for a granddaughter last week. She has trained her daughters to be wonderful housekeepers. Two[12] of them have a most charming café[13] across the road from her. 'Bob' set them up in it – a log cabin hung round with ships' models & full of interesting curios, & all so bright & tasteful – orange curtains & blue tablecloths & excellent meals & pretty nieces to serve them.

Here is a full moon coming up over Signal Hill. ...

1 28 September 1935.
2 Fred Anderton.
3 Edna Virginia Anderton (1902–1977).
4 Parkas.
5 Quidi Vidi village, near St John's.
6 Joseph Murphy (1861–1944). Arrived in Brigus in 1911 and was parish priest there for thirty-three years.
7 Ezra Broughton (1876–1958). Born in England. President of the Newfoundland Methodist Conference, 1924–5.
8 Mary (Leamon) Bartlett.

9 Robert Abram Bartlett (1875–1946). Commanded the *Roosevelt* in the American explorer Robert E. Peary's polar expeditions of 1905–6 and 1908–9.
10 North Pole.
11 This refers to the April 1909 final leg of Peary's expedition to the North Pole. In fact, he did not travel alone but with the African-American Matthew A. Henson.
12 Eleanor and Emma.
13 Benville Tea Rooms.

J.H.S. to Greta, St John's, 12 October 1935

... *Private* ... I am sending in my resignation as from 16th February next – the end of my second year. There are various official reasons for this, and other private ones. Of the latter, the chief is our desire to live in closer proximity to our various relatives. We both feel it a grievance that we see so little of our children. We are gradually getting on in life and are entitled to a quiet time in touch with those we love before the end. Of course, we shall have to live in very much simpler fashion than ever before. ... It will be a case for a cottage in the country. ... If I can get any kind of reasonable arrangement in London, we should probably think of Sussex or Surrey. Otherwise, Dorset or the Lakes. ...

Officially, we are having a bad time. The fish markets abroad are out of joint ... and, very naturally, the people are discontented and critical and querulous. We, as a Commission, are passing through a bad piece. That is really the sole reason for my hesitation in sending in my resignation. It looks like getting out of difficulty by running away.

We have our normal social engagements, which I do not much enjoy. We also have a number of official functions – opening fairs, attending meetings, occasionally making public speeches. I have just written a long-ish account of the operations of my department, which is appearing in the press in instalments,[1] and leading, of course, to criticism by the press. Either it says, 'We told you so long ago'; or, 'Why have you not done this? or that? or the other?' One paper attacks me vigorously for failure to borrow $10 or $15 million for 'development.' That is the system they followed, as long as they could borrow, and which resulted in the present condition of affairs. ...

1 See *Evening Telegram*, St John's,   1935, 7; 26 October 1935, 5;
   12 October 1935, 9, 11; 21 October   28 October 1935, 6.

Q.H.S. to Maisie, Newfoundland Hotel, 12 and 14 October 1935
... All the big merchants here have combined & signed an appeal for a case, that was decided by the Commission here, to be carried to England for reconsideration. It is a question of the dismissal of one of the government employees – a captain[1] of a ship in Mr. Lodge's department. He was accused of smuggling – almost caught in the act, but he was acquitted on insufficient evidence tho' *he confessed to having smuggled on previous occasions*. It was well known that he did smuggle, and the customs officer had been just waiting for a chance to convict him. The government dismissed him, & he appealed against his dismissal because he had been acquitted of that particular act. Mr. Lodge is very unpopular, & this has been seized upon as an opportunity to embarrass him & the Commission. If the appeal is allowed to go home & the Dominions Office takes any action in the matter beyond routine turning of it down as not their job but the Commission's own business, if they desire to take any action (which is most unlikely as it would be as good as saying, 'The men we have put in

charge of the government are not fit for their job'), then the whole Commission – except possibly Alderdice – would resign in a body.

Sunday 13th. ... Daddy is sending his resignation in this week by the mail. I shall not pin my plans to its acceptance because I think it possible the present international position may make it awkward for the Dominions Office to accept it just now. Every day, people say things that make one feel bad about thinking of leaving just now; the people who really care about the condition of the poor here feel that John & his dept. are the ones who are really doing something radically helpful, & I fear they will be greatly discouraged. But either he or Mr. Lodge must go in February, because neither of them will consider staying on a fourth year, & they can't both go the same year. And Mr. Lodge will not go this year because he wants another (& better) job after, & so must put in three years here or he might have a bad mark against him. And the foundations of the work have been well & truly laid; another man, with perhaps less experience, could carry on. But Daddy says to the Dominions Office, 'Not at the salary.' They must pay their English Commissioners more. They cut English income tax off our salaries before we get them.

Such a heavenly Sunday! I thought it was going to be wet. It was such an exquisite silvery sunrise – silver sky, silver sea & harbour, silver light over all the world, and such a sweet, fresh, damp wind blowing. But now the sun is shining and the sky blue and all the land so clear-cut, every little farmhouse crisply black & white against the green hillsides and shadows chasing on land & sea. ...

We have just been across to the Lodges' room to listen to the news from England at 1 o'c. We had an early lunch, with cream cheese sent in by a friend who makes it. Yesterday, we had fresh corn from a friend – grown in St. John's. Fancy it ripening here. It was delicious. This afternoon, we are going about 42 miles to Father Duffy's[2] well. It used to be just an untidy roadside well – not 'made' in any way. No one knows anything about it except that it is about half-way between the old French capital, 'Placentia,' & St. John's, and that it has always been called Father Duffy's well. Daddy suggested that it should be tidied up by our forest officer's people & this has been done, & now the R.C.s have taken up the idea & the Knights of Columbus have put a stone surround with the name on it, & the foresters have cleared the forest round it, & today the Knights of Columbus are having a formal opening & dedication, & I expect it will become a place of pilgrimage & cures will be announced presently. It is just fresh, wholesome water – very restoring to the man who has to travel the 80 miles on foot. This is a great country for walking. Women think little of walking 80 miles to sell their knitting in St. John's, & they pay for their lodging by their knitting on the way. ...

Another glorious day today. ... Tell John[3] we look from Cabot Tower up there away over the ocean to you all. We often go up there – we drive up or we walk up – it is only about 550 ft. high – a wonderful outlet just at our door. A line of old, many-coloured wooden houses straggles up the roadside part way – then you get onto a plateau with blue lakes and a long valley, & then, when you have crossed a ridge, you climb again to the hilltop, which is a ridge along the cliff tops with Cabot Tower on the highest point & the remains of old fortification & an emplacement with 6 old cannon commanding the Narrows. And a path to the north leads you round the rocks to a point where you look down on Cockles Cove[4] – a magnificent creek with red cliffs rising sheer out of green depths, & the sea surging in & dashing up the rocks. And all along that ridge, you look out towards England and south to Cape Spear ... which truly runs far out into the sea like the head of a lance. Mrs. Lodge is not a good walker or we should go up oftener. She had two big operations 3 & 5 years ago. She usually comes in here to smoke her morning cigarette or, if the weather is good, we have a walk together. We are a great comfort to each other. We love to talk of our children & grandchildren & gloat on the photos & snaps! Can't you see us! ...

1 Westbury Kean (1886–1974).
2 James W. Duffy (1798–1860). Born County Monaghan, Ireland. Assistant priest at Ferryland in 1834 with responsibility for area from

Fermeuse to St Mary's Bay. Priest at St Mary's, 1837–43.
3 John Macaulay, her grandson.
4 Cuckolds Cove.

Q.H.S. to Ian and Sheila, Newfoundland Hotel, 14 October 1935

No letters from you for such a long time. ... At the moment the flags are up on Cabot Tower signalling the Furness Withy boat from Boston to Halifax, the *Newfoundland*, which will take our letters to England tomorrow. It always gives me a thrill when the two flags go up for our two direct mails by the *Nova Scotia* & the *Newfoundland*. To think that in 6 days, no, 7 – on Wednesday of next week – this letter should be in your hands! ...

Here she comes – the lovely ship. She is right in the harbour. It will be half an hour before she docks – they are so careful now. Did I tell you that twice this year the landing stage has been smashed up? Luckily, no one was hurt. The last time, I was meeting friends & was busy till the last moment. Then I saw her right in the Narrows, hurried into my coat & hat, & rushed down, &, behold, the dock alongside was matchwood! It made me realize the danger of a badly wounded animal. I shall always watch it at a respectful distance & with a quick retreat available. Luckily, no one was on that particular landing stage at the moment, as it was under repair & the workmen were away. It was a horrible sight. Now they are terribly careful. I believe there has been some change in the current, & old captains have been taken unawares.

Tuesday 15th. We dined at Government House last night to meet a Dr. Leicester (or Lester)[1] from the Carnegie Foundation in New York. He has come to enquire into helping with the foundation here of guilds for men & women, on the model, in some measure, of women's institutes. Lady Anderson is planning them for the island. What wonderful work the Carnegie & the Rockefeller Institutes are doing. I believe the Carnegie will never help unless the people themselves are ready to bear a share, & the Rockefeller people insist on the same thing. ...

We have just had a visit from such a keen, eager man, an old-looking man but such an eager fellow & so slim & alert – a Scotchman, tho' his name is Jones,[2] a chemist. He came up immediately after breakfast and sat till 10.30, talking about mines & the mining possibilities here & mines all over the world. He was tremendously interesting. ... He says that the development of gold deposits in this country would be a most paying proposition, & England would back any such projects that could be advised by the Commission's experts: 'We know you men can be trusted to make true reports.' He has been sent out here in response to a false report from a prospector, & he has just found it a waste of time. But he is enthusiastic about other mineral development possibilities he sees in this island. ... We have watched with great regret the demolition of a powder magazine up on Signal Hill, the beautifully faced stone being used to build a wall in the town. The Commission has no control over the municipality; it has its own government. ... Tomorrow, we have to go to Heart's Content, 80 miles away, to open another exhibition – Heart's Content, Heart's Delight & Heart's Desire have joined in this effort. ...

1 Robert M. Lester (1889–1969).

2 W. Jones left St John's for Liverpool on 15 October 1935 on the S.S. *Newfoundland*.

Q.H.S. to Bel, Newfoundland Hotel, 19 October 1935

... John & I are both very well. I am so thankful to be free of those dizzy attacks. My temptation now is to be greedy; I do enjoy my morning porridge here. I make my breakfast off it, & it is certainly fattening. I have gone up 1 stone since I came out! ... We are quite spoilt here. Last year, when I had to be so careful, they started making me split toast (you know the very thinnest crispest toast), and John liked it too, & so we always have it now with every meal. John's breakfast is just orange juice – a tumbler full (!) – and this toast. I have a small glassful of orange juice too, but that is at least the juice of two oranges – John's must be four at least. Then we make our own tea up here half an hour after every meal; I pour it straight off the leaves as soon as made – no 2 minutes brewing – and it is such a different drink from the ordinary brew, and I am sure it is much better for John, who drinks it so strong. The people here are so thoughtful & kind. If they notice, as they always do, that we like anything, they do it without being asked – like the toast. And I chanced once to say that I did not care to play bridge for money, & I am never asked; word has been passed around.

We have had a very busy time lately, entertaining & being entertained, & doing expeditions on business. We have had to go far out into the country at least 5 times in the last fortnight. The last was to open an agricultural exhibition at Heart's Content, more than 86 miles away. That was an experience. It was a terrible day of storm & rain. It was bad enough going in the daylight, but coming back was really dreadful – a fearful strain on John driving through it. We had the sea on our bonnet[1] twice, and had to drive through huge pools, so that the water blinded us, and the rain was so heavy that the lights shining on it made a curtain like thick fog. And up on the moors, the wind was roaring, so that we had to shout at each other, tho' we were side by side in the closed car, & we felt as tho' we must be blown right away. But the exhibitions are a great encouragement to the people. Heart's Content was one of the down & out places. Now the villages all along that coast are cooperating & breaking up land & keeping sheep & pigs & poultry, and are weaving & spinning their own wool & making their clothes. John has got the St. John's merchants to form committees to help the people to cooperate, & is backing their efforts with government financial support. He is against giving anything for nothing. The people must do their part, & the government will help them. So here 1,500 people have been lifted out of dole conditions – there, 500; there, another 1,000; & so on. There are already 6 of these committees at work in different parts of the island, and on the Labrador the same policy is backing a big commercial venture² that is giving employment to another 500 men & their families & is developing the resources of the country. But there will have to be a lot of dole again this winter, not for these people but for the many who have not yet been touched by these schemes, & for many fishermen & families where the fishery has either failed or has been so badly paid that the men, in spite of hard work & good fishing, have not made anything to carry them through the winter. The papers are clamouring for 'work instead of dole,' but it costs about 5 times as much and at the end you are still in the same position. Mr. Lodge's road-making plans will eventually bring much improvement in conditions, but this sort of road-making does not give a great deal of direct employment. The papers clamour for road-making instead of dole, but the local roads on which gangs of men would be set to work have to be within reach of their homes, and a road from one little settlement to another, or just a patch of road leading nowhere, is useless. The settlements communicate more satisfactorily by boat, as there is not enough traffic between most of them to justify the cost of making a road. When we go by train, we see the bits of roads leading nowhere; sometimes there are miles of beautiful roads now grass-grown – never used – made as a political response to this same plea. So that it comes to this: the country must be developed with a view to the future. We have only got a certain amount of money to work with – English borrowed money too – & it has to be laid out so as to get the best return – increasing returns – not dead-end work. But the people can't be allowed to starve while the country is being rehabilitated, & so, much as we dislike & disapprove a system of dole, it has to go on. But not as before. With more honest supervision & with the people's conscience stirring against dependence, there should not be nearly so many on the dole this year, tho' conditions in the fishing business are worse than they have ever been – so many markets closed; so many competitors, & they suffering in the same way & competing more strenuously. It is going to be a dreadful winter, but I do think the masses are more hopeful & feel that government is doing something that has not been attempted before. ...

   The country is looking lovely with the autumn colouring; the ground is ruby-red with blueberry leaves, & there is the rose-red of wild pear & cherry, & the ash leaves here turn from golden to red, & the berries are marvellous this year. But loveliest of all are the golden birch & poplar. There is one exquisite ... turn of the road, where golden birches shiver over pools. We watch for it, but it is always a breath-taking surprise. It can't be long now before the snow comes; meanwhile, we are enjoying all the air we can get. Mrs. Lodge & I try to get out for a walk every day. When the snow comes, she does not walk; it is so dangerous, & she has sprained her foot badly more than once & has to have massage every day. ...

1 The bonnet (hood) of their car.
2 The logging operation of the Labrador Development Company at

Alexis River. This company was started by J.O. Williams of Cardiff, Wales.

J.H.S. to Ian and Sheila, Newfoundland Hotel, 20 October 1935
... *Private.* Our chief item of news is that I have given notice to the Dominions Office that I will resign my appointment at the end of my second year on 16th February next. This has to be kept confidential until it is announced at home. I do not, of course, know what line the Secretary of State[1] will take – whether they will be glad of the opportunity, or will urge that I stay on for another year. If they make a point of that, it will be difficult to persist, and I do not want to put them into an embarrassing position. My department is a heavy one and I shall be sending you a copy of the report which we have just published. It is not very long and gives a concise account of what really means an enormous lot of work. ...

One of the charms of this place is the amount of sunshine. You wake in a gale of wind and rain, and, by midday, the whole place is bathed in sunshine – and vice versa. This of course makes for colour in the landscape. Looking out of the window, in front of which I am writing, there is alternate sunshine and shadow racing across the hills. But I fear that summer is over, and autumn near its end, for we have news of ice closing in on the Labrador coast.

We have had dinners on Friday & Saturday.[2] Friday's was rather heavy, as we had a quaint mixture of guests, chiefly educational; they did not click too well, and the Principal[3] of the Memorial College has no fund of interesting conversation. Yesterday, we had a staff dinner – the heads of the various divisions of the department[4] and their wives and the Secretary of the Commission, Carew, and Mrs. Carew.[5] That was a much pleasanter function. They were simple people, ready to enjoy themselves, and after dinner we had a couple of tables of bridge and one of Michigan Bank (Newmarket) and subsequently sevens.[6] Today, we give a small lunch party. Entertaining is necessary and is a heavy tax. We should be given an entertainment allowance, but in fact we are not. ...

1 For Dominion Affairs.
2 18 and 19 October 1935.
3 Albert G. Hatcher (1886–1954),

President of Memorial University College, 1933–49, and Memorial University, 1949–52.

4 Of Natural Resources.   6 Card-games.
5 William J. and Mary Florence
   (Channing) Carew.

Q.H.S. to Maisie and Blair, Newfoundland Hotel, 26 October 1935

... I have been getting a roundabout little lady, Mrs. Beckett, to try on
some knitted suits for me. ... These suits are really beautifully made and
look so smart & are so comfortable. ... There is tremendous demand for
the Nonia work in America now; they can't keep pace with the orders. All
the tourists buy them & send back further orders from friends. The bother
of ordering is that it takes about a couple of months to get it, though Mrs.
Beckett, who is in charge of the work & has taught many of the women &
has insisted on a high standard of work, is so kind. ... She comes from Liverpool
– lost her husband in the war, & her 5-year-old boy was run over by a motor
truck. Poor soul, Poor soul! How can a woman survive such grief?

We have been having such wild storms here, but today and all this week
it has been mild & most days very lovely. These clear autumn days are such a
joy. It is curious here that, tho' fog hangs all round 'the banks,' 80 miles away,
& often drifts towards the southeast coast, we get, as a rule, no 'atmosphere' – the distance is intensely clear. At the moment, I can see for miles
in the distance as clear as the foreground; it is only a question of perspective *and* your own sight how much you can see. I see every little house &
the windows in it and all the individual trees & shrubs on the hillsides. ...

Evening. I have been for a walk. I hoped Daddy could get a half day
off, but here it is after 5.15 & he is not back yet. Mr. & Mrs. Lodge took the
afternoon off & went into the country, but I wanted a walk & declined
their invitation – thought it would be more rest for Mr. Lodge to have his
wife to himself. I had planned to go to the English cemetery.[1] You never
know what interesting people you may find in the cemetery in a strange
place, & I like to poke about and let the people of the past feel that even
strangers think of them sometimes. However, it is a long walk & the
afternoon turned chilly, so I made a circle for two miles & came back
through the town. On all sides, I heard: 'Gettin' cold now! Soon have the
snow. Shouldn't be surprised if we saw it tonight.' ...

1 The Anglican cemetery, Forest Rd.

Q.H.S. to Ian and Sheila, Newfoundland Hotel, 26 October 1935

... I wonder whether you are having an Indian summer after all the storms.

Here it is wonderfully mild & we are having lovely days. Daddy's diary shows the same story for last year at this time, but more so, as he seldom notes the weather in his diary & he mentions it as specially lovely. Today, the sea & Quidi Vidi Lake are royal blue, & white cirrus clouds are lying still against the blue sky. The hillsides are mostly faded to buff, & the plain woods are almost black against them. But here & there, as on the banks of Quidi Vidi, the grass is very green, and there are bright green stretches on the hillsides that I think must be still unripened crops. In the gardens round about them are hardwood trees, & there are all shades of gold & red. Out in the country, the colours are gorgeous. I have never seen such lovely golden poplars – they are like a dream where they droop above a pool, reflected in the water. The woods are all mixed, with birch & poplar & fir. Where fir is cut down, birch springs up, as I expect you know. And there is great variety of birch & poplar in this country. ... But ... round many of the settlements that once were beautifully wooded, the hills are barren wastes – all the soil washed off them. It is so sad because gardens (which here mean only vegetables) are almost impossible in many places. All the hills round St. John's used to be thickly afforested; now there are only patches & fringes of old forest here & there in the gullies & dotted about the more distant hills. Signal Hill & South Side Hills are quite bare. But – how beautiful it is! There is a quarry up on the side of Signal Hill, but the road has been so roughly hewn that it is no disfigurement; the sun is on it now, and it is golden & purple & silver. Above it are higher slopes, with Cabot Tower & the Marconi aerial and the guns & the old arsenal; below are cultivated fields sloping steeply to quaint wooden houses climbing winding roads. I find these wooden houses most picturesque; the colours are delicately lovely – faded reds & blues & greens & greys – & the roofs all up & down, & no two houses ever alike or quite in line. And all along the shore of the hill are the fishermen's flakes, and on the rocks at the entrance to the harbour the waves dash up & fall back in white foam that spreads far out over the blue. There is a lovely red-sailed schooner tacking through the Narrows now.

I do love living above a harbour. I shall miss it much when we leave. I never tire of watching the ships coming & going, and all the life of the port. I don't suppose many harbours have so many schooners coming & going. There are often 3 schooners at once in the Narrows. I always wonder they don't collide. ...

Monday. I expect Daddy writes of the difficulties & perplexities here. I think that one of the root troubles in this country is that there is no aristocracy. The top layer of society here are merchant shopkeepers, busy men, none of them, I should think, ... who have ever got beyond the 3rd form[1] stage of school education, as we should measure it in England. When they can afford it, and they make sacrifices to afford it in many cases, they send their boys & girls to England to school at about 15. But they are content to give them the cheapest preparatory school training here – cheap & bad, because the teachers are inadequately paid and the equipment of the schools is insufficient. It amazes me that wealthy parents think no shame that the overworked & underpaid teachers have to add to their work by organizing sales & entertainments to get necessary repairs done to the buildings or to provide necessary equipment. They have a splendid Englishwoman, Miss Cherrington, at the head of Spencer College, the girls' C. of E. school, where there are 300 girls, & she has brought out a friend to help her as matron of a girls' hostel.[2] She found a broken-down sort of boarding house in use and it did not pay! She & her mother had to mend all the beds with their own hands – there was not one decent whole one (as an instance) – and the food was atrocious. She & her friend together have made a beautiful hostel now – a house where the girls learn how a decent house should be & can be ordered. And not only does it support itself, but there is a substantial balance. And tho' it is by their own hard work and private efforts that this has been achieved, that balance is not theirs for use in Spencer school & hostel; it has to go into the united funds of Spencer & Feild[3] (the boys' school), which is excessively badly run & mismanaged. Isn't it disheartening? And there is the boys' old hostel[4] that was so badly run & mismanaged that it has stood deserted for two or three years; and when they were asked to clear it up this summer, they found unimaginable filth – everything left as it had been left 3 years ago, & left shockingly, & the linen green with mould. It never seems to be anyone's business here to tidy up.

But I got off the point. My point is this: the children who should be getting the training for potential leaders of this island community don't get the preparatory training that would make them ready to profit by the English school opportunity. The foundations are as cheap as possible; how can you expect the final structure to be sound? I was saying this to Daddy yesterday; it has struck me so much going to the schools, talking to the teachers, listening to the parents complaining of the fees(!), and noting the type & standards of the men who should presumably be leaders here. We were washing our hands, preparing for lunch, when I broke forth on the subject. And at lunch, we had a curious confirmation. A man who was lunching with us was telling us about his daughter – how well she had done at school here, always 1st or 2nd in her class, never lower than third all the way through till he sent her to school in England at 15. And there she is never *above* 9th or 10th. 'I can't understand it; I'm disappointed in her or maybe the school's at fault.' Maybe! Maybe!

All these leading men have their merchant businesses, but they have also their shops on Water Street in St. John's – Bowrings, Jobs, Bairds, Knowling, etc. – innumerable general stores – the best far below the standard of any shop you would ever deal with in England – the standard of the stores you find in the sort of street in England where you get fried fish shops – squalid. The shop assistants are not paid a decent – not a living – wage in many cases – and they have terribly long hours & they have no freedom; they dare not complain or they would lose their jobs, & there are no others – they are serfs. You don't meet Mr. Bowring or Mr. Job & company in these shops; in fact, I think they are ashamed of acknowledging any connection with them. But these are the shops where the fishermen *must* buy their stores. These shops are, I suppose, one of the main factors of the wealth of these leading men. It all seems to me to come back to rotten foundations. The Commission is moving steadily along, doing what it can; trying to create a new social conscience – reforming, building up new structures. But now, when they are getting at foundation facts and laying them bare and proving the need for revolutionary changes, the merchants & the bankers are in a panic. And yet, the only salvation for them is revolutionary measures. The truck system, which filled their pockets, is emptying them fast now. I must stop this letter. Please consider it private. ...

1 Junior high school.
2 Spencer Lodge.

3 Bishop Feild College.
4 Feild Hall, Forest Rd.

J.H.S. to Maisie and Blair, St John's, 27 October 1935

... *Private. Jacta est alea.*[1] I have given notice that I shall exercise my option to retire February next. I have as yet had no reply, but expect that one is now on the water, and that it will contain a protest. But I am going to be firm about it. *Very strictly between ourselves*: we are having a small difference of opinion with the home government as to the constitutional position of our government, and I do not propose, under any circumstances, to stay out here not as a member of an independent government but as a superior civil servant under control of the Secretary of State.[2] Do not mention this to anyone. The matter has not yet come forward officially. It is simmering, perhaps brewing. My retirement will make Downing St.

think about it very seriously. So, D.V., you will see us home before next spring, and we shall be looking for an economical shack in which to spend the evening of our lives.

In view of this possibility – probability – I wrote Otto Niemeyer[3] of the Bank of England, suggesting to him that I would be available if they are looking for a man as director of some company! I got a very nice letter back, saying that they all know me and are all wishful to help and that I am to let him know when the matter is finally decided. If I can get a directorship with £400 or £500 a year as salary, we should doubtless settle somewhere within reach of London. We should be compelled to, so that I should be handy for my work. And Quita would like that. She is in truth a town bird – for she loves the theatre and the shops and her fellow man. I am a clodhopper. I love the country and all it implies, and do not care if I never saw a person except those I care for: you children & our friends. But if I can earn four or five hundred a year, it will make all the difference. It will mean, for instance, a car, which will not be possible with no earned income. And Quita and I both love a car.

Such a lovely day. We have been having an enormous deal of rain during the last two months. In September, we had 22 days rain. This month, we have had several days of lovely sunshine, but a good many of heavy rain. Economically, things in the island are very bad. The wet season has prevented decent curing of fish, which demands sun. Two cargoes which went to Portugal were so bad that the exporters had to accept a reduction of £1,600 in the price of the first on 500 tons. I have not heard the amount in the second case, but it will be much the same. Then the foreign markets are dreadful. The Italian market is, of course, closed, and it usually takes 9,000 to 10,000 tons. That has to be directed elsewhere, and that again means rock-bottom prices, which are passed on to the fisherman. The great mass of the fishermen (and they are thought to number 30,000 families) will have nothing at all on which to commence the winter. They will be forced onto the dole. On the south coast, things are particularly bad. All the merchants save two are said to be insolvent, & I heard that over one long stretch there is no flour to be had. The picture generally is very black. There are one or two gleams of sunshine. The lobster pack is a great improvement on last year. The export of herring is much more promising. And there is some real promise in the mining areas. Our great iron mine,[4] which was working two days a week when we came here, and four days a week last winter, is now working six days a week. Then we have three large American companies examining quite seriously areas where there are molybdenite, and sulphur and lead. This does not mean immediate employment, but if the examination is successful, which seems likely in at least two of the three cases, there will be employment for two or three thousand families. And we are pushing agriculture all we can. This is all part of our long-range policy to get away from entire dependence on salt codfish. It is, however, a long-range policy, and meanwhile we are faced with a very bad winter. So you see that life is full of anxieties.

It is curious how work comes in rushes. This last week has been rather a nightmare. The worst time is, but only very occasionally, in the middle of the night, when I wake up and think out problems. As a rule, I sleep very well. ...

1 The die is cast.
2 For Dominion Affairs.

3 Sir Otto (Ernst) Niemeyer
   (1883–1971).
4 At Bell Island, Conception Bay.

J.H.S. to Greta, St John's, 27 October 1935

... Like you, we have been suffering from a great deal of rain. September had 22 wet days. October has been better, for, though there has been a lot of rain and two howling gales, we have had quite a number of lovely days of sunshine – like today – and they make up for much of the other kind. This place is most lovely in the sunshine – so much so that it is difficult to settle down to steady writing in this sitting–room of ours. We can see the harbour & the Narrows, and the blue sea breaking on the brown rocks into foamy masses of lace. On the other side, we look out onto the hills where the Bally Haly Golf Club has its clubhouse and course, among the farms and below the forest. Quita's writing-table is in the window, & she carries on a conversation about the movement of schooners in the Narrows, and the changes of colour on the hill, and the racing clouds, and their shadows tearing over the fields, in intervals of writing to Auntie Bel, or, as at present, to Sheila.[1] ...

We are, officially, still passing through a bad patch. ... It is the problem of this winter, and of next year's fishery which is causing us most anxiety.

This is in many ways a very remarkable island. There are 25½ million dollars in small savings deposits – an average of £80 per family. Lives are insured for another 56 millions. Yet half of the population lives in a state of poverty which at home would be regarded as appalling. In part, this means maldistribution of wealth. In part, however, it means that no matter how much a family will starve, it will refuse absolutely to withdraw one cent from its savings account. In that, they are extraordinary people. They are a curious people in many ways – highly religious in church – not outside. Very little backbone. Very little persistence. They work very hard for a short time, but cannot keep it up, apparently. They are ill-disciplined &, I think, not very truthful. They are very hospitable. In fact, the root trouble is lack of education, and things will not be right till we get a good educational system, run by the state, not the churches. We have inserted the edge of the wedge, but our education Commissioner[2] is a nervous person and will not apply the hammer except with gentle taps, and then only when his ruthless U.K. colleagues become impatient and drive him to it. ...

1 Sheila (Gonner), wife of J.B. (Ian)   2 Frederick C. Alderdice.
  Hope Simpson.

J.H.S. to Betty, St John's, 2 November 1935

... Here we are having a difficult and anxious time. The fishery position is very bad – bad weather meaning bad fish, and bad markets meaning bad prices. The actual fishermen are getting nothing more than the cost of their supplies as a rule – nothing extra for the winter. So we expect to have 20,000 more on relief than we had last year. And when you have that kind of poverty and the hopelessness of that outlook, people are naturally discontented and disappointed. There was a public meeting this week calling for the abolition of the Commission. It was run by nonentities, and the speeches amounted to personal abuse of the Commissioners, without any criticism of policy or constructive suggestions at all. It was a crowded meeting, with an overflow outside, but, in effect, its influence, insofar as it had any influence, was favourable to the Commission. The thinking people were quite disgusted.

We have other difficulties and anxieties, and life is not an easy matter, but the peace of God which passeth understanding keeps our hearts and minds, and the anxiety is confined to the office. At home, we have perfect happiness. Quita is very well and very happy, and where she is, there is contentment and quiet satisfaction.

We have had a quieter time than usual, I am thankful to say. The last month has been rather a racket, and an expensive racket, and our bank balance is lower than it has been since March 1934. That does not worry. We have all that heart can desire or reasonable man can need.

At the moment, we are enjoying Mrs. Beckett's radio. She has gone to Corner Brook. Now I have the Empire Broadcast – someone is talking about cricket. ... The Lodges, with whom we usually have a game of bridge when we are both at home, are out after dinner. He also is having a bad time. He is subject to the most scurrilous and libellous attacks, but meets them with perfect equanimity. He is a difficult man to move. The thing he particularly hates is vacillation. And that is present in a marked degree in Mr. Alderdice, so that we occasionally have quite interesting passages of arms in Commission. ...

Q.H.S. to darling Benjamina [Betty], Newfoundland Hotel, 2 November 1935

... It is such a heavenly day. All this week has been glorious. We can hardly believe this is November, it is so warm. I wakened at 6.30 this morning and, as always, I sat up to see how the dawn was breaking. Signal Hill & the South Hill were in silhouette – just a few electric lights pricking the blackness of the hillside & a dim spark in the window of the tower. The harbour was dim silvery grey. Along the horizon was a low band of smoky fog, breaking upward into flaming orange that lost itself in the deepest blue of the empyrean, with the morning star like a little sun blazing high in the blue. I have never seen anything like that morning star – it blots out or dims every other star, & makes its own silver path on the sea. I just thought, 'I must not forget to tell Betty about this; she will be able to picture it.' How I wish I could paint! I have been trying to do a little sketch from the window, but it is very bad. ...

Mrs. Lodge has been along to see me – she comes here to smoke her mid-morning cigarette & we sometimes go for a walk together. We are getting out as much as we can before the snow comes. Mrs. Crawford¹ rang up here asking me to go to bridge. No thank you. I don't accept afternoon bridge parties, or I should never be in for Daddy. It is about the only use I am here. He does like to find me here.

Private. There are all sorts of excitements going on here. The Abyssinian question is quite dwarfed by the local excitements. There was a public meeting called this week by some people who call themselves 'The Crusaders.' They demand the abolition of the Commission. Who is Sir John H.S.? What qualifications has he for being in charge of the fisheries? What qualifications has he for development of mineral resource, etc., etc.? Here is his record from *Who's Who.* He was a magistrate in India (a magistrate here is a very subordinate person). He was a relieving officer in China (a relieving officer here is a still more inferior person), etc., etc. The men running the meeting are all men who are either professional agitators or persons who want jobs or who have been discharged from jobs for mal-practice. There was no one of any weight taking part. But, of course, it will be advertised abroad, & questions will be asked in Parliament. ...

1 Probably Dorothy Crawford, wife   the Browning Harvey biscuit
   of James Crawford. He was with   factory.

Q.H.S. to Greta, St John's, 13 November 1935

... Isn't it lovely that we expect to be home for Xmas. What a pity we have no home to open for the month. I think our best plan will be to do as we did last year – take rooms at the Royal Hotel at Waterloo.[1] Or perhaps we should make our Xmas. in the south this year. ... I am afraid John will have to be in London most of the time. He needs a holiday, and will have to husband his strength. He will not get much rest in London. ... The great thing is that we are coming home for one month, & can have Xmas. with some of our children, & see them all, we hope.

You seem to be having bad weather in England. We had a glorious armistice day,[2] tho' there was a nip in the air. We have really had lovely mild weather – not muggy but just delicious. It makes me feel so well. In fact, I have taken to dancing about our room. You would laugh. So do I. But I can't help feeling intensely happy, when the weather is so invigorat-ing, and the outlook on the harbour so beautiful & so changeful, and all well at home among you children, and the prospect of seeing you all soon! I feel ashamed of being so happy over it all when there is such dire distress in this island, and Daddy is so overburdened with anxiety. I shall be thankful to get him away for a time. ... And things here are really the limit. Here is an instance of what happens. One of the partners of a big firm here told the Governor (& this man & others are spreading the report) that no tenders were asked for the blankets for all the new hospitals, and, as a result, this man's firm is having to close down its woollen mills.[3] Now the hospitals are under the Dept. of Health & Welfare (one of the N.F.L. Commissioners, Puddester, who is hated), but all supplies orders go through Mr. Lodge's dept. The Governor asked Mr. Lodge about it, greatly dis-tressed that such a thing should have been done. Mr. Lodge's reply was to produce a letter from the partner: 'In reply to your request for tenders, we beg to quote our terms for blankets' – or words to this effect. It was an absolute lie that they had not been asked to tender. The tenders had been asked for, but this firm's prices were so far above the tender accepted that they were quite out of the question. If their firm's prices had been at all reasonable, the order would have been given to them in preference to a lower tender from outside the island because naturally the Commission's aim & end is to develop every possible industry within the island. But that is typical N.F.L. Such shortsighted policies; the people sacrifice far-reaching development possibilities to immediate & individual selfish gain. The firm involved in this case is Job's, & the partner concerned is Harold Macpherson, who, I should have thought, is a decent fellow; he is a cousin of Fraser Bond. You don't know where you are with any of them, it seems to me.

And the lies that go about continually – lies to down the Commissioners. And none of these agitators against the Commission have any constructive suggestion to offer. All they can suggest is the old game of borrowing (and they have exhausted all those resources – no one will lend to N.F.L. under control of a native N.F.L. government). It would be easy for the Commission to create a spurious prosperity on those lines, using English money for which they are trustees, & landing this country in even deeper & deeper morasses of debt. Things are in a terrible state here – there is no doubt of that. But whose fault is it? Surely this is the result of 40 years of spendthrift living; it can't be cured in a year. And what a year! To begin with, even in good times the fishery could not support anything like the number of families that are dependent on it, and this year the fishery has been very bad. And even where men have had good hauls, the prices are so low it has not been worthwhile to fish. And yet, the N.F.L.er will not believe that there is any limit to the number of fishermen who can be employed round the coasts. He thinks it is just bad government, bad management. He scorns all the Commission's efforts to get the fisherman onto the land, to get the wood & the fur trade developed & mining possibilities explored. They seem to think the English loan[4] is an inexhaustible mine of wealth from which millions can be drawn for any purpose.

The reason we are coming home sooner than we intended is that the Dominions Office have wired out asking Daddy to stay on till August, in view of the fact that the new Governor is coming here on January 9th & it would be difficult for him to have to start with a new Commission too. They asked John to come home at once for a month, & offer him all the leave that is due to him at the end of his time on full pay. That suits us well, tho' Daddy would have preferred to get away altogether in February, as he suggested.

And the reason they want him home at once is on account of the Kean[5] case. I must have told you about this. It is not Daddy's dept., but the whole Commission is involved. Capt. Kean, the son of the old sealing captain, was accused of smuggling skins out of the country. He was really caught in the act, but the evidence was not conclusive & he was acquitted. But, in his evidence, he acknowledged that he had smuggled on other occasions. On account of this, he was judged by Mr. Lodge (in whose dept. he is employed) as not a fit person to be entrusted with a government ship, and he was dismissed with the approval of the *whole* Commission. He appealed to the Governor, and the Governor in Commission brought the case for consideration again; & again, on the evidence, the whole Commission upheld Mr. Lodge's dismissal. Then an agitation was got up in St. John's in favour of this man, & Mr. Walter Monroe,[6] a former prime minister here, wrote to the Dominions Office about it, & the Dominions Office asked the Governor for particulars. That, in brief, is an outline of what happened. The position is now: 'Has the Secretary of State a right to interfere in domestic affairs of this island?' England's money is being spent out here, & the Secretary of State has a right, by the terms of the agreement with N.F.L., to know how the money is being spent; but, quite definitely, according to that document, he has no right to interfere or to ask for explanations of a case like this. It is patently absurd. Every inefficient charwoman could appeal against dismissal to the English Secretary of State. But because this Capt. Kean is the son of the old sealing captain[7] & a friend of Mr. Alderdice, Mr. Alderdice (who himself agreed with the Commission on the 3 occasions on which the case was considered) has identified himself with the agitation & told Capt. Kean that a gross injustice had been done & called Mr. Lodge 'a pigheaded Englishman' to Capt. K. But all the rest of the Commission will resign if the Secretary of State insists on having the facts of this case. It is not a question now of whether this man was unjustly dismissed; it is a question of constitutional importance whether the Commissioners are governors or civil servants under the Secretary of State. A very carefully considered & carefully worded letter statement of the Commission position is going home this mail. The Secretary of State will either have to climb down or *dismiss* the Commissioners as a Commission; that would include the Governor, and he has just been appointed to New South Wales! What is going to happen? It is a good thing Daddy is coming home. He is tactful, and if anyone can do it, I think he can smooth the way so that the government at home can accept the limitations of their control of the Commission without creating a hostile and embittered atmosphere at home. ...

The Lodges are off to America on Sunday[8] for the conference on the new airways service.[9] Poor Mrs. Lodge is not looking a bit well, & she is homesick for her children and anxious about them. ...

1 Near Liverpool.

2 11 November.

3 Riverside Woollen Mills, Ltd, at Mackinsons, near Brigus, Conception Bay, was run by the Macpherson family of St John's.

4 From the U.K. Colonial Development Fund.

5 Westbury Kean.

6 1871–1952. Prime minister of Newfoundland, 1924–8.

7 Abram Kean.

8 17 November 1935.

9 Proposed transatlantic service.

Q.H.S. to Betty, Newfoundland Hotel, 16 November 1935

Isn't it lovely! – isn't it lovely!! ISN'T it LOVELY!!! We are coming home! We are coming home!! WE ARE COMING HOME!!! Hurrah! Hurrah!! Hurrah!!!

17th. I can hardly believe it. We have just been seeing Mr. & Mrs. Lodge off to America by train for the conference on airways across the Atlantic. Poor Mrs. Lodge wept when we were talking about coming home the other day: 'I do want to see my children.' Of course she does. And they are having such a horrid time, with everyone telling lies & spreading lies about them, trying to down Mr. Lodge. Mrs. Lodge unfortunately gave an interview in London when she was at home (all the dominion ministers' wives were doing it, & it seemed that Newfoundland's representative should not refuse). She said nothing that is not simple truth about the terrible poverty in the outports & the lack of education, but these people can't bear any criticism or unbaring of their nakedness. It is natural, but if they are to have the help they need – & really want – they can't get it & things can't be cured by hiding the poverty & ignorance. The result has been a storm of attacks on her in the papers. I think that it was certainly injudicious to give an interview – we women of the commission have to keep our fingers out of pies for the sake of helping our husbands in a negative way. It sounds lazy (& is), but it seems as tho' if we do anything, we just make their work more difficult.

It is such a lovely day again. We are having a wonderful autumn – you might almost call it the spring of winter – glorious sunny days with just a nip in the air to make you feel full of energy and wanting to sing & dance in spite of all the trouble in the world. ...

This morning, there is a sprinkling of snow on the roofs and on the shady side it still lies, tho' it is midday. John put the car away for the winter last night – was not that lucky? Quite a lot of people had their cars frozen last night. I protested against putting it away till Monday, as I thought we might have a last drive today & Sunday. ...

I have been trying to paint a bit lately – most unsuccessful in result but still a joy, in spite of the despair over results. Nevertheless, I have had a thrill out of it too. ... Fraser Bond came in one afternoon, when genius was burning & my fingers wet with paint from squeezing the brushes (instead of putting them in my mouth as you do), & he was fearfully pleased with my efforts. ... I had just been splashing in my memory of a dawn. ... Prof. Fraser Bond said, 'Why not send that to Miss Holloway[1] & get her to take a photograph of it?' I took his suggestion & very apologetically asked Miss H. to see what she could do with it. The result is really rather delightful – it makes a charming little picture for a Xmas. card. So I am having some done. It is far nicer than my sketch, tho' Venus comes out as a dirty smudge. ...

Professor Fraser Bond gave us such a delightful lecture on Masefield[2] this week, at the Memorial College. He is a first-class lecturer, so simple & humorous & such a poet himself. ... He did what I have never heard any other lecturer do – he not only recited but he gave every recitation twice over to allow the music & the sense of the words to sink in. He does not use a note, as he is, as I told you, almost blind – just waiting for the operation for cataract. ...

---

1 Elsie Holloway (1882–1971). Her photographic studio was on Bates Hill, St John's.

2 John Masefield (1878–1967) was appointed poet laureate by King George V in 1930.

J.H.S. to Maisie, St John's, 17 November 1935

... It is now 10.45 a.m. We went to see the Lodges off at 10. They are gone on duty to Ottawa, Washington & New York and will not be back, I expect, before Christmas. He is having a bad time. He is the subject of the most vicious kind of attack. The reason is partly that he is supposed to be atheist, but in fact mainly because he does what he believes to be right, no matter whose feelings are affected. All kinds of scurrilous accusations are made, and they do not confine themselves to Lodge. They allege that Mrs. Lodge has been travelling round with him to New York and to London & both of which places he has been called on duty at the expense of the N.F.L.

government. Of course that is utterly untrue. He pays every penny of her expenses.

Altogether, we are having a bad time. The fishery has been in part a failure, and the weather for 'making'[1] the fish has been dreadful. ... And there is a universal demand for more liberal dole and for 'work for the unemployed.' If you get hold of the critic and ask him to tell you what work he suggests and how it should be supervised and how financed, he is of course stumped. But you cannot argue with leading articles. A great deal of the burden falls on me, as fisheries are in my department, and the fishermen think I am responsible for bad fishery, bad weather, bad markets, and bad prices. They say, 'What have you done about it?' If I reply, 'What can I do?,' the natural reply is, 'That is up to you.'

So sometimes I lie awake at night and think the thing over and over without getting any farther.

We are in for a bad winter, but the climax will be next February and March, by which time I shall have had my month of absence and shall be fresher for it.

Private. We are also having a very serious disagreement with the home government about the constitutional position. That is really why I am coming home. It seems to me that the chances are about three to one on the breakdown of Commission government on this question. No. I had better avoid discussion of the question. Please keep this item of news absolutely confidential. ...

1 Preserving by salting and drying.

J.H.S. to Betty, St John's, 17 November 1935

Mother is trying to get London on the wireless at 8.55 p.m. this Sunday evening. It is a cold night. ... This morning we went to see the Lodges off. They have gone on government business to Ottawa, Washington and New York. It is in connection with the transatlantic air route which is expected to begin for mail next summer. There is some idea that we shall have an air mail from Canada during the winter, but I doubt it very much. They have not got any airport ready yet, and Quidi Vidi is too small for the machines they will use. The Air Force[1] man who came out here told me that the first machines that come out will weigh 20 tons and the larger machines later will weigh 70 or 80 tons. That means a good deal of preparation of the ground before they can begin. ...

We have not had much this week in the way of social engagements and

have little in prospect. There is a big dinner at Government House the 21st
– white tie and decorations – and that is all. ...

1   Royal Air Force.

J.H.S. to Ian and Sheila, St John's, 18 November 1935
... Last year, I remember hearing a lecture by a Catholic professor[1] of St.
Francis Xavier University in Nova Scotia. He was speaking to the Rotary
Club and had as his audience representatives of the businessmen of St.
John's. He began somewhat as follows: 'A state of society in which the
great majority of the people have no say whatever in the price of what
they buy, and equally no say whatever in the price of what they sell, is
fundamentally immoral.' You can imagine the effect of dropping that brick.
The statement applied quite literally to affairs in this haven of iniquity.
The fishermen have no say whatever in the price of their supplies, which
they obtain on credit from their merchants, and no say whatever in the
price allowed to them for the fish, with which their accounts are settled.
Yet the problem is very complicated. If you wish to put a stop to the
system, you must replace the merchant. That would mean so many millions of money that the government cannot face the step. Also, the government would be the worst possible agent for marketing the fish. And an
evil feature of N.F.L. is the unquestioned fact that the people have become used to looking upon an advance from the government as not being
repayable.

I have got away a fair distance from my text – I fear the conditions of
the year. We are in for a bad winter and I fear a worse spring. We are making
every effort to widen the base – the economic base of prosperity in the island
– pushing agriculture, forests, fur, game, mines. But all this is bound to be
a slow process. And the problem of supporting life and preventing utter
demoralisation is one for immediate solution. It means, of course, the dole.
But if we could invent a dole without concomitant loss of morale, we
should solve our problem. We should also be super-governors! ...

1   A.B. MacDonald.

Q.H.S. to Ian and Sheila, Newfoundland Hotel, 18 November 1935
Isn't it lovely for us to be coming home for Christmas? I am so excited &
delighted. It seems too good to be true. ...

Daddy is very tired – we shall have to do things as easily as we can, but we must see as much of you all as we can. I am sorry we have to come out again. I am a bit afraid of Daddy breaking down. He is wonderfully brisk & young in his ways, but the anxieties of this place are great & weigh upon him. And we feel it very strongly that we are not wanted here. All they want is the English money, & they resent it being controlled by Englishmen. The attacks on Mr. and Mrs. Lodge are disgraceful. They make out that they are making fortunes out of this job (the British government pays the British Commissioners), and when they went to England last year, the rumour flew around that he had decamped with public funds. They have tales of what he has done in the past – he was actually a very wealthy man who worked with Nansen for years as an honorary financier – going with him to Russia, etc., & getting wealthy friends in London to help in all sorts of extraordinarily generous ways, & neither he nor they ever got a word of thanks from the League of Nations, & even Nansen was never heartily supported by them. The *Norwegian* government offered Mr. Lodge a decoration – the only one he would have appreciated, but our government would not allow him to accept it – I think because Norway was a neutral nation in the war.

I do hope Daddy will be allowed to accept the Chinese decoration. We have heard nothing further about it yet. ...

1936

**Q.H.S. to Greta, R.M.S. *Newfoundland*, near Newfoundland,
15 January 1936**
Tomorrow, we hope to land. It is getting colder & colder, but the sun
came out for half an hour just now. We hear of intense cold in London, &
think of you. The news of mild weather in Newfoundland made everyone
in the lounge prick up their ears. It was amusing to have it on the wireless.
I expect it was a compliment to the new Governor.[1] It seems we may
expect to see green land instead of snow-swept wastes. If only the sun will
shine for our arrival, I don't mind whether it is a green or a white world.
We feel so jealous for the first impression that our nice Government House
party will get. ...

We like our new Governor & his family & party; he sits next to me at
table, & at first sight he was very much on guard, but he is friendly enough
now. She[2] is pretty & attractive in a sort of French style, & she is very
friendly & pleasant. She seems a bit childish, but has quite a lot of experience of entertaining & running committees, etc. The son,[3] 22, who is to be
his father's A.D.C., is a most attractive fellow. They are all so happy to be
together. The secretary is Captain Schwerdt,[4] & he has his wife[5] & two
little girls[6] – a very attractive party, & I am glad they are to be in our hotel.
The children ... love John & would attach themselves to him like leeches
but for their good manners & their parents' watchful care. But their eyes
follow him wherever he goes, & they are always planning little surprises
for him. They are such sweet things. The mother is ... very daintily formed.

We play bridge with the Emersons[7] & sometimes with Mrs. Howley,[8]
but the latter is not at all well, & Mrs. Emerson is not a good sailor & has
not been up much.

The ship is pitching & rolling, & it is difficult to write. This may catch the Thursday night mail via Canada. ...

1 Vice-Admiral Sir Humphrey (Thomas) Walwyn (1879–1957), Governor of Newfoundland, 1936–46.
2 Eileen Mary (van Straubenzee) Walwyn (1883–1973).
3 James H. Walwyn (1913–1986).
4 Charles Maxwell Richard Schwerdt (1889–1968).
5 Violet Vere Charlotte (Dent) Schwerdt.
6 Pamela and Rosemary.
7 L.E. and Ruby Emerson.
8 Mary Howley, wife of William R. Howley.

J.H.S. to Greta, St John's, 21 January 1936

The offices are closed today, and I am at home on an afternoon of gloom in more sense than one. I have just had a deputation from four of the outports round Brigus,[1] where 275 fishermen have been left with 900 tons of fish which they cannot sell. They want the government to buy it from them. Alternatively, they want the government to sell it for them 'at a reasonable price.' That means that the government should sell it for them at any it likes, as long as they get at least £12 a ton. They say that, unless this can be done, they will be forced on to the dole, to which they have hitherto never resorted. I cannot sell their fish for them, and we certainly cannot favour Brigus by giving them a dollar a hundredweight as a bounty on their fish. If we did, the whole island would quite properly demand the same treatment. It is a bad method – indeed, a thoroughly bad method. The French practise it, and, incidentally, ruin our Greek market by unfair competition.

Outside, there is a bitter gale of wind. I walked up to my office today with difficulty. At one point, I was blown across the road. The ice underfoot was so slippery that I could not stop myself. Fortunately, I ran into a heap of snow brushed off the side path & so steadied myself. But it was a fight against a bitter wind all the way. Quita went down to the shops, but did not attempt walking. She went in the tram. Yesterday, the tram-lines became so slippery that the trams could not run at one period, and six of them stuck one behind the other. The bad weather commenced on Monday.[2] Sunday was a perfectly lovely day of sunshine, and Quita and I drove out to Topsail,[3] and on to Manuels, about 15 miles. It was most lovely – brilliant sunshine and the whole landscape under snow. It made the sea look quite grey.

Our new Governor is quite different from Murray Anderson. He is a pusher. I dare say it is good for us. He is rather impatient of our deliberate methods in Commission. Today, we had our first meeting. Naturally, a good deal of it was taken up by arrangements in connection with the death of King George[4] and the proclamation of King Edward.[5] That takes place tomorrow, but if the weather is going to be at all like today, I cannot see anyone who can avoid it turning out to hear the proclamation read. ...

1 Conception Bay.	4 George V.
2 20 January 1936.	5 Edward VIII (1894–1972).
3 Conception Bay.	

J.H.S. to Betty, St John's, 26 January 1936

I am in the sitting-room with the window wide open, and the whole place covered with snow. It was a glorious morning, but now, 20 to eleven, has clouded over, and it looks like more snow. We have had a good many lovely days since we got back last Thursday week, and some rather miserable ones of gale and snow. Last Monday and Tuesday were bad days, but Wednesday,[1] when the proclamation was read, was a magnificent day of sunshine, though the wind was cold.

That was a great function. The invited people came to my room at the Colonial Building, at 10.30. The table and one desk had been taken out and chairs put in for 30 or 35. The Governor sat where I usually sit. He was sworn in by the Chief Justice, and then he, the Governor, swore in each of the Commissioners. Then the proclamation was signed by the Governor, all the Judges, the R.C. Archbishop and all the heads of clergy, all the Commissioners, the Mayor, the Chief Justice, and the President of the Board of Trade. Things went faster than we expected, though Trentham became ill and very nearly fainted. He was so ill that he could not get up to sign his name, and had to leave the room. He was attended by Dr. Macpherson in the rest room.

Monday. I have had rather a poor night. I was awake for some time, but the time was not wasted, as I prayed about some of the problems we have to solve. Some are very difficult; some seem insoluble. Then, when I was asleep, I had a series of nightmares, which I can remember quite well. ...

We were at St. Thomas's yesterday. The service was in nature a memorial service for King George, with the church draped in black & purple, the Dead March and special prayers. There was a crowded congregation, & the new Governor was there for the first time. The official memorial service is at the cathedral tomorrow.

Wednesday. This is a letter of snippets – written as I get the time. Now it is a lovely sunny morning, with deep snow everywhere. Yesterday, we had a gale with heavy, driving snow – a dreadful day for the funeral services. There were 8,000 people at the R.C. cathedral, and the cathedral[2] was crammed. The service was at 11 o'clock. We drove down in a ramshackle taxi, and had quite a little wait in the gale & snow before we could get in. Bad luck in my top hat. We had the Windsor service on the wireless, and the processions from Buckingham Palace to Paddington, & from the station at Windsor to St. George's Chapel.

Now we have a new King, God help him. I expect that he will turn out well.

Here we have a new & very promising Governor. His whole entourage (wife & son who is A.D.C. – private secretary with wife and two little girls) is very pleasant and attractive. The Governor himself is a man of force of character. I think that he will be very popular, and I feel already that he is going to be a strong support. ...

I must stop & get ready for office. We have a Commission meeting today with an enormous agenda. ...

1   22 January 1936.   2   Anglican Cathedral of
                                            St John the Baptist.

Q.H.S. to Betty, Newfoundland Hotel, 27 January 1936

Are not these wonderful days we are sharing? Could anything have been more fitting than the records that the B.B.C. has broadcasted for us at this time? First, there was the note of anxiety, not stressed – but warning us. And then, as the days passed so quickly, we shared the watch, tho' so far away. And then, on that last day, the beautiful message repeated hour after hour, 'The King's life is drawing peacefully to its close'; so simple, so moving, so dignified – a king still leading his people, as he went down into the valley of the shadow of death. All over the world – not only in the Empire – the nations have watched & waited, and have felt that a great man has passed on his way. It is curious to note the surprise with which the acknowledgement of his greatness is made. That character – the simplicity & honesty & kindliness, the devotion to duty, and the wisdom and understanding that came to him through this, have brought him to the stature of a great king. I wonder where you have been these days – whether you have been able to listen in. ...

Do you know we have had such marvellously lovely weather since we came out. It snowed just before we arrived, so that N.F.L. was looking angelic when we arrived, in her first winter coat of spotless purity; and ever since it has snowed a little now and then, so that her purity is still unsmirched – 13 days of glorious weather – sunshine and snow and three of the dirtiest days imaginable – snow & sleet blizzards. Today is one of them.

Wednesday 29. Another glorious day! Sunshine & fresh snow on all the world, and a west wind blowing instead of yesterday's icy northeasterly blizzard. What a climate it is! But it is worth while having blizzards three days out of 14 when the days between are so marvellous. I can't get past the joy of all this sunshine & beauty. It was so cold yesterday that, even with all the heat on, it was not too warm in our rooms, with the east wind on these windows & the window ledges piled with snow. But during the night, when all the heat was turned off, I woke to find myself far too hot, & had to take off the eiderdown & open the windows wide (I had left only the bathroom window open wide & the sitting-room a little). The sun is so hot this morning that I have no heat on. Outside, the snow is dazzling and the sound of sleigh bells delights my ear.

And what a happy time the children have! The toboggans come shooting down the Signal Hill roads. But they don't stick to country roads. Everywhere in the town, the children are tobogganing and skating & skiing & sliding and snowballing. It really is a *children's* paradise. No one says them 'nay.' The tall policeman takes no notice. And it is horribly dangerous for themselves as well as other people. One lady told me that, when she was a child, she was tobogganing home from school & did what was forbidden – crossed a road – & shot between the legs of a horse. When she got home, there were visitors on a sleigh, & they were describing to her parents this awful experience. Luckily for her, she had not been recognized.

It is such fun to see the variety of equipage nowadays. The farmers, of course, come in on sleighs & slides, the man standing to drive & a woman perched on top of the goods. They usually come in twos & threes, & they go home at the gallop. Little trucks of coal go round on slides – the funniest little baker's van – ancient victorias¹ are taken off their wheels & put on sleighs. The Newfoundland dogs come into their own these days. You see them singly or in pairs, harnessed to little sleighs carrying children, or even a man, or a load, galloping along, scattering the snow as tho' they loved it. I saw two horses just now rolling in the snow on Signal Hill.

All day yesterday and last night, men were at work trying to keep the tennis courts (now the skating rink) clear of snow. We thought it hopeless & stupid because the snow was so heavy & falling all day. But this morning, the rink is in perfect order, ready for the skaters, & mountains of snow are piled up to the top of the surrounding poles. Little children are having a glorious time sliding down. Prams are taken off their wheels & put on slides, and many little children are just rolled up like mummies & strapped onto slides instead of being laid in prams. ...

1 A four-wheel carriage with a
   collapsible hood.

J.H.S. to Ian and Sheila, St John's, 30 January 1936

We have not had, and could not expect, any home letters since we left. That is one of the drawbacks of our inaccessible country, and will not be remedied while we are here. I think that next year there will be a transatlantic air service for mails, but not for passengers. And, in any case, I hope that we shall not be here to see it. It will make a very great difference to Newfoundland. ... Yesterday, we had a Commission meeting with an enormous agenda, but our new Governor is a very live wire and we finished in 2½ hours. Personally, I anticipated that we should have had two sittings to get through the work. I am not sure that he is not pushing us too fast. Lodge is not yet back, and I am anticipating with a great deal of interest and a certain apprehension his reaction to the new Governor.

Quita is remarkably well. She has her days full with correspondence and visits and assistance in various directions. At the moment, 6.30 p.m., she has with her an Australian member of the nursing service,[1] whose hand is against every man and who smells intrigue in every quarter. I have escaped after an hour of it. The lady is a Napoleoness who wanted to run not only the nursing service but everything else in her district, and strode along treading on the corns of everyone. She is an excellent woman in many ways, but I should certainly not like to have her in my department. Her own boss, the Commissioner for Public Health & Welfare, has refused to see her – probably with good reason. It would be very difficult to get her out, once having got her in. I have my own worries in that respect, as two of my subordinates have turned out inefficient, and it is difficult to get rid of a man in public service once he has been recruited.

We are having a very difficult time at present, and prospects in many directions are gloomy. This island resembles a hedgehog with a problem in every prickle. One does not lack work. There are certain bright spots, but quite a number of dark patches, and it is the dark patch that sets the tone,

though I personally try to advertise and perhaps to magnify the bright
spots in the public interest. ...

1 Possibly (Clara) Beatrice
  McKeague, the nurse at Lamaline.

J.H.S. to Maisie, St John's, 31 January 1936

I have taken an hour off this snowy afternoon, in part because the Walwyns
kindly had us to lunch and in part because the *Newfoundland* is lying at
the quay and sails for England late tonight, and I do not want it to travel
without at least a note from me to Shubra.[1] The ship also takes our forest
officer, Jack Turner (who is by the way a poet of some parts),[2] to whom I
have given a letter to Blair.[3] Turner knows no one in Liverpool, where
some of his time must be spent. ... If you could have him, say, to lunch on
Sunday, or to tea one afternoon, I am sure he would be grateful. He is
rather shy, but is a very nice fellow when you get through the crust. He is
to investigate the possibilities for our timber in England.

Quita has just gone to patronize a lady's working party. I hope she will
not get roped in to work herself. That is quite possible for she is that kind.

We have a new & very energetic Governor who, I think, hopes to make
us sit up. ... But I have a certain fear that he may fall foul of his departments. We cannot allow the Governor to do or order anything, though we
shall be grateful for suggestions or for support. He was the admiral in
charge of the Indian navy, & before that he commanded a battleship, in
both of which capacities he said 'Go' and they went, or 'Do this' and it
was done. As Governor, he has to shed that aspect of authority if he wants
to avoid trouble. ...

1 Residence of Blair and Mary
  (Hope Simpson) Macaulay at
  Great Crosby, Liverpool.
2 Author of *Buddy's Blighty, and*

Other Verses from the Trenches
(Boston c. 1918).
3 Blair Macaulay, Sir John's
  son-in-law.

Q.H.S. to Greta, Newfoundland Hotel, 4 February 1936

Sunshine on now blue sky and a glorious world! Aren't you jealous?
There was ice drifting into the harbour this morning, & every little bay is
frozen up, but the sun is hot & I have no heat on – I must correct this – I

thought I had no heat on & wondered why the room was so comfortable, because the air is icy and the sun is only on the bedroom & bathroom windows. I find that, tho' I have not turned the heat on at all in here today, the pipes are warm at the pipe end. Also, the whole hotel is kept so warm that our rooms keep warm from the surrounding heat. For the air is truly icy – quite different from anything we experience in England. I went up to the office with John this morning, & I just thought, 'We'll have to beware of frost-bite.' We took a snapshot of one of our huge policemen to send to you – he looked fine against the snow. We have also taken some photos of the slides. I want to take lots of snaps of the quaint vehicles & costumes in the snow. I saw a small girl wrapped from toe to crown, only the small encirclement of eyes, nose & mouth showing, & she was eating a cone of ice cream as she dragged her slide over the snow up the hill!

We had such a hurricane on Friday[1] night that the *Newfoundland* could not leave till morning. ...

Daddy is well, but very much weighed down at times with anxiety about the plans for the future of the fishery. Other things are doing well – developing wonderfully – but the question of the fisheries touches such a large proportion of the population, & is so involved & so desperate, that any mistake in handling the problem might cause disaster.

We lunched with the Walwyns last week – just ourselves. We like them all very much. They are so keen & so prepared to be happy and to do their best. ...

The skating rink below is very much patronized. It is a job to keep it cleared because, every day & night, fresh snow falls, & often the snow has to be shovelled off before the big ash-pans can be used; then it has to be swept. It seems an impossible task at times, but the men work all night and, in the morning, on fine days, the surface is perfect. Every few hours, too, the rink is closed for scraping & flooding again. There is 'God Save the King' now, & the music has stopped & everyone is clearing off for a few hours more clearing of the ice. ...

Tuesday 5th. Another even more glorious day; the sea is clear of ice and clear blue-green, touched with flecks – a lively sea – not stormy. Long icicles hang from the roofs, tho' the sun is shining full on them. The wind is icy. I have just come in.

1 31 January 1936.

J.H.S. to Greta, St John's, 6 February 1936
... You would love the winter here. We are having days of brilliant sun-

light, and quite warm sunshine, with a keen frosty wind and, of course, snow everywhere. ...

Quita likes this place. The view of the harbour from our windows is a constant delight, and the keenness of the air and brilliance of the sunshine are a great attraction. And she is remarkably well.

I am very busy, and we are having somewhat of an anxious time with the Governor. He is a nice fellow, but he has never been used to being a figurehead. He wants to *do* something. And constitutionally he cannot. We Commissioners are the people who do things, and we can accept no gubernatorial interference and no gubernatorial orders. I have told him so! I do not think that he likes the position, but he has the grace to understand it. ...

Another six months and, D.V., I shall be a free man! I am looking forward to that consummation with much anticipation. ...

Q.H.S. to Ian and Sheila, Newfoundland Hotel, 7 February 1936
How you would all enjoy three weeks of weather such as we have had since we landed three weeks ago. It really is glorious – sunlight & dry clean snow and arctic clearness of atmosphere. Today, there is a north wind, and the snow is driving like smoke off Signal Hill – just as we saw it in those pictures of Everest – snow streaming like pennons from the peaks. How your boys[1] would love it – skiing, skating, tobogganing, sleighing, sliding; every day & all day long the cold is intense. I go up to the office with John nearly every day, & I go out in the afternoon too. But I sometimes wonder whether I shall have to turn back – my hands go dead inside my thick lined gloves, and when I face the wind, I wonder whether my nose will freeze. But it is so healthy. The children don't feel the cold as I do, I know. I saw a child eating an ice cream cone in the snow one day, when I was wondering whether there were icicles pendant from my nose. ...

I do feel so sorry for the poor these days. It must be awful to have no warm clothes & insufficient firing, & to have to walk 7 miles there & back in this icy wind to get your dole – or worse, to row in an open boat over stormy seas to get it. It is bad enough to have to go on the dole, but in many areas it is not such an easy life as some would think. ...

There is a *Daily Mail* paper boat[2] leaving for England today, & she is taking the mail. Such an unexpected opportunity. We have taken to posting regularly instead of waiting for direct boats, as they are so infrequent now. The Commission has built big sheds for the paper company[3] (Grand Falls) so that they can carry on all through the winter. At Grand Falls, the sea at Botwood (their port) freezes up. This is the first winter the ships have been here, & it is jolly that they are to carry mails. I expect they will bring them back too, the *Geraldine Mary* & the *Esmond*. ...

I forgot to tell you that, out of the 20 days since we came, 3 have been blizzardy – the 20th, when the King was dying; the following Tuesday, when he was being laid to rest; and last Friday, when the *Newfoundland* could not sail till next day. They have been real hurricanes. It is so strange to lie at night & hear the wind tearing at the foundations of the house, & to think with grief of the poor fishermen on that wicked south coast – & then suddenly to find oneself awake to glorious day again. Today is not so good – after a wonderful sunrise, the snow has gathered up and now it is driving in fine flakes thick over all the land. We can't expect to have sunshine all the time, & the beauty of the place is that it may be like this now, but in half an hour the sun may break through, & the clouds drive away from blue skies. And all through these days, we have had fresh snow every day or night at some time, so that it is always spotless. ...

1 Pupils at Hartnells House, Clifton
   Junior School.
2 S.S. *Esmond*.

3 Anglo-Newfoundland Development
   Company.

J.H.S. to Betty, St John's, 8 February 1936
... We are having rather a difficult time at the moment, while the new Governor finds his feet. He is a 'live wire,' and wants to do something himself. Now Governors cannot *do* anything. *We* have to do the doing, and if he tries to interfere, we are bound to prevent him. It is just a question of the tact necessary to obtain that result without offence. Specially as he is so anxious to do good and effective work.

We have been having cold weather. The footpaths are sheets of solid ice, covered with snow, & walking is quite dangerous unless you are careful. Yesterday was very cold with high wind and driving snow – but we have had a lot of brilliant sunshine in the course of the last week or ten days.

I am particularly busy, as Claude Fraser (my secretary) and Jack Turner (forest officer) are both away at the moment. Fraser is in Canada, Turner in England. And there is a lot of additional work to be done. Prospects are not too bright. The fishing industry is passing through a very bad time. I am having my own particular difficulties with two of my superior official subordinates, who will have to go, and whose removal is going to be painful.

However, God's in His Heaven. Though things may look black, as long as we are doing what we believe to be God's will, we are not responsible for the results. They are in His hands. ...

Q.H.S. to Betty, Newfoundland Hotel, 16 February 1936

It is just two years ago today since the Commission of Government took over here, & two years ago yesterday since we arrived in this country. Well, I think the Commission has justified its appointment over & over again. There is criticism here, naturally, but as many of the critics point out – where would N.F.L. have been today but for the Commission? The country was bankrupt & in despair. Now, capital is flowing in, new industries are developing, administration has been put on a new & more solid basis by the creation of a civil service, by the appointment of magistrates all over the island, & by the creation of the Ranger force; the land is being developed as it has never been before; the mineral possibilities are being carefully & systematically examined, & old mines are being worked & new mines opened up; the wildlife of the island is being preserved, & the fur trade controlled & developed. Roads are being flung across the island, opening up new possibilities of trade & traffic – fishing & shooting is being organized for tourists. And, above all, the people are being helped onto a better level through better education & more of it, & through better health & social services. And there it is that our biggest problem lies. The standards of morality are so low. Dishonesty is at the root of most of the troubles of this island, & dishonesty is at the root of most of the difficulties the government has to deal with in the matter of reconstruction.

As an example. Bad as the year has been for the fishery on account of 1) poor fishing, 2) bad season for curing (it was so wet & foggy during the drying season), & 3) bad markets (the loss of the Italian markets, increased competition & low prices), the dishonesty in handling the fish for the markets abroad caused heavy losses. 'Packets' of fish labelled 'prime' would contain all sorts & sizes of fish – bad & good, small & large, & fish that were not 'fish' at all. The dealers in Europe have plenty of choice in the people with whom they will deal, & if Scandinavia & Iceland will sell them fish that they can depend upon to be what their labels declare them to be, it is not likely they will deal with N.F.L. We have had two N.F.L.ers' out in Spain & Portugal this autumn examining the question, & they report frankly that a great deal of the depression in the fisheries is due to this dishonest trading. Another point they make is that the N.F.L. traders bid against each other & force down their own country's prices. They are such selfish individualists in trade & so shortsighted.

It is the same in the logging trade. Daddy went ahead to Liverpool, you remember, to examine for himself some cargoes of wood that had just come over. He found one absolutely rotten & the Liverpool lumberman said, 'We expect a lot of that sort of stuff from N.F.L. We can depend upon the Scandinavian wood to be what it purports to be.' And yet, we have the finest wood for certain purposes, & we have the most sought-after 'fish' when it is properly cured & marketed.

February 17. Monday. Such a glorious day again. I have been up to the office with Daddy, & we have fed the pigeons there, & are delighted because they know us now, & get excited when they see us coming, and swoop down from the cornice & feed on the ice at our feet. They will soon, I hope, feed from our hands – if the N.F.L.ers do not catch them & wring their necks; you know how they can't resist killing everything that gives them a chance. That is why the pigeons were so wild at first. ...

The harbour is full of slob ice now. Yesterday, the *Geraldine Mary* came in and had to cut a path through it. Beyond the beacon rock, there is open water still. I hear that an iceberg has been seen already; it is very early. ...

Here is a poor schooner coming in festooned & draped with icicles. Her flag is at half-mast. I wonder what is wrong. I have been watching the tug trying to hack a way through the ice to her.

1 Raymond Gushue and
   John T. Cheeseman.

J.H.S. to Ian and Sheila, St John's, 16 February 1936
... Today is the second birthday of the Commission of Government, and the papers are dwelling on the sins of omission and commission. They conveniently forget the pit from which the island was digged. We have made quite remarkable progress in these two years of cultivation. And our wisdom has largely been in the self-restraint that we have exercised. Reform cannot be imposed. It must come with the acceptance of the society it affects. We are just about to enact regulations of a very severe nature governing marketing of fish abroad. These regulations will now be welcomed. If we had attempted them two years ago, they would have been bitterly resented.

The question of Newfoundland is, as I have always said, a moral question. Things will never be right until we get a generation decently educated, and until the standard of personal and commercial honesty changes entirely. The present dishonesty is appalling. If a fisherman, or a merchant, can sell second-class fish as first-class and get away with it, he is regarded as a clever & successful fellow. They occasionally can the wild rabbit and label it 'Salmon,' and there is a case on record in which a tin of lobster was opened & found to contain the head of a codfish. This year, an attempt was made to open a new market for blueberries in Chicago, and the consignment was found to contain rocks & earth (to increase weight) and brushwood and a woman's ragged jumper (to increase bulk). How is it possible to improve the export trade (which is vital to the country) when such things are done?

These are the real, practical difficulties with which the Commission of Government is faced. Nothing permanent is possible in the way of reform until the people themselves undergo a change of heart. Yet they are, in observance, a most religious people. They attend their churches regularly and are bitterly sectarian. And if you told them they are immoral (which in fact their practices prove them to be), they would probably throw you into St. John's harbour.

We are suffering at the moment, I am sure very temporarily, from overzeal on the part of our new Governor. He is an admiral with a fine quarterdeck manner, and an astonishingly free use of the broadside. He is rapidly becoming chastened, and learning that, as Governor, he is impotent to do or to order anything, and, as chairman of Commission, in effective possession of one vote only, like every other Commissioner, unless there is equality, when he has a casting vote. *Le pauvre homme.*[1] He came here expecting and determined to do something which would put things right at once. He has already learned that he is tied and bound by the chain of constitutional practice and is limited to suggestion, which may or may not be acceptable to his colleagues. I have been the tactful agent who has explained the position and brought it home to him, and suspect that, though he may be grateful, he is not pleased. However, it was quite essential that he should understand the position before Lodge arrives. Otherwise, there would have been a series of volcanic explosions before peace ensued.

Last Sunday,[2] I spoke to a society of young people, the Antlers,[3] to whom I had spoken last year. Then it was in a room to 50 or 60. Last Sunday, it was in a theatre to an audience of 1,000! They seemed to accept what I said to them with appreciation. I spoke on 'The Outlook' – beginning with the general, political and economic, and then concentrating on

Newfoundland. I cannot think that the speech was satisfactory to the general public. The only thing they would appreciate would be a statement that the British government was prepared to give them one million, or preferably two million, pounds sterling. ...

Last night, we went to the Prince's Rink[4] to see the final hockey match between the team from Halifax (N.S.) and St. John's.[5] They had played two previous matches this week, each winning one. So last night excitement ran high. We won 2–0, both our goals being scored in the last 20-minute period. It is a lovely game, and the skating is marvellous. The pace is terrific, and they all seem able to skate backwards as fast as forwards, and to stop dead when going full speed. The rink was crammed. It is a wooden rink and, if it went on fire, I cannot think that anyone would escape from the galleries, or many from the parterre.

Monday morning.[6] 8.30. Such a heavenly day – glorious warm sunshine – not a cloud in the sky – and the harbour covered with ice. Yesterday afternoon, we drove 18 or 20 miles over a road cleared by snowplough, to Portugal Cove & back. Very interesting & very lovely, but somewhat difficult when on one occasion we met traffic. Either side were snow-banks, six feet deep, and we had to back to the nearest cleared-from road.

I had a painful job on Saturday, hearing the reply of one of my officers to various charges made against him. He denied some and explained others, and suggested an enquiry, which would have been very difficult, as it would have meant enquiring from his subordinates. Fortunately, he thought better of it and last night submitted his resignation!

Now the new week has begun. It will bring its own problems, but at least one welcome event, for the Lodges return on Thursday. ...

1 The poor fellow.
2 9 February 1936.
3 The Newfoundland Order of
   Antlers was started by Philip E.
   Outerbridge to raise funds for
   playgrounds. The meeting was held
   at the Queen Theatre.

4 On Factory Lane, behind the
   Newfoundland Hotel.
5 The City All-Stars versus the
   Canadiens Juniors of Halifax.
6 17 February 1936.

Q.H.S. to Noton,[1] Newfoundland Hotel, 18 February 1936
We shall be thinking of you tomorrow, when King Edward VIII lays his sword on your shoulder and creates you one of his first knights – perhaps

the very first, as BARClay may be the first name on the list. Well, he could not have a worthier knight. ...

By the bye, do you know Miss Geen, who is, I believe, in charge of social work of some sort in Manchester – I think it is in connection with unemployed women? Her sister[2] is in charge of child welfare here – a very nice woman, able & tactful. ... It is a difficult job she has here, & all the more difficult because women ... get very little recognition in this country. I hope things are going to be pleasanter for Miss Geen & other women who are doing fine work here. ...

1 Her brother, (Robert) Noton Barclay (1872–1957), Lord Mayor of Manchester, 1929–30. Export

   shipping merchant with Robert Barclay & Co., Ltd.

2 Dorothy Geen.

Q.H.S. to Greta, Newfoundland Hotel, 20 February 1936

... *Friday* 21. Another perfect day. The air is full of tiny sparklets of ice like motes in the sunshine – rising all the time. I try to catch some on my hand; they are more like tiny squares of thin glass – they melt before I can examine them. Nearly every day, I notice this – especially in the mornings. The temperature is below zero every night, and the harbour is frozen over. But I have the windows wide open, & the sun is hot now. The railway is responsible for keeping the harbour open, and it is most interesting to see the little tugs labouring to make a pathway for a schooner. I watched one at work one day; it pushed into the ice & stuck, then it backed & tried another plan till it stuck again – four times it tried before it got through the thickest ice and reached the waiting schooner & then proudly towed her through the path of open water. ...

I do miss the wireless. It has gone back to the Lodges. It costs too much to buy a set that would be any use here, as we have so short a time now. The Vincent Joneses[1] hired one for a week at £1. That would soon mount up!

We are going to see the *Fort Amherst* today & lunch on board. She is one of the new Furness Withy boats.

Your ... & our Christmas cards are being most useful. I have done such an attractive scrap-book for Lourdes[2] that I can hardly bear to part with it. It is a school drawing book, & I have pasted the outside with flowers from a catalogue. It is quite a job preparing the cards – cutting them all down, arranging them so as to have suitable subjects & styles & colours grouped together. And I have racked my brains, & all the poetry books & children's books I could get hold of, for suitable poems & songs & sayings to illustrate the pictures. It is great fun. The cutting alone took me 4 hours! But these cards will fill lots of books. And I spent a happy hour in the new public library,[3] rooting among the poetry. I have never seen a library so well used. It was opened only about 3 months ago. Every table was full of readers, & crowds were coming & going, borrowing books to take home. It is a revelation of the hunger of these people for education. 'Water Street' said no one would use a public library here! It is not just fiction. There is more solid literature taken out than stories. I was amused to find that my corner – the poetry – was evidently a rendezvous for young lovers – very young ones. They were reading in couples!

Another great boon to the town is the unemployment centre. The Y.M.C.A. has gone bust, & the Commission has taken over the Y.M.C.A. quarters[4] for these men – all except the bowling alley, which is let to help the funds. But they have the use of big warmed rooms & little rooms & a library & lots of magazines & papers, & games, & there are classes in navigation & in reading & writing & a fine gym & a swimming bath. The men are so grateful. Mr. Van Bommel,[5] who is in charge, is a splendid fellow and very experienced. He came from Canada, where he had done similar work.

We had a great scoop in this matter. We asked Mr. V.B. if there was anything they needed specially, as we wanted to help. He said the men liked jigsaw puzzles, & they were short of them. I suggested we should try to get hold of a fretwork machine & let the men make their own. But that very day, we saw an advertisement of custom house remainders to be sold & among them a 'Carton' of jigsaw puzzles. We authorised Mr. Van B. to try for us and he got 6 *dozen*, of which 2 dozen were very fine big pictures, for $3.80, i.e., 15/.! I am sure those big ones would cost 7/6 each. Wasn't it luck! ...

1 Vincent S. and Mary Jones.
2 Land settlement on the west coast of the island.
3 The Gosling Memorial Library was opened on 9 January 1936 in the museum building on Duckworth St. It was named in honour of William Gilbert Gosling (1863–1930), Mayor of St John's, 1916–20, and author of *Labrador* (Alston Rivers 1910) and *The Life of Sir Humphrey Gilbert* (London 1911).
4 In the King George V Seamen's Institute.
5 D.J. Van Bommell, manager of the community centre.

J.H.S. to Greta, St John's, 21 February 1936

... Quita is out at a tea-party. I am just back from a meeting of exporters of codfish, held for the new Governor. He is a man determined to *do* something. That is liable to be a nuisance. He interviews everybody, and thought he had discovered something valuable in an idea of a central marketing authority. Unfortunately, I produced a note submitted to and accepted by the Salt Codfish Board[1] on 14th December last, proposing exactly that measure. However, I called a meeting for him, and he addressed it this evening, and his drive will unquestionably help in getting things through. But we are all agreed that his desire to do something will land him into difficulty. He can neither do anything himself nor order anything to be done. It is the Commissioner in charge of the department who does and orders things. And every Commissioner would at once resent and resist any attempt on the Governor's part to do or order anything in his department. Naturally, that is disheartening to an active man desirous of pushing things along – but it is the true position, and I have had to tell him so twice already.

The Lodges arrived on Wednesday[2] night by the new boat *Fort Amherst*. She is a beautiful little boat. There was a private view today for the Governor and the government. I went over the whole boat and spent quite a time down in the engine room. When I came up, I found Quita and the rest of our little party partaking of cocktails in the cabin of the engineer.

We have had marvellous weather the last ten days – cold & sunshiny – with the exception of a day of ferocious gale on Tuesday which caught the Lodges between Halifax & St. John's.

Saturday 22nd. Such a storm. Rain & gale & the wretched *Incemore* sailing into it tonight. It is a cold-blooded proceeding to sail quite deliberately out of a sheltered harbour into a ferocious gale. ...

I must stop. It is after 9 & I am due at office at 9.30. ...

1 Established by the Salt Codfish Act,   2 19 February 1936.
   1935, of 13 June 1935.

J.H.S. to Betty, St John's, 23 February 1936

... We are having a mild and windy spell after some lovely cold, sunny weather. The harbour has been quite busy. ... You know that they are despatching paper from Grand Falls via St. John's in winter. It gives a good revenue to the railway and some work in St. John's, though the longshoreman's union[1] is liable to stop the trade by demanding excessive wages and inequitable conditions of labour.

1 Longshoremen's Protective Union.

J.H.S. to Ian and Sheila, St John's, 23 February 1936

... We are still in the trough of the depression, and there are only faint gleams of improvement. Most of the island is bankrupt. The merchants' resources seem exhausted, and the fishermen have nothing on which to fall back. They depend on the merchants for supply, and I fear there will be a great shrinkage in supply this year. Economically, that will perhaps be sound, for we are carrying over 15,000 tons of unsold net fish this winter. Still, it cannot but mean distress if 15,000 tons less is caught in 1936. It would mean £240,000 less coming into the island. ...

We had one of our aeroplane pilots – Kent[1] – to dinner a couple of days ago with his wife. One of our planes was utterly destroyed in a storm last August. They were both anchored when the storm came on, and a great motor barge broke loose and came down on them, and crushed them both. One escaped, repairable. The other was just matchwood. Kent flies the repaired one – now on skis. It is extraordinarily useful. The cooperative man[2] had to go out to Grates Cove (Bay de Verde) last week. It took him two days to get there, as both road & rail were blocked with snow. We sent the plane for him, & he was back inside of an hour. Since then, he has been there & back & held a meeting – leaving here after 11 and being back by five the same day.

There is great competition for the plane. We are getting a second, which the R.A.F. is going to use for upper air observations. We shall have the use of it for the cost of the gasoline & oil of our trips. That is good business for us. Directly the snow is off, we are to begin to construct the aerodrome[3] for the transatlantic flights. It is to have six runways, each 1,500 yards long and four hundred yards broad – star-shaped, so that landing may be possible with the wind in any direction. It will cost £200,000. They evidently mean real business and we are to have trial flights this summer. They do not plan to take passengers, at least for the first two years. ...

1 Captain Clifford F. Kent of Imperial Airways Ltd.

2 W.D. Beveridge.

3 The future Newfoundland Airport at Gander.

Q.H.S. to Betty, Newfoundland Hotel, 6 March 1936

I think of the primroses out in England now! The snowdrops must be over – the daffodils must be just starting. I expect there are lots of primroses in the fields at Godington.¹ ...

We are having pretty difficult times here. Mr. Alderdice died suddenly,² and the question is who is to be the new Commissioner. A lot of people want another Englishman, I am told. But the constitution would not allow that, I think. A Newfoundlander it must be, and a Church of England man, as the other two N.F.L. Commissioners are Roman Catholic (Howley) & Wesleyan (Puddester). But the question is, who is there? Nobody suitable apparently. It seems as tho' they would have to leave a vacancy or appoint a nonentity! It is extraordinary how few men there are here who have the necessary education and knowledge & character which are really required. I say, why not appoint Mr. Harold Mitchell, who has always worked hard for his country and is doing a big & excellent piece of work on the Trinity Bay coast re-establishing the fisher folk through land development & organized fishing? But he is a Presbyterian, & the N.F.L.ers would not stand a second Nonconformist. Then I say – Daddy too in both cases – why not take ... Fraser Bond, who would like it, who is an educated man & loves his country & has character? But he has spent most of his life in America, & tho' he has a lovely place at Whitbourne, he hates Markland & will not do a thing to help the people there. His uncle, Sir Robert Bond, was an outstanding prime minister of Newfoundland – remembered for his probity and fine character, & his name would help Fraser Bond, & I believe Fraser Bond himself would throw himself heart & soul into the Commission work. Mr. Trentham says N.F.L.ers would think it an insult to appoint a man who is practically an American. Anyway, the appointment is in the Governor's hands – not mine!

We have got thaw at last – real thaw. But some mornings we have silver thaw. Do you know what that is? I thought it was just frost over all the world. But it is something rare & far more lovely. The sun shines on a world standing in shining armour. Every tree, every branch, every twig, every wire is coated in ice. The poplars hold up shining silver spears, the branching trees are hung with shining silver catkins; every telegraph wire is strung with diamonds. You have no idea what a shining, glorious world it is. And such a marvel because the sun is hot now; an icy air & wind holds it an enchanted world – there is not a drip from the icicles. But today is an ugly thaw – the roofs are black & bare again, & great black patches show on the hills. The snow is all slushy on top of ice, & walking is dangerous. Motorcars keep to the tram-lines, which have been kept clear with salt, but they splash filthy salt water all over one as they pass. There is an iceboat skimming over Quidi Vidi; it must be D. Fraser's[3] – he builds boats there.

The sealers will be leaving in a few days. Daddy & the Governor are going to see the ships this afternoon. ...

The Sidney Webbs[4] have sent us their new book, *Soviet Communism: A New Civilisation?*, with such a nice inscription to us both. I have not tackled it yet. ...

Here is the sun again, & the mist is driving away over Signal Hill. We should soon see icebergs again. ...

1 In Oxfordshire, England.
2 On 26 February 1936.
3 Douglas C. Fraser (1904–1990), pioneer Newfoundland aviator.

Established Old Colony Airways, 1931, and Fraser Airways, 1932.
4 Sidney James Webb, Baron Passfield (1859–1947), and (Martha) Beatrice (Potter) Webb (1858–1943).

Q.H.S. to Bel, Newfoundland Hotel, 7 March 1936

... We ought to be at a party just now – the 'Puds' (Puddester, originally Poindexter!) are having a reception for the Governor & Lady Walwyn, & all the world is there. Invitations are always by telephone here, so I did not know it was semi-official, & declined, as we always do decline invitations for Sunday; we like to keep our Sundays for the rest John so much needs and for his home letters to the children. But we simply skip with delight at the thought that we have escaped. If we had known it was to meet the Walwyns, we should have had to accept.

I don't think I am very popular. I won't play bridge in the afternoon, & I always hurry home from tea-parties to be with John. He hates me being out. And what is the good of me if I can't shape my life here to be of any little help I can to him in this discouraging & anxious job. ...

Q.H.S. to Ian and Sheila, Newfoundland Hotel, 7 March 1936

... We have lost one of our Commissioners, you may have heard, Mr. Alderdice. He died on the 26th. I thought there would be a lot of illness after the funeral. Everyone walked at a less than funeral pace, the hearse horses making a good meal of the flowers on the wreath-carrier in front. No ladies go, but the procession was about a mile long. It was a raw day &

raining. I did feel sorry for the little scouts in their scanty attire. It was one of the most foolish-looking things I have ever seen to turn children out in khaki drill & shorts for such a purpose on such a day. They had to stand outside about an hour while the service was held in the church & the whole ceremony took about 3 hours for them. ...

All very private ... The new Governor ... came out believing that he was to be an ordinary Governor and full of energy & belief in his powers ... to put everything right in a very short time. And he can't do a thing – except involve the Commission & himself in embarrassing situations. Daddy is doing all he can to help him to an understanding of the position & to some knowledge of conditions; he is most energetic, & rushes about all day long inspecting businesses & offices & interviewing people, listening to everyone and believing everything everyone tells him. It is a great surprise to him to find that he is not admiral of this ship, & cannot command the Commissioners. He is terribly puzzled & out of his depth. It was a shame to let him come out to this job in this babe-unborn condition; his attention ought to have been called to the constitution. You would think he would have found out for himself – I suppose he just took it for granted. But there was some queer work about it – Mr. Lodge & Daddy were at home, & the Dominions Office never made any attempt to bring them together – in fact seems to have wished to keep them apart. Very queer doings, I think. ...

Hullo! Hullo! I noticed my windows are all hung with icicles again, & the air is so cold that I could not bear the window open in this room – I had to open the door into my bedroom, & keep fresh with a secondary supply. But now – magic fingers clothing the trees again in ice – silver frost again. ...

J.H.S. to Ian, St John's, 8 March 1936
... I have had a busy and difficult week. The Italian situation, both as to sanctions¹ and as to exchange, has resulted in that country taking from us very little codfish. Usually, she takes some 9,000 tons. She is also taking very little from Norway & Iceland. So we, in common with those countries, have to sell in other markets, and they have become glutted, and prices of course have fallen. So our merchants are left with large quantities of fish – which they consider that the government should take over at a price remunerative to the merchants and of which it should dispose otherwhere than in the market – i.e., in the sea!, which is of course absurd. But the fisheries have been so pampered and so spoon-fed for the last

20 years that those engaged in them cannot see the absurdity. We are at the moment engaged in an attempt entirely to reorganize the control of production and of marketing. This was accepted by the licensed exporters at a meeting addressed by the Governor (in true nautical style), but now they are inclined to bargain for a subsidy as the price of reorganization. Which again is absurd. One of our troubles is extreme individualism. Every individual merchant thinks only of how his particular interest is affected by any provision of law or of regulation, and has no interest whatever in the general welfare.

Another of our outstanding troubles is the number of people depending on the fishery. There are 34,000 people recorded as so dependent at the recent census. They export about 60,000 tons of fish, worth £1,500,000. The actual profit recorded by the producers seldom exceeds £2 per ton. In very good years, it reaches £4 per ton. Taking this maximum, the actual profit on normal export received by the producers might be £240,000. A simple arithmetical exercise £240,000/34,000 gives you about £7.10^2 per producer as the profit from his year's operations. Of course, that is an impossible figure. They get a little more from salmon & herring & halibut and squid, and from their gardens. But the standard of the average fisherman's life is deplorable, and things will not be right till we get the numbers fishing down by 50% and the production up by another 50%. When I argue on these lines, people think that I am mad. Fishing is the local fetish. The island has always lived on the fish & therefore must always so live. The methods adopted in the fishery are sanctioned by 300 years of use, and so have proved that they are inevitable and right – and so on. And when I point out that what is required is not knowledge of fishing, but knowledge of arithmetic and the application of a little common sense, I am regarded as still less sane.

We have been busy this week. Apart from the ordinary dinner & lunch engagements, which are of course restricted by official mourning,[3] the special features of the week were a visit to the sealing fleet on Friday with the Governor & a visit to Markland yesterday. The sealing fleet sailed yesterday morning. It consisted of three modern steel steamers and four ancient wooden steamers, of which one had been with Scott in the Antarctic. ... The old ships were the *Neptune*, *Eagle*, *Thetis* & *Terra Nova*. Another ancient ship – the *Ranger* – left four days ago. One of the five, I forget which, was built in 1863, another in 1871. The conditions on these ships must be abominable. They are crowded with men, who sleep between decks. I thought of them as I lay in bed last night & a southwesterly gale tried to beat in our windows. There is no accommodation on board for washing and no adequate sanitary arrangement, and conditions must become progressively disgusting. When you add to this the nature of the freight – raw sealskins covered with blubber – you can possibly imagine what a sealer is like when it returns from its voyage in four to six weeks.

Yesterday's trip to Markland was an experience I should not like often to repeat. We left by special train to Whitbourne at 9, arriving there about 11. Rain came on as we were driving open sleighs the 6 miles to our destination. That was not too bad, though not comfortable. We did our various visits of inspection to houses, barns, staff house, sawmill & schools, & had lunch in one of the last, cooked & served by the children & an excellent meal. Then, about 4.15, we started back to the station. It was raining hard and freezing hard. When we got to the station, my hat was frozen as hard as a tile and had a frieze of icicles all round it, & my waterproof[4] was plated with plaques of ice. We were not frost-bitten, but might well have been. It is what they call here a 'silver thaw' – the upper-air temperature being too warm for snow, while the lower layers are below freezing point. It is lovely to look at, for everything is glittering white with frozen rain and tiny icicles. But it is desperately uncomfortable. Walking was very difficult, & climbing up & down steps was dangerous. One of the party fell down a flight of steps & had a very nasty bump, with his spine against the edge of one of them.

I wish I could get away, but there is a good time coming, and October should see us safely home, D.V. ...

1 On 18 November 1935 the League of Nations voted to apply economic sanctions against Italy because of that country's attack on Ethiopia. In response, Italy cut economic ties with participating countries and brought in a system of control for food and raw materials.

2 £6.10 in the original. Corrected there (not by J.H.S.) to £7.10.

3 For George V.

4 Raincoat.

Q.H.S. to Greta, Newfoundland Hotel, 9 March 1936

I have just been watching the *Newfoundland* come in from Halifax – in fact she is not yet alongside; she looked lovely crossing the mouth of the Narrows, half-way to the horizon, with the sun shining on her white bridges. I thought she was an iceberg at first – until I got my glasses on to her. Coming from the south, she has to go quite a little way north before she swings round to take the Narrows, so we lose sight of her again for half an hour at least before she puts her nose in at our gates. And already the office has very kindly rung me up to tell me that she sails again this evening instead of tomorrow. And it is 4.30 now, & J.H.S. will be in for tea at 5 o'c. ...

We were so sorry for the sealing vessels. They sailed on Saturday[1] morning in calm weather, but by evening there was a raging storm, and all night long it shook the hotel and tore great slabs of ice off the roof with a sound of big guns. However, the ships have survived it and are at the Funks.[2]

I watched them all start – seven little ships; there used to be between 20 & 30. *Neptune*, the oldest ship, built 65 years ago, led the way – then came the *Terra Nova* ... & the *Beothic,* old Captain Kean's ship; he is 80, & he leads the fleet. All the other captains think he has some special sense for finding the seals; he brought in his 1,000,000th the first year we were here[3] and J.H.S. suggested him for a medal, of which he is very proud. He has 3 wigs – brown for his work on the ships, gold for presiding at meetings, & silver for church & parties. One of the lift boys who brought me upstairs just now is called 'Dominy,' & I asked him if the captain[4] of the *Neptune* was his father. 'No, that's me uncle.' Captain Winsor[5] of the S.S. *Ungava* was a parliament man under the old government & was in the cabinet – & speaker. When John mentioned this to the Governor on introducing Capt. Winsor, Admiral Walwyn ejaculated, 'Good Lord!!!,' & never noticed he had said anything a bit questionable.

There was such a sirening when the seven little ships moved out to sea; every boat in the harbour saluted them, & there were crowds on Signal Hill. There was a delay when they were ready to start – 25 stowaways hidden in coal bunkers, in addition to the 1,400 men they carried legitimately. These lads were well laughed at when they were put ashore. ...

You know the seals have to come up onto the ice-pans for the birth of their babies, and it is the baby white-coats that the sealers are after; they are the ones that are dyed for women's coats. But they change colour after the 10th day, so it has to be smart work on the ships. No one knows where the seals will be, & when the ice is sighted ... the men are all out clinging to any high points they can reach. Then, once a clump of seals is spotted, the ship puts her armoured nose into the ice & pushes in as far as she can go. Then overboard go the men with their poles & flags, racing over the ice, leaping from floe to floe.

It is dangerous as well as hard work. Sometimes fog comes down & cuts the men off; one of Captain Kean's captain sons[6] lost 75 men one voyage; fog came down, and then a gale sprang up, & the ice broke up, & the men drifted away and were not found for several days. They were all dead.

The ships will be away about 6 weeks, & by that time all the white-coats will be born, & their white-coats will be turned to brown.

The ships are all separated already by the gale, and they come straggling home. But not a ship fails to get its greeting of siren singing. I shall not forget the noise that greeted Capt. Kean's return that first year.

It is like a summer evening – such still, quiet, flooding sunlight. ...

1 7 March 1936.
2 Funk Island is situated approximately 60 km. (38 miles) northeast of Cape Freels.
3 See Q.H.S. to Greta, Newfoundland Hotel, 5 April 1934.
4 Captain J.C. Dominy.
5 William C. Winsor (1876–1963), member of the House of Assembly for Bay de Verde, 1904–8, for Bonavista, 1908–13 and 1924–8, and for Bonavista North, 1932–4. Minister of Marine and Fisheries, 1924–8, and of Posts and Telegraphs, 1932–4.
6 Westbury Kean was captain of the *Newfoundland* in 1914 when seventy-eight members of its crew were lost on the ice.

J.H.S. to Betty, St John's, 12 March 1936

It is Thursday morning at 7.25, and I have done over an hour's work. I am sitting in my office, with the window wide open. It is a pearly, hazy, morning, with the sun veiled in slight mist. The harbour is still, and there is practically no wind. Signal Hill is almost clear of snow, and the Southside Hill, the opposite side of the harbour, is also fast losing its snow. It looks very much as if we were at the end of the winter, though that seems too good to be true.

This letter will travel on the same boat as Quita. We have suddenly decided that she should go home for a month. ... She will get to England on the 22nd or 23rd, and leave again for N.F.L., 'as at present advised,' by the *Nova Scotia* on 16th April. ...

The Lodges are going home on the same boat as Quita. He is going on duty. He gave a very fine lecture last night, 'Impressions of two years,' which has created quite a sensation.

15/3. Sunday ... On Friday, we had a little dinner – the Governor's party & the Charles Harveys, Miss Cherrington & Mr. Watson.¹ Quite informal & very pleasant. But the Governor is a very different person from Murray Anderson – much more unpleasant and extraordinarily vigorous & impetuous – and stupid. A bad combination. Unless he changes a great deal, he is going to be an unsatisfactory Governor. I sympathize with him in his

energetic desire to *do* something. But under the present constitution he
cannot *do* anything. We are the people who do things. He has just one
vote out of seven in the meetings of the Commission. That is the limit of
his power. And he dislikes that intensely. ...

1 Probably Ernest Watson, a St John's
   accountant.

J.H.S. to Maisie, St John's, 16 March 1936

Here I am, a grass widower, with our dear one about a hundred miles away
on her journey to you all, you fortunate ones. She started about half past one
in a fog after a lovely morning. All that can be said is that the sea is quite calm
– a satisfactory beginning for a voyage. There were only four or five passengers. The Lodges (which makes me still more bereft) and one Beveridge, who
was director of cooperation and has left very much in disgrace. He is the
second senior official in my department of whom I have had to get rid
within the last month – painful processes both. I hate getting rid of a man,
for I cannot help thinking and wondering what will happen to them. ...

Officially, things go on with difficulties at every turn. The fishing industry thinks that the government should support it with bonuses and
subventions. It is hopelessly disorganized and does not wish to suffer the
necessary trials of reorganization. It looks to the government to keep it
alive as it is. Why should we? I suppose because the government has done
this for the last 20 years. The newspapers write as if we had untold millions to play with. In fact, we are living at the expense of the generosity of
the British taxpayer. If we did not, we should be in the soup to the extent
of about 2 million dollars a year. Barring the fisheries, things are not too
bad. Mines & forests, agriculture and game, all are looking up. But the
fishery affects a third of the whole population. That is why a knock in the
fishery affects us so severely and so rapidly. ...

I will stop & get to reading. Soviet communism.[1] Heavy and long, but
very interesting. ...

1 *Soviet Communism: A New*
   Civilisation? by Sidney and Beatrice
   Webb.

J.H.S. to Greta, Newfoundland Hotel, 22 March 1936

There have been no letters since Quita left last Monday.[1] I think of her
arriving in Liverpool today, and I expect that she has had a fine voyage.

Here we have had marvellous weather – just like summer. The day before yesterday, it was 72° in the shade and 100° in the sun. The *Geraldine Mary* – the big paper boat – arrived here from England yesterday, and I met one of the passengers who told me that they had had a good voyage. So I expect that the *Nova Scotia* had the same. ...

Here we are having a very difficult and anxious time. It is largely due to the instability of the people. They are like weathercocks. They remind me of the Greeks and in many ways also of the Chinese, though they have not the unremitting application of the Chinese. At the moment we are trying to push through a reorganization plan for the fishery, by consent. It is impossible to obtain consent. One day you get it, and the next day you find that the merchants have shifted their ground and that things are anything but what they seem. I have had a most difficult week of meetings and interviews, & though I have not heard officially the result of last night's meeting of the reorganization committee, I understand that they have gone back on the proposals which they had already accepted, & that a week of delicate negotiation has been a waste of time. ...

1 16 March 1936.

J.H.S. to Ian and Sheila, St John's, 27 March 1936

I am a lonely and solitary bird at the moment while Quita is peacocking at home. ... Since she left, I have had one home mail, but nothing from you. I hope that all goes well. ... The wireless is on – the B.B.C. orchestra is playing the 'Yeomen of the Guard,' so you can see how close this place is to Daventry[1] at least. ...

I am having a very difficult time and am having to bear a heavy burden at present. I think I must have told you about the failure of this year's fishery – or rather of its disorganization owing, *inter alia*, to sanctions. We have been engaged during the last month in negotiations for the constitution of a central fisheries board, with very drastic powers, to put an end to the internecine competition among exporters. We have got it through at last and sent home for approval. The fish merchants do not know what they are in for! This has been a very bad year. Yet when you look at the revenue, it has not been so bad really. We reduced taxation at a rate which implied the loss of a million dollars a year. In fact, we are only down $175,000 on last year so far. That does not look like depression. But there is a depressed feeling among the merchants – due to fish. They are pressing us to put up money to help them out, as they have not been able to sell the last season's fish. I am not going to give them anything. Some of them will go west, but the fishery has been propped up by annual subventions from the government for many years past. This year we are going to find out, by refusal to help them, exactly where the fishery really stands.

I am doing some public speaking. On Tuesday, I spoke to the unemployed at the community centre.[2] They are a most attentive and sympathetic audience, and actually cheered at the end, though little I said could have been of much help to them. But they were the kindest kind of audience.

Yesterday, I spoke at the Memorial University College. Another very kind audience. I always like talking to that crowd. I spoke for an hour! They appeared to enjoy it and were very enthusiastic at the end. I spoke very freely and told them what I believe to be at the bottom of most of the Newfoundland trouble – the want of fundamental honesty. It is humiliating when you find Newfoundland wood turned down because they include all kinds of rotten stuff – and the Newfoundland fish losing its market because a barrel marked no. 1 turns out to be number 2 or number 3 – and when you open a tin of lobster and find it contains a rabbit's head. That is the kind of thing that happens frequently and makes it so difficult to stimulate an export trade.

I am speaking twice next week – once on the fisheries at Rotary, which will have to be a *most* carefully prepared speech as it is an official pronouncement. The other is a reply for the toast 'Newfoundland' at the centenary of St. Andrew's Masonic Lodge.

So you see that I am not only lonely but busy. Perhaps it is as well. ...

1 Northampton, England. Site of B.B.C. shortwave transmitter.

2 In the King George V Seamen's Institute.

J.H.S. to Maisie, St John's, 30 March 1936

... It is difficult to write a letter knowing that you have probably had all the news from Quita already. However, you will just have to put up with repetition. First, weather. We were in glorious spring ten days ago, but about four days ago the temperature fell and cold rain came, and then on Saturday night – the night before last – there was a heavy fall of snow, so that I trudged to early service yesterday in snow up to the ankles of my snowboots. Most of it melted quickly, but some is still lying, and today the wind is bitter and there are what they call 'snow-flurries.' Also, there is a thick mist about a couple of hundred feet above sea level.

Our little problems and anxieties are poor things compared with yours at home. Things in Europe are dreadfully menacing. What with the war spirit of Hitler & Mussolini on one side, and the unreasonableness of France on the other, Anthony Eden[1] must have his hands full. ...

Here, as I say, our anxieties, such as they are, are comparatively unimportant, but sufficient for an ordinary mortal like myself. Our chief problem is the truck system and the indebtedness of the fishing population. The system is that a merchant advances supplies to a fisherman – who is already in debt – at exorbitant credit prices, to permit him to go fishing. At the end of the voyage, the fisherman hands over his catch, for which he is credited by the merchant *at a price fixed by the merchant*. If there is more than enough to settle the a/c, the merchant probably places the bulk of it to back debt, and gives the man a little supply towards his winter keep. This year, the great majority of the fishermen have come straight on to the dole at the end of the season. What is happening, though one dare not say it in public, is that the mass of the people are being exploited by a small group of capitalists, of whom a number are very wealthy men. That is the problem we are supposed to solve, and it is extraordinarily difficult to see any solution except through years of effort. I am making a pronouncement at Rotary luncheon on Thursday. They will probably assassinate me before I have finished! ...

1 (Robert) Anthony Eden (1897–1977),   British Foreign Secretary
   first Earl of Avon. Appointed   22 December 1935.

J.H.S. to Ian and Sheila, St John's, 7 April 1936

... I sent you a copy of rather a drastic speech I made last week. This country is 200 years behind the times. A third of the population tries to live off salt codfish, which it makes, and catches, as its great-great-grandfathers did. If you had time to read the speech, you will have marvelled how the people can hope to live on the amount of fish they produce. They are always hoping for an enormous catch and a big price. These are in fact incompatible, and things will not be right till we reduce the number of fishermen by half, while maintaining the amount caught at the present figure, *and enormously improving its quality*. That will mean an improvement in price. I am thoroughly unpopular in many quarters, but my facts have not been impugned in any of the quarters. They cannot be, for the speech was thoroughly documented. I am to speak next month on Newfoundland prospects apart from fish.

I am having an easy [time] after a very difficult period of negotiations, which have resulted in mussolinizing[1] the fishing industry. Yesterday and today, I was drafting the legislation necessary for a statutory fisheries board, which is going to have quite dictatorial powers. The difficulty is the personnel. Here in N.F.L. it is almost impossible to find a strong and honest man. Indeed, to find a strong *or* honest man in the fishing industry. ...

We have had one tragedy. One of my Rangers[2] went out on patrol alone to cross the northern peninsula.[3] He was on snowshoes and took three days' supply. He got lost and, 15 days after he started, was found by one of four search parties we sent out. He had both feet frost-bitten. They got him to the nearest hospital – St. Anthony – 100 miles away. On Saturday, they had to amputate both feet, & he got tetanus. We sent anti-tetanus serum by plane, & it reached St. Anthony on Sunday, but I got a wire this morning (Tuesday) to say that he died this morning. The first casualty among the Rangers and a life thrown away. He should never have started on that patrol alone. ...

1 Making over in the manner of the Italian dictator, Benito Mussolini (1883–1945).

2 Constable Dan Corcoran.

3 Great Northern Peninsula.

J.H.S. to Betty, St John's, 11 April 1936

... We are having lovely weather – cold but brilliant sunshine. Yesterday, the Schwerdts[1] took me round by Portugal Cove and the Bauline Line to Pouch Cove and Flatrock and Torbay and then home by the Marine Drive. I expect you remember that drive. We did it together, but we missed out Flatrock and took the straight road from Bauline to Torbay. ... At Pouch Cove, we got out to inspect the new fish store, put up by the Cooperative Society. 300 of the fishermen of Bauline, Pouch Cove and Flatrock have joined together to try to escape from the clutches of the merchants. I do not know how they will succeed, but they are showing real energy at present. All the work in the large store (it is 72 feet by 36) was done gratuitously by the members of the society. *But* they owe the merchant $18,000 – and I much fear that, when the fish comes in, the merchant will issue a writ and try to take the fish. The men say that they are willing to pay the merchant as they can afford it. At present, the merchant takes the whole of their catch and leaves them to go on the dole for the winter. I am afraid that is the custom in the majority of the outports. The economic conditions of this island are so bad that it almost drives me into communism. It looks here as if the whole population were working for the benefit of a few hundred wealthy or well-to-do capitalists at the top. The poverty of the outports – and indeed of a lot of the city – is appalling, and I wonder that they have not had a revolution long ago.

I am having a solitary time. Since Quita left, four weeks ago last Monday, I have been out three evenings only. ...

Work does not get any easier, but I think that we are gradually getting more recognition. We have refused to be stampeded, and so we are being recognized as at the least stable. But this country has a long way to go before we have stability. We are trying hard to develop every avenue of revenue and of employment, but we have a terrible legacy of incompetence, political immorality and debt. And there is always that dreadful commercial immorality with which it is difficult to contend. Sometimes it seems as if nothing one could do would be of any good. Yet I am convinced that ultimately even N.F.L. will come through – if we begin at the bottom. That means education. ...

1 C.M.R. Schwerdt, secretary to the
  governor, and family.

J.H.S. to Maisie, St John's, 12 April 1936
... I am having a very lonely Easterday. I went to church this morning & took communion – thinking of each one of you. Church was full and not less than 200 stayed to communion. That was the third communion service of the day. The first, at 6 a.m., was crowded. Then there was another at 8.

I think that marriage ruins one for solitude. I remember 1895 – 40 years ago – when I was subdivisional officer ... I was absolutely alone but not lonely. Now I feel just like a lost dog. ...

Monday morning. 8.30. ...

When we leave N.F.L. next autumn, we will carry away a lot of pleasant memories, of which I think the chief will be of sunshine. This is a wonderful country for sunshine, and, even on the worst days, you are never certain that the sun will not break through. It did yesterday, and today, though there is a southerly gale and it is *very* cold, the sun is shining bravely. ...

J.H.S. to Greta, St John's, 14 April 1936
Yesterday was bitter, and when I went to bed, there was a row of icicles hanging from the upper sash of my window. Today, there is nearly a foot of snow on the street. ...

The icebergs are on the move. Four big ones have been seen 200 miles N.E. of St. John's, and Atlantic shipping has been diverted to the B route, 70 miles south of the present one. By the time Quita gets there – a month hence – the iceberg stream will be in full swing. I wish that she had been able to come earlier – not because of icebergs, but because I miss her so.

I am having a busy time and an anxious one. The N.F.L.er is a fickle person, and at the moment pressure on us is heavy to remove sanctions.[1] They have caused loss to the merchant, of course, and to the merchant here profit, however obtained, seems to weigh far more than morality, national or commercial. At least that seems to be the case with many of them. I spoke at Rotary last week and they did not like it. But what I said was true and had to be said. I have to speak tonight at a dinner. We are going to start a branch of Chatham House.[2] I am not greatly hopeful of its success unless the professors of the Memorial College, a number of whom are British & Canadian, come in and run it. What is most needed is a good secretary. Our civil service secretaries are much too busy to take it on as a sideline. And a young lawyer [would] expect a salary. That we shall never be able to pay. ... I am replying for N.F.L. at a centenary banquet of some of the lodges here. The people of this island love public meetings, but I think they are bad for them. They are a relic of the old political regime – an intellectual stimulant and narcotic exercise. This is very marked in church attendance. The sermons are very direct and eagerly followed. If the minister castigates the audience, as frequently happens, he is popular. And then he and the audience leave the church and things are exactly as they were before. It is purely a temporary excitement, that has no effect on daily life. This is the aspect of the local character that encourages pessimism in one's estimate of the future. One always hopes that things will improve – that people will carry out their promises – that they will exert themselves to pay their debts – and the hope is always disappointed. The truth is that we have to begin at the bottom – with the children and their education. ... And there we strike the most difficult of snags in the churches and the denominational system. ...

A good deal of my work at the moment is connected with the new fisheries board. The legislation for it has to be prepared and framed, but as it is the duty of the Department of Justice and said department is extraordinarily slow, I have done the drafting, or got it done, outside the department, and then taken the drafts to the Commissioner for Justice, and discussed and settled the draft with him. I spent two or three hours yesterday and an hour with him this morning. I fear I am regarded in the justice department as a nuisance, but if you want something out of that dept., you have to make yourself a nuisance. ...

1 The economic sanctions the League
of Nations had imposed on Italy.

2 St James's Square, London, England, headquarters of the Royal
Institute of International Affairs.

J.H.S. to Ian and Sheila, St John's, 15 April 1936
I am listening to a concert from Warsaw – rebroadcasted by Daventry.[1] Rather remarkable, but not too good in reproduction. ...

Yesterday, we had a dinner at which we started a branch of Chatham House. I was the speaker, and I expect that I shall also be the mainspring. But not for long, for my service ends on August 12 – less than four months now. I think it will be a very good thing to have this branch in N.F.L., for the country is so self-centred that anything which turns people's thoughts to matters outside N.F.L. is of value. It is for that reason that I am always pressing to have the wireless telephone to Canada.[2] It would cost us about £2,500 a year, but I am sure that it would more than repay the cost in the advantage of contact with the world. It is difficult for anyone who does not know this country to realize its incredible self-centredness. And the pride of the people. They admit the faults of the place in conversation in private, but utterly resent any adverse criticism from an outsider.

I have had a busy week in drafting the legislation necessary for the new fisheries board. That is now ready and should be passed at tomorrow's meeting of the Commission, as should the shop hours act.[3] This latter is a most contentious matter, which could not possibly have been passed by a political government. We limit hours for young people and females to eight a day – others 54[4] – a weekly half holiday on Wednesday – a maximum 5-hour shift – seats for attendants – adequate sanitary conveniences. Every one of these items is revolutionary in the eyes of the St. John's storekeeper. And the legislation is due to insistence by the U.K. Commissioners, though it is in the Department of Home Affairs, which is the charge of a N.F.L. Commissioner.[5] I wish that one of us had education. That is where drastic reform is most needed, and it will never happen under a Newfoundland Commissioner. Things will not commence to progress till we get rid of this damnable denominational education. ...

1 Northampton, England. Site of
B.B.C. transmitter.

2 A radio telephone link with Canada
was eventually established in

288 20 April 1936

January 1939, through the cooperation of the Canadian Marconi
Company and the Avalon Telephone Company. This gave
Newfoundlanders, for the first time,
direct voice communication not
only with the neighbouring
dominion but, through Canada,
with many other countries of the
world.

3 The Shop Closing Hour Act,
St John's, became law on 9 May 1936

and took force as from midnight 10
May 1936.

4 Weekly maximum for anyone.

5 James Alexander Winter (1886–1971),
who succeeded Frederick C.
Alderdice on the Commission of
Government. Winter was Commis-
sioner for Home Affairs and
Education, 1936–41.

J.H.S. to Maisie, St John's, 20 April 1936

I have a free half hour – *mirabile dictu*[1] – in office. At least it appears at
present to be free. Outside, the sun is shining brightly, though there are
heavy white clouds driving through a blue, blue sky. A strong & cold west
wind is blowing. ...

We have had a hectic time officially. We passed a shop hours act in the
most approved form ... and we have a tornado blowing round us in consequence. This is not reform but revolution. Their grandfathers and great-
grandfathers never needed this kind of legislation. We may legislate if we
like, but the law will be ignored – &c. &c. &c. We are going to reconsider
the legislation in the light of this agitation, but on the reform side of it
(which is the side to which they object), I am adamant.

Then we have also a difficult job with the constitution of a fisheries
board. That is a dictatorial body deliberately designed to dragoon an un-
ruly crowd of merchants, each of whom has, of course, only his own
pocket to consider. He wants to sell fish at a profit to himself. If the price
abroad comes down, he wants to maintain the same standard of profit to
himself, and so he passes the fall in price on to the fisherman. If there is
competition to sell, he offers at lower & lower prices, to undersell his
competitors, and yet hopes for the same old profit. And the fisherman is
helpless. We are going to stop this system by the fisheries board, which
will refuse to license fish for export except on such conditions as the board
thinks fit. From the board's decision there is an appeal to the Commissioner, and he will, of course, tend to support the board. There will be
another tornado directly the legislation is published. But we are in a very

strong position. Neither of these measures could possibly have been passed by a political government dependent on votes and funds provided by the wealthy – that is, the merchants. We hope for great things from both of these measures.

I have been having quite a number of engagements recently. People are just beginning to realize that Quita is away and that there is an unattached man available for a four, when wanted. I have had dinner engagements every day from last Tuesday[2] on, and have four this week. ... Last night, I dined *en famille*[3] at Government House, and after dinner Lady Walwyn and I spent a pleasant hour at the piano – I playing accompaniments for her & she singing. As she had not sung for years or I played, the effect was remarkable.

We are having quite a time with our Governor. He is an admiral & cannot understand why he cannot issue orders. He has just circulated a memorandum, demanding a new procedure in the matter of despatches to the Dominions Office, and desires 'that this new procedure should be put into effect as soon as possible.' And I am asked to inform the secretary of the Commission[4] as to the date on which my department will bring it into effect. I have not replied, but have put up a memorandum to the Commission pointing out that this is a matter which requires orders of the Commission, not of the Governor (though I do not say that in so many words), and that I do not propose to change the procedure until the Commission has considered the question and come to a resolution on the subject! So, at the next meeting, the fat will be in the fire. I am very glad that Lodge is not here. Had he been, an explosion could not have been avoided, as he would have written a caustic memorandum refusing point blank to do anything. In fact, something has to be done, and the Governor has every right to propose to *the Commission* that it should be done, but none at all to order individual Commissioners, or the Commission as a whole, to do anything whatever. The Governor cannot yet understand the position, or why, as an admiral, he could give orders to his fleet, but, as a Governor, is prevented from giving orders to his Commission. I have tried to explain, and have told him quite definitely that he cannot, and that if he tried it on with me, I should politely but firmly refuse to obey, and should refer the matter to the Commission for its decision. In Commission, as chairman, he has one vote. There are six others, each of whom has one vote, and a vote of equal value. ...

1 Wonderful to relate.   3 With the family.
2 14 April 1936.   4 William J. Carew (1890–1990).

J.H.S. to Ian and Sheila, St John's, 24 April 1936

... We have been through a very difficult time in connection with the organization of the Newfoundland Fisheries Board, and today has set the seal on everything, for the act was published tonight, and this evening also we got a despatch from the Dominions Office accepting our proposals as to personnel. But just as I was rejoicing, the Commissioner for Justice rang up and told me he thought we had made one serious omission. We have provided that the board shall license or refuse to license export of fish, but we have not provided any sanction in the case in which a man exports without a licence! So we got hold of the chairman[1] of the new board, and the Commissioner for Justice came over, and we had a heart-to-heart confabulation. We shall have tomorrow to amend the act we passed today. Still, it is better to do that than to have a lacuna, which would be discovered by someone who did not like the board and might give us a lot of trouble later. I shall be very glad indeed when the board is functioning properly. It will take a lot of work off the shoulders of my department and, incidentally, a lot of administration also. It is great to have that buffer between the department and the trade.

Yesterday, St. George's Day, we had a holiday. I combined business with pleasure. Schwerdt, who is private secretary to the Governor, drove me and a friend to a place[2] 40 miles away, where the forest division is doing a pit-prop and saw-log operation. We took our rods and tried to fish, but there was a cold gale of wind, and the fish would not look at a fly, though another man there caught 14 sea trout on the worm. However, it was a great day. We walked about a mile through the woods and came to a 'pond' – all lakes are called ponds – which we crossed in a small boat. We then crossed a narrow spit of land and got into a motorboat and went three or four miles to where they have built a ... dam – to raise the water and so get a head for the drive which begins next week. We have to drive about 28,000 tons of wood down the river – the pit-props to the sea, where they will be loaded on ships for Barry,[3] the saw-logs to our mill lower down the river on which operations have been going on. I only wish that we could undertake four or five more of these operations. They are good for the forest, which deteriorates rapidly once it gets past its period of maximum growth. They are also excellent as an example to the ordinary contractors, whose operations are run on the truck system (whereas ours are on a cash basis), and are beneath contempt from the technical standpoint. ...

1 Raymond Gushue.
2 On the Back River, a tributary of the Salmonier River.
3 Near Cardiff, Wales.

J.H.S. to Ian, Newfoundland Hotel, 3 May 1936

Your letter of 19th caught the direct mail all right. The *Incemore* had a dreadful voyage, and did not arrive till 1st May, 10 days out of Liverpool. Another ship that came in for the same storm – the *St. Quentin* – is in harbour here. I went to see her this afternoon. You never saw such a mess. The officers' cabins were crushed in and the whole of the upper works. They are built of iron plate, and it was beat in and smashed from the attachment to the deck. The boats were carried away, and the davits torn clean out of their sockets, and the iron bulwarks of the ship were bent in as if there had been a collision. It was all done by one colossal sea. ...

We are making progress here. The fisheries board,[1] a dictatorial organization devised by J.H.S., is in being & has begun well. Mineral development is booming. Our revenue is extraordinary. We reduced the tariff to lose a million dollars a year on an arithmetical calculation, & have had bad fishery markets. Yet in February, March & April we are $397,000 ahead of last year in our revenue. And motorcars are appearing on the streets like peas falling out of a pod. We are 20 per cent up in motors in the last two years. Please explain this. Yet we have 25% of the population on able-bodied relief. ...

1 The Newfoundland Fisheries Board.
  Created by the Newfoundland
  Fisheries Board Act, 1936, of 24
  April 1936.

J.H.S. to Maisie, St John's, 5 May 1936

I have just been reading the morning papers describing the orgies of Addis Ababa.[1] The end of a tragedy, and possibly the end of an honest effort to secure international peace by collective action. Also, possibly the end of the League,[2] which France and Italy have never loved, and from which the small and weak nations have not benefited as they should. It may be that our civilization is passing. ...

It looks as if we were back in 1913 with Italy for Germany. And how small our parochial problems in N.F.L. seem when compared with these enormous world problems. We are suffering here from sanctions. The people who made the special type of fish that Italy wants are going into bankruptcy, and the hundreds of fishermen who make fish for them are going on to the dole. The fishery is a perilous support for a very large number of people. More than a third of the population are engaged in it, more or less, and even under the best of circumstances, cannot get a living from it. The markets have this year been dreadful – fish selling at less than cost price, and the fisherman getting no profit. Yet our revenue may be described as 'buoyant.' I cannot understand it at all. ... It looks as if, from the revenue point of view, the fisheries are less important than we think. ...

Last night, we had the Governor to dinner to meet the doctor from the wilds of Twillingate hospital and his very charming wife. Name of Olds.[3] They are Americans and have a difficult time, for the secretary of the Dept. of Public Health[4] is jealous of them, and takes it out by not sending their salary for months. Once he sent nothing for four months. Scandalous.

We have a mild day of heavy rain after a bitter weekend. Yesterday, we had a 'silver thaw' – a lovely phenomenon. When the upper air is warm, the rain falls, and the lower air is freezing, and the rain turns into icicles. That is the most dangerous weather for flying. Ice forms on the wings.

I must away. ...

1 Refers to the capture of the
   Ethiopian capital by Italian forces.
2 Of Nations.

3 John and Elizabeth Olds.
4 Harris Munden Mosdell
   (1883?–1944).

J.H.S. to Greta, St John's, 7 May 1936

... I have been busy, both officially & socially. Last Saturday[1] night, we had our departmental dinner, and they took the opportunity to spring a surprise on me. The staff presented me with a silver-plated model of a caribou. They know, of course – though it has not been announced – that I am leaving in the autumn. After dinner, there was bridge and there was dancing and there was 'Auction forty-fives'[2] – the national card-game. I played bridge for an hour, & then was roped in to dance, & the girls were very complimentary, and actually took the leap-year privilege of asking me – and (though it is difficult to believe) seemed to enjoy it. Or they were very good actors. It was a very successful function, and I have a *very* nice staff. 62 sat down to dinner – every kind – skippers of the trawlers, foremen from the forest, game wardens, clerks & inspectors, stenotypists & secretaries.

Yesterday, I went out to inspect our forest operations & the game park.[3] It was a *lovely* day though bitterly cold, but I dressed to suit the weather and was very comfortable. We did some heavy walking through dense jungle and marshes, & I had had enough by the evening. We saw two beaver houses, & walked in the track of a large caribou, and found its droppings.

9/5/36. Just after breakfast – and I was interrupted, and it is now after dinner, & we have had a snowstorm going on for the last nine hours. I took the afternoon off, and started at 12 for Seal Cove[4] to get some fishing. It commenced to snow as I drove there and was snowing hard when I got there 20 to one. I ate my lunch, got into a boat, and fished in the snow for half an hour. No rises and my hands were blocks of ice. So I started home. I had no chains, and something ... went wrong with the engine, so that I got back with great difficulty. By that time, there were six inches of snow. Now, there must be a foot, and the traffic is quite disorganized. ...

Quita sailed last night. A new steamer[5] that we have built on the Clyde for the coastal traffic is on the way across [and] today wirelessed that she is in a fierce westerly gale, which is keeping her back – so I fear that the *Newfoundland* must be having the same experience.

Sunday 10/5. *Such* a glorious day. Brilliant sunshine. Not a cloud in the sky and water rushing from every street, from the melting snow. ...

After a good deal of anxiety over various questions, we seem to be having a quiet interval ahead. But in this quaint island you can never tell. One rejoices with a certain amount of anxiety. A storm might blow up tomorrow. I think, however, that looking well ahead, things are distinctly more promising. We are having important mineral developments. At Bell Island,[6] we have, I believe, the largest iron mine in the world, with 3,000 million tons of ore proved. Two years ago, the export was 124,000 tons. Last year, it was 660,000. This year, it will certainly be a million and a quarter & may be a million and a half. The wages will have risen to 50,000 dollars a week. Of course, that only means local prosperity, but 40% of the wages come back to the treasury in taxation of various kinds, and the company pays 10 cents a ton royalty. On $2½ million wages, therefore, we get about $1 million in taxes, plus $150,000 in royalty. Then there is a fluorspar mine,[7] which began to export 2 years ago with 2,000 tons. This year, it is exporting 10,000 – next year, it will be 25,000. The Buchans lead-zinc mine has exported stuff this year worth 2 millions more than the year before. A talc mine[8] is opening this year with a trial shipment of 6,000 tons. Then we have parties working at gold, molybdenite, and sulphur – each with apparently reasonable prospects. Finally, we are just getting a mineral survey of 20,000 square miles of the Labrador done by a Canadian company.[9] *That is for the moment confidential.* Probably it will no longer be confidential when this reaches you, as all we await is a telegram from the Dominions Office.

I am taking a fortnight leave in June and six weeks in August-September. After which we come home, D.V. I do not know what we shall then do. Between ourselves, I do not contemplate complete idleness with complete equanimity. Yet I shall be 68 in July, and that is getting rather close to the end. We shall have enough to live upon, in a very quiet way, but I should like to earn something to help out with other people who are facing financial difficulty. ... So I think I must look round for some easy billet, suitable for an old gentleman, and with adequate salary attached thereto. Not too easy to find. ...

1 2 May 1936.
2 Popular local card-game.
3 On the Salmonier Line.
4 Conception Bay.
5 The *Northern Ranger*.
6 Conception Bay.
7 At St Lawrence.
8 Near Manuels, Conception Bay.
9 Weaver (Minerals) Ltd of Toronto and Montreal. The work was carried out by the Labrador Mining & Exploration Co., Ltd. J.H. Colville was president of both companies.

Q.H.S. to Ian and Sheila, R.M.S *Newfoundland*, 10 May 1936

... We had such a lovely day to start. Maisie[1] & the children saw me on board, but we did not start till 8.30. Yesterday was glorious – the sea almost dead calm and everyone up on deck playing games & lying about in long chairs – more like the Mediterranean than the Atlantic as I have known it before. Today, we have quite a big sea, but the sun shines and the air is delicious. ...

1 Mary (Hope Simpson) Macaulay.

Q.H.S. to Bel, R.M.S. *Newfoundland*, 13 May 1936

Here we are well on our way. Tomorrow, we expect to be in the iceberg belt, & we hope to land on Friday[1] morning. We have had rough weather the last three days. A storm struck us on Monday morning very early. It was so sudden; I had my port wide open, and before I could get to it, the opposite berth was soaked & rain & spray had blown through the room soaking everything in its way. The sea has been so rough, and we have had to stow down, so we shall be a day late in St. John's. It is raining today so that the decks are wet, but I have had a good walk this morning. It has been too dangerous to walk about before. But our first day out was lovely; we might have been on the Mediterranean.

We have about 60 passengers 1st class, so it is quite lively now that the sea has calmed down. The nicest people on board are the Campbells. She is a sweet person, a Norwegian, & he is a naval man who was leader of an expedition to the South Pole, and brought his party safely through a terrible winter that they had to spend in an *igloo* in which they could not stand upright. He made them do physical drill, & he told stories, & repeated all the poetry he had ever learnt – turned out stores of his mind that he did not know were there. They have a farm on the west coast of N.F.L.,[2] and come out every year and always spend a few days at Government House, so we have met them often, but I have not known them so well before. They always want us to go over & spend a holiday with them, as they have beautiful fishing. Major Wise[3] is on board too – he has a farm next to the Campbells & is a great friend of theirs. He spends the summer in N.F.L. 'playing at farming' & the winters in the Transvaal, where he has a serious farm. It is interesting hearing about their lives. Mrs. C. has just been telling me about her house in Norway – it is described in Sigrid Undset's[4] [title missing] – the farm that Sigrid comes down to over the mountains with her father when she is a little girl.[5] She came to England for school for two years – then she was maid of honour to the queen, and she has had all sorts of interesting experiences. ...

There is an old French nun fast asleep beside me. She is going out to St. Pierre, an island that still belongs to the French – off N.F.L. St. Pierre & Miquelon are the last vestiges of the French hold on N.F.L. ...

1 15 May 1936.
2 At Black Duck.
3 Douglas Wise.
4 Sigrid Undset (1882–1949), Norwegian author, winner of the Nobel Prize for literature in 1928.

5 Possibly refers to an episode in *The Bridal Wreath*, the first volume of *Kristin Lavransdatter*. The central character of this book, however, is called Kristin rather than Sigrid.

Q.H.S. to Greta, R.M.S. *Newfoundland*, 14 May 1936

Here we are in the Arctic current, so we are on the lookout for icebergs, & it is bitterly cold. I have got a hot-water bottle between my feet. The captain[1] was not down for lunch; he is on the bridge all the time now till we get in. It is an anxious lap of this voyage. And a mist has come down, which makes it more difficult. Luckily, we came along at a good pace yesterday, and so have this lane of icebergs in the daylight. But we have had to slow down now. ... It will be lovely to get in & find Daddy waiting. Isn't it queer to think how easily we come & go and how hardly those voyagers of 300 years ago did this same trip. The poor women! How did they fare? And here I am – it is only three months since a mist came down shutting out my view of the hotel & our bedroom window where Daddy was waving to me, & today I shall be watching for my first view of the figures waiting on the quay. We *hope* to get in in daylight, but if this mist thickens, it may be tomorrow. The sea is getting up a bit. ...

1 Thomas H. Webber.

J.H.S. to Betty, St John's, 16 May 1936

... This place has the quaintest kind of climate. I have just been reading out the weather from my diary – such [a] lot of 'lovely days' and 'perfect days' and then, suddenly, 'snow,' 'heavy snow' and 'bitter.' The truth is that we have a great deal of sunshine. Yet the leaves are not out, though the lilac buds are green and the bulbs are in flower. The Claude Frasers' garden has been a mass of blossom. ...

On Thursday,[1] Quita arrived. They said the boat was coming in about 7, but they ran into fog, and for an hour they lay without moving. Then they came out of the fog into beautiful clear weather. Quita said that it was like coming through a wall. Thick fog and then absolutely clear weather.

Yesterday was showery but today has been lovely, with fog now & then. This morning, we went to inspect the new ship *Northern Ranger*, which we have bought for the coastal service. She is a beautiful little ship and must be a good sea boat, for she had a gale ahead for five days on the way out from Glasgow and appears to have been quite comfortable. ...

Tonight I have been broadcasting. It is 'Save the Forest Week,' and there have been broadcasts every day and articles in the papers and speeches in the schools. We have it every year. I think it is good propaganda. ...

1 14 May 1936.

J.H.S. to Ian and Sheila, St John's, 18 May 1936

... We are just off to a glee club concert at the Memorial University College, at which one of the soloists is the ex-Greshamian,[1] John Colman.[2] He is a very nice fellow, and likes dropping in to see Quita from time to time. I must stop.

9.40. We are back. The concert only lasted an hour. The glee singing was *excellent*, and John Colman has a beautiful voice. I have never seen such a lot of plain faces as in the chorus; 54 girls and not one of them even approaching good looks. The same with the men, of whom there were 24. But they were very well trained, and sang delightfully.

It is jolly to have Quita back. It makes an immense difference. She is very well, and has received the warmest of welcomes from everybody. Since she came, the giddy social round has begun again. Last night, we supped at Government House, and there are at least three other engagements this week. My most serious one is another pronouncement at the Rotary Club, on Thursday.[3] I am taking on 'Newfoundland – Other than Fish,'[4] and am going to try to hearten people a little. The fishery depression is exaggerated. Of course, it touches a very large number of people. There are about 114,000 out of a total population of 289,000 more or less dependent on the fishery. Yet the value of exported codfish is only about six million dollars of total exports of 28 million. So, from the national economic standpoint, it is not so important as it is from the social standpoint. Failure of the fishery does not mean overwhelming loss to the country as a whole, though it does mean immediate and necessary expansion of the social services – especially dole. There are lots of bull points. Minerals are going ahead rapidly. We have the largest iron mine in the world, with established reserves of 3,000 million tons. The export has increased by 500% in the last two years and will again be doubled this year. Wages are now paid at the rate of 50,000 dollars a week, against $10,000 in 1934. Other mines are going ahead also. So is timber. So is agriculture. Thus, we are hoping that before long the fishery will become of minor importance. There is also a prospective export of fur running into millions, and tourist traffic has scarcely been touched. ...

1 Former pupil at Gresham's School, Holt, Norfolk, England.
2 Born 1906. Taught biology at the Memorial University College, 1933–6. A Harvard Ph.D.
3 21 May 1936.
4 For his speech see the *Evening Telegram*, St John's, 21 May 1936, 6.

J.H.S. to Greta, Newfoundland Hotel, 21 May 1936

... This is an exquisite morning. It is now 25 past seven, and I am sitting in my little office room in the hotel, with the window on my left wide open and the harbour full of life. Two steamers have sailed through the narrows – one the *Fort Townshend* from New York. The other a German boat, from where?

We have had trouble in the harbour this week, for the longshoremen's union has refused to handle a consignment of fish for Spain which should have left by the *Incemore* on the ground that it was packed at an outport, Carbonear, by non-union labour. The Carbonear union, which has recently been organised, consists of 120 scallywags on the dole. Decent workmen refuse to join it. So we are faced with rather a difficult labour problem. Furness Withy were afraid of a strike, so refused to allow the stuff to be put on board by non-union labour, even though we guaranteed police protection. Under these circumstances there was nothing to be done. The firm in question fits out some 400 men for the fishery and now says it is going to do no outfitting. That means some 2,000 people on the dole. ...

Here, Quita and I are looking forward to a fortnight of leave in June, and to six weeks from 21st August. Then we shall return for ten days, give over charge, and get home (D.V.) by the boat leaving here on 12th October. I put in the D.V. as I have no official information, but I believe (though you must not repeat it) that Ewbank,[1] who, you may remember, was secretary of the India Colonies Committee,[2] is to relieve me here. That would be a good appointment.

Apart from the fishery, things here are not unpromising. ... We have two important prospects at present confidential. One is that the Hudson's Bay Company may institute fur farming on a large scale in N.F.L. The other that a large Canadian mineral company[3] has applied for a concession of rights of exploration over 20,000 miles of the Labrador. They would do an aeroplane survey and intensive mineral exploration. This would cost us nothing. They would spend a million dollars and would want exclusive mineral rights over 2,000 square miles as their *quid pro quo*. We should charge them a minimum rent of $64,000 per annum and royalties on all minerals produced. It sounds too good to be true. And the part of the Labrador in question is most inaccessible, and will certainly not be developed by anyone else. That may come any day now, but is confidential till published officially. ...

1 Robert Benson Ewbank (1883–1967), Commissioner for Natural Resources, 1936–9.

2 Committee Hope Simpson had chaired while a member of Parliament.

3 Weaver (Minerals) Ltd of Toronto and Montreal.

Q.H.S. to Bel, Newfoundland Hotel, 26 May 1936
... I dare say you heard of N.F.L. on the wireless a few days ago. There is a man[1] here who acts as correspondent for the Labour papers,[2] & he seizes

upon any little excitement to make a story & cause enquiry in Parliament – anything to embarrass the Commission. So he had wired home that there were riots among the fishermen at Carbonear, & that 500 police had been sent from St. John's to quell the disturbance. What really happened was that at Carbonear (the largest outport) there is a union of stevedores – 154 men, of whom all except 17 are on the dole & most are just riff-raff. The decent fishermen will not have anything to do with this union. Mr. Moores,[3] a very good merchant there who pays union wages, employs, & has employed for generations, men who are not union men. He can't force them to join – in fact, some of the best men say they would go back on the dole rather than join the union. So Moores's fish was shipped to St. John's by non-union men to be transshipped to the *Incemore* for transport to England. The union men have refused to handle it. The Commission said, 'We can't take sides, but if either side choose to handle the fish, we will protect them.' But Furness Withy refused to allow Moores to employ non-union men – they would not risk a strike among the union men here who could hold up the ship & lose them thousands of pounds. So the fish had to go back to Carbonear. Of course, the fishermen are furious, & want to break the union at Carbonear, & they held a big meeting at Carbonear. But there was no riot, & they are furious that anything of the sort should have been reported to England. Howley – the N.F.L. Commissioner for Justice – is a feeble person, & he sent off 50 police to Carbonear *in case of trouble*. If J.H.S. had been the Commissioner in charge of justice, he would have sent out one of his own Rangers, with perhaps a couple of other men. You know the story of the riot somewhere in Canada? The mayor wired for help to quell it, & he and the town council met the train on which the detachment of soldiers was expected to arrive. One little Tommy[4] stepped out of the train. 'Where's the detachment?' asked the mayor. 'What detachment?' 'To quell the riot.' 'Well, there's only one riot isn't there? – one riot, one soldier.'

Here is the sun again. We have had three days without a glimpse. Monday, being Empire Day, was a holiday & that gave two whole holidays together. We took the car & went about 54 miles up north to Brigus. It is one of the oldest settlements and is very picturesque, and people often spend holidays there. So we telephoned for a room at the hotel, 'The Cabot'[5] (if we stay here for a holiday, John gets no rest). It was a bitterly cold, dull day, but the drive is most beautiful in any weather – in & out & around about beautiful lochs & bays & over Brigus barrens, where you feel on top of the world – looking out over what must have been high mountain tops before the Atlantic washed out the lower levels and cut this land off from the American mainland, washing in & out too among the mountains and making this remarkable 6,000 miles of coastline. We always love this drive – there cannot be a more beautiful drive anywhere I think – specially when the sea is blue & the distance clear.

The hotel is set back from the road & darkened by three of the few trees in the place. Exceedingly dull. Oilcloth on the floor with a few hooked mats. German highly coloured prints – 'oleographs,' I think they are called – and texts. Not a window in the place would open. In the sitting-room, an immense stove that made the room like an oven for half an hour and then went out if not constantly replenished with logs. No bathroom – no drinking water in bedroom, no hot water provided – a w.c. whose plug a notice instructed you not to pull except in case of real necessity, as the sanitary arrangements were under repair. The notice was yellow & fly-blown, & we found it has been up for at least two years. We had quite decent food, & the bed was clean, but we decided to get away early next day (we had engaged our room for the night). This is typical of the sort of accommodation you get when there is anything that calls itself a hotel, except here & at Corner Brook & a guest house at Grand Falls. At one place where we stay, the w.c. is three minutes walk up the road & is right on the road, & in only two lodging houses that I know is there a w.c. indoors & one of them has just last year been installed. So you can see, tho' N.F.L. is an ideal place for a camping holiday, a lot will have to happen before you can make it comfortable for tourists. I don't think Newfoundlanders mind these discomforts – possibly Americans & Canadians don't either – except the wealthy travelling Americans. There are only three places where you can be really comfortable – most of the rest are below the level of cottage accommodation in England. I think this must be why N.F.L.ers do not travel in their own country – they have shacks for the summer a few miles out of St. John's.

After lunch, we snoozed in the hot room & woke chilled when the fire went out. Then we went for a walk round the harbour & climbed a hill & met a little grey man with a big grey bobtailed sheep-dog. He was obviously not a real Brigus man. He turned out to be, as I suspected, a Mr. White,[6] who settled here when he retired from the Grand Falls paper mills to be with his great friend,[7] also retired from G.F., who was also an artist. The artist is dead, but his work lives on, & everywhere you see his lovely pictures of Brigus & the country round. Mr. White invited us to his house – a most charming little house under a cliff & sheltered from the winds but with a lovely view up the bay. It is over 100 years old & is well built &

planned for a wooden house. The doors are so low we had to stoop to them. The paint is all white & the walls hung round with real good water-colours – Stanhope Forbes[8] & others – & the furniture is old & charming. The little man does everything for himself, and the place is beautifully kept. I was amused to see that he has the comforts of life – electric light, a hot-water boiler & bathroom. His little garden was sweet too – 10 apple trees growing in a bit of a meadow below, and flowers in terraced beds here & there. I saw boxes of seedlings in the bathroom all so healthy ready for planting out in their eggshells.

Then we went down into the little town again & called on old Mrs. Bartlett,[9] mother of the town's hero and also American hero Bob Bartlett, who was captain of the ship that took Peary to the furthest point – then Peary would have no one with him to share the glory of being first there. We always have to call on the old lady. She is 84 & brisk & bright as possible. We had tea with her & then went to church at the United Church, where we were much embarrassed to be welcomed by name from the pulpit!

We were very glad that Monday was much warmer – dull still however. We drove quickly along, exploring some bays we had never been into before & fishing & lunching on the way. We asked the way at one place: 'You can go by Cat*choos*.' 'Cat*choos*,' I said. 'How do you spell it?' 'Kate Hughes,'[10] it turned out to be! That shows you how names of places arise sometimes. I find everyone calls it Cat*choos*.

I had an interesting time one day seeing Scott's[11] ship, the *Terra Nova*. A different story that. I went with Captain & Mrs. Campbell – he was captain of that ship on the Scott expedition. Scott's cabin is kept just as it was, and Captain C. showed us how everything was arranged – where the ponies were kept – in the fo'c's'le, & the dogs on the deck – such a crowd it must have been, & such discomfort! And the smell! The *Terra Nova* is one of Job's ships, & returned to sealing after her heroic adventures. She had just been cleaned up after her last trip. She was built in 1884. She is humping a bit. The *Ranger*, which is older, has 'kept her figure.' She was lying alongside. Such little bits of ships they look to carry so many precious lives into such dangerous seas. The bulwarks were carried away by ice last voyage. 'That happened when we were in the Antarctic too,' said Capt. Campbell. The *Terra Nova* carried 155 men this year, I believe. ...

1 Probably John T. Meaney.
2 Newspapers supporting the British Labour Party.
3 Silas Moores of W. & J. Moores Ltd. For this whole episode see *Evening Telegram*, St John's,

19 May 1936, 4; 20 May 1936, 4; 21 May 1936, 4; 22 May 1936, 4; 23 May 1936, 7; and the report by A.J. Walsh in Provincial Archives of Newfoundland and Labrador, GN 38/S6-1-5A, file 6.

4 British soldier.

5 The Cabot Hotel at Brigus was run by Roy and Elsie Rabbitts.

6 George White.

7 Albert Edward Harris (1875?–1933), general manager of the Anglo-Newfoundland Development Company, Grand Falls, 1920–9.

8 1857–1947. British painter.

9 Mary Bartlett.

10 Kitchuses, Conception Bay.

11 Robert F. Scott.

Q.H.S. to Maisie, Newfoundland Hotel, 28 May 1936

Here come the *Newfoundland* – from Boston & Halifax on her way home to England. So pretty she looks! You could hardly believe it if you have not seen her in this little narrow harbour. She looks like a great liner here and is so beautifully proportioned – long & slim & so clean & smart – such a joyous sight – shining too, making one's heart beat faster & one's eyes brighten. I can hardly believe that it is only a fortnight today since she brought me back – I seem never to have been away, so quickly & easily I have slipped back into my place. ...

I can't boast of our weather lately. We have had three days without a glint of sun, & one day of fog. But yesterday was perfectly glorious again – clear as crystal air & blue sea & sky, with a bank of thick white fog along the horizon. Today is uncertain – sunshine & cloud & misty along the horizon. But in an hour it may be glorious. ...

Daddy has had a worrying time – but he will tell you all about it. It was amazing the wireless reporting riots that never occurred and 500 police turning out to quell them. ... Then the merchants have been trying to harry Daddy into subsidizing the fishery. They said they could not supply the fishermen unless the government guaranteed them. But Daddy has stood firm, & the schooners have all gone off to the banks last night & today – such a pretty sight & a grateful sight to the anxious Commissioner. The merchants have always relied on the government to protect them against what they call loss – i.e., anything below what profit they *want* to make. Daddy says the fishery must stand or fall on its own legs or it is radically unsound. But it is hard to stand firm when it seems as tho' decent fishermen may be ruined. So the actual sailing of so many schooners is an enormous relief. ...

J.H.S. to Greta, St John's, 28 May 1936

It is 6.15 a.m. The foghorn is mooing at the Narrows, but it is clear on the water, and the mist is on the hilltops. Indeed, the sun is trying to come through. I am sitting in my office room in the hotel. You know that I have a little private office there, next to our bedroom. The window is on my left as I face the writing-desk, and the schooners that have come in for salt and for supplies for the fishery are sailing down the Narrows, one after another, such a pretty sight. I am glad to see them going, for we have been on the verge of trouble. Year after year, the government has been giving subsidies of one sort or another to the fisheries. We went into the matter thoroughly this year, and I found that in the last three years the amount had been roughly $1,300,000, and that the actual fishermen for whom the help was intended were no better off, indeed were worse off, than they were in 1933. All that the relief had done was to secure the profit of the merchants. So, this year, we have refused subsidies of any kind. The merchants have exerted every kind of pressure. The last move was to induce the fishermen to believe that nothing was being done for the fisheries, because we were wasting money on the civil service. On Tuesday,[1] there were about 60 schooners here with some 500 fishermen, and they threatened to hold a protest meeting last night and to have a procession (which might easily have developed into a riot) to my office this morning. I interviewed the leading agitator at great length on Tuesday. Yesterday, we held a Commission meeting, reconsidered the whole policy, and reaffirmed it, saying that we were not going to guarantee or to supply, and that supply was a matter between fisherman and merchants. There was no meeting last night, there will be no procession this morning, and I heard from the police last night that all except four of the schooners had got their supplies. And now they are streaming out of the harbour, so that incident is safely closed.

The merchants are one of our serious problems. For many generations, the fishery has been run on what is called 'the supply system,' which in plain English means on truck. The merchant advances to the fisherman supplies of salt & other things for his voyage, on credit and often at outrageous prices. The fisherman is then bound to hand over his catch to the merchant at prices fixed by the merchant. As a result, practically every fisherman is permanently in debt to his merchant. I once heard a very fine man, Professor MacDonald of Antigonish St. Francis Xavier (Catholic) University, speak here to the Rotary Club. He began by saying that a system under which the great majority of the people had no say whatever in the price of what they buy, and equally no say whatever in the price of what they sell, is fundamentally immoral. That is just the N.F.L. truck system, and the bulk of his audience consisted of merchants who were responsible for it and living on it. You may imagine the warmth with which the statement was received. The system has been in existence for hundreds of years. The merchant class has exploited the fishing class for all that time, and now you have a small group of wealthy men who have been and are being supported by a mass of poverty-stricken, indeed destitute, fishermen, who are tied and bound by their debts to the merchants. It is an enormous problem, and one which is most difficult to tackle.

Forgive my lecture, which is on a subject which forms my daily bread! I am thinking of the problem all the time, and all the time devising some way or ways to get around or over it. We are stimulating every possible attempt to deal in cash. Gradually, things are getting better – not in the fishery, which is the most difficult part of the problem, but in other directions. In the forests and in the mines, transactions are increasingly in cash. We have, however, a demoralized population which has been brought up with the system, knows nothing else, and is easily persuaded that any attempt at reform is animated by vicious or machiavellian motive. Witness the argument about the civil service.

Our own plans are gradually crystallizing, & I have heard officially *but confidentially* that Ewbank is going to succeed me in N.F.L. Of this I am more glad than I can say, for it means continuity of policy. He has the same mentality and training as I have. ...

The Governor is away on tour – a blessed relief – but returns tomorrow, and I do not doubt will be full of energy and proposals on which we will have to sit heavily. He is gradually realizing that a Governor is powerless, however powerful a Governor in Commission may be. As chairman of the Commission, he has one vote in seven. He began not only by saying what he was going to do, but by writing memoranda to the Commission containing such expressions as, 'I have decided that, &c.,' until he learnt that he, of himself, can do just nothing, and that he may decide what he likes but that the decision has no effect whatever unless it is also the decision of the six obstructionists who form the Commission. I thoroughly sympathize with the feelings of an active, somewhat unintelligent and irascible naval officer who discovers, for the first time in his life, that he cannot give an order, and is fundamentally impotent. Fortunately, I have lots of tact, and he is not too old to learn. ...

1   26 May 1936.

Q.H.S. to Greta, Newfoundland Hotel, 28 May 1936

... I am so sorry I did not see any friends outside family this time, but it was no use trying to – I wanted to see as much of you as possible & get odd jobs done, & London always makes me so tired at first. Besides, I had just had flu. ... Everyone here says, 'Did you see Lady Anderson?' – or, of course, you would see Lady Hastings, or Mrs. Dunn[1] or Barbara Grieve. They seem to think England & Scotland & Ireland together are about the size of St. John's. But this is a jolly place to come back to. Everyone rushes up to greet you – in the hotel, the page-boys, the lift-boys, the maids, the men say, 'Glad to see you back again. Hope you had a good trip. Did you leave your sister better?'[2] And in the streets & shops it is the same. Everyone knows you have been away & welcomes you back & seems really glad to see you and knows all your business. It is most amusing, but very heartwarming & pleasant. How cold & unfriendly England must seem to these friendly people. ...

1 Elizabeth Anderson Dunn, wife of Peter Douglas Hay Dunn (1892–1965). A British official, P.D.H. Dunn was seconded to Newfoundland in 1934 as customs adviser. He was Chairman of the Newfoundland Board of Customs, 1935–7, and Commissioner for Natural Resources, 1941–5.

2 She had gone home to visit her ailing older sister, Isabel. See above 14, 279.

Q.H.S. to Sheila, Newfoundland Hotel, 29 May 1936

... We are having difficult times here, but not what the papers in England have credited us with – riots. John is standing firm in his refusal to bolster up the fish merchants. They said they could not supply the schooners to go out to the banks for their season's fishing unless the government would guarantee them against loss. Loss to them means anything short of the profit they want to get. I believe the rest of the Commission would have given way – wanted to give way & subsidize them. It is difficult and anxious when you know that, if you don't, there is probability that hundreds of fishermen will be unable to go to the fishery. So it was an enormous relief when, on Wednesday[1] evening, we saw schooner after schooner sailing out, & all day yesterday they were leaving. Things in this country will never be healthy till the people learn to rely upon themselves & not upon the government.

We hear that Daddy's successor, Mr. Ewbank's appointment, was announced on the wireless last night. We have known of it for some time. He is such a nice fellow. He was Daddy's secretary on the ... [India] Colonies Committee, and he and Mrs. E.[2] stayed with us at Blagroves[3] more than once I think. They will be much liked here, and I should think he is just the man for the job.

Does Ian[4] remember a Miss Phillips at Oxford – Lady Margaret?[5] Her sister, Miss Phillips,[6] has bought a school here. She is a Girtonian[7] herself, but left after a year in 1916 to be a V.A.D.[8] She is having a pretty difficult time, I should think. The school is not at all what it was advertised to be, & she has lost a lawsuit over it. But she has all the little children of the more educated classes. I doubt whether it will ever pay; people here will not pay for good education – not enough of them. ...

The foghorn is blowing as the fog is sweeping in on St. John's, & one brave little ship, the *Newfoundland,* has to go out into it. ...

1 27 May 1936.
2 Frances Helen (Simpson) Ewbank.
3 Their house near Oake, Somerset.
4 J.B. Hope Simpson, her son.
5 Lady Margaret Hall, Oxford University.
6 Gwendolyn M. Phillips ran Rockford School.
7 Former student at Girton College, Cambridge University.
8 A First World War service organization.

J.H.S. to Betty, St John's, 1 June 1936

First of June. 6.45 a.m. A lovely morning, and I am sitting in my office room at the hotel and a stream of schooners is pouring out of the harbour through the Narrows. I suppose 15 or 20 have left this morning. I am much relieved to see them sailing out, for this day last week, Monday,[1] we were threatened with a hostile demonstration and a strike, because we refused, quite firmly, to guarantee the merchants against loss and the merchants appeared to try to force our hands by refusal to supply. However, we stood firm and all the schooners have been supplied except four. This dole is a curse. No one in the country should starve, for there [is] food available for everyone for the taking. Herring & potatoes and seals and turr[2] and fish and vegetables. But the people have become demoralized, and many of them lazy, and they seem to prefer to sit down and eat flour and drink tea, rather than attempt to get their living for themselves.

I think I must have told you before this of the mystery of this island. We reduced the tariff to lose a million dollars of revenue this year. We have had a bad fishery, and markets have been most difficult. Yet our revenue is steadily above our estimate. The revised estimates were made last November, and we are $400,000 ahead of them. The estimate for last month was $430,000, and we are well over $500,000. No one can explain this. Also, motorcars are flowing in an uninterrupted stream. Where are people getting the money to buy them? It is a dreadful island in some ways. Bitter destitution and poverty in one stratum – ample luxury and wealth in another.

The chief problem is the moral problem. What is needed is conversion – a turn right round. It is the problem of the individual applied to the mass. One of the difficulties is the position of the churches. As you know, the people are great church-goers. But when they get outside the church door, they seem to leave the influence in the building. Mr. Dunn could tell us a good deal about the honesty of many pillars of the church. I am as bad as any of them! ...

Yesterday, Sunday, we went to church in the morning, and drove to Topsail in the afternoon and had tea. ... It was a lovely afternoon, though cold. We were in a queue of cars all the way there. I cannot guess how many cars there were on the road, but it must have been hundreds. They have red and green lights at Rawlins Cross[3] now, but they are moved by the policeman on point duty.

Things are gradually approaching our climax next September. The official announcement of Ewbank's appointment as my successor was made on Friday,[4] and since then I have been damned with faint praise – though possibly with more than I deserve. I am very glad that Ewbank follows me, as it will mean continuity of policy, which is important. Our plans are to take a fortnight holiday this month, leaving for Black Duck next Sunday week. Then we stay in St. John's till 21st August, when the Ewbanks arrive. We then leave on September 8th and have a holiday in Canada and the States, to say goodbye to friends and relations, and get home somewhere towards the end of October. Where we then settle depends on what happens to J.H.S. I suppose I am really too old for new jobs, but it will be difficult to settle down to idleness. ...

1 25 May 1936.   3 A major St John's intersection.
2 A common sea-bird.   4 29 May 1936.

J.H.S. to Maisie, St John's, 1 June 1936

... Officially, we are passing through a very difficult time in various directions. The new fisheries board is up against great opposition from Portugal and also from a small number of recalcitrant exporters here. I have little doubt but that we shall work through the difficulty satisfactorily, but it is giving us considerable anxiety at the moment. Another difficulty is the personality of the new Governor, who wants to 'do' things himself, which is constitutionally impossible, and also suffers from the weakness of desire to be universally popular, which is incompatible with anything like strong administration. He is learning, but it is a painful process both to him and to his instructors, of whom I am the chief!

We submitted our budget for 1936–37 to London for approval the last week of April. It was based on the figures of income and expenditure in 1935–36 to the end of March. Our year begins on 1st July, so we had to revise the estimates for 1935–36 on the March figures, plus our anticipation – say guess if you like – of what would happen in April, May and June. The guess has been seriously wrong, but fortunately in the right direction, for our income for these three months is turning out to be between $600,000 and $700,000 *more* than we expected. This means that, instead of ending the year on the 30th of this month with an exchequer balance of $400,000, we shall have more than a million in hand. London may not be as pleased as we are, for on the 'guess' we asked for a grant-in-aid, which I have no doubt they have sanctioned, which will be a good deal more than we shall in fact need next year.

This buoyancy of the revenue is the more remarkable as we had last year probably the worst year on record in the fishing industry, which is always regarded (I think erroneously) as the most important industry of the country. We have been making an enquiry into the source of this inflated revenue. We thought it might be due to luxury spending. The opposite turns out to be the case. It is due to the importation of larger amounts of foodstuffs and clothing, in large measure. This means that the people generally are eating more sugar and molasses and meats, and clothing themselves better. Which again means that, with the exception of the fishing community, the rest of the island is living better. That is most satisfactory.

Socially, we are having a quiet time – occasional small dinners, occasional small bridge parties. Today, we took Andrew Grieve and his two boys to Holyrood – 30 miles away, on Conception Bay – for lunch. It was a heavenly day and Conception Bay reminded us, as it always does on a fine day, of Greece. The sea was as blue as the Mediterranean. ...

It is time to go to bed. Quita is very well and very happy. She loves this island and, above all, the view from our bedroom window over the harbour, with the myriad schooners coming and going through the Narrows. ...

Q.H.S. to Greta, Newfoundland Hotel, [June 1936]

... We too have had a hot spell & have been wearing our thinnest garments. These rooms are the greatest comfort – the coolest suite in the hotel, on the N.E./S.W. corner & 5 stories up on a hill high over the town & harbour, so that we get every breeze that blows (& it is very, very seldom that no breeze blows on even the hottest days) and only the early morning sun shines in at our windows. A friend from the other end of the hotel came in one afternoon: 'O!' she exclaimed – 'how heavenly cool! I've simply been melting all day – it's hardly bearable.' So we are lucky. I do hope the Ewbanks will get these rooms when we leave; it is much the most convenient arrangement – far better than having a house when you are here just for a couple or three years. Maids have to be taught their job – having no training at all, coming from homes that are often empty of even what we would consider the necessities of the simplest cottage life, and whose mothers are as ignorant as the children. If you get a good maid, she learns very quickly & is wonderfully good, but you may have to spend your energies on half a dozen before you find a good one. It is expensive living in a hotel, but we only have to pay for our rooms when we are away & we have no responsibility for a household to be considered. And nowhere else could we get such a position. Another thing is [that] here we are safeguarded against intrusion by beggars & place-seekers. It is not that one wants to cut oneself off from human contacts with trouble, but John's time would be wasted & we should have no peace or rest for him.

Thursday 11th. We had the Lodges back just for one day – they had to go on at once to America. We miss them very much. ...

Did you see any account of the wreck of the *Magnhild* off Mistaken Point Head?[1] She was bringing us 800 head of cattle & sheep etc., & all are lost except about 12 sheep. It is a great misfortune because, tho' it is all insured, the people who had managed to scrape together enough to buy a pig at the price they then were cannot afford $1 extra, which is the price now. And there is also the loss of so many weeks during the summer when feed is plentiful. But the worst thing about the loss of the *Magnhild* is the way the inhabitants of the surrounding outports treated the wreck. The Norwegian crew managed to get ashore safely, but the ship was surrounded by small boats & looted – stripped of every moveable thing – seamen's clothes & money stolen. It really reads like a story of the South Sea Islands 100 years or more ago. And Mistaken Point is not more than 80 miles from St. John's – not far from Cape Race. There are men living now who have been knighted [and] who made their money from wrecking, Andrew Grieve tells us. ... And all down that coast the people have wonderfully good

blankets for their beds – the product of wrecks. They used to pray for
wrecks in church, I believe. A friend told us a few days before this wreck
that, when she was down at Trepassey, a man told her that 'that there
contraption on Signal Hill (the wireless) has spoilt their business.' The
papers are outspoken on the *Magnhild* business, I am glad to say. They
point out what a bad name this will give to Newfoundland – that even a
foreign ship wrecked on its shores is treated like this. So let us hope the
thieves will be shamed into restoring the lost property before the law gets
at them. And let's hope that the law will not be lenient. ...

We are off to Black Duck to the Campbells' for a few days fishing. We
leave on Saturday[2] night & are picked up by the mail on Sunday & arrive
early on Monday. From the Campbells', we go on for two or three days
more somewhere else, & back by the following Monday. We were to have
had a fortnight, but we shall have to take another week in July instead, at
Gleneagles, as the new Commissioner, Mr. Alex Winter, is ordered to take
a holiday by his doctor. I think Daddy needs his fortnight much more. ...

1 Mistaken Point, near Cape Race.   2 13 June 1936.
   For this whole episode see *Evening*
   Telegram, St John's, 8 June 1936, 6.

Q.H.S. to Bel, Newfoundland Hotel, 8 June 1936

... Here we have an early summer. Last week, it suddenly turned really
hot, and we are wearing our coolest garments – cooler than I wear in
England as a rule; in fact I don't think I ever wear a thin nainsook[1] chemise
& no vest or wool of any sort in England as I do here – & my thinnest silk
frocks. It is really very delightful to feel the air on your skin – such soft
balmy breezes. It is early for such a warm spell here; the trees have rushed
out the last few days, & the gardens are full of tulips – the daffodils are
over. It is lovely having a second spring this year.

John is having a very difficult time. There are all sorts of problems that
you can hardly imagine, not knowing this country. The latest is that this
morning comes news of trouble at Markland – one of the new agricultural
settlements that are doing so well. There are close to 200 families there
now, and six new families are giving trouble. The Marklanders themselves
decide who shall be allowed to settle in their community; one of the
conditions of being admitted is that the children shall attend the community school, which is non–sectarian. One of the women refuses to let her
children go to the school. The governors say, if you do not obey the law
of the community, you must get out; these six ... households, who support

the woman, have their notice to quit, & they will not quit. We don't want
to bring the police in to evict, but the rest of the community are so mad
with these 6 that they will probably evict them themselves. And we don't
want a riot. And now the head of the police[2] tells us that the woman who
is the instigator of the business has been in prison for arson, and of all
things that are dreaded in those woods & wooden houses, fire is the worst.
It would be terrible. The woods are thick, and the houses are scattered
through the woods in all directions round a square of about 8 miles. The
community is doing so well. Some of the families are almost independent
after only 2 years last April. All the experts who come to see it say it is the
finest agricultural settlement they have seen – so enthusiastic – & the
educational side is one of the chief features of it; it is the salvation of those
slum dwellers. Their faces tell a tale of happiness achieved. The school is
the community centre. The children love it. They learn to be clean & to
obey & to cook & to keep clean houses, as well as the three Rs. And they
learn to buy their food & to note how much every meal costs. And in the
afternoons, the women come to learn to sew & make their clothes, etc.,
and to have some fun together like a women's institute – & the men have
lectures & classes in the evening. And the beautiful thing is that the principal school – & the first – was built by the men themselves in their off time;
it is *their* school, & they are so proud of it. ...

We have been out to see the experimental & demonstration farm several
times. That is another of John's babies – 'Mount Pearl.' There is a farmer[3] in
charge under the direction of the agriculture department, & he has about 20
pupils & assistants. One of the experiments is mink farming – they are doing
well. I think we got 50 mink over from Canada for a start. Also silver fox
farming. The mink babies are arriving now, & we saw some of them, but no
one is allowed to look for them until they are brought out by the mother;
otherwise she would kill them. The silver fox babies are due too. The Governor took his dog with him to the farm & the mink were terrified, & we fear
there may have been loss of babies, and Lady Walwyn took him to the fox
farm & the same thing happened. Isn't it idiotic? Then we saw a bed being
prepared for cranberry growing. And of course all the ordinary farm work
goes on, & they have beautiful imported sheep & rams & a stallion. ...

1 Fine, soft cotton fabric, originally   2 Patrick J. O'Neill.
   Indian.   3 James Sparkes (1884–1971).

J.H.S. to Ian and Sheila, St John's, 12 June 1936
It is 7 a.m. and I am sitting in my little office room at the hotel with a

window open over the harbour to my left and streams of motorboats coming in through the Narrows with the catch of the cod traps for the night. It is a lazy life. They set their traps at the beginning of the season, visit them and haul them each morning, and, if the fish are running, evening as well, & bring home the fish. Last year, when fishing was bad, I saw men go out to the traps at seven a.m., come home at eight with perhaps half a dozen fish, [and] loaf at home all day and till next morning, when they repeated the performance. The cod trap and the 'depression' have combined to stimulate inertia in the fishermen.

It has been a difficult and anxious week. We were engaged in negotiations in Portugal, where the government buying agency[1] refused to deal with the selling unit[2] which had been constituted here by agreement of the exporting merchants. As the new fish is piling up, the merchants here became desperate, and urged us to revoke the new constitution. We were as firm as was practicable with opposition in front and mutiny in the ranks, and at midnight last night we got reassuring information from Portugal. We shall not get our plan in toto, but we have stood pat on a unified selling agency here. This replaces five individual agencies, which used to compete among themselves, much to the advantage of the Portuguese buying agency. This competition among sellers brought down the price this time last year from £33 a ton to £25 a ton in the course of a month. £25 a ton for made fish in Portugal does not cover the fisherman's costs. I have little doubt that, as a result of the negotiations just completed, the price will rise to £30 a ton, and eventually go higher. The exporting merchants are a poor crowd. They sign agreements for joint action, and observe the agreement just as long as they consider it to their advantage and no longer. That has been one of the elements of difficulty. We never knew when we should not be torpedoed by our own side. ...

We are approaching the end of the fiscal year, and our Commissioner for Finance is embarrassed. I may have told you about it, but in that case forgive me. Our year begins on 1st July, and we have to send home the budget for sanction of H.M.G. early in April. We get the actual figures up to 31st March, guess the income & expenditure for the next three months to the end of June, and base our estimates for 1936–37 on the result. The guess of the probable income for April, May & June has been seriously inaccurate, and we have about $500,000 *more* than we expected. The estimate of income for 1936–37 is thus probably far too conservative, but the immediate trouble is that, expecting half a million less than we have actually collected, we have asked for a grant-in-aid from Great Britain of £430,000, where we could have done with less than £400,000. Also, we told them we would have an exchequer balance of $840,000 on 30th June, and it is going to be $1,400,000! It is good to be on the safe side, but the Treasury at home will conclude that we have been unduly cautious, and this may have adverse results in years to come. This is the second time we have cried 'Wolf.' Last year, we had to spend a million more than was in our budget, as our exchequer balance was well over two million. The money was put into reproductive expenditure, for $300,000 went in roads, $400,000 in a new steamer which we needed, and the balance in railway renewals. By the way, this year, *for the first time in history*, the railway shows a surplus. One year, the deficit was 2 million dollars.

Generally, things are going well, though we have constant criticism from many directions. I have no doubt whatever as to the ultimate result, but when the country is solvent and the Commission clears out and the politician comes back, matters will rapidly deteriorate again. It is a question of national rectitude. That is a *very* weak plant in Newfoundland. ...

1 The grémio; a guild of importers controlled by the Portuguese government.
2 Hawes and Moreira. Hawes and Company was founded in 1909 by the British commodity broker George Hawes. It was long established as the principal agent for the sale in Europe of Newfoundland saltfish.

Q.H.S. to Betty, Newfoundland Hotel, 12 June 1936

... I wish you were here now. The weather is so glorious. And you would love working at that window looking out over the harbour in Daddy's office.

Daddy & I are off for a week's holiday tomorrow, Saturday. We go tacked onto a freight train, I think, as far as Bishop's Falls. Then, on Sunday night, the mail picks us up and takes us on to Black Duck on the west coast, where we arrive early on Monday morning. We are going to stay with the Campbells for a few days. They have a sweet place – a farm – & they are on the Codroy River, where the salmon fishing will be about at its best, I think. We go on for another two or three days to another point on the river, and keep the car as our home, & return on ... Monday. ...

I have just been collecting my things for tomorrow. I shall take that little paintbox, but I don't suppose I shall do anything worth the trouble. I wish I could do this sky! – such lovely masses of white cloud against the blue, sailing out of the west over the Atlantic. Take my love to darlings over the ocean, you lovely ships.

We have been up to Mount Pearl often lately. It is the new government experimental & demonstration farm. ... It had been neglected for years, & it was like walking on air cushions, there was such depth of dry grass beneath last year's growth. It has been burnt off now, and a lot of land has been ploughed up & sown. We watched the farmer sowing ten days ago, & when we went yesterday, the farm was green all over the sown land. The farmer they have put in to manage is a splendid-looking fellow – fair & sunburnt & blue-eyed & such a happy face. He may well be; he has 10[1] splendid sons, three of them working with him, the rest at school or too young, & 3 daughters, & this is a great opportunity for him. The house is in the middle of the farm & is not very big. The farmer's family occupies the ground floor, & 15[2] students live above, & the farmer's wife[3] feeds the lot. So she must be a busy woman, with one little maid to help her.

Yesterday, we saw the new cows that have just arrived from England – such beauties; 4 of them cost £600. The stock will soon improve. They have a fine bull too. The new lambs had just been shorn, & they looked almost as big without their fleeces. ... On the whole, things look very bright on the farm. ...

1 There were, in fact, nine sons.
2 There were ten students.

3 Emily (Beecham) Sparkes (1887–1976).

J.H.S. to Betty, St John's, 13 June 1936

... Quita and I start on a week of holiday tonight! Think of that. We are first going to the Campbells' at Black Duck, on Harry's River on the west coast, for three days. Then we are going somewhere in the private car for another three days, salmon fishing. I am going to have a real rest. We have been passing through a very difficult time in the reorganization of the fisheries. The merchants are, as you know, a quaint crowd. They asked for a sales unit for the Portuguese trade. That was organized, and the Portuguese, who have an official buying agency, refused to deal with the organization! We should have stood out against this attempt to dictate who we should employ as our sales agents, but the merchants got the wind up, were afraid that they would be left with fish on their hands, and compelled us to compromise with Portugal. That has been done amicably, and I hope that things will be all right now, but in this country you can never be sure! It has been anxious work.

And we are having trouble at Markland. Some agitators got in and engineered a strike. We gave the ringleaders notice to quit, but they refused to budge. We do not want to have to go to court to eject them, but that will ultimately prove necessary, I think. The Squires[1] party are behind them and are delighted. Squires is a clever fellow. When the Governor went to inspect at Harbour Grace, he engineered it so that he – H.E. – had to take a trip with Squires on his yacht. And, of course, that was put in the papers. The Governor has very noticeable limitations. He means well, but is in many ways a nuisance. He is always butting in, but as he has no executive power under the constitution, that only means trouble for the Commissioner concerned. And Lady Walwyn looks upon herself as a vicereine[2] – like the wife of the Governor-General of India – and just as important. It is so ridiculous in a little place like this. It will not worry us for long. Ewbank arrives on 27th August. We leave on 8th September. And it is curious to think that, after we leave, we shall probably be entirely forgotten. The Andersons[3] are scarcely mentioned now. I do not believe more than a few ever think of them. Memories are very short. ...

1 Sir Richard A. Squires.
2 Viceroy's wife.
3 The former governor and his wife.

Q.H.S. to Maisie, on board the *Terra Nova* carriage, on the way across Newfoundland, 14 June 1936

... Here we are in the observation car of our carriage attached to a freight train. About a mile of line stretches away behind us, disappearing over a rise; the track is green with a wealth of grass & seedling trees, & buttercups & every variety of spring life for 15 yards on either side. Then come the roughly cleaved pine poles that are the telegraph posts, carrying four wires at this point. And we are in a cloud of butterflies – large yellow ones with black edges to the wings – black body & black tip to tail. ...

We came on board at 8 o'c. last night & had a very bumpy night. I don't suppose the freight train drivers are as expert as the passenger drivers. I wakened this morning at 7 and drew my blind & gave a gasp of delight. It was such a glorious morning, & the sun was shining on a blaze of colour – masses of wild azalea (the air is all quivering over the line & the butterflies dancing up & down in it & chasing each other). We were running along near a lake that twisted & turned about wooded inlets, & on all the open ground were carpets of azalea/rhodora in blossom – such full blossom. ...

Isn't it a remarkable thing that in a country that is considered mountainous – & that always strikes us as mountainous, tho' we know there is nothing as high as Snowdon[1] – we have a railway flung across 550 miles of the island & there is not a tunnel all the way? The line slides up & over rises where there would be a cutting on an ordinary line, & it puffs & pants & sometimes takes a run back *pour mieux sauter*[2] – up the steep hills. Looking back over the line, it undulates gently till it slides on an incline & vanishes. The line was laid very fast – just pebbles & dust flung on the cleared track, & the sleepers are not more than a foot apart.

1 o'c. Now we are at *Bishop's Falls*, in a siding, & have been dismembered from the freight train, & here we wait till about 9.30 tonight, when we shall be attached to the mail & shall hope to reach Black Duck, our destination, about 5 tomorrow morning. We shall be put in a siding there, and our hosts, the Campbells, will come to fetch us after breakfast.

This place, Bishop's Falls, is a junction, & there must be about 200 little houses scattered about. The Exploits River flows beside the station, & the far side is all green jungle. Here are some children coming up from bathing: a little girl in a blue suit & cap, & her brother – must be the station-master's children. ...

There goes another child down to bathe – and here is a timber train – the engine ringing-ringing its bell as it passes through. The 'peeled'[3] timber is a lovely sight – golden in the sunshine. All the way along the line, at intervals, you pass stacks of timber waiting to be loaded, and on the rivers you see stores of timber in the water, bound round so that they cannot escape to the sea. On rivers like the Exploits, there are acres & acres of it in the great bays – a shining, gleaming, golden horde. ...

1 Highest peak in Wales.   3 Barked.
2 Better to jump ahead.

J.H.S. to Greta, in the 'Business Car' on a siding at Bishop's Falls, 14 June 1936

We are on a holiday! We left St. John's last night at eight o'clock, attached to a goods train, and are to be picked up here – 230 miles from St. John's – by the overland limited tonight. The reason is that they do not like the platform at the end of the overland to be masked by another car attached behind the train. This 'Business Car' has an observation section at the end – then two sleeping cabins and lavatory – then dining-room and then kitchen. The beds are real beds and very comfortable. Today is real mid-summer – brilliant sunshine and hot – and the black flies and mosquitoes are busy. Of course, our windows are screened, but every time the door opens they flood in, and it takes quite numerous reminders on their part before you get rid of the last of them. Quita's ring-finger is swollen, so that she has removed her wedding-ring. The part of my anatomy they chose is among the hairs of my hand.

The reason for last night's goods train was the transatlantic flights. We are to have a sea-drome at Botwoood and an aerodrome at Cobb's Camp, some thirty miles east of this place. On the train, we had the survey party who have gone to lay out the plan of the aerodrome. They had masses of stuff with them, for they are starting on the work right out in the jungle, and they will have to house the whole staff. They will have bunkhouses for the workmen and, as there will be anything up to 350 employed when they begin, that will mean seven large or fourteen small bunkhouses. They had the rubberoid roofing with them. Then they had to have all the supplies for board. It is a great business. The runways are 1,500 yards long and 400 *yards* broad, and they have to be faced with some tar solution. ... The aerodrome will not be ready this year, but the trial flights are to be made to Botwood, by seaplanes. Botwood is just a few miles from here, on Exploits Bay. ...

Officially, we have passed through rather a difficult and anxious time this last fortnight. There have been two special points of difficulty – Fisheries Board and Markland. The Fisheries Board nominated Hawes & Moreira as a sales unit for Portugal. This was done on the resolution of the Portuguese association, which contains all the exporters to Portugal. In Portugal, all the buying is done by a grémio – a guild of importers controlled by the government. The new arrangement put a number of brokers out of the Newfoundland business. This was the object, for it was due to competition among brokers to make sales that the price of Newfoundland fish fell to a point where there was no living in it for the fishermen. But the eliminated brokers exerted strong political pressure in Portugal, and the grémio refused to buy any fish at all at any price whatever from the new unit. Meanwhile, a lot of new fish has been made, and the fishermen were desperate to sell. So on one side we had the recalcitrant grémio, and on the other the disgruntled fishermen. Finally, we arranged for terms of compensation for excluded brokers, and the grémio agreed, and I expect that tomorrow we shall make our first sales and, perhaps, everyone will be happy. But it will depend on the price. The grémio made a tentative offer of 25 shillings a hundredweight for first-class fish. We are standing out for 30 shillings. If we could sell a very large quantity, we would accept 28.

The Markland matter is small, but was causing great trouble. One family refused to send its children to school. This was the fault of the mother, who is a terror and has a bad police record, of which we knew nothing when they came to Markland. The father is a decent, quite hard-working fellow. It is a law of the Medes and Persians[1] that every child *must* go to school. So the management told this family that it must quit Markland. They got up an agitation, and some agitators there (we have two or three) called a meeting. They were told they could have their meeting, but not in working hours. They held it, against orders, in working hours. The manager[2] gave five of the ringleaders notice to quit. They refused to quit. We have waited six weeks in the hope of local public opinion inducing them, but, as in the case of the League,[3] though the rest of the community would throw them out by force if we allowed it, the pressure of public opinion is insufficient. So we shall possibly have to go to court to eject them, which we naturally want to avoid. They are being used by Squires as political pawns – something with which to discredit the government by commission. A case in court would be a grand opportunity for *suggestio falsi*[4] in innumerable matters. Just before I left, I heard that two of the families are planning to leave. So, perhaps before I get back, the matter may be settled. ... The Lodges are coming back from New York this week, arriving at St. John's on Saturday.[5] I shall be glad to see them back for many reasons. He has only been here one day for the last seven months. He had work in Montreal & New York, & then was in England when we came home in December. He stayed there, working till May, came out in the *Nova Scotia*, and went on to Boston in her next day for a meeting of directors of the International Power & Paper Company in New York. And is now returning.

I am already enjoying this holiday. I am not going to think of anything, D.V., official, until I get back, unless telegrams come, and I can trust my secretary not to send out anything unless it is desperately urgent.

I must have told you about the unexpected buoyancy of our revenue. We shall be $600,000 better off on 30th June than we expected. But London has heard of it, and, *strictly between ourselves until 29th June*, they have reduced the grant-in-aid for next year by £70,000 = $350,000. However, I cannot see how we shall need even the whole of the balance. The buoyancy goes on merrily, and meanwhile developments are taking place which will increase it. Our iron mines are working as they have not done for the last 15 years. That means direct income from royalty and indirect from customs. The two paper companies are working to capacity, and have raised their rate of wages. The fluorspar mine is more than doubling its output. Buchans (lead and zinc) has had a very prosperous year, has increased wages, and will pay a big dollop in royalty. And now we have just heard that a molybdenite deposit on the south coast,[6] which is being explored, is proving very promising, and that arrangements are being made for the export of marble from Canada Bay! So it looks as if we are at the beginning of an era of real development, even if the fisheries do not recover. Even there, however, prospects are much better this year. And, finally, there is more land under crop this year than has been the case for 15 years.

I shall not be here to see Newfoundland booming, but I finally believe that it will not be long before she does. ...

1 An immutable law.
2 A.C. Badcock (b. 1911), who succeeded R.H.K. Cochius.
3 League of Nations.

4 Misrepresentation.
5 20 June 1936.
6 At Rencontre.

J.H.S. to Maisie, Spruce Brook, 18 June 1936

... Home again 24/6/36.

It is dreadful to think that practically a week has passed since I began this epistle, and that we are back and in the thick of the fight again. Black Duck, where we spent the first three days of our holiday, is on Harry's River, and is a charming little farm, carved out of the forest by Captain Campbell (R.N. retired). I am sure that Quita will have told you all about them. He was with Scott at the Antarctic, and was lost, with his party of six, for seven months, during which they lived in a cave they dug into the ice. Of course they should all have died, and would have done so but for the amazing endurance of the men and the pluck of Campbell, their leader.

His wife is Norwegian – very charming - who was lady-in-waiting to Queen Maud[1] of Norway and is an intimate of our own royal family. She has a number of little personal gifts from Queen Alexandra.[2] Altogether, the Campbells move in circles to which we are unaccustomed, but they are delightful hosts.

The resource of Black Duck for the visitor is fishing. The river was far too high, and while we were there the only fish taken was a 17-pound salmon caught by Campbell. We left them on Wednesday night & slept in our carriage, which was taken back 12 or 15 miles to Spruce Brook, where we left the car next morning. Quita will have told you all about that too. On Thursday morning, I fished a pool at the end of the Nine Mile Lake,[3] which is in front of the Spruce Brook hotel (a log hut hotel with 23 bedrooms!). The pool is 2½ miles from the hotel by water, and it took 40 minutes to row down there & 40 minutes back, so [it] is really somewhat inaccessible. I saw no salmon but caught 2 trout. Not much fun on salmon tackle. I got badly bitten by black fly.

Next day, I went down towards Spruce Brook, some six or seven miles on a 'speeder,'[4] and fished North Brook Pool and Faunce's Pool.[5] In the former, I caught a 22-pounder. At Faunce's, a very fine salmon rose to me and was on for about 15 seconds but was not properly hooked & got away.

I fished the same pools on Saturday, without a rise of any kind. Evidently, the salmon were on the move, and had passed on up to the lake. Also, it is rather early for Harry's River, and I do not think many salmon had got up so far.

We left Spruce Brook on Sunday, and the Lodges were on the train as far as Grand Falls – say, from two o'clock to eight. They are coming back after 7 months absence! They have, however, not been idle, though I do not know how much result there will be from his exertions. They are, I hope, arriving here on Saturday.[6]

We are a much depleted staff. Howley is sick. Winter is away resting. Puddester is away on inspection. Lodge has not yet arrived in St. John's. That leaves Trentham and myself. Trentham goes on leave on Friday of next week. We take our week's holiday from the following Sunday. The Governor leaves for some leave the same day. Indeed, there is going to be difficulty about the Governor. And Howley's sickness is causing serious embarrassment, as he is responsible for drafting legislation and we need quite a number of laws.

We are having marvellous weather now, after having rain last week. This is aesthetically the most lovely position in which to live. The harbour on my left, as I write, is live with motor fishing boats returning with their morning's catch, and schooners coming in with lumber, or to get supplies.

Quita is very well. So am I. We are both looking forward to release from N.F.L., though we shall look back on its beauty with regret. ...

1 Wife of King Haakon VII (1872–1957).
2 1844–1925. Wife of King Edward VII (1841–1910).
3 Georges Lake.
4 Small railway vehicle used by workmen.
5 On Harry's River.
6 27 June 1936.

J.H.S. to Greta, St John's, 26 June 1936
... Since we got back, I have been having a difficult and anxious time with fish! Our new Fisheries Board is up against extreme opposition from vested

interests, supported by the official buying agency in Portugal. The fight is still on, but I think we are now winning. The grémio, the buying agency in Oporto, refused to buy our fish except at a ruinous price. We have stood out for £5 a ton more than they were willing to pay. Now the position is that Portugal has only three weeks' supply in hand – that Norway (like ourselves) refuses to sell at the price they offer – and that Portugal cannot get the fish anywhere else. Our weak point lay in our exporters wanting to sell at any price, but the Fisheries Board refused them licences and has fought their battle. If we win, as appears now to be almost certain, the board's position will be enormously strengthened. But it has been touch and go, and I have been most unpopular in many quarters.

The future is most attractive! We spend this weekend with Fraser Bond at Whitbourne. Then, on Sunday the 5th, we go for another week of our holiday to Gleneagles. On the 6th August, we expect Ian for a fortnight. Then, on 28th August, my successor arrives, and, on 8th September, we leave for the rest of our holiday. The first ten days will be spent on the upper Humber. From there, we shall go on to Canada – Montreal, Ottawa, and Toronto – then to Boston ... then to New York for a few days, & then home for good.

This week my Chinese decoration has arrived – the Brilliant Jade. The Foreign Office has refused to recommend to the King that I be allowed to wear it, on the quite mistaken ground that I was a servant of the League![1] That decision I am fighting – on principle – for I could never wear it. It is a flaring pendant, with a crude red white and blue ribbon. But I can get a miniature made for my bar. ...

1 League of Nations.

Q.H.S. to Betty, Newfoundland Hotel, 29 June 1936

... We are beginning to feel quite hustled – the end of our time here drawing near. ...

The Lodges are back again, & it is good to have them here. Mr. Trentham goes off to England for a holiday, leaving next Friday by this mail. Mr. Howley is in bed having all his teeth out. Dr. Mosdell's house has been burned down. ... Mr. Dunn is running the hotel now. Mr. Cochius has left Markland; having received a legacy in Holland, he has had to go back there. ...

We had such a pleasant little visit to ... Fraser Bond (the half-blind professor) at Whitbourne this Sunday. We drove over after office on Sat-

urday evening & spent the night there. He was listening for us, & was out
at the gate before we could get out of the car – so pleased to see us – such a
kind welcome. We had a glorious sunset on the lake, & he took us all
round the garden & up to the barn to see the magnificent western view
from the great barn doorway looking away to Mount Spread Eagle.[1] Then
talk, talk, talk – all so interesting. On Sunday morning, we went to the
little church at Whitbourne & stayed for communion & thought of all the
dear ones. ... Then we inspected the new Ranger barracks, & I called on
Mrs. Anderton, who is living in a shack that was the messing shack till the
barracks were built. We got back in time for dinner here.

The country is looking lovely now. The blue irises are out everywhere,
& the buttercups & the red sorrel make a wonderful tapestry of colour –
blue, red, & gold; and the moon daisies are just swimming on a green sea
of meadow-grass – so lovely. ...

1 Spread Eagle Peak.

J.H.S. to Ian, St John's, 29 June 1936

Things are going with a tremendous rush. You will be leaving home before
another mail can reach you. Indeed, you will be coming out – and returning home – by the ship that takes this letter. And my successor will arrive
less than nine weeks from now. I am much looking forward to your
fortnight here, and we shall do all possible to make it a happy success. ...

We have been having another anxious official week. The new fish is
ready for market, and Portugal, which buys through a unified government
agency, is offering a price which means nothing for the fisherman. Yet
they *must* sell to get the money with which to continue fishing. The Fisheries Board (stiffened by this department)[1] is refusing export licences until
the price is raised sufficiently to pay at least something to the fishermen.
This has meant severe agitation, but we have been firm and have actually
given a guarantee that, if the fish is held, we shall assume at least the price
now offered. It looks as if we were going to win, for Portugal only has
three weeks' supply in hand, and nothing afloat, and both Norway and
Iceland are standing pat for considerably higher prices. But it is an anxious
business. If we do not succeed, it means the end of the Fisheries Board. ...

Our year ends tomorrow. The revenue has turned out to be $500,000
more than last year, though we reduced the tariff to sacrifice a million
dollars, and the year has been a bad one for fish. Altogether, I think that
things are definitely much better, though we have a long way to go before

they will be right. I have just read a note on the railway returns. For the first time in history, the railway has paid expenses and given a small surplus. When you realize that on one occasion the deficit was two million dollars, & that in the year 1933–34, when we came here, it was $300,000, you can see how decent administration has justified itself. The same features are discernible in the post office, which is within measurable distance of giving a surplus in place of serious deficits in the past, and in the customs, where decent administration has resulted in an enormous decrease in smuggling and consequent increase in revenue. But the concert of carping criticism still goes on. I do not let it affect my sleep. And, in another nine weeks, it will be a thing of the past. Of one thing I am sure that the country is convinced, namely, that it has an honest administration and that we are out for nothing except the good of the country. But efficient administration is a new and uncomfortable experience, and the man who has poached deer every winter and eaten fresh meat regularly, and who now finds that this implies prosecution and loss of his rifle, is not likely to be particularly fond of the administration which compels obedience to the law. In the past, lawlessness, in the sense of failing to obey the law, was universal. Now, with the help of the new magistracy and of the Ranger force, things are rapidly changing. But the people do not yet understand why the law should be obeyed if it can be avoided.

I am writing in our sitting-room at the hotel. I began in office. It is very pleasant to think that in five weeks you may be sitting here with us, enjoying our after-dinner cup of tea. ...

1 Of Natural Resources.

Q.H.S. to Maisie, Newfoundland Hotel, 1 July 1936
... This is a holiday, being the memorial day for the N.F.L.ers killed at Beaumont Hamel, July 1, 1916.[1] ...

We have been at the service twice, so today we are taking Mr. Trentham & Mr. Douglas to Brigus for lunch – a lovely run of about 56 miles. The day is uncertain: ten minutes ago it was glorious; now the sky is covered with clouds. Mr. Trentham is off to England for two months' holiday, leaving by the mail of the 3rd.

I wonder whether you have strawberries now, or are they over? We had our first taste here yesterday, & I expect we may pick some up today on our way, as they are grown by a few people at Topsail & the children sell them by the roadside. Usually, they are hardly worth buying, they are so dirty. There is a lot of diphtheria about, but I don't fancy strawberries would be carriers. ...

Evening. We have had a perfectly glorious day. The dark clouds soon cleared, and it could not have been more beautiful. As we came down over the hill to Conception Bay, it was heavenly; blue irises & buttercups by the roadside, a mountain stream dancing over the rocks beside us – water-falls tumbling down from the woods to join the stream, poplars in their sweet fresh green hanging over the road; & below, the great bay, sapphire blue, with dancing flecks of white spray, & Bell Island & the Clapper[2] & Little Bell & Kellys Islands, all clear as under a magnifying glass, their sharp cliffs overhanging the water like mushrooms at some points; and, away beyond, the mountains & coastline, blue as the irises & stretching away into the Atlantic. Our route took us in & out among the bays & over high moorland, the barrens, & then down again to the bay and thro' little settlements set among woods & green fields, moon daisies swimming on the green sea of meadow-grass. We got to Brigus at 1, & lunched at the café[3] kept by Bob Bartlett's sisters. Bob himself (Peary's captain), with the famous *Morrissey*,[4] was due in Brigus bay this afternoon. All along the way, children were out on the road selling strawberries to the passing cars; even up on the barrens, there were children with cups & glasses full of wild strawberries. We collected several boxes full for our friends, on the way home. Now we have drunk your health, my darling, and have had our dinner, & Mr. & Mrs. Lodge are coming in to play bridge.

Thursday 2. Here comes the *Newfoundland* from Boston to Halifax, on her way to England, carrying our mail. Lovely, lovely ship! I feel nearer you all at once, as I see her coming through the Narrows – she looks like one of the big Atlantic liners, a regular *Queen Mary* among the small craft here.

We had a pleasant week on the west coast. The Campbells are delightful hosts. Their log cabin home is about 1¹/₂ miles from the railway, along a rough but lovely road of their own, which branches off to another farm, Major Wise, who is also a friend & in & out all the time, he & Capt. C. consulting over their farming. Both log cabins are near the river & about 1 mile apart. ... Then Nigel, Capt. C.'s grown-up son (Mrs. C. is second wife), has a bungalow alongside, with another spare room, and there is a bedroom bungalow for extra guests too. The farmland is all round the three sides, and the servants' shacks & farm buildings make a charming homestead. Mrs. Campbell has her spinning wheel in the lounge & her loom in the bedroom, & spins & weaves for her own costumes, & teaches

the women round. Her Norwegian maid married the son of their head
man & is now the cook, & the children are godchildren of the big house.
We had to visit all the servants in their houses, and were welcomed with
lovely courtesy. Mrs. C. was lady-in-waiting to Queen Maud, I expect I
told you, & the house is full of gifts from her & Queen Alexandra &
Princess Victoria⁵ – lots of little personal things that make one realize how
intimate she was & how fond they were of her, as well as wedding pre-
sents. The house is full of mementos & pictures of the Scott expedition to
the Antarctic, & Capt. C. was so interesting about it. He is ordinarily a
very quiet man, but he is a charming & simple & friendly host. ...

1 On the first day of the Battle of the Somme.

2 Land formation at the western end of Bell Island.

3 Benville Tea Rooms.

4 The *Effie M. Morrissey.*

5 Born 1868. Daughter of Edward VII and Queen Alexandra.

Q.H.S. to Ian, Newfoundland Hotel, 3 July 1936

Four weeks today, you start – five weeks yesterday, you are due! It is
lovely. ...

O! it is so lovely these days! Fresh green of spruce & birch & all this
jungle, & red sprouts of berry bushes all over the rock country – & marshes
– & buttercups & blue irises & red sorrel, making a wonderful tapestry of
colours everywhere – & moon daisies swimming on seas of meadow-grass.
And the sunshine. Four days out of these last five have been glories. That
is the sort of weather we have here. I am looking out over the harbour, and
it is blue and sparkling, & Quidi Vidi lies like a sapphire below the hills.
There is a French man-of-war lying in the harbour & a French gunboat at
the wharf below, and the *Newfoundland* is getting ready to sail, her red
funnels & her upper decks showing above the roofs of the houses below
us. ...

Q.H.S. to Bel, Gleneagles, Glenwood, 7 July 1936

Here we are away in the wilds again for another week. I am sitting in a
wired-in verandah of the log cabin, looking out over 16 miles of lake, and
the tiny waves make a constant shshsh on the shore, & the rustle of the
young birch is like soft silk. It is a glorious day - hot with a cool breeze.
The little garden is gay with lupins & columbines, but the blaze of colour
is still to come. On the little lawn in front is a gay umbrella, with camp-

326 7 July 1936

chairs under it. I once tried sitting out there, but was eaten up with mosquitoes & sandflies. Mrs. Reid tells me she puts it up just for the patch of colour on the green. ...

I may tell you that I am woefully disappointed today. I was to have gone with John canoeing down the river, as we did last year, but last night, when things were being packed for our camping, Dr. Keegan came in with such a tale of mosquitoes & sandflies & black flies that I decided I must not venture. I seem to be a bad subject too – my neck & face are swollen up now & my legs are maddening. John got bitten too, but the poison does not seem to affect him so much. I get quite feverish with it. It is not worthwhile going to be miserable. So I saw J.H.S. off in *his* canoe with *his* guide at 7.30; then I had my breakfast in my cabin & have done an hour's weeding & an hour's Spanish. Dr. Keegan has gone off too. He is a wonder. He has a wooden leg & is as strong as possible & always so sweet, with his sleek white hair & long fine nose & strong mouth. *And* he has, as his guide, our one-armed Cecil,[1] John's guide of last year, who is a still greater marvel. He is the best guide on the river – poles & paddles, lands the fish when caught, pitches a tent, rigs a sail – even ties the doctor's shoes for him! It is a mutual admiration society.

A plane has just gone over – one of the new planes which is being used now for weather, meteorological & atmosphere observations. We have 2 planes, & they are in constant use. There was a good deal of opposition to this – even Mr. Lodge was against it at first. But it is making an astonishing difference to the country. There are, I think, 9 geological parties out prospecting in different parts of the island, and the professor[2] in charge of the whole work flies to all the different parts to inspect the work, there being everywhere lots of lakes & ponds to land on, & he does, in a few hours, journeys that would ordinarily have taken him a fortnight there & back. And the forest officers use the planes in the same way, & in case of forest fires, the planes are a tremendous advantage in fighting the fires. The same with the police and with important people from Canada & England wanting to get to the Labrador & back quickly. Indeed there is far much more than the two planes can accomplish, but this is all we can afford at present.

Mrs. Reid (such a nice girl), our hostess, has brought me some of her first strawberries. They are delicious – not like the tasteless Canadian berries. When we left St. John's on Sunday morning, the fox expert, Mr. Douglas[3] (who has been lent to N.F.L. by Canada), came to see us off & brought in a big box of strawberries, so we have been eating those ever since, keeping them on ice here. Then, Mr. Reid's father[4] brought us a big can of cream & a big joint of veal (their own calf) for the Reids' party here.

And we brought chocolate & a bottle of rum. So we are well provisioned. The Sunday mail is one of the island entertainments – in fact, the 3 weekly (summer, 2 in winter) mails are. The St. John's station was crowded, & little children, gay in their summer muslins, were running along the lines, & people were standing on the steps & platforms of waiting trains & carriages just to see the mail start. And all along the way, at every wayside station & halt through which we ran, even if we did not stop there, were crowds, &, running through settlements, the householders were all out to see us pass. It is so amusing.

And it is such a funny little train – narrow gauge. But it is most comfortable – far better than the connecting trains in Canada, I am told. And certainly the food arrangements are much superior to our English ones. Half an hour before the meal, the waiter comes round with the menu and you choose your meal, as you would on board a ship, *à la carte*. And yet we must have had quite as many people dining & lunching as you get on an express in England. And the food is excellent. We prepare light meals ourselves – omelettes & strawberries & excellent cream – but most people have soup & fish & steak & onions or chops or joint, so all tastes are catered for. We usually have a private coach with our own kitchen & cook & dining & observation car & 2 bedrooms. But this time, as we were only going to have one day on the train, we came by the ordinary coaches. Going back, they are sending a special coach for us, so that we can get on to it when we like & be attached to the mail train, which passes about 12.30 on Sunday night. So we do it very comfortably.

It was very lovely coming along – buttercups & blue irises everywhere in profusion, & moon daisies on the meadows, & yellow water-lilies on every lake & pond, ferns unfolding, rowans¹ in flower, pitcher plants holding up their ruby cups on the marshes, making pools of colour, and the views were glorious. No doubt about it, this is a very lovely country. And so full of interest – the caplin fish are in now – a little fish, the size of a sprat, & it is like living in a Bible story to see the fishermen drawing their nets so full of fish that, as they ladle them into the boats close to the shore (sometimes on the shore), the boats are in danger of sinking. The fish are piled on the shore to be dealt with later, as the fishermen return to spread their nets again & again, & there they lie everywhere along the shores – glittering lakes & mounds of fish among the grass as we look down on the bays & inlets. This harvest lasts only about a fortnight. It does not matter that the fish rot as they lie in the sun; presently, they will be carted away and spread on the fields just as they are, and the air will be fouled with the rotting smell. Such a waste it seems – good food for man & the earth, if dealt with scientifically. It is a nicer fish than sprats to eat fresh, and it would make wonderful fish-meal & manure. This plan of manuring with the whole fish as it comes from the sea is not only wasteful but evidently sours the land, I am told.

There goes the plane again on its return from afar. We have been out watching it pass. And Mrs. Reid has just been showing me a foxglove that has a Canterbury bell as its top flower. The flowers below the end one are ordinary foxgloves. The same thing happened on the plant last year, and she has a beautiful photo of it.

Another thing I must tell you about our journey. At Whitbourne, when we stopped for a few minutes, there were the usual crowds, and we moved out on our way & were just gathering speed when the conductor saw a car coming at full speed to cut us off at a crossing – the passenger waving frantically. We reached & crossed the road just before the car, but the conductor had seen it & he rushed along the train & signalled the engine driver, who stopped & slowly backed, & we took on a Mrs. Bruce, a gay young spark, who had missed the train 40 miles back at Holyrood and had hoped to catch it up at Whitbourne. Isn't it amusing to think of a mail train chased by a motorcar & backing to pick up the passenger?

Another rather striking thing was at Holyrood itself – or, rather, at the next bay – there were about 8 boats crossing it, *loaded* with passengers returning from church at Holyrood, and yet there is not a house to be seen on that bay, & on weekdays the bay is always deserted, except during the season of squids (which is just due), when all the Holyrood boats are gathered there, jigging squids as fast as they can – it is the best bait & commands high prices in the States & Canada as well as here.

I must tell you another thing that would strike you travelling in this island – the piles of stones collected round most of the fields, like a sea beach. The poor folk who clear the fields for cultivation have a hard job even when it is not mostly rock.

Lunch-time – lettuce & tomato & cheese cream salad with lobster – apples baked with a filling of raisins – coffee. That does not sound like the wilds! ...

1 Cecil Pelley.
2 A.K. Snelgrove, government geologist. Taught at Princeton University.
3 W.O. Douglas was in charge of the Hudson's Bay Company fur farms in Canada.
4 Robert Gillespie Reid Jr.
5 Mountain ash.

Q.H.S. to Maisie and Blair, Gleneagles, Glenwood, 11 July 1936

... There: I have just put the finishing touches on a little sketch I have done
for Mrs. Reid. ... It is extraordinarily bad, but she & 'Robin' are delighted
with it & have made me sign it! I did one of the cabin last year, & she
begged for it & has framed it. The frame improves it enormously. This one
is the Gleneagles bay with the horse ferry & one of the bedroom shacks,
with the hills behind & sunset glow on the lake! ... I have just touched in
the daisies in the grass & the foxgloves along the edge of the shore. That
anything so thoroughly bad should give so much pleasure! It is well worthwhile, even tho' I heartily dislike my own effort & have *no* illusions about
it. And I have spent two happy afternoons over it. ...

July 17 [Newfoundland Hotel]. ...
Did I tell you about the northern lights we saw at Gleneagles? It was an
astonishing sight. Crossing over from the log cabin to our bedroom shack
at 11 o'c. at night, I was startled almost to fear by the gigantic ribs of light
meeting in the depths of the starry night – soft, misty chiffon – like mists
blowing out from the ribs, the wind, or the light, blowing up the ribs,
tearing out the chiffon that changed shapes all the time, melting and forming again into torn chiffon shapes clinging to the umbrella ribs, always
blowing in some heavenly breeze. Dr. Keegan told me that he had once
driven though coloured northern lights; he said he was so terrified – they
were playing all around & about him. Another man told me he had had
the same experience near here.

I have just started working at Spanish. ... Lots of people here know
Spanish on account of the trade in fish. ...

Such a row here last night! Sirens blowing – shouts – crowds running,
the roar of fire engines – thousands of people collecting in the street below. Only a chimney on fire! No one ever seems to have a chimney
cleaned except in this way. And when a chimney goes on fire, the fire
brigade has to be called. And in this town of wooden houses the danger is
very great. We watched one chimney in a house below blazing for half an
hour one night. It was a horrible sight – flames pouring out, & a roaring
wind scattering burning soot all over the adjoining roofs. It looked as tho'
the roof must fall in & disclose a roaring furnace. After the last fire of 1892,
when the town was half burnt-out, a law was passed that no wooden
houses should be built. There are hardly any others. This hotel is concrete,
& the Bishop's 'palace,'[1] a little red brick villa, & the court-house & the
English cathedral are of stone; the rest of the town looks like a wooden
English town of the 15th century. ...

1 Bishop's Court, residence of the
   Church of England bishop, King's
   Bridge Road.

J.H.S. to Maisie, St John's, 16 July 1936

... This whole island seethes with children. That is the biggest problem. They are not being educated at all adequately, and many of them are not going to school at all. And what is to become of them all? We are doing all we can in the matter of development, but there are probably 40,000 too many dependent on the fishery for whom we must make some provision, and each year tens of thousands grow up to employable age for whom at present there is no employment. Birth control is very badly wanted, but is anathema to the Catholics (one-third of the population) and to the C. of E. (another third). The combination of destitution and a seething population of children is very remarkable. Of course, a large portion of the population should emigrate, but all emigration has ceased, and a lot of the emigrants have come back – expelled from U.S.A. and Canada.

We are rapidly reaching the end of our lap. Three weeks tomorrow, Ian arrives. Six weeks today, my successor arrives. ...

J.H.S. to Sheila, in office, 28 July 1936

By the time this gets home, Ian will have left. ... We are both getting quite excited. ... We expect him on Thursday[1] of next week. I have arranged for him to go to Gleneagles on the Gander – just above Glenwood station – for a week's fishing. ...

Here a complete change has come over things recently, with the result that I am having an incredibly easy time – so much so that I suspect a storm must be brewing. We had a long and difficult fight with Portugal on one side and some of our fish exporters on the other, with the object of getting a better price for our fish. Friday[2] we won, and have since sold 4,000 tons of fish at a price £2 a ton higher than the Portuguese were prepared to pay. Though this means a considerable improvement not only in immediate returns but in prospects for the future, there has been no word of commendation & satisfaction here, though there was any amount of criticism while the fight was on.

If it were not that so many people are dependent on an inadequate return from the fishery, things would not be so bad in this island. We finished our year 1935–36 on 30th June, with $500,000 more in the till than we had expected at the end of March. And the revenue continues to come in much better than we anticipated. But conditions cannot be satisfactory as long as more than a third of the population depend in the main on an industry which, under the best possible circumstances, cannot give them an adequate living. We are settling about 200 families on the land, and encouraging others to settle themselves, but it will be many years before this has an appreciable effect. Yet it is the only cure that we can foresee, unless, as is possible, there is important mineral development. We now have about ten geological parties making a survey in the hope of discovering minerals in paying quantities. ...

1   6 August 1936.   2   24 July 1936.

Q.H.S. to Greta, Newfoundland Hotel, 30 July 1936

... Well, our days here are drawing rapidly to an end. We are having a marvellous summer to end up with. But indeed, as you may have noticed(!), I can find no fault with the climate & the weather here. It is just the people themselves, I think – a curiously shiftless, improvident people, ignorant, ruined by nearly 100 years of self-government for which they were entirely unfit, lacking the necessary education and lacking also any class of educated & leisured people who could act as leaders. Have I told you before how our experience of conditions in this island has made us realize the enormous debt England owes to men & women all over the country whose privileges of position & education & wealth have been recognized by them as opportunities for service? The amount of voluntary service in England is astonishing. And, in the great mass of cases, it is not done as a duty but rather as of course or as a privilege. ... I do honour them. I do think our England is a garden where some of the loveliest flowers of all time are grown. I know – I know – about those terrible blots *on* the face of the land. But at least they are not hidden – and men & women are doing their utmost to help to wipe them out or change them into something which shall no longer be a shame to us.

I think it must be a question of years of honest government here and a revolution in education. The trouble is that it can't be done quickly. You must carry the people with you. Here there are thousands of children getting no education at all and money being wasted on sectarian & denominational schools – 3 schools where one could do the job infinitely better with one good building & well-paid teachers. The R.C.s and the Anglican Bishop are bitterly hostile to the change that must come sooner or later. And the government will not scoop out English money to finance R.C. schools or any other which they cannot control or inspect. But we are moving slowly towards something better, & the people are beginning to demand it. Compulsory education for all the children of the island is a first necessity. But some will have to be by correspondence, as in Australia & New Zealand. And another great difficulty is what is to be done about the existing schools, buildings, & teachers. It will cost millions to take over the buildings. And all the poor incompetents will be thrown out of employment. It is all extraordinarily difficult. Of course, education is not Daddy's department – it was Mr. Alderdice's & he did nothing; the only thing done was by the Commission as a whole – the thin edge of the wedge – a head of the educational work appointed on his merits & irrespective of creed, a Canadian.[1] The new N.F.L. Commissioner for education is Mr. Alec Winter[2] – a man with children of his own, an Anglican, but not a devotee of the Bishop's, so I hope he may get a move on.

This is the season of picnics here. All the world gets out into the country on every possible occasion. Nearly everyone has a friend out from home or America some time during the summer, and this is the occasion for endless excursions. I have been to a good many. The invitation is always by word of mouth or telephone (practically all invitations here are, except formal Government House parties) & the form is: 'I'm going to boil a kettle out at Hogan's Pond[3] on Monday; can you come?' And always these kind people arrange for anyone who has not the use of a car to be called for by someone who has. One *very* hot day, there were 33 ladies 'boiling a kettle' down at Beachy Cove.[4] On the way, we saw the *Hindenburg*[5] sailing over Conception Bay. We got out of our cars & ran up onto some open ground &, as she passed overhead, we waved & yelled to her. (She went on & flew round quite low over St. John's.) Then we went on our way & gathered on cliffs looking out from under little pine woods across to Bell Island. It was a lovely spot – green sward & cushiony tussocks. ... But here we looked out over blue, blue sea & down into a chine where the sea worked in clear as an emerald over red & yellow rocks. And on the shore & up & down among the rocks were little lakes & pools of silver fish – masses of caplin waiting to be carted up the steep cliff path to be spread on the fields for manure. Then another day this week, I went with fourteen other ladies, & we boiled our kettle on a shady sward by the side of a lake. And first, some of the ladies bathed – this is usually part of the programme, but it is too cold for me. The masses of pink & white foxgloves on the bank above the pond were a lovely sight. I don't think they grow wild here, but these had overflowed from a garden. There are three bungalows on this pond – about 3 miles apart, however. I must say these picnics are very jolly: so free & easy & everyone so friendly. ...

Here we had to go to tea at Government House. H.E. is away on the *Scarborough*, & she[6] & 'James'[7] are alone. We sat out in the garden, which is very sweet & parklike, and she showed us the little farm they have started. And here is a big bunch of roses & sweet peas she has just sent in. ...

1 Lloyd W. Shaw.
2 J.A. Winter.
3 Northwest of St John's.
4 Conception Bay.

5 German zeppelin.
6 Lady Walwyn.
7 James H. Walwyn.

J.H.S. to Greta, St John's, 31 July 1936

... Time is rushing by. Ian sails today and arrives next Thursday. Three weeks later, Ewbank arrives, and the following Thursday – 3rd September, four weeks next Thursday – I give over charge and we leave for the Humber.[1] I hope that trip will not be too much for Quita. Last year, when I went up, it was a case of sleeping on the ground, on spruce boughs, in a tent – washing in the river, generally by bathing, and outdoor sanitation in any convenient thicket in the woods, with a hope that no inquisitive bear would come along. Now I have had four log cabins put up at the various stages, so things will be less primitive. Still, it is rough going, and some of the rapids are fearsome things. I have also had a trail cleared all the way up one bank, but that will not be of much use to us, as we are going up by canoe. Quita is a very good traveller and demands very little, so that one is apt to forget that she will be 66 this next December. It would be a great disappointment to both of us if she were to miss this last experience of camping in N.F.L. She will be the first woman who has gone up the Humber to the place where it leaves the hills. I am hoping not only to catch a lot of salmon, but to shoot a moose, and perhaps a bear.

We have been pretty busy with parties and engagements recently, and last night I made a public pronouncement at a meeting of the teachers' association.[2] It was a perfectly appalling night of rain, sheets of it, just like India. Yet there were about 500 at the meeting. The trouble was getting out, for the people at the door would not go on into the rain, and the passage became more & more blocked as the rest of the audience came out of the hall. Quita always hates a crowd and was very nervous of the pushing and pressing. I suppose it took us quarter of an hour to get from the hall to the street. I then sympathized with the people who were block-ing the doorway, for, though our car was just outside, it was raining so hard that it came through my coat sleeves and trouser legs to my skin before I got into the driver's seat.

The Governor is away on tour, which means peace. He is a nervous, jumpy, active person – not at all the kind to be Governor at all. Both he & Lady Walwyn love talking in public, and they both talk drivel. That would not matter so much if he would avoid telling his audience what he pro-poses to do, for he cannot 'do' anything at all. The only people that can do anything are the Commissioners, and if the Governor wants anything done, he has to get the Commissioners concerned to agree to it. I have had considerable difficulty in this particular matter – the final decisive instance being when he wrote a memorandum containing the words 'I have de-cided' and directing a certain procedure to be introduced at once. I did not introduce it, but put up a memorandum to the Commission pointing out that nothing could be done without the orders of the Commission – and the Governor was in the chair & disliked it intensely. The Governor's 'decision' was in part entirely turned down. However, he is learning and, though he cannot but always be a difficulty, he is much less liable to attempt to issue orders than he was. Of course, the general public, spe-cially in the outports, does not realize the position, and the Governor is very liable to be looked upon as a person who makes promises which subsequently he cannot carry out.

One of the beauty spots of St. John's is our model farm. It is six miles out and is really a lovely spot with a trout stream running through the farm and its woods. The drive up is through a long avenue of trees. This was just a jungle, but we have cleared it up, and now there are vistas through the woods all the way. ... The hay is just in. We got it in before the rain, in perfect condition. The rain has done lots of good. We needed it badly. Last week, we had 17 forest fires going on at the same time. Now all is well in the forests.

We take all our friends out to see the farm, and it is becoming so popular that I think we shall have to start a café there! ...

1 Humber River, western   2 The Newfoundland Teachers'
   Newfoundland.   Association.

Q.H.S. to Sheila, Newfoundland Hotel, 4 August 1936

The day after tomorrow, Ian is due here! We are so excited & delighted.

We have been counting the days like children; now we are counting the hours.

O! Such an armful of roses! A friend has just put his head at the door. 'May I come in so early in the morning? I just wanted to bring you these fresh from the garden.' Such a glory! & such a joy! I have just laid them in a bowl until I can arrange them – but I think flowers are always better for lying to soak right up to the bloom for awhile after gathering. ...

I do hope we shall not come to the end of the summer weather before Ian arrives. It has been a marvellous summer, & no matter what weather we have now the fact remains. But I do want Ian to see the country as near its best as can be after the first exquisite spring & summer flush of leaf and flower is over. Tomorrow is the great event of the year for St. John's sites – the boat races,[1] and they say that it always marks a change for the worse in the weather. I do want him to see the cliffs & headlands in full sunshine as he approaches the coast, & St. John's itself, which really is most striking, with Cabot Tower crowning our Gibraltar at the entrance to the Narrows, & the R.C. cathedral, with its twin towers, dominating the harbour.

The tennis tournament is in full swing on the courts below, and we are very gay. ...

1 Regatta.

J.H.S. to Greta, St John's, 11 August 1936

... Ian arrived on a lovely evening last Thursday.[1] He had enjoyed the voyage thoroughly, though they had had bad weather until the last day. He is, as always, full of beans, and he brought us the latest news. ...

Ian left for the Gander on Saturday. We drove him out 70 miles to Whitbourne, and he got on the train there. It was crammed – the largest number who have ever travelled on the overland in the history of the island. We had reserved a seat for him, but I doubt very much whether he got it, for everything was occupied – even the platforms between the carriages. One little group of passengers – but they were in the baggage car – consisted of two beavers, one with two and the other with three young ones. They are being transported to an area on the west of the island to start beavers there. The beaver population has been almost exterminated by poaching. We have stopped that now. There is one little area on the Avalon Peninsula where there are still a large number, and we are moving the surplus to other places. We have so far moved a hundred, 93 to Tug Pond and Come by Chance, and now seven, the first instalment of the second hundred, to Howley reserve. It is just luck that we arrived in time to prevent the entire destruction of the beaver population.

The game and fur prospects of the island are much improved. Caribou and moose had been poached mercilessly. Now that has stopped, and there is no doubt that they are increasing rapidly all over the island. In another five years there should be a great supply.

Socially, we are very busy. Dinners & lunches & tea-parties most days. ... Today, the Lodges come back, and we shall dine together. Tomorrow, there is a party on H.M.S. *Scarborough*. On Thursday,[2] we dine at the Alec Winters' – he is our Commissioner vice[3] Alderdice. Then there is a big garden party at Government House. ...

We go up the Humber for ten days or a fortnight – fishing and to shoot a moose and perhaps some bear. ...

1   6 August 1936.   3   In succession to.
2   13 August 1936.

Q.H.S. to Maisie, Newfoundland Hotel, 18 August 1936

... *Friday 21 August.* The *Nova Scotia* is lying down below, & her cranes have been going hard all morning & most of the night, and soon she will be off with our beloved boy on board.

We had a glorious day on Wednesday – a blazing hot day with a breeze. We started at 9 & drove round about by Salmonier, as J.H.S. wanted to inspect his new sawmill[1] out there & I wanted to leave *The Princess & the Goblin*[2] for little Gertrude Murray[3] out at their fishing bungalow, so we had [a] short visit there & then to Whitbourne to inspect the Ranger force at 12 o'c. There is a new batch of men being trained, & John had a word with every man & then addressed them & said goodbye to the new force. Then we went out to Markland & lunched on the river, & then the manager showed us the new work that is going on; there are more than 500 people settled there now and their 'gardens' are a joy to see – acres of potatoes, & some have all sorts of vegetables & even a show of flowers. Then we rushed back to meet Ian's train at 3.15, & we took him to tea with Fraser Bond, (the blind young professor), & then back by Brigus, where we dined & met crowds of friends taking advantage of the glorious holiday, and arrived here at about 10 – a long tiring day but so enjoyable.

Yesterday, there was a garden party at Government House, & it was a dull day threatening rain. It actually did rain a bit but not much during the party, & we thoroughly enjoyed introducing Ian to our friends & acquaintances. ...

1 On the Back River.   3 Daughter of Andrew and
2 By George MacDonald (1824–1905).   Janet Murray.

Q.H.S. to Greta, Little Falls, Humber River, 6 September 1936
September 3 is three days behind us now – the day of freedom that John has been so much looking forward to. He is no longer a N.F.L. Commissioner – no longer an 'Honourable,' as he says. We had a very busy last fortnight, farewell parties, etc., & everyone so kind & seeming really sorry we were going. Of course, the 'everybody' does not include the people who have the bad taste not to like us & who are glad to see us depart. To my intense amusement, some of them turned up to see us off; how they must have disliked it! But they just had to or they would not have been 'it.' The Walwyns have been very kind & friendly, doing all they could to make us feel that they appreciate J.H.S. & really regret losing him. I think H.E. feels that his stay & support & father confessor has deserted him. They gave us a wonderful farewell dinner – full dress & decorations – & a very happy & really kind thought – they asked us to choose 6 of the guests, some special friends. So that made it particularly pleasant for us. Of course, all the Commissioners & wives were invited, & the high court judges & other necessary people, so we did not need to consider them.

And on Thursday morning[1] (we left by the evening train), Lady Walwyn came to say goodbye to me & left me with kisses, and later on H.E. came over with John from the Commission meeting to say goodbye to me, & they sent the A.D.C. in full uniform to take us in their car to the station & see us off. So they did us proud.

We had a great see-off – & loads of flowers & gifts – & some of our friends really weeping, and all along the line at the stations there were friends waiting to wave to us & shout farewells as we passed – some of them running after our coach, as we were on the back of the train with an observation car, so that we could run out onto the platform & have a farewell shout. It was such a lovely day & a lovely see–off, & a perfectly lovely journey from 5 o'c. till dark, when the moon came up like an angry red lozenge.

Next day, we woke to heavy rain – really battering, pounding rain – and it went on till evening. We left the train at Deer Lake, & our kind friends had arranged for us to spend the night in the staff bungalow house of the I.P.P. power-station – such a relief. So instead of starting off on our long trek up the river 10 miles to the first 'shack,' we spent the night in a comfortable little house all to ourselves & had hot baths & English beds & good meals at the staff house.

Next day, Saturday, yesterday, was glorious and we came on, starting at 8 in the morning. There was a rainbow spanning the river & it was all too lovely for words, *and* everybody shook their heads about the forecast. The first 2 miles we did by motor launch, but at Nicholsville (the stretch of river where the 7 or 10 Nichols families [live] – the father of the clan & the eldest son being our guides) we picked up our canoes (6 of them) and loaded all our stores & luggage into them. Some of our luggage is going straight home, with the car also – most of the rest we left at Deer Lake station – a suitcase each & a rug bag & fishing tackle we brought on. Mr. Jo Goodyear[2] has arranged everything for us & accompanied us, so we have a canoe each with a guide each, another canoe for the gear, [and] a fifth for a lot of stores, etc., that have to go up to the shacks to complete them. A 6th canoe came on as far as our first lunch landing, & then a lot of the stuff was repacked & rearranged & the 6th canoe went back.

So we had our 'mug up'[3] at 11 o'c., and after that we really felt we were fairly started. It is a most beautiful river – far bigger than the Gander – & the forests more beautiful – finer timber & more variety. The birches are just turning, & here & there a bunch of gold shines among the green. And here & there are maples glowing rose-red, & the wild currant is as brilliant as Virginia creeper. There are masses of Michaelmas daisies, white, pink, & blue. We had to walk two miles along an old track yesterday, and when we were not diving through thick jungle, our way was through such flowering meadows (wild) it was like a wild garden – so very lovely.

I have made a great mistake in not buying breeches & thigh-high waders. I did buy long wellingtons,[4] but never thought of anything more, which was stupid. But the more is really a necessity for this trip. I do my best by tucking my petticoat into my knickers & safety-pinning my skirt up to my belt well above my knees. We have to wade along the edge of the rapids that are too rapid for one guide to pole passengers up them. In most places, the jungle is too thick & too close to the river for any alternative, and in parts the edge is too deep for wellingtons. Yesterday, we took the trail for 2 miles, but today the trail was inaccessible from the river, so we had tremendous scrambles, & I had to hang on by birch boughs & alder branches & feel my way along as much of a steep bank as my feet could find, John & Mr. Goodyear helping me over difficult places, sometimes over slippery submerged rocks, & once I plunged & had to do the rest of the way with a wellington half full of water.

My guide has been making me bough beds. He cuts hundreds of young spruce ends & lays them in lines, the second line almost crossing the first, so that in the end you have a deep spruce bed. These shacks are so pretty – my guide has had the job of building them, 5 shacks, & of making the trail. He tells me it takes about 20 men a fortnight to clear the ground & build & finish a shack. They are all alike, set in a good clearing with a few trees left along the back, but so high they do not impede the view. There is a pretty, railed verandah in front – a porch, one big room, & a little pantry continuous of the porch division, & behind, two bedrooms, with plank beds & a shelf for a basin. The big room just has a table (rough planks), & 2 benches, & a stove. The pantry has a shelf for a washing basin. All the cooking is done on the stove, & big pots are boiled over a fire outside.

Daddy has fished on the way for half an hour once each day & in the evening, yesterday, & caught a small salmon each time – 3½ & 5 lbs. But we are hurrying to get up – above the Grand Falls, where there will be more chance of seeing big game. ...

I have bought the cheapest Brownie⁵ and wish I had done it long ago. I am getting some excellent photos. I hope the ones on this trip will turn out well. ...

1 3 September 1936.	4 Rubber boots.
2 Josiah Goodyear (d. 1965).	5 Type of camera.
3 A cup or mug of tea and a snack.	

Q.H.S. to Ian, Little Falls, Humber River, 11 September 1936

... How we have been wishing that you could have been with us for this trip! It is really a great holiday. I have never had anything to compare with it, and you would have loved it. Just fancy! I have myself seen 5 moose and have stared straight into the face of a 6th – [a] cow moose within 10 ft. & could not see it! And I have seen 3 beaver houses & bear droppings & wild black duck & teal and, of course, kingfishers & jays (moose jays) galore, & chickadees & twillocks, of course. This Humber country beyond the Grand Falls is just a great water park – lakes & lovely islands, great birch trees & fine firs of the smaller variety but growing to 80 ft. – exquisite, flowery banks, covered with all sorts of ferns, & studded in some places so thick with cracker berries¹ that they look as tho' masses of scarlet beads had been flung down. And the wide flats or marshes, where the river spreads over a wide valley with reeds for the wild black duck & teal, & seas of water lilies, & alder-grown islands, where the moose feed, and behind all, blue mountains – blue as sapphire – & the river itself so often blue as the sky, & still, mirroring such a lovely world.

Today, I went off alone with Roy Nichols, my guide, such a nice young fellow, fair & lean & clean & hard. I wanted to explore up an arm I had not been in. It was too lovely for words. We started in thick mist & took 2 rapids & crossed the great marsh before the sun broke through, & the first thing was the cracking of a branch in the alder beside us. We were moving very quietly, but Roy stopped at once & we lay still as still & presently there was another crack & I saw the branches moving. The moose went on feeding, but we drifted down a bit, and, as I say, she saw us – looked straight at me from 10 ft. (Roy says 8 ft.) away & I never saw her, tho' I was staring into the alders where she was. She moved away & we went on – up lovely reaches overhung with birch that has splashes of gold upon it now. And here & there are maples glowing rose-red. And here & there massed foam, floating down the river like fleets of white ducks or like little icebergs.

By 11 o'c., I was up in a lovely lake under the foothills and startled a black duck in the rushes. I was just deciding that I must turn back but must just see what lay beyond an island, when, on the shore beyond the island about 100 yds. away, a great bull moose came strolling along. He was a beautiful creature – I could hardly believe his horns – a glorious red in the sunshine & such a great mass I could hardly believe they were horns. We drifted along & gently paddled a little nearer. He took a good look at us and suddenly shook his mighty horns. I thought he was trying to shake them off, but Roy quietly backwatered &, when he shook them again, he continued to backwater. Then the bull came walking on towards us – along the shore – wading & swimming, & then up he lifted onto the shore again & strolled off up a birch-hung gully. Roy said, 'For two pins that fellow would have come after us. I didn't like the look in his eye.' But wasn't that a wonderful experience. It was such a picture.

I am afraid I have put John off killing a moose. After I had seen those two lovely young things one day, it seemed dreadful to think of killing a king beast for the sake of a 'head.' I did not tell you about those two.

Our guides & Mr. Goodyear (our friend who has arranged everything) are all tremendous talkers, and it seemed to me if I stayed with them, I should see nothing – you can hear their voices half a mile away. So I asked Roy Nichols, my guide, to go ahead with me quietly to try to get some photos. So off we went on a roundabout route among some islands. J.H.S.

had already got away by himself, but we were all going for the same place in the end by different ways. We heard a moose eating its way among a group of alders, & I saw the red horns – so like the alder branches in shape. It moved off, & we went on. Then, just as we were coming out into the main river, there was a crashing among the woods on an island under which we were passing, and first a great young bull came out, & then, two or three yards behind, a cow, & they crossed the ford within 20 ft. of us – such a lovely sight, the two beautiful animals against the blue of the lake beyond, stopping in mid-stream to look at us, & then splashing on & up the far bank. Then, when we got into the main river, I saw J.H.S. about ¼ mile ahead, & the rest of the party came up to join me, very excited – explaining that they had made a great noise to frighten them up to me.

Then, in the distance, J.H.S. held up his hand, & we all fell still & silent as we watched him cross to the far side. A bull moose was barking in the woods there. He & his guide slipped in under the shade of a great birch, & now & then we got a glimpse of the guide's light shirt as they climbed about the hillside, the guide (John tells me) barking in imitation of the bull to call it. But we saw the trees moving as the moose went away over the hill. But then another moose came out into the reeds & trotted along the shore & swam across the river about 100 yds. from us. Such a glorious day & such a lovely day rich in delight.

Today. 12th. We have come another stop on our way back, as J.H.S. is afraid of being belated for our train tomorrow, Sunday night. We have had such a day! We were wakened by a moose calling – our camp at Silent Rapid was an old moose lodge – and a bull went up through the camp in the early morning. The day was grey & threatened rain, & soon after we got off at 9 o'c., it came down in buckets. The 'steadies'[2] were like a great plain, with armies of Halma soldiers[3] hopping up & down & losing their shining heads – others springing up in millions to take their place & lose their heads. After 8 hours of this, we pulled into a wood & lighted a fire to warm ourselves as we rested. Then on again, & after a time the rain stopped & the sun came out. Coming down the rapids to Big Falls *was* an experience. We *walked* about 3 miles up the trail on our way because the going is too difficult with passengers as well as all the luggage & stores on that stretch. In some places, one of the guides must clamber on the rocks & float a rope down to the canoes, & then they are helped up by the guiding rope. But going down we were told to sit still. It was thrilling. There is nothing approaching the Humber rapids on the Gander; a single mistake or error of judgment & over could go the canoe – & you & your guide with it forever. You edge & nose & twist your way through the upper rapid, then on you go on a giant sweep of water down into a boiling rapid, the waves threatening to swallow your little craft. The whole way was a succession of these vicious rapids, & then, when we neared the Big Falls, it was too exciting – being swept on, nearer & nearer, the whisper going to a roar & the cloud of spray rising nearer & nearer as we were swept along almost to the brink – then, just in time, we nicked round into a cave with a ladder up the cliff, & one after another, as the canoes swept in, the first arrivals caught them & helped them in to safe harbourage until all were in, packed nose to nose in the tiny cave.

Another comfortable fire & a mug up of tea & bread & cheese. John & I climbed up onto the cliff & watched the canoes being portaged with ropes round the rock & over the falls; & tho' the spawning season is really over (or is it the salmon running season?), we counted 53 fish trying the falls in the ten minutes we watched them & not one got up. So we decided they must be weaklings that had been trying to get up all summer & were tired out.

This is a very egotistical letter, but I think you may be interested, & we have talked so much about you & longed to share it with you. ...

1 Dward cornel (*cornus canadensis*).   3 Used in a board game.
2 A steady is a stretch of still water in
  a brook or river.

J.H.S. to Greta, c/o the Bairds,[1] Government Farm, Nappan, Nova Scotia, 16 September 1936

... Last Sunday, the 13th, ... we came back to the semi-civilization of Deer Lake.

That was a grand day. We left the Little Falls cabin in the morning, about 9.30, and came down rapids – some of them very fierce – all the way to Deer Lake. Or rather, to where we found the motorboat, four miles up river from the lake. On the way, there were two portages, one at the Little Falls and one at Big Falls, where we had to get out and climb over bluffs through which the river had cut its passage through the ages. ...

You have no idea of the skill of those guides in bringing a canoe down the rapids. They are a seething mass of rushing water tumbling down an incline very freely sprinkled with large rocks, some protruding from the water, others just covered. The guide stands in the stern of the canoe with a pole, with which he guides and checks the canoe. His job is to keep the canoe in a clear channel. That implies sometimes that he checks the canoe and at the same time guides it sideways until there is a passage ahead for a short distance, when he does the same thing over again. ... The current is running eight to ten miles an hour. The whole place is boiling. How the guide can see ahead far enough and fast enough and accurately enough to keep his canoe from striking visible and invisible rocks, I cannot imagine. That is where his skill comes in. He does not always miss them. Once my canoe was within an ace of being upset, and another time it made a ferocious bump against an invisible rock, and several times we scraped the rocks. This last is a most curious sensation. The canoe is very flexible, and you feel the bottom arching its back like a caterpillar as it slips over the rock. It feels rather as if there were a submarine earthquake in the river. I suppose that last Sunday, in the 14 miles from Little Falls cabin to the motorboat, we had ten miles of rapids. We got down to the boat at 4 o'clock. It took us about 5½ hours to do the 14 miles, apart from the hour we spent at lunch.

We got to Deer Lake about six o'clock and again stopped in the bungalow attached to the staff house. Our train was due at 1.40 a.m. – a disgusting hour. We got to the station about ten past one, and the train did not arrive until 2.15! Fortunately, we had reserved a drawing-room, so we got to bed at once and the train did not catch up time as we feared. This meant that we slept till a quarter to eight; then got up and dressed and had our breakfast before we got to Port aux Basques. ...

1   Whylie Wellington and Anita Elliott
    (Hill) Baird (1886–1985).

**J.H.S. to Ian and Sheila, Cornwallis Inn, Kentville, Nova Scotia,
19 September 1936**
... It was glorious sunshine when we got to Port aux Basques, but there was a strong N.E. wind blowing, and the *Caribou* rolled all the way across the Strait[1] – 90 miles. There was a big crowd on board – about 120 passengers – but only 9 turned up to lunch. Quita was not sick but she took Mothersill and kept quiet in her bunk. They dressed the ship with flags for us as we came into Sydney harbour, and the customs & immigration people took their cue accordingly, & we had no examination. ...

1   Cabot Strait.

Select Bibliography on the History of Newfoundland and Labrador in the 1930s

Readers wishing more detailed bibliographical information on the period should consult my *Newfoundland in the North Atlantic World, 1929–1949* (Kingston and Montreal 1988), 427–38; Agnes O'Dea, comp., and Anne Alexander, ed., *Bibliography of Newfoundland* (Toronto 1986); and the listings of the Centre for Newfoundland Studies, Queen Elizabeth II Library, Memorial University, St John's. For current Newfoundland and Labrador bibliography see: 'Recent Publications Relating to the History of the Atlantic Region,' in *Acadiensis*; 'Recent Publications Relating to Canada,' in the *Canadian Historical Review*; 'Publications and Works Relating to Newfoundland' in *Newfoundland Studies*; and the 'Bibliographie d'histoire de l'Amérique française,' in the *Revue d'histoire de l'Amérique française*.

Alexander, David. *Atlantic Canada and Confederation: Essays in Canadian Political Economy*. Eric W. Sager, Lewis R. Fischer, and Stuart O. Pierson, comps. Toronto 1983.
- *The Decay of Trade: An Economic History of the Newfoundland Saltfish Trade, 1935–1965*. Memorial University, Institute of Social and Economic Research 1977.
Andrews, Ralph L. *Integration and Other Developments in Newfoundland Education, 1915–1949*. St John's 1985.
Baker, Melvin. 'In Search of the "New Jerusalem": Slum Clearance in St. John's, 1921–1944.' *Newfoundland Quarterly* 79/2 (Fall 1983), 23–32, 35.
Bassler, Gerhard P. 'Attempts to Settle Jewish Refugees in Newfoundland and Labrador, 1934–1939.' *Simon Wiesenthal Centre Annual* 5 (1988), 121–44.
- '"Deemed Undesirable": Newfoundland's Immigration Policy, 1900–49.' In James Hiller and Peter Neary, eds., *Twentieth-Century Newfoundland: Explorations*, 153–77. St John's 1994.

– *Sanctuary Denied: Refugees from the Third Reich and Newfoundland Immigration Policy, 1906–1949.* St John's 1992.

Cadigan, Sean. 'Battle Harbour in Transition: Merchants, Fishermen, and the State in the Struggle for Relief in a Labrador Community during the 1930s.' *Labour/Le Travail* 26 (Fall 1990), 125–50.

Campbell, Victor. *The Wicked Mate: The Antarctic Diary of Victor Campbell.* H.G.R. King, ed., with a foreword by Lord Shackleton. Aldburgh 1988.

Clark, Richard L. 'Newfoundland, 1934–1949: A Study of the Commission of Government and Confederation with Canada.' Unpublished Ph. D. thesis, UCLA 1951.

Cuff, Harry A. 'The Commission of Government in Newfoundland: A Preliminary Survey.' Unpublished M.A. thesis, Acadia University 1959.

Dawson, Rhoda. 'The Wharves of St. John's, Newfoundland.' Intro. by Peter Neary. *Canadian Parliamentary Review* 15/2 (Summer 1992), 2–5.

Digby, Margaret. *Report on the Opportunities for Co-operative Organisation in Newfoundland and Labrador.* London 1934.

Ewbank, R.W. *Public Affairs in Newfoundland.* Cardiff 1939.

Feder, Alison. *Margaret Duley: Newfoundland Novelist.* St John's 1983.

Forestell, Nancy M. 'Times Were Hard: The Pattern of Women's Paid Labour in St. John's between the Two World Wars.' *Labour/Le Travail* 24 (Fall 1989), 147–66.

– 'Women's Paid Labour in St. John's between the Two World Wars.' Unpublished M.A. thesis, Memorial University 1987.

Fraser, A.M. 'Government-By-Commission (1934–6): A Survey.' *Canadian Journal of Economics and Political Science* 3/1 (February 1937), 71–83.

Gilmore, William C. *Newfoundland and Dominion Status: The External Affairs Competence and International Law Status of Newfoundland, 1855–1934.* Toronto 1988.

Godfrey, Stuart R. *Human Rights and Social Policy in Newfoundland, 1832–1982.* St John's 1985.

Gorvin, J.H. *Papers Relating to a Long Range Reconstruction Policy in Newfoundland,* 2 vols. Vol. 1, *Interim Report of J.H. Gorvin C.B.E.*; Vol. 2, [Supporting Documents]. St John's 1938.

– *Report on Land Settlements in Newfoundland.* Department of Agriculture and Rural Reconstruction. Economic Series no. 1. St John's 1938.

Gosse, John S.R. *Whitbourne: Newfoundland's First Inland Town.* Whitbourne 1985.

Greenwood, Robert. 'The Origins of NAPE: The Civil Service Association during the Commission of Government: 1936–49.' *Newfoundland Quarterly* 82/1 (Summer 1986), 22–6.

Gwyn, Richard. *Smallwood: The Unlikely Revolutionary*, rev. ed. Toronto 1972.

Handcock, Gordon. 'The Commission of Government's Land Settlement Scheme in Newfoundland.' In James Hiller and Peter Neary, eds., *Twentieth-Century Newfoundland: Explorations*, 123–51. St John's 1994.

– 'The Origins and Development of Commission of Government Land Settlements in Newfoundland, 1934–1969.' Unpublished M.A. thesis, Memorial University 1970.

Hiller, James. 'The Career of F. Gordon Bradley.' *Newfoundland Studies* 4/2 (Fall 1988), 163–80.

– 'The Politics of Newsprint: The Newfoundland Pulp and Paper Industry, 1915–1939.' *Acadiensis* 19/2 (Spring 1990), 3–39.

Hiller, James, and Peter Neary, eds. *Newfoundland in the Nineteenth and Twentieth Centuries: Essays in Interpretation*. Toronto 1980.

Hiscock, Philip D. 'Folklore and Popular Culture in Early Newfoundland Radio Broadcasting: An Analysis of Occupational Narrative, Oral History and Song Repertoire.' Unpublished M.A. thesis, Memorial University 1986.

– 'The "Irene B. Mellon" Radio Programme, 1934–1941.' In Gerald Thomas and J.D.A. Widdowson, eds., *Studies in Newfoundland Folklore: Community and Process*, 177–90. St John's 1991.

Horwood, Harold. *A History of the Newfoundland Ranger Force*. St John's 1986.

– *Joey: The Life and Political Times of Joey Smallwood*. Toronto 1989.

House, Edgar. *The Way Out: The Story of NONIA in Newfoundland, 1920–1990*. St John's 1990.

Innis, H.A. 'Basic Problems of Government in Newfoundland.' *Canadian Journal of Economics and Political Science* 3/1 (February 1937), 83–5.

Kealey, Linda, ed. *Pursuing Equality: Historical Perspectives on Women in Newfoundland and Labrador*. St John's 1993.

Liddell, T.K. *Industrial Survey of Newfoundland*. St John's 1940.

Lodge, Thomas. *Dictatorship in Newfoundland*. London 1939.

McCann, Philip. 'The Educational Policy of the Commission of Government.' *Newfoundland Studies* 3/2 (Fall 1987), 201–15.

McCorquodale, Susan. 'Public Administration in Newfoundland during the Period of the Commission of Government: A Question of Political Development.' Unpublished Ph. D. thesis, Queen's University 1973.

MacKay, R.A., ed. *Newfoundland: Economic, Diplomatic and Strategic Studies*. Toronto 1946.

McKim, William A., ed. *The Vexed Question: Denominational Education in a Secular Age*. St John's 1988.

MacKinnon, Robert. 'Farming the Rock: The Evolution of Commercial Agriculture around St. John's, Newfoundland, to 1945.' *Acadiensis* 20/2 (Spring 1991), 32–61.

- 'The Growth of Commercial Agriculture around St. John's, 1800–1935: A Study of Local Trade in Response to Urban Demand.' Unpublished M.A. thesis, Memorial University 1981.
Macleod, Malcolm. *A Bridge Built Halfway: A History of Memorial University College, 1925–1950*. Kingston and Montreal 1990.
- 'You Must Go Home Again: A Newfoundland–Canada Quarrel over Deportations, 1932–1933.' *Newfoundland Quarterly* 78/4 (Spring 1983), 23–5.
Neary, Peter. 'Canadian Immigration Policy and the Newfoundlanders, 1912–1939.' *Acadiensis* 11/2 (Spring 1982), 69–83.
- 'Ebb and Flow: Citizenship in Newfoundland, 1929–1949.' In William Kaplan, ed., *Belonging: The Meaning and Future of Canadian Citizenship*, 79–103. Montreal and Kingston 1993.
- *Newfoundland in the North Atlantic World, 1929–1949*. Kingston and Montreal 1988.
- '"Wry Comment": Rhoda Dawson's Cartoon of Newfoundland Society, 1936.' *Newfoundland Studies* 8/1 (Spring 1992), 1–14.
Neary, Peter, ed. 'The Bradley Report on Logging Operations in Newfoundland, 1934: A Suppressed Document.' *Labour/Le Travail* 16 (Fall 1985), 193–232.
- 'J.B. Hope Simpson's account of Sir John Hope Simpson's Newfoundland Career, 1934–6.' Document. *Newfoundland Studies* 6/1 (Spring 1990), 74–110.
- *The Political Economy of Newfoundland, 1929–1972*. Toronto 1973.
- '"With great regret and after the most anxious consideration": Newfoundland's 1932 Plan to Reschedule Interest Payments.' *Newfoundland Studies* 10/2 (Fall 1994), 250–9.
Neary, Peter, and Patrick O'Flaherty. *Part of the Main: An Illustrated History of Newfoundland and Labrador*. St John's 1983.
Newfoundland Royal Commission 1933 Report. Cmd. 4480. London 1933.
Noel, S.J.R. *Politics in Newfoundland*. Toronto 1971.
O'Flaherty, Patrick. 'Looking Backwards: The Milieu of the Old Newfoundland Outports.' *Journal of Canadian Studies* 10/1 (February 1975), 3–9.
- *The Rock Observed: Studies in the Literature of Newfoundland*. Toronto 1979.
Overton, James. 'Economic Crisis and the End of Democracy: Politics in Newfoundland during the Great Depression.' *Labour/Le Travail* 26 (Fall 1990), 85–124.
- 'The Politics of Hope in Newfoundland in Two Depressions.' *Newfoundland Studies* 9/1 (Spring 1993), 26–57.
- 'Public Relief and Social Unrest in Newfoundland in the 1930s: An Evaluation of the Ideas of Piven and Clowes.' In Gregory S. Kealey, ed., *Class, Gender and Region: Essays in Canadian Historical Sociology*, 153–66. St John's 1988.
- 'Riots, Raids and Relief, Police, Prisons and Parsimony: The Political

Economy of Public Order in Newfoundland in the 1930s.' In Elliott Leyton, William O'Grady, and James Overton, *Violence and Public Anxiety: A Canadian Case*, 195–334. St John's 1992.

– 'Self-Help, Charity, and Individual Responsibility: The Political Economy of Social Policy in Newfoundland in the 1920s.' In James Hiller and Peter Neary, eds., *Twentieth-Century Newfoundland: Explorations*, 79–122. St John's 1994.

Panting, G.E. 'Newfoundland's Loss of Responsible Government.' In J.M. Bumsted, ed., *Documentary Problems in Canadian History*, Vol. 2, *Post-Confederation*, 241–62. Georgetown 1969.

Plumptre, A.F.W. 'The Amulree Report (1933): A Review.' *Canadian Journal of Economics and Political Science* 3/1 (February 1937), 58–71.

Pocius, Gerald L. 'Tourists, Health Seekers and Sportsmen: Luring Americans to Newfoundland in the Early Twentieth Century.' In James Hiller and Peter Neary, eds., *Twentieth-Century Newfoundland: Explorations*, 47–77. St John's 1994.

Richard, Agnes M. *Threads of Gold: The History of the Jubilee Guilds and Women's Institutes in Newfoundland*. St John's 1989.

Robison, Houston. 'Newfoundland's Surrender of Dominion Status in the British Empire, 1918–1934.' Unpublished Ph. D. thesis, University of Chicago 1949.

Rompkey, Ronald. *Grenfell of Labrador: A Biography*. Toronto 1991.

Rusted, Nigel. *It's Devil Deep Down There: 50 Years Ago on the M.V. Lady Anderson, a Mobile Clinic on the S.W. Coast of Newfoundland*. St John's 1985.

Saunders, Gary L. *Doctor Olds of Twillingate: Portrait of an American Surgeon in Newfoundland*. St John's 1994.

– *Rattles and Steadies: Memoirs of a Gander River Man*. St John's 1986.

Smallwood, J.R. *I Chose Canada: The Memoirs of the Honourable Joseph R. 'Joey' Smallwood*. Toronto 1973.

– *The New Newfoundland*. New York 1931.

Summers, Valerie A. *Regime Change in a Resource Economy: The Politics of Underdevelopment in Newfoundland (1825–1993)*. St John's 1993.

Sutherland, Dufferin. '"The Men Went to Work by the Stars and Returned by Them": The Experience of Work in the Newfoundland Woods during the 1930s.' *Newfoundland Studies* 7/2 (Fall 1991), 143–72.

– 'Newfoundland Loggers Respond to the Great Depression.' *Labour/Le Travail* 29 (Spring 1992), 82–115.

– 'A Social History of Pulpwood Logging in Newfoundland during the Great Depression.' Unpublished M.A. thesis, Memorial University 1988.

Tuck, Alice M. 'The Newfoundland Ranger Force, 1935–1950.' Unpublished M.A. thesis. Memorial University 1983.

Wade, Mason, ed., *Regionalism in the Canadian Community, 1867–1967.* Toronto 1969.

Winter, Harry Anderson. 'Memoirs of Harry Anderson Winter.' Intro. by A.B. Perlin. Parts I and II, *Newfoundland Quarterly* 72/2 (March 1976), 15–24. Part III, *Newfoundland Quarterly* 72/3 (July 1976), 17–22.

Woodworth-Lynan, C.M.J. 'Victor Campbell: Newfoundland's Connection with Captain Scott's Last Antarctic Expedition, 1910–1913." In Donald H. Steele, ed., *Early Science in Newfoundland and Labrador,* 63–84. St John's 1987.

Index

200–1; on Orange Order, 176; on painting, joys of, in Newfoundland, 121, 313, 329; on Paradise, 224; on 'Phippards' (Southeast Placentia), 84; on picnics, season of, 332–3; on place-names, 185; on Placentia, 104–5; on poaching, 116–17; on police, 71; on political corruption, 38, 42, 73, 77; on population problem, 49, 73, 92, 163; on Port Hope Simpson, 122; on public finance, 180; on radio, 32, 56, 83, 99, 233, 258, 269; on Remembrance Day (1 July), 105, 323; on her role as spouse of Commissioner, 188; on Roman Catholics, 73, 101, 163, 224, 233; on St John's, 30, 50, 78, 89; on St Pierre, 51; on Salmonier Line development, 177–8; on Salvation Army, 187–8; on sanitation, 53, 93; on scenery, 30, 41–3, 44, 49, 51, 65, 75–6, 77, 84, 90–1, 104, 107, 146, 157–8, 164, 169, 171, 179, 181, 185, 191, 197, 198, 202–3, 224, 233, 237, 240, 299–300, 315–16, 321–2, 324, 327–8; on seal fishery, 43, 64–6, 73–4, 81, 274, 278–9; on seal flippers, 64; on Service League of Newfoundland, 38, 50–1; on shop assistants, work conditions of, 146, 242; on silver thaw, 273; on 'Skin Daddies,' 94; on social scene, 38–9, 56, 59, 98, 103–4, 121, 122, 188, 220, 228, 274, 336–7; on South Coast trip (May 1935), 157–61; on South Coast trip (July 1935), 194–201, 202–5; on Spanish, her study of, 329; on speculation, 42; on speech of Newfoundlanders, 44, 160; on Spencer Lodge, 153; on status of women, 67, 173, 204, 269; on stones, piles of, 328; on strawberries,

323–4, 326; on summer and sun time, 159; on *Terra Nova* (ship), 301; on tidal wave of 1929, 196–7, 203; on tourism, 197, 300; on transatlantic travel, 25, 81, 143–3, 255–6, 294–6; on transportation and communication, 30, 32, 41, 63, 66, 71, 74, 77, 80–1, 83, 97, 122, 164, 180, 233–4, 237, 259, 262, 315–16, 326, 327, 328; on the unemployed, 177; on unemployment centre (St John's), 270; on voluntary service, virtue of, 331; on wildlife, cruelty to, 266; on winter pastimes, 30, 41, 259–60, 262, 263; on women's institutes, 92; on Y.M.C.A, 29, 39–40, 43, 270; on Y.W.C.A., 29, 77–8, 39–40

Hope-Simpson, (Robert) Edgar, xvi, 10

Hope Simpson, Sheila, xv, 83, 84 n3, 244, 245 n1

Horse Chops, 118 n6

Horwood, Julie (Hutchinson), 36 n3

Horwood, William, 31 n3, 135, 141, 257

Hotel Vanderbilt (South Kensington), 134

House, Anna, 162, 163 n2

House, Arthur, 162, 162 n2

House, Claude K. 62 n2

Housman, Laurence, 194, 197 n1

Howley, Mary, 255, 256 n8

Howley, William R., xvi, 7, 14, 139, 140, 141 n1, 145, 165, 166, 170, 256 n8, 273, 286, 299, 320, 321

Howley reserve, 336

How to Tell Stories to Children, 158

Hudson's Bay Company, 82, 104 n1, 119, 298

Hughes, Richard Arthur Warren, 197 n4

Credits

The maps were drawn by David Mercer of the Cartographic Section (Director, Patricia Chalk), Department of Geography, University of Western Ontario.

Photographs appear courtesy of the following: Gertrude Crosbie: Beside the Salmonier River; Clare (Cochius) Gillingham: Markland schoolhouse, Clare Cochius and her Markland pupils, children took turns, enthusiasts at the settlement; Sandra Gwyn: Claude, Ruth, and Sandra Fraser; Dr Mary Macaulay: wedding day, Quita with Maisie and Greta, outside Buckingham Palace; Cyril Pelley: Newfoundlander's Newfoundlander; Daphne Hope Simpson (now Shannon): Robin and Jean Reid, J.B. (Ian) Hope Simpson; L.G. Sparkes: Emily and James Sparkes; Frederic F. Thompson: The Grange; Richard Wallington: St John's in 1936, Rhoda Dawson's cartoon; and the Provincial Archives of Newfoundland and Labrador: The Newfoundland Hotel, A17-3; in the grounds of Government House, B18-11 NA 2203; Newfoundland Rangers, MG621 VA 127 17-1; Sir Humphrey and Lady Walwyn, A48-26.

The quotations in the preface (p. xiii) from Robert Manson Myers, *The Children of Pride: A True Story of Georgia and the Civil War* (New Haven and London 1972), pp. xi and xii, are copyright Yale University Press and are used by permission of the publisher.